The C++ Workshop

Learn to write clean, maintainable code in C++ and advance your career in software engineering

Dale Green

Kurt Guntheroth

Shaun Ross Mitchell

The C++ Workshop

Authors: Dale Green, Kurt Guntheroth, and Shaun Ross Mitchell

Reviewers: Anil Achary, Brent Arnold, Andrew Dent, Paras Gaba, and Archit Goyal

Managing Editor: Mahesh Dhyani

Acquisitions Editor: Alicia Wooding

Production Editor: Samita Warang

Editorial Board: Shubhopriya Banerjee, Bharat Botle, Ewan Buckingham, Megan Carlisle, Mahesh Dhyani, Manasa Kumar, Alex Mazonowicz, Bridget Neale, Dominic Pereira, Shiny Poojary, Abhishek Rane, Brendan Rodrigues, Erol Staveley, Ankita Thakur, Nitesh Thakur, and Jonathan Wray

First published: February 2020

Production reference: 3220221

ISBN 978-1-83921-662-6

Published by Packt Publishing Ltd.

Livery Place, 35 Livery Street

Birmingham B3 2PB, UK

Why Learn with a Packt Workshop?

Learn by Doing

Packt Workshops are built around the idea that the best way to learn something new is by getting hands-on experience. We know that learning a language or technology isn't just an academic pursuit. It's a journey towards the effective use of a new tool—whether that's to kickstart your career, automate repetitive tasks, or just build some cool stuff.

That's why Workshops are designed to get you writing code from the very beginning. You'll start fairly small—learning how to implement some basic functionality—but once you've completed that, you'll have the confidence and understanding to move onto something slightly more advanced.

As you work through each chapter, you'll build your understanding in a coherent, logical way, adding new skills to your toolkit and working on increasingly complex and challenging problems.

Context is Key

All new concepts are introduced in the context of realistic use-cases, and then demonstrated practically with guided exercises. At the end of each chapter, you'll find an activity that challenges you to draw together what you've learned and apply your new skills to solve a problem or build something new.

We believe this is the most effective way of building your understanding and confidence. Experiencing real applications of the code will help you get used to the syntax and see how the tools and techniques are applied in real projects.

Build Real-World Understanding

Of course, you do need some theory. But unlike many tutorials, which force you to wade through pages and pages of dry technical explanations and assume too much prior knowledge, Workshops only tell you what you actually need to know to be able to get started making things. Explanations are clear, simple, and to-the-point. So you don't need to worry about how everything works under the hood; you can just get on and use it.

Written by industry professionals, you'll see how concepts are relevant to real-world work, helping to get you beyond "Hello, world!" and build relevant, productive skills. Whether you're studying web development, data science, or a core programming language, you'll start to think like a problem solver and build your understanding and confidence through contextual, targeted practice.

Enjoy the Journey

Learning something new is a journey from where you are now to where you want to be, and this Workshop is just a vehicle to get you there. We hope that you find it to be a productive and enjoyable learning experience.

Packt has a wide range of different Workshops available, covering the following topic areas:

- Programming languages
- Web development
- Data science, machine learning, and artificial intelligence
- Containers

Once you've worked your way through this Workshop, why not continue your journey with another? You can find the full range online at http://packt.live/2MNkuyl.

If you could leave us a review while you're there, that would be great. We value all feedback. It helps us to continually improve and make better books for our readers, and also helps prospective customers make an informed decision about their purchase.

Thank you,
The Packt Workshop Team

Table of Contents

Chapter 4: Operators   137

Chapter 5: Pointers and References   173

Chapter 6: Dynamic Variables   211

Chapter 9: Object-Oriented Principles   335

Preface

About

This section briefly introduces this course and software requirements in order to complete all of the included activities and exercises.

About the Book

C++ is the backbone of many games, GUI-based applications, and operating systems. Learning C++ effectively is more than a matter of simply reading through theory, as the real challenge is understanding the fundamentals in depth and being able to use them in the real world. If you're looking to learn C++ programming efficiently, this Workshop is a comprehensive guide that covers all the core features of C++ and how to apply them. It will help you take the next big step toward writing efficient, reliable C++ programs.

The C++ Workshop begins by explaining the basic structure of a C++ application, showing you how to write and run your first program to understand data types, operators, variables and the flow of control structures. You'll also see how to make smarter decisions when it comes to using storage space by declaring dynamic variables during program runtime.

Moving ahead, you'll use object-oriented programming (OOP) techniques such as inheritance, polymorphism, and class hierarchies to make your code structure organized and efficient. Finally, you'll use the C++ standard library's built-in functions and templates to speed up different programming tasks.

By the end of this C++ book, you will have the knowledge and skills to confidently tackle your own ambitious projects and advance your career as a C++ developer.

About the Chapters

Chapter 1, Your first C++ Application, will equip you with the fundamental tools and techniques required to get started building basic C++ applications.

Chapter 2, Control Flow, presents various tools and techniques that are used to control the flow of execution throughout applications.

Chapter 3, Built-in Data Types, presents the built-in data types provided by C++, including their fundamental properties and use within vectors and arrays. These are then utilized in the creation of a real-world sign-up application.

Chapter 4, Operators, presents a variety of operators provided by C++, describing what they do and how they can allow us to manipulate our data.

Chapter 5, Pointers and References, presents a variety of operators provided by C++, describing what they do and how they can allow us to manipulate our data.

Chapter 6, Dynamic Variables, introduces dynamic variables – that is, variables that can be created when needed and can hold an arbitrarily large amount of data that is limited only by the memory that is available.

Chapter 7, Ownership and Lifetime Of Dynamic Variables, makes the use of pointers in C++ programs safer and easier to understand.

Chapter 8, Classes and Structs, presents the fundamentals of structs and classes with the aid of practical examples and exercises.

Chapter 9, Object-Oriented Principles, presents best practices for designing classes and will give you an overview of abstraction and encapsulation, where to use them, and how they can benefit your custom C++ types.

Chapter 10, Advanced Object-Oriented Principles, presents a number of advanced object-oriented principles, including inheritance and polymorphism, that will allow us to build more dynamic and powerful C++ applications.

Chapter 11, Templates, covers an overview of templates and gives some examples of how they can be used and where and teaches you how to implement template types and functions.

Chapter 12, Containers and Iterators, provides an overview of using the containers and iterators provided by the C++ standard library.

Chapter 13, Exception Handling, covers exception handling, the mechanism used by C++ for reporting and recovering from unexpected events in a program.

Conventions

Code words in text are shown as follows: "The **#include <typeinfo>** line gives access to the name of the passed-in type through the **name()** function."

A block of code is set as follows:

```cpp
#include <iostream>
#include <string.h>

using namespace std;

template<typename T>
bool compare(T t1, T t2)
{
    return t1 == t2;
}
```

New terms and important words are shown like this: "In the previous chapters, **object-oriented programming (OOP)** was introduced, along with examples and use cases."

Long code snippets are truncated and the corresponding names of the code files on GitHub are placed at the top of the truncated code. The permalinks to the entire code are placed below the code snippet. It should look as follows:

Example09_1.cpp

```
23      string getName()
24      {
25          return m_trackName;
26      }
27
28      void setName(string newTrackName)
29      {
30          // if S-Club is not found set the track name - otherwise do nothing
31          if (newTrackName.find("S-Club") == string::npos)
32          {
33              m_trackName = newTrackName;
34          }
35      }
36
37      void setLength(float newTrackLength)
38      {
39          if (newTrackLength < MAX_TRACK_LENGTH && newTrackLength > 0)
40          // no prog metal for us!
41          {
42              m_lengthInSeconds = newTrackLength;
43          }
44      }
```

The complete code for this example can be found at: https://packt.live/2DLDVQf

Before You Begin

There are many tools we can use to compile our C++ programs, too many to cover here, so here are some recommendations and a guide on getting started:

Online Compilers

cpp.sh is an online C++ compiler and the one the authors extensively used in this book. Visit cpp.sh and ensure the options are set up as shown:

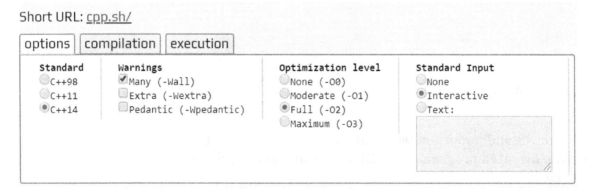

Figure 0.1: Screenshot of the cpp.sh online compiler

That is all we need to do to get started using this compiler. Simply write out your code and hit the run button. Any errors will appear in the compilation tab, and interactive standard input and output will be located on the execution tab. Here is a partial list of online C++ compilers you can use while working on the exercises. If the one you are using becomes sluggish, or you can't find it at all, try another:

Tutorialspoint C++ compiler: This website allows you to compile a C++ program contained in a single file. It prints error messages from the operating system. You can find it at https://www.tutorialspoint.com/compile_cpp_online.php.

godbolt compiler explorer: This website allows you to compile a single file on many different compilers and shows the output assembly language; its UI is a little subtle for some tastes. It prints error messages from the operating system. You can find it at https://godbolt.org/.

coliru: This website allows you to compile a single file. It prints error messages from the operating system. You can find it at http://coliru.stacked-crooked.com/.

repl.it: This website allows you to compile multiple files. You can find it at https://repl.it/languages/cpp.

Rextester: This website lets you compile a single file using Microsoft Visual C++. You can find it at https://rextester.com/.

Installing the Code Bundle

Download the code files from GitHub at https://github.com/PacktWorkshops/The-CPP-Workshop and place them in a new folder called `C:\Code`. Refer to these code files for the complete code bundle.

If you face any trouble with installation or with getting the code up and running, please reach out to the team at workshops@packt.com.

1

Your First C++ Application

Overview

This chapter equips you with the fundamental tools and techniques required to get started building basic C++ applications. We'll start by breaking a C++ application into its core components, identifying each by their role(s). We'll then take a look at the core language that defines C++, including pre-processor directives—statements that let us perform actions before our code is compiled. Finally, we'll look at how we get information in and out of our applications (I/O) before putting this all together in a final exercise in which you will write and run your own C++ application in an online compiler.

Introduction

As the world becomes smarter, so do our devices. Everything from watches to our refrigerators now have the capacity to run code, a large portion of which is C++. Between 1972 and 1973 Dennis Richie authored the C programming language while working at Bell Labs. While great for efficiency, thanks to features such as low-level memory access, C is a procedural language and so does not provide object-orientated features. In response to this, Bjarne Stroustup, also while working at Bell Labs, began working on "C with classes" in 1979. In 1983, the language was renamed C++, and it saw its first commercial release two years later in 1985. Since then, it has gone through many standardizations, the last in December 2017, and continues to be governed by the International Organization for Standardization.

Utilized in everything from operating systems to cutting-edge 3D game engines, C++ is the backbone of countless systems and industries, not least because of its high-performance capabilities, flexibility, and portability. C++ puts you close to the hardware, so it is often the tool of choice for performance-critical applications.

The goal of this course is to demystify the C++ programming language, and to get you writing quality code as quickly as possible through a very pragmatic approach. While theory is certainly required, and will be covered where necessary, we'll mainly be focusing on practical application–learning by tackling real-world exercises and activities.

To start our journey, we looked at a brief history of the language. While this alone won't make you a better programmer, it's always good to have context for what we're doing and why. By learning the origins of the language and how it's used in industry, we will set ourselves up with an informed starting point for the journey ahead.

We're then going to jump right into dissecting a basic C++ application. By breaking an application down into its constituent parts, we can gain an understanding of the main pieces that it comprises. We'll then expand on this basic understanding by looking at each part in more detail throughout the rest of this introductory chapter.

When we've concluded this chapter, we'll not only have an understanding of the origin of the language; we'll also be familiar with the different core parts of an application. We'll be able to look at an example C++ application with a sense of meaning and understanding. We'll then use this basic understanding to springboard into the next chapter, where we'll look deeper into the language at specific features and functionality.

Advantages of C++

Before we dive into the structure of a C++ program, let's have a look at a few key benefits of the language:

- **Performance**: By putting the programmer close to the hardware, C++ allows us to write very efficient programs. Along with low-level memory access, the abstraction between code and what the machine will do is smaller than in most other languages, meaning you can manipulate the system better.

- **Portability**: C++ can be cross-compiled to a wide array of platforms, and runs on everything from watches to televisions. If you're writing an application or library for more than one platform, C++ shines.

- **General purpose**: C++ is a general-purpose programming language, and is used in everything from video games to enterprise. With a rich feature set spanning everything from direct memory management to classes and other Object-Oriented Programming (OOP) principles, you can make C++ work for you.

- **Large libraries**: Since the language is used in so many applications, there's an abundance of libraries to choose from. With hundreds of open source repositories, the wealth of information (and the support systems that come with it) is vast.

C++ is a double-edged sword, however, and as the famous saying goes, "*With great power comes great responsibility*". C++ gives you enough room to do great things, but also to get yourself into trouble if used incorrectly. Bjarne himself once said of the language, "*C makes it easy to shoot yourself in the foot; C++ makes it harder, but when you do it blows your whole leg off.*" That's not to say by any means that C++ should be avoided, just that it should be used deliberately and with consideration—something the following chapter will impart.

Anatomy of a C++ Application

With a brief understanding of the history of the language, we're going to start our journey by delving into a basic C++ program to see what we're working with. There's no more fitting a start than Hello World!. This famous program prints the words `Hello World!` to the console, and has served as the starting point for scores of programmers before you. While basic, it contains all the key components of a C++ application, so will prove a great example for us to de-construct and learn from.

Let's start by taking a look at the program in its entirety:

```cpp
// Hello world example.
#include <iostream>

int main()
{
    std::cout << "Hello World!";
    return 0;
}
```

Consisting of just seven lines of code, this small program contains everything we need to look at the basic anatomy of a C++ program. We're going to cover each aspect of this program in more detail over the coming chapters, so don't worry if not everything makes perfect sense as we break this program down. The aim here is simply to familiarize ourselves with some core concepts before covering them in more detail as we progress.

Starting from the top, we have a **preprocessor directive**:

```cpp
#include <iostream>
```

Preprocessor directives are statements that allow us to perform certain operations before the program is built. The **include** directive is a very common directive that you'll see in most C++ files, and it means "copy here." So, in this case, we're going to copy the contents of the **iostream header file** into our application, and in doing so, allow ourselves to use input/output functionality it provides.

Next, we have our entry point, **main()**:

```cpp
int main()
```

The **main()** function is where your C++ application will kick-off. All applications will have this function defined and it marks the start of our application—the first code that will be run. This is typically your outer-most loop because as soon as the code in this function is complete, your application will close.

Next, we have an IO statement that will output some text to the console:

```
std::cout << "Hello World!";
```

Because we have included the **iostream** header at the start of our application, we have access to various input and output functionality. In this case, **std::cout**. **cout** allows us to send text to the console, so when we run our application, we see that the text **"Hello World!"** is printed. We'll cover data types in more detail in the coming chapters.

Finally, we have a **return** statement:

```
return 0;
```

This signals that we're done in the current function. The value that you return will depend on the function, but in this case, we return **0** to denote that the application ran without error. Since this is the only function in our application, it will end as soon as we return.

And that's our first C++ application; there's not too much to it. From here, the sky is the limit, and we can build applications that are as big and complex as we like, but the fundamentals covered here will stay the same throughout.

Seeing this application typed out is one thing, but let's get it running in our first exercise.

Exercise 1: Compiling Our First Application

In this exercise, we are going to compile and run our first C++ application. We're going to be using an online compiler throughout the course of this book (and the reasons for doing so will be explained after this exercise) but for now, let's get that compiler up and running. Perform the following steps to complete the exercise:

> **Note**
>
> The code file for this exercise can be found here: https://packt.live/2QEHoal.

1. Head to cpp.sh and take a look around. This is the compiler that we'll be using. Once you go to the address, you should observe the following window:

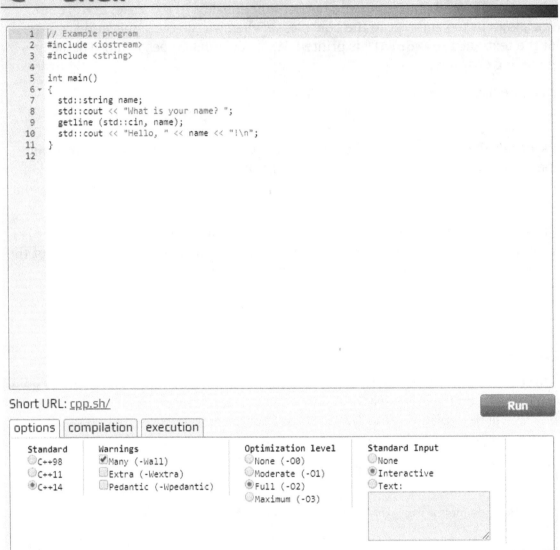

Figure 1.1: C++ shell, the online compiler we'll be using

Options: This allows us to change various compilation settings. We won't be touching this.

Compilation: This shows us the status of our program. If there are any compilation issues, they'll be shown here so we can address them.

Execution: This window is our console, allowing us to interact with the application. We'll input our values here and view the output of the application.

For our first program, we'll run the "`Hello World!`" application we deconstructed in the preceding section.

2. Type the following code into the code window, replacing all the content that's already there, and then hit **Run**:

```
//Hello world example.
#include <iostream>

int main()
{
    std::cout <<"Hello World!";
    return 0;
}
```

As you can see, the console now contains the text **Hello World!**, meaning our program ran without issue:

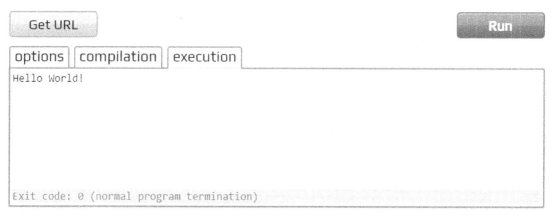

Figure 1.2: Output of our "Hello World" program

Try changing the text to something unique and run the program again.

> **Note**
>
> Here is a partial list of online C++ compilers you can use while working on the exercises. If the one you are using becomes sluggish, or you can't find it at all, try another. Online compilers are useful because they reduce the amount of stuff you have to learn to almost nothing beyond the programming language.
>
> Tutorialspoint C++ compiler: This website allows you to compile a C++ program contained in a single file. It prints error messages from the operating system. You can find it at https://www.tutorialspoint.com/compile_cpp_online.php.
>
> cpp.sh: This website allows you to pick a C++ language version and warning level, and compile a single file. However, it does not print error messages from the operating system. You can find it at http://cpp.sh/.
>
> godbolt compiler explorer: This website allows you to compile a single file on many different compilers and shows the output assembly language; its UI is a little subtle for some tastes. It prints error messages from the operating system. You can find it at https://godbolt.org/.
>
> coliru: This website allows you to compile a single file. It prints error messages from the operating system. You can find it at http://coliru.stacked-crooked.com/.
>
> repl.it: This website allows you to compile multiple files. You can find it at https://repl.it/languages/cpp.
>
> Rextester: This website lets you compile a single file using Microsoft Visual C++. You can find it at https://rextester.com/.

C++ Build Pipeline

Before we go any further, let's take a moment to discuss the build pipeline. This is the process that turns the code that we write into an executable that our machines are capable of running. When we write our C++ code, we're writing a highly abstracted set of instructions. Our machines don't natively read C++ as we do, and likewise, they're unable to run our C++ files as we write them. They first have to be compiled into an executable. This process consists of a number of discrete steps and transforms our code into a more machine-friendly format along the way:

- **Preprocessor**: As the name implies, it runs through our code before it's compiled, resolving any preprocessor directives that we may have used. These include things such as `include` statements, which we saw previously, and others such as macros and defines that we'll look at later in this chapter.

Our files are still human-readable at this point. Think of the preprocessor as a useful editor that will run through your code, doing all the little jobs you've marked, preparing our code for the next step–the compiler.

- **Compilation**: The compiler takes our human-readable files and converts them into a format that the computer can work with–that is, binary. These are stored in object files that end with `.o` or `.obj`, depending on the platform. Consider the small **Hello World !** application we dissected earlier. All that code lives in a single file, main.cpp. If we were to pass that to a compiler, we would get back main.o; an object file containing the binary version of our source code that the machine can run. This isn't quite ready to run yet, and you can't directly execute an object file. Before we can execute our application, we need to look at the final step of the pipeline–the linker.

- **Linker**: The linker is the last step in producing our executable. Once the compiler has turned our source code into binary objects, the linker comes through and links them all together, putting together our final executable.

The aforementioned steps have been visualized in the following process flow diagram:

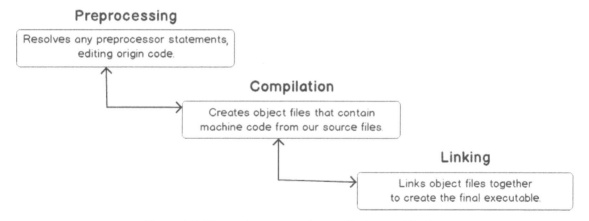

Figure 1.3: The various step of compilation and linking

These three steps are what every C++ application goes through, be it a single-file program such as the "Hello World!" program we've already discussed, or a multi-thousand-file application that you might see in real-world applications; these fundamental steps remain the same.

Different operating systems have different toolsets that perform these actions, and covering them all would not only take focus away from writing C++ itself, but potentially create different experiences, depending on the setup, especially because they're always changing. That's why in this book we'll be using an online compiler. Not only can we jump straight into writing code, but we can be sure that everyone will have the same results.

This overview of these processes has hopefully provided a solid overview of the fundamentals, so that when you do look to compile your applications in the future, the process will be familiar and you'll understand what's going on behind the scenes.

C++ Keywords

Keywords are words that are reserved by C++. Thus, we cannot use them in our applications for anything other than their intended purposes. For example, a common keyword is **if**, so you would not be able to define a variable or function of that name. It's these keywords that structure the C++ language, and it's through their use that we instruct our program on what it should be doing.

There are many keywords defined in the language, and covering them all at this early stage is not necessary. Instead, let's take a look at the keywords that we'll encounter over the coming chapters.

Some of these words define basic types, (**bool**, **char**, **int**, and so on), some of them are statements to define program flow (**if**, **else**, **switch**, and so on), and others define objects and scope (**class**, **struct**, **namespace**, and so on).

We'll be using these throughout the book, but for now we just need to know that these words are reserved by C++. You'll be able to tell because most modern text editors will highlight these words thereby making them stand out. Let's take a look at how keywords are distinguished in our code editor. Observe the following program:

```cpp
// Keywords example.
#include <iostream>

#include <string>

int main()
{
    // Data type keywords.
    int myInt = 1;
    double myDouble = 1.5;
    char myChar = 'c';
    bool myBool = true;

    // Program flow keywords.
    if (myBool)
    {
        std::cout << "true";
    }
    else
```

```
    {
        std::cout << "false";
    }


    struct myStruct
    {
        int myInt = 1;
    };
}
```

On the compiler window, the preceding code would appear as follows:

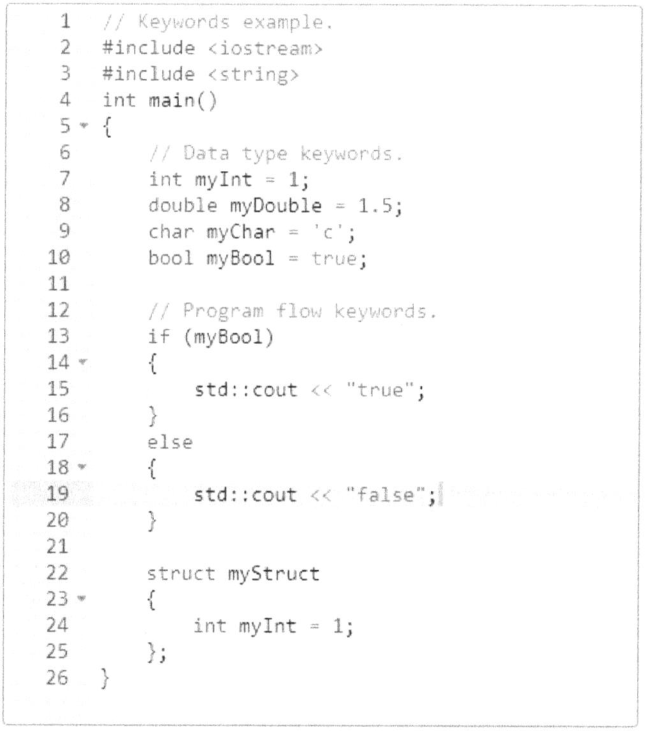

```
1    // Keywords example.
2    #include <iostream>
3    #include <string>
4    int main()
5  ▾ {
6            // Data type keywords.
7            int myInt = 1;
8            double myDouble = 1.5;
9            char myChar = 'c';
10           bool myBool = true;
11
12           // Program flow keywords.
13           if (myBool)
14 ▾         {
15               std::cout << "true";
16           }
17           else
18 ▾         {
19               std::cout << "false";
20           }
21
22           struct myStruct
23 ▾         {
24               int myInt = 1;
25           };
26   }
```

Figure 1.4: Keywords and their highlighting

We can see that the keywords in this program are given special presentation in the editor, usually a different color, to denote their status. This will differ between IDEs.

Note

IDE stands for Integrated Development Environment and is the software that we use to develop our applications. Example IDEs include Visual Studio and CLion.

Keyword Examples

Running through each keyword individually isn't necessary. We'll cover them as we go, but we can quickly take a look at some common keyword groups and what they do.

Type keywords denote the basic variable types provided by C++. These include **int**, **bool**, **char**, **double**, and **float**:

```cpp
int myInt = 1;
char myChar = 'a';
bool myBool = true;
double myDouble = 1.5;
float myFloat = 1.5f;
```

Program flow keywords allow us to structure the logic of the application. These include **if**, **else**, **then**, and **switch**, as shown in the following snippet:

```cpp
if (expression)
{
    // do this
}
else
{
    // do this instead.
}
```

Access modifiers determine what other classes and components can and can't see our C++ variables and functions. When building classes (something we'll look at shortly) we have three to choose from: **public**, **protected**, and **private**. The correct use of these modifiers plays a big part in building robust systems, ensuring our data and functionality isn't open to abuse or dangerous misuse. Here is an example:

```cpp
class MyClass()
{
public:
    int var1; // Accessible to the class, everything that can see MyClass.

protected:
    int var2; // Accessible to the class, and any child classes.

private:
    int var3; // Accessible to the class only.
}
```

Modifier types change the properties of our variables. These include **const**, **static**, **signed**, and **unsigned**. By putting these in front of our variables and functions, we can change the way they behave in our application, as shown in the following example:

```
unsigned int var1 = 1;        // Unsigned means it can only be positive.
signed int var2 = -1;         // Signed can be both positive or negative.
const std::string var3 = "Hello World"; // Const means the value
                                        // cannot be modified
static char var4 = 'c';       // Static means the value is shared
                              // between all instances of a given class.
```

Preprocessor Directives

We've come across this term a few times now, so let's look at what it means. A preprocessor directive is a statement that runs before our code is compiled. This is incredibly useful for a range of different things, from header files to selective code compilation.

Include

One of the most common directives, **#include**, we've already looked at; it means "*copy here.*" When the preprocess runs, it will literally copy and paste the contents of the included file in its place. This means that any functions, variables, classes, and so on defined in that header are now also accessible by the class containing the **include** directive.

There are two variations you'll see with this directive:

```
// Include example.
// Version 1 - Generally for system files.
#include <headerfile>

// Version 2 - Generally for programmer files.
#include "headerfile"
```

In **Version 1**, you're directing the preprocessor to look for the file using pre-defined search paths. This is typically used for system headers, and these paths might be set by your IDE, for example; they're implementation-defined.

In **Version 2**, you're directing the preprocessor to start its search locally where the file itself sits. This is generally used to include your own project headers. If this search fails, it will then resort to using the same paths as **Version 1**.

Macros

The **#define/#undef** directives allow us to define macros in our programs. A macro works similar to the **#include** statement in that it replaces content. You define a name, follow it with either some data or functionality, and then whenever you want to use that code you can refer to it by its defined name instead. When the pre-compiler runs, it will simply replace the instances of the macro name with this defined content.

A macro is defined as follows:

```
#define name content
```

With this in place, any instance of **name** in the preceding code will be directly replaced with **content**. Let's take this simple example of defining a word:

```cpp
// Macro example 1 - Defining a value.
#include <iostream>
#include <string>

#define HELLO_WORLD "Hello World!"

int main()
{
    std::cout << HELLO_WORLD;
}
```

With our macro in place, our output line is the direct equivalent of the following:

```cpp
    std::cout << "Hello World!";
```

We can see this if we run this code in the online compiler. As you can see, we get the output **Hello World!** Anywhere we want to use that string, we can use the macro instead.

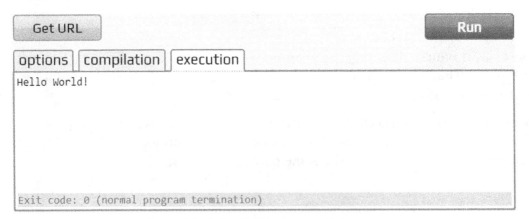

Figure 1.5: Hello World output using macro

As well as defining single values, we can also define functionality as shown in the following snippet:

```cpp
// Macro example 2 - Defining functionality
#include <iostream>

#define MULTIPLY(a,b) (a * b)

int main()
{
    std::cout << MULTIPLY(3, 4);
}
```

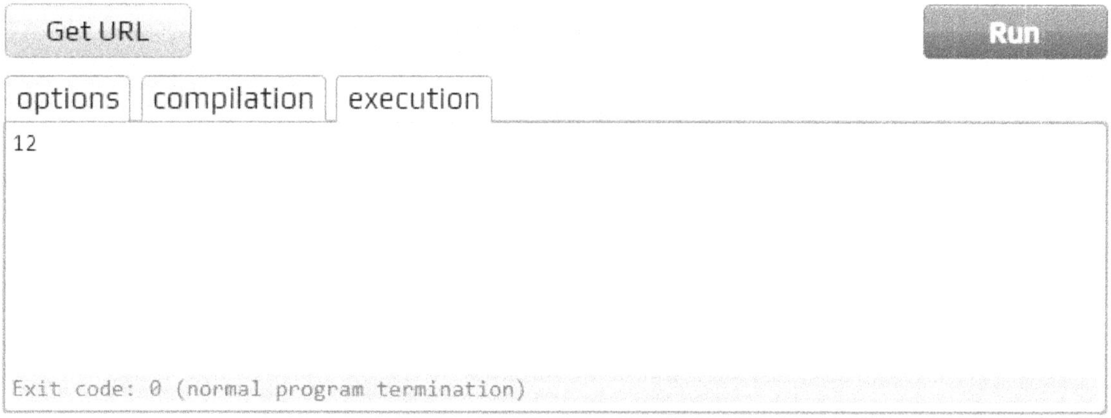

Get URL		Run
options	compilation	execution

```
12




Exit code: 0 (normal program termination)
```

Figure 1.6: Using a macro to define multiply functionality

> **Note**
>
> A significant benefit of defining functionality through macros is speed, as it reduces the overhead of function calls. There's a better way to achieve this, however, through the use of inline functions.

Once defined, a macro can be undefined using the **#undef** directive. This will remove the value/functionality assigned to the macro. If this macro is then called anywhere, an error will occur as it no longer holds a valid value.

We can see this using our first example. Let's say we make two calls to **std::cout** using the macro, but in between them we undefine the macro:

```
// Macro example 3 - Undefined macro.
#include <iostream>
#include <string>

#define HELLO_WORLD "Hello World!"

int main()
{
    std::cout << HELLO_WORLD;
    #undef HELLO_WORLD
    std::cout << HELLO_WORLD;
}
```

What behavior would you expect when we run our code this time?

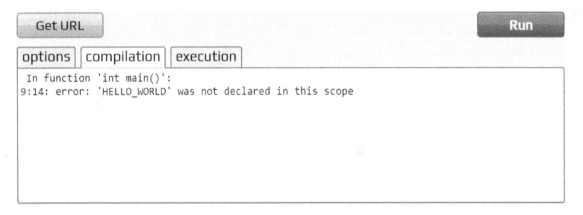

Figure 1.7: Compilation error as 'HELLO_WORLD' is undefined

As we can see, the first call remains fine. At the point the compiler hits that line, **HELLO_WORLD** is still defined. When we hit the second call, however, **HELLO_WORLD** has been undefined, so the compiler throws an error. An example of where macros such as this might be used is with debug behavior. You could define a macro, **DEBUG**, equal to **1**, and use this to produce debug code in your application where needed, and **#undef** it where not.

It's critical that macros are defined when we go to use them, so let's look at how we can ensure that's the case.

Conditional Compilation

We've just seen that if we try to use a macro that isn't defined, the compiler will throw an error. Thankfully, we have the **#ifdef/#endif** directives to help us guard against this by letting us check whether a given value is currently defined.

If we take the last example where we were getting a compiler error but safeguard against this by using these new statements, we can satisfy the compiler, as shown in the following code:

```cpp
// Macro example 4 - Ifdef macro.
#include <iostream>
#include <string>

#define HELLO_WORLD "Hello World!"

int main()
{
    #ifdef HELLO_WORLD
        std::cout << HELLO_WORLD;
    #endif

    #undef HELLO_WORLD

    #ifdef HELLO_WORLD
        std::cout << HELLO_WORLD;
    #endif
}
```

If we modify our program and run the preceding code, we can see that the compiler is now satisfied and will run the program correctly, skipping the second output altogether:

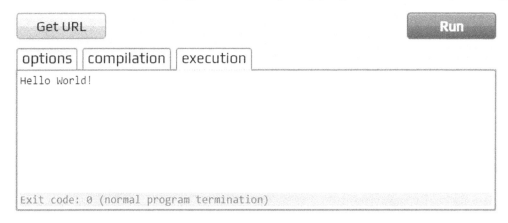

Figure 1.8: Safeguarded against the use of an undefined macro

What happens here is the code inside the **#ifdef/else** directives isn't compiled into our final program if the macro specified isn't defined at that time. We also have the **#ifndef** directive available, which checks that the value is not defined. This is used in the same way as **#ifdef**, but obviously returns the opposite value; **true** when the value is not defined, **false** if it is.

As you can imagine, we can use these for lots of things, and there are other directives that allow us to do this with any **constant** expression, not just checking whether something is defined. These are **#if**, **#else**, and **#elif**.

> **Note**
>
> A constant expression is just an expression where its value can be determined at compile time (before the program is run).

The following program shows an example of how these preprocessor directives can be used to manipulate what code gets compiled into our program:

```cpp
// Conditional compilation example.
#include <iostream>

#define LEVEL 3

int main()
{
    #if LEVEL == 0
        #define SCORE 0
    #else
    #if LEVEL == 1
        #define SCORE 15
    #endif
    #endif
```

```cpp
    #if LEVEL == 2
        #define SCORE 30
    #elif LEVEL == 3
        #define SCORE 45
    #endif

    #ifdef SCORE
        std::cout << SCORE;
    #endif
}
```

Here, we use the value of our **LEVEL** macro to determine what value we give our **SCORE** macro. Let's copy this code into the compiler and see how it behaves. Change the value of **LEVEL** and see how that affects the output.

> **Note**
>
> If we use **#if** and **#else**, each need their own matching call to **#endif**. This is not the case with **#elif**.

Figure 1.9: We can use macros to determine what code gets compiled

As we can see, by changing the value of **LEVEL**, we can change what code actually ends up being compiled into our application. One common use of this in practice is to compile platform-specific versions of things.

Let's say you've got a function that needs to do slightly different things between OSX and Windows. One way to solve this is by wrapping each function definition inside a platform define so the correct function gets compiled for each platform. Here is an example of this functionality:

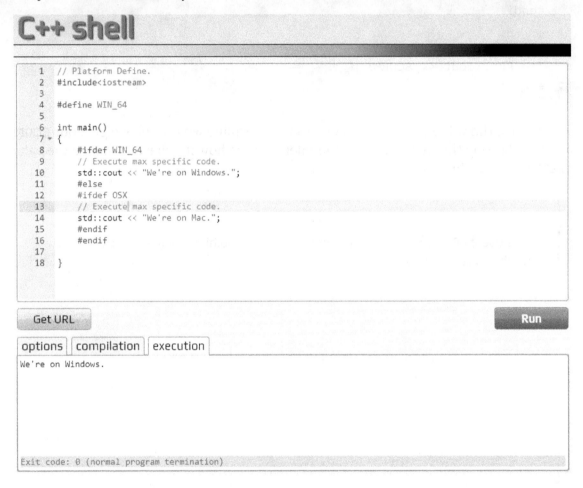

```cpp
1    // Platform Define.
2    #include<iostream>
3
4    #define WIN_64
5
6    int main()
7  ▾ {
8        #ifdef WIN_64
9        // Execute max specific code.
10       std::cout << "We're on Windows.";
11       #else
12       #ifdef OSX
13       // Execute max specific code.
14       std::cout << "We're on Mac.";
15       #endif
16       #endif
17
18   }
```

Get URL   Run

| options | compilation | execution |

```
We're on Windows.
```

```
Exit code: 0 (normal program termination)
```

Figure 1.10: Using defines to run certain code based on OS

> **Note**
>
> There is no equivalent of **#elif** when using **#ifdef**. Instead, we have to just chain **#ifdef/#endif** statements.

Now that we have a basic understanding of preprocessor directives, we will apply some of the concepts we've learned by writing a program that defines values through them.

Exercise 2: Defining Values with Preprocessor Directives

In this exercise, we're going to build a small application that will give a test score a letter grade. We'll define score thresholds in macros and use them to assign grades:

> **Note**
>
> The complete code for this exercise can be found here: https://packt.live/2rZFyqB.

1. We'll start by including our **iostream** and string headers, and defining our grade macros:

```
// Preprocessor directives activity.
#include <iostream>
#include <string>

#define GRADE_C_THRESHOLD 25
#define GRADE_B_THRESHOLD 50
#define GRADE_A_THRESHOLD 75
```

Define these thresholds as you see fit.

2. Allow the user of the program to input their test score by typing in the following code:

```
int main()
{
    int value = 0;

    std::cout << "Please enter test score (0 - 100): ";
    std:: cin >> value;
```

Don't worry that we've not yet covered the IO statements that we're about to use. We'll be covering them next.

3. Output the grade the user got based on their test score.

This is where we use the values we defined earlier. By defining these in macros, we can easily update them at a later date. This is nice as it allows us to modify the thresholds in a single location. Everywhere those macros are used will be updated as a result. Use the following code to do this:

```
    if (value < GRADE_C_THRESHOLD)
    {
        std::cout << "Fail";
```

```
    }
    else if (value < GRADE_B_THRESHOLD)
    {
        std::cout << "Pass: Grade C";
    }
    else if (value < GRADE_A_THRESHOLD)
    {
        std::cout << "Pass: Grade B";
    }
    else
    {
        std::cout << "Pass: Grade A";
    }
}
```

4. The complete code looks like this:

```cpp
// Preprocessor directives activity.
#include <iostream>
#include <string>

#define GRADE_C_THRESHOLD 25
#define GRADE_B_THRESHOLD 50
#define GRADE_A_THRESHOLD 75

int main()
{
    int value = 0;
    std::cout << "Please enter test score (0 - 100): ";
    std::cin >> value;
    if (value < GRADE_C_THRESHOLD)
    {
        std::cout << "Fail";
    }
    else if (value < GRADE_B_THRESHOLD)
    {
        std::cout << "Pass: Grade C";
    }
    else if (value < GRADE_A_THRESHOLD)
    {
        std::cout << "Pass: Grade B";
    }
    else
```

```
    {
         std::cout << "Pass: Grade A";
    }
  }
```

5. Now let's run our program. If a user inputs a score between 1-100, we can provide them with a letter grade. For an input of **50**, you will obtain the following output:

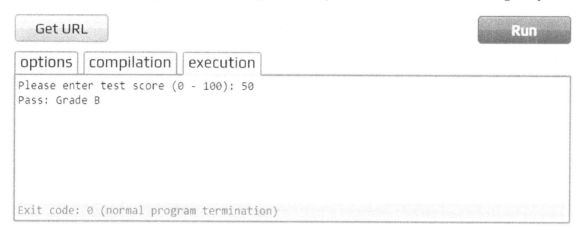

Figure 1.11: Assigning a letter grade to a user's test score

Basic I/O Statements

I/O stands for **input/output** and is how we get information in and out of our programs. This can take many forms, from inputting text via a keyboard, to clicking buttons with our mouse, to loading a file, and so on. In this chapter, and in general moving forward, we're going to be sticking with text input/output. For this, we'll use the **iostream** header.

Throughout this section, we'll be reading directly from input with little to no data validation. In a working application, however, input would be strictly validated to ensure it's of the correct format, among other things. Our lack of this is strictly for example purposes only.

The **iostream** header contains everything we need to interface with our applications via the keyboard, allowing us to get data in and out of our application. This is accomplished through the **std::cin** and **std::cout** objects.

> **Note**
>
> The **std::** prefix here denotes a namespace. This will be looked at in more depth later in the book, but for now we can just know they're used to group code.

There's a couple of ways we can read data from our keyboard. First, we can use **std::cin** with the extraction operator:

```
std::cin >> myVar
```

This will put your input into the **myVar** variable and works for both string and integer types.

Observe the following code that has an **std::cin** object included:

```cpp
// Input example.
#include <iostream>
#include <string>

int main()
{
    std::string name;
    int age;

    std::cout << "Please enter your name: ";
    std::cin >> name;
    std::cout << "Please enter you age: ";
    std::cin >> age;

    std::cout << name << std::endl;
    std::cout << age;
}
```

If we run this code in our compiler, we can see that we can enter our details and have them printed back to us:

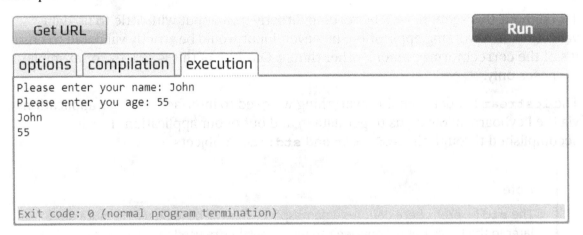

Figure 1.12: Basic IO

If you tried to enter a name with a space in, you'll have run into an issue where only the first name was captured. This gives us more insight into how **std::cin** is working; namely that it will stop capturing input when it encounters a terminating character (space, tab, or new line). We can see now why only our first name was captured properly.

It's also useful to know that extractions, the **>>** operator, can be chained. This means that the following two examples of code are equivalent:

Example 1:

```
std::cin >> myVar1;
std::cin >> myVar2;
```

Example 2:

```
std::cin >> myVar1 >> myVar2;
```

To avoid our strings being cut off when a terminating character, such as space, is encountered, we can pull the entirety of the users input into a single variable by using the **getline** function. Let's update our code using this function to get the user's name:

```
std::cout << "Please enter your name: ";
getline(std::cin, name);
```

If we run the code again, we can now see that we're able to use spaces in our name and **getline()** will capture the whole input. Using **getline()** is nicer because it means we don't have to worry about the line issues that can come with using **cin** extraction directly.

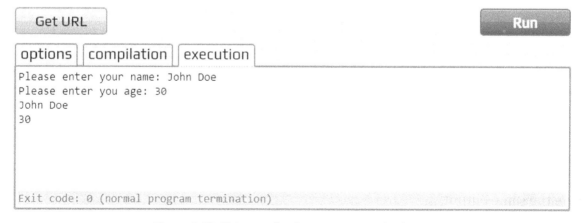

Figure 1.13: Using getline() to capture entire input

When we use **getline()**, we read our user's input into a string, but that doesn't mean we can't use it to read integer values. To convert a string value into its integer equivalent, we have the **std::stoi** function. For example, the string "**1**" would be returned as **int 1**. Combining it with **getline()** is a good way to parse integer inputs:

```
std::string inputString = "";
int inputInt = 0;

getline(std::cin, inputString);
inputInt = std::stoi(inputString);
```

Regardless of which method we use, we need to ensure that we handle strings and numerical values correctly. For example, perhaps we have some code that expects the user to input a number:

```
int number;

std::cout << "Please enter a number between 1-10: ";
std::cin >> number;
```

If the user inputs a string here, maybe they type **five** instead of inputting the number, the program won't crash, but our **number** variable won't be assigned a value. This is something we need to be aware of when getting input from our users. We need to ensure it's of the correct format before we try to use it in our programs.

Outputting text is as simple as making a call to **std::cout**, using the insertion operator, **<<**, to pass our data. This will accept both string and numerical values, so both the following code snippets will work as intended:

```
std::cout << "Hello World";
std::cout << 1;
```

As with the extraction operation, the insertion operator can be chained to build more complex outputs:

```
std::cout << "Your age is " << age;
```

Finally, when outputting text there are times where we want to either start a new line or insert a blank one. For this, we have two options, **\n** and **std::endl**. Both of these will end the current line and move to the next. Given this, the following code snippets give the same output:

```
std::cout << "Hello\nWorld\n!";
std::cout << "Hello" << std::endl << "World" << std::endl << "!";endl
```

As mentioned earlier, there are other types of input and output associated with applications; however, most of the time, IO will be facilitated through some form of UI. For our purposes, these two basic objects, **std::cin/std::cout**, will suffice.

We will apply our knowledge of the **getline()** method and the **std::cin, std:cout,** and **std::endl** objects in the next exercise.

Exercise 3: Reading User Details

In this exercise, we're going to write an application that will allow you to input your full name and age. We'll then print this information out, formatting it into complete sentences. Perform the following steps to complete the exercise:

> **Note**
>
> The complete code for this exercise can be found here: https://packt.live/37qJdhF.

1. Define the **firstName, lastName**, and **age** variables, which will hold our user's inputs, as shown in the following snippet:

```
// IO Exercise.
#include <iostream>
#include <string>

int main()
{
    std::string firstName;
    std::string lastName;
    int age;
```

> **Note**
>
> We're going to be covering data types in their own chapter later, so don't worry if the exact nature of these variable types isn't clear at this point.

2. Type in the following code, which will request the user to input their first name:

```
std::cout << "Please enter your first name(s): ";
getline(std::cin, firstName);
```

3. We'll do the same for surnames, again using **getline()** using the following snippet:

```
std::cout << "Please enter your surname: ";
getline(std::cin, lastName);
```

For our final input, we'll allow the users to input their age. For this, we can use **cin** directly because it's our last input, so we need not worry about terminating lines characters, and we're expecting a single numerical value.

4. Type the following code to have the user input their age:

```
std::cout << "Please enter your age: ";
std::cin >> age;
```

> **Note**
>
> Again, it's only because we're writing simple example programs that we're trusting our users to input the correct data and not doing any validation. In a production environment, all user input data would be strictly validated before use.

5. Finally, we'll present this information back to the user, making use of chained insertions to format complete strings and sentences using the following code:

```
std::cout << std::endl;
std::cout << "Welcome " << firstName << " " << lastName
          << std::endl;
std::cout << "You are " << age << " years old." << std::endl;
```

6. The complete code looks like this:

```
// IO Exercise.
#include <iostream>

#include <string>

int main()
{
    std::string firstName;
    std::string lastName;
    int age;
```

```
        std::cout << "Please enter your first name(s): ";
        getline(std::cin, firstName);
        std::cout << "Please enter your surname: ";
        getline(std::cin, lastName);
        std::cout << "Please enter your age: ";
        std::cin >> age;
        std::cout << std::endl;
        std::cout << "Welcome " << firstName << " " << lastName
                  << std::endl;
        std::cout << "You are " << age << " years old." << std::endl;
    }
```

7. Run our application now and test it with some data.

    For our test data (John S Doe, Age: 30), we obtain the following output:

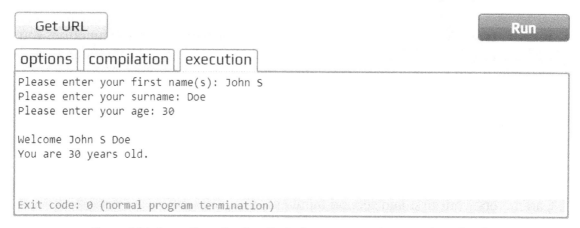

Figure 1.14: A small application that allows users to input various details

Thus, with the completion of this exercise, we have put together, through basic IO, a little program that allows users to enter some personal details. We will now move on the next topic–functions.

Functions

Functions in C++ encapsulate our code into logical units of functionality. We can then call these functions instead of having duplicate code throughout our project. For example, consider a small application that asks users for their name, greets them, and then stores that name in a list, as shown in the following snippet:

```
// Get name.
std::cout << "Please enter your name: " << "\n";
getline(std::cin, name);
std::cout << "Welcome " << name << ".\n";
names.push_back(name);
```

This is code that we will probably want to call multiple times during our application's lifetime, so it is a good candidate to be put into a function. The benefit in doing so is that it reduces duplicate code through our applications, giving us a single place where we can maintain the code and fix any bugs. If it was duplicated throughout the code base, anytime you want to upgrade it or fix something, you'd have to find all instances and do it to each.

A function is split into two parts: a **declaration** and a **definition**. In a function declaration, you're declaring the most basic information about how that function will work–namely–the type of value the function will return, the name of the function, and any parameters. The actual logic of the function's behavior is then dictated by the definition. Let's break a function declaration down.

A function is declared as follows:

```
return_type function_name(parameters);
```

- **return_type**: This is the type of value that you will return from the function. You can also return **void**, a C++ keyword, if you don't want to return anything. For example, if you had a function that added two numbers together, the return type might be **integer**.

- **function_name**: This is the name of the function and is how you'll reference it in code.

- **parameters**: These are an optional set of values that you pass into a function. Again, taking the example of adding two numbers, you would have two **integer** parameters: your first and second numbers.

This declaration usually lives in a header file (`.h`) along with other functions declarations, and they're then defined in a `.cpp` file. *This is why we see the #include directive so often.* We declare our objects' functionality in header files, then actually define how they work in `.cpp` files. We usually separate these into individual files because it allows us to hide implementation details. It's often the case that header files are made public, so we can see an object's functionality and use it, but the exact implementation of that function is kept private.

> **Note**
>
> We're not going to worry about this for now. Since we're working in a single file, we're just going to define and declare functions at the same time, not separately.

Taking this back to our previous example, we can take the snippet of code that allows a user to input their name, and define it in a function as shown in the following snippet:

```
void GetNextName()
{
    std::string name;
    std::cout << "Please enter your name: " << "\n";
    getline(std::cin, name);
    std::cout << "Welcome " << name << ".\n";
    names.push_back(name);
}
```

Now, each time we need this functionality, we can just call this function instead. The function provides its own variable, **name**, for us to use, but note that the **names** variable is being used from the main program. This is possible as it's within scope of the function. Scope is something that will be covered in detail in a later chapter, but for now we can just observe that the **name** variable is defined inside the function, while **names** is defined outside of it.

It's easy to imagine how much tidier this is now that we don't have duplicate code, just multiple calls to the same function. This makes our code more readable, maintainable, and easier to debug. This process of restructuring our code is called refactoring. We should always aim to write code that's easy to maintain, debug, and extend, and having good structure plays a big part in this.

Passing by Value, Passing by Reference

Function arguments are values that we pass into our function. If we think of our function as a discrete bit of functionality, then our parameters allow us to give it what it needs to run. There are two ways of passing parameters into functions, by value and by reference, and it's important to understand the difference.

When we pass an argument into a function by value, this means we're making a copy, and will be working with that. The easiest way to visualize this is by writing a small test application. Observe the following code:

```
// Pass by value-by-reference example.
#include <iostream>
#include <string>

void Modify(int a)
{
    a = a - 1;
}
```

```cpp
int main()
{
    int a = 10;

    Modify(a);

    std::cout << a;
}
```

In this simple program, we define a number to be 10, pass it to a function that will subtract 1 from it, and then print that value. Since we started with 10 and are subtracting 1, it would be reasonable to expect the output to be 9. However, when we run the preceding snippet, we obtain the following output:

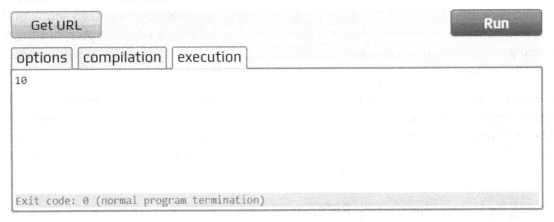

Figure 1.15: Passing by value means the change doesn't stick

Why Are We Outputting 10?

Because when we passed our **a** variable into our function, it was passed by value. The function made a local copy of **a**, in this case 10, and then anything it does to that value is completely separate from the original **a** value we passed in.

Passing by reference is the opposite of this and means, "Actually work on this variable; don't make a copy." Again, it's easiest to see this in action. Let's make the following amendment to our code:

```cpp
void Modify(int& a)
```

A very subtle change, but what we've done here is added **&** after our **int** type in the function. This symbol means "the address of." We have chapters later in the book that will cover memory in much more detail, so we'll keep it light here, but in practical terms it means, "Don't make a copy; actually use that value."

Let's re-run the code with this change in place.

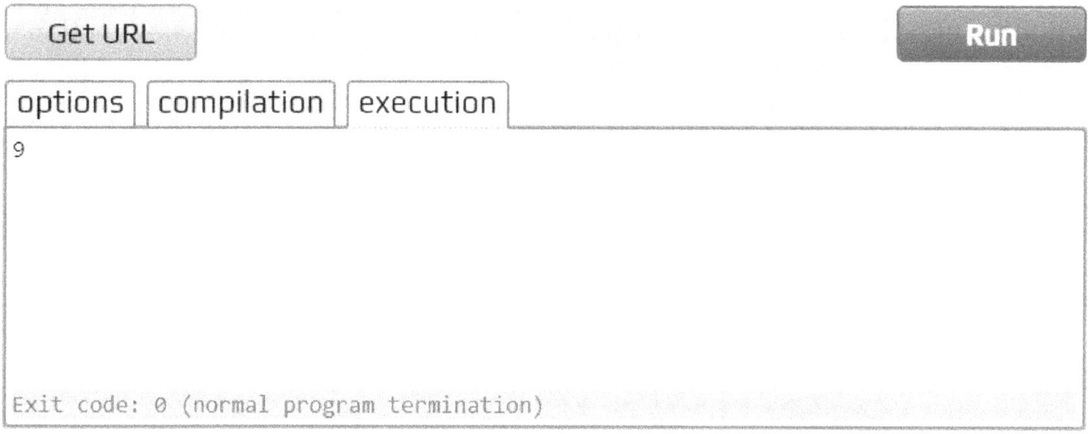

Figure 1.16: Since we're now passing by reference, the change does stick

Passing by value or by reference is an important concept to understand. If you're working with big objects, passing by value can be expensive because temporary objects have to be constructed/deconstructed. This is another topic that will be covered in later chapters. For now, taking away the fact that values can be passed either by value or by reference (as we've seen here) is sufficient. We'll build on this later.

Function Overloading

Writing functions to encapsulate our behaviors is a great step towards creating versatile and maintainable code. We can do more however; we can overload them. Overloading, in this context, means providing more than one version of the function. Let's say we define a simple function to multiply two numbers:

```
int Multiply(int a, int b)
{
    return a * b;
}
```

This function's arguments are of type **int**, so what happens if we wanted to multiply **float** types or **double**? In this case, they'd be converted to integers and we'd lose precision, not something we generally want. In order to solve this, we can provide another declaration of the function, with the same name, that can use those types. Our function declarations would look like this:

```
int Multiply(int a, int b);
float Multiply(float a, float b);
double Multiply(double a, double b);
```

What's great is we don't need to worry about calling the correct version of this function. Given we provide the correct types, the compiler will automatically call the appropriate function for us. We can see this in action with a simple test. We can create function definitions for each of these and add a unique output to each so we can tell which one's been hit.

Here is an example of how to do this:

```cpp
// Function overloading example.
#include <iostream>
#include <string>

int Multiply(int a, int b)
{
    std::cout << "Called the int overload." << std::endl;
    return a * b;
}

float Multiply(float a, float b)
{
    std::cout << "Called the float overload." << std::endl;
    return a * b;
}

double Multiply(double a, double b)
{
    std::cout << "Called the double overload." << std::endl;
    return a * b;
}

int main()
{
    Multiply(3, 4);
    Multiply(4.f, 6.f);
    Multiply(5.0, 3.0);

    return 0;
}
```

In the preceding code, we have our overloaded function and three calls to it, each with a different type. When you run this application, the following output is obtained:

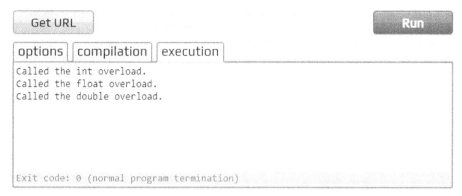

Figure 1.17: The compiler knows which version of the function to call

As we can see, the compiler knew which version of the function to call since we matched the specified parameter types in each case. A **multiply** function is a bit redundant, and certainly a simple use case of this, but demonstrates nicely how we can make our functions more useful and flexible.

Another way to achieve this flexibility is through templates. Instead of overloading a function for each individual type, with a template you create a single, highly generic version of the function that can accept any type. Templates will be covered in a later chapter.

Default Parameters

Another way we can make our functions more flexible is with default parameters. This allows us to make some of our parameters optional, and we do so by giving them a default value in the declaration as follows:

```
return_type function_name(type parameter1, type parameter2 = default
value);
```

This function could now be called in two ways:

```
function_name(value1, value2);
```

In this case, both parameter values are passed into the function as normal:

```
function_name(value1);
```

In this case, since the second parameter has been omitted, the default value will be used instead. Having the ability to provide default parameters allows us to make our functions more flexible in what they can do, but there's a limit to this. The point of a function is to neatly encapsulate a certain behavior, so we don't want to make it so flexible that it starts being responsible for multiple behaviors. In this case, it would be better to create a new discrete function.

Let's have a quick look at an example of this with another exercise.

Exercise 4: Functions

In this exercise, we're going to define and use a function that will output the larger of two numbers. This function will require a return type and two parameters. Perform the following steps to complete the exercise:

> **Note**
>
> The complete code for this exercise can be found here: https://packt.live/346VDJv.

1. Declare the function, assigning its return type, name, and parameters:

```cpp
#include<iostream>
int Max(int a, int b)
```

As we saw earlier, if we were purely declaring this function in a header file, we would add a semicolon to the end of that and define it elsewhere. Since that's not the case, however, we open our curly braces straight away and define our functionality.

2. Define the behavior of the function. We want to return the number that has the highest value, so the logic for this is easy, as shown in the following example:

```cpp
int Max(int a, int b)
{
    if (a > b)
    {
        return a;
    }
    else
    {
        return b;
    }
}
```

3. Now all we need to do is get two numbers from our users. We've covered IO earlier in this chapter, so we should be comfortable with that:

```
int main()
{
    int value1 = 0;
    int value2 = 0;

    std::cout << "Please input number 1: ";
    std::cin >> value1;

    std::cout << "Please input number 2: ";
    std::cin >> value2;
```

4. Finally, we need to output the answer to the user. We've covered this before as well, but this time, instead of using a variable in our **cout** statement, we'll make a call to our new function, passing in the user's numbers:

```
    std::cout << "The highest number is " << Max(value1, value2);
}
```

5. The complete code looks like this:

```
// IO Exercise.
#include <iostream>

#include <string>

int Max(int a, int b)
{
    if (a > b)
    {
        return a;
    }
    else
    {
        return b;
    }
}

int main()
{
    int value1 = 0;
    int value2 = 0;
```

```
        std::cout << "Please input number 1: ";
        std::cin >> value1;
        std::cout << "Please input number 2: ";
        std::cin >> value2;
        std::cout << "The highest number is " << Max(value1, value2);
    }
```

6. Run this in the compiler and test it with some numbers.

    For our test case (1 and 10), we obtain the following output:

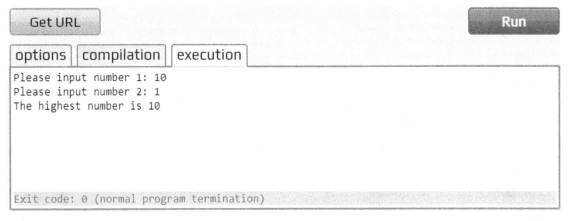

Figure 1.18: We can treat our function as its return type, in this case int, and output that value

By pulling our code into functions like this, we're able to get a wide range of functionality from little code. Not only that, but by having that functionality localized to a single function, we give ourselves a single point of failure, which is easier to debug. We also—in theory—get a re-usable chunk of code that we can deploy anywhere. Good program architecture is an art, a skill that develops with time and experience.

> **Note**
>
> I say "in theory" because while in this very simple case the code can be easily moved and re-used, it's often not the case in larger systems. Even simple functionality ends up being so ingrained into the system (and tied up in dependencies) that it's not easy to just pick it up and re-use it elsewhere.

With the core elements of a C++ application broken down, let's look at writing our own small application from scratch, putting into practice everything we've learned in this first chapter.

Activity 1: Writing Your Own C++ Application

The aim of the activity is to write a system that will ask users for their first name and age. Users will be placed into groups based on their age, and we'll use macros to define these age brackets. We'll print the user's information back to them, along with their assigned group (the name of which is also at your discretion), using functions to encapsulate any repeated functionality. Our desired outcome will be a small program that will be able to sort users into groups, as shown in the following screenshot:

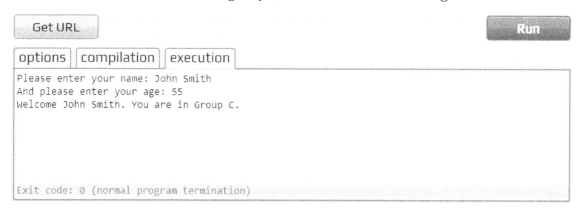

Figure 1.19: Our program asked for the user's name and age,
and assigned them to the appropriate group

Before you begin, ensure that all previous exercises have been completed because this activity will test a number of the topics that we've covered in this introductory chapter. Here are the steps to complete the activity:

> **Note**
>
> The code for this activity can be found here: https://packt.live/2QD64k4.

1. Define your age bracket thresholds using **#defines**.

2. Define a name for each group using **#defines**.

    Hint: Review *Exercise 2, Defining values with Preprocessor Directives* to complete this step.

3. Output text asking the user for their name and capture the response in a variable.

4. Output text asking the user for their age and capture the response in a variable.

5. Write a function that will accept age as a parameter and return the appropriate group name.

6. Output the user's name and the group that they have been assigned to.

    Hint: Review *Exercises* 2 and 3 to complete steps 4, 5, and 6.

This small program touches on a little bit of everything that we've covered in this introductory chapter. We've used preprocessor statements to define some application data, used IO statements to get data in and out of our app, and encapsulated code neatly within functions. Feel free to spend some time with this application before moving on, extending it as you see fit.

> **Note**
>
> The solution for this activity can be found on page 514.

Summary

In this first chapter, we've learned a little about the history of C++, covered its various applications throughout multiple industries, and deconstructed an example program. This allowed us to identify the core components and concepts that comprise a C++ application.

First, we discussed the history of the language, looking at the problems that it was designed to solve. With that context in place, we deconstructed an example application, identifying the key features of a C++ application.

With those key concepts now identified, we moved onto looking at each in greater detail. We learned some common C++ keywords and what they do. We looked at preprocessor directives and how we can use them to perform operations before our code is compiled. We then looked at basic IO statements, using `std::cin` and `std::cout` to get information in and out of our applications. And finally, we looked at functions, ways in which we can encapsulate behaviors into nice re-usable blocks of code.

To put all of this into practice, we ended with a programming task in which we constructed an application from a set brief. By developing an application that allows users to input their details, and then sorting them into groups, we put into practice the skills we've learned.

With this fundamental understanding of the anatomy of a C++ application, we can now start to delve into C++'s language features and tools. Gaining this initial understanding of an application was necessary so that we understand how our applications are built and run. Next, we're going to be looking at control flow—the means by which we control which code executes and when, allowing us to build bigger and more complex applications.

Control Flow

Overview

This chapter presents various tools and techniques that are used to control the flow of execution throughout applications. This includes, but is not limited to: if statements, switch statements, and various loops. We will also look at how we control the lifetime of our applications using these techniques, and how they are to be used efficiently. The chapter will end with the creation of a number guessing that that will implement various loops and conditional statements.

Introduction

In the first chapter, we covered the absolute essentials of C++ and looked at the key components of a C++ application. We looked at how applications run, how they're built, and how we can get information in and out of them with some basic I/O. Up until this point, the applications we've built have mainly run sequentially; that is, the code we've written has been executed line by line, sequentially. While that's great for demonstration purposes, this generally isn't how real-world applications work.

In order to represent logical systems correctly, we need to be flexible in what we do and when. For example, we may only want to perform a certain action if a given statement is true or to return to an earlier piece of code again. Manipulating execution in this manner is known as control flow (or program flow), and is the topic of this chapter.

To begin with, we are going to look at the humble **if** statement, one of the most fundamental logic statements. We'll then branch out into looking at **switch** statements, a nice alternative to long chains of **if/else** statements. Next, we'll look at loops. Specifically, we'll see how we can use them to repeat code execution, and how we can make them more efficient and precise with **break** and **continue** statements.

The chapter will conclude with a fun activity in which we'll create a number-guessing game from the ground up. This will not only require the skills we learned in *Chapter 1, Your First C++ Application*, but also the program flow skills that we're about to cover. When this chapter is finished, not only will you have a solid understanding of the core logic statements and loops, but you will have also implemented them within practical exercises.

if/else

One of the most basic, yet most important, control flow statements is if. This simple keyword is at the heart of all logic, allowing us to perform a given action only if a specified condition is true. By chaining these **if** statements together in creative ways, we can model any logical system.

The syntax for an **if** statement is as follows:

```
if (condition) { // do stuff. }
```

If the statement we use as our condition resolves to **true**, then the code within the curly braces will be executed. If the statement is **false**, then it will be skipped. Our condition can be anything that can be either true or false. This can be something simple, such as checking the value of a Boolean, or something more complex, such as the result of another operation or function.

We also have the **else** statement. This allows code to be executed if, and only if, a preceding **if** statement's condition evaluates to **false**. If the condition evaluates to true, however, and the **if** statement is thereby executed, the code within the **else** statement will not be executed. Here's an example:

```
if (MyBool1)
{
    // Do something.
}
else
{
    // Do something else.
}
```

In this example, if **MyBool1** was **true**, then we'd execute the **// Do something** code but not **// Do something else**. If **MyBool1** evaluated to **false**, however, we'd execute the **// Do something else** code but not **// Do something**.

An **else** statement can also be used together with an **if** statement. With an **else/if** block in place, should the first **if** check fail, then the second will be evaluated. Here is an example:

```
if (MyBool1)
{
    // Do something.
}
else if (MyBool2)
{
    // Do something else.
}
```

In this example, **MyBool1** will be checked first. If that returns **true**, then the **// Do Something** code will be executed but **// Do something else** will not. If **MyBool1** was **false**, however, **MyBool2** would then be checked, and the same rules would apply: if **MyBool2** was true, then **// Do something else** would execute. So, if **MyBool1** and **MyBool2** were both false, then neither code would be executed.

It's also possible to place **if** statements inside one another. This practice is referred to as nesting. Here's an example:

```
if (MyBool1)
{
    if (MyBool2)
    {
        // Do something
    }
}
```

In this example, if **MyBool1** returns **true**, then the second **if** statement will be evaluated. If **MyBool2** is also **true**, then **// Do Something** will be executed; otherwise, nothing will get executed. C++ allows us to nest many levels deep. The standard suggests 256 (although this isn't enforced), but the more levels deep you go, generally, the more confusing the code. It's good practice to minimize nesting where possible.

Now, let's get some code written and see these **if / else** statements in action.

Exercise 5: Implementing if/else Statements

In this exercise, we will write a simple application that will output a certain string based on an input value. The user will input a number, and the application will use **if/else** statements to determine whether it's either above or below 10.

Follows these steps to complete the exercise:

> **Note**
>
> The complete code can be found here: https://packt.live/2qnQHRV.

1. Enter the **main()** function and then define a variable called **number**:

```
// if/else example 1.
#include <iostream>
#include <string>

int main()
{
    std::string input;
    int number;
```

2. Write code that prints the **Please enter a number:** string, gets the user input, and then assigns it to the **number** variable:

```
std::cout << "Please enter a number: ";
getline (std::cin, input);
number = std::stoi(input);
```

> **Note**
>
> We've used the **std::stoi** function here, which we first saw in *Chapter 1, Your First C++ Application*. This function converts a string value into its integer equivalent. For example, the string **1** would be returned as **int 1**. Combining it with **getline**, as we did previously, is a good way to parse integer inputs.

3. Use **if/else** statements to evaluate the condition based on the user input and then print either **The number you've entered was less than 10!** or **The number you've entered was greater than 10!**:

```
if (number < 10)
{
    std::cout << "The number you entered was less than 10!\n";
}
else if (number > 10)
{
    std::cout << "The number you entered was greater than 10!\n";
}
return 0;
}
```

4. The complete code looks like this:

```
// if/else example 1.
#include <iostream>
#include <string>

int main()
{
    std::string input;
    int number;
    std::cout << "Please enter a number: ";
    getline(std::cin, input);
    number = std::stoi(input);
    if (number < 10)
```

```
    {
        std::cout << "The number you entered was less than 10!\n";
    }
    else if (number > 10)
    {
        std::cout << "The number you entered was greater than 10!\n";
    }

    return 0;
}
```

5. Run the complete code in your editor. You will see that it evaluates the statements and outputs the correct string, as shown in the following screenshot:

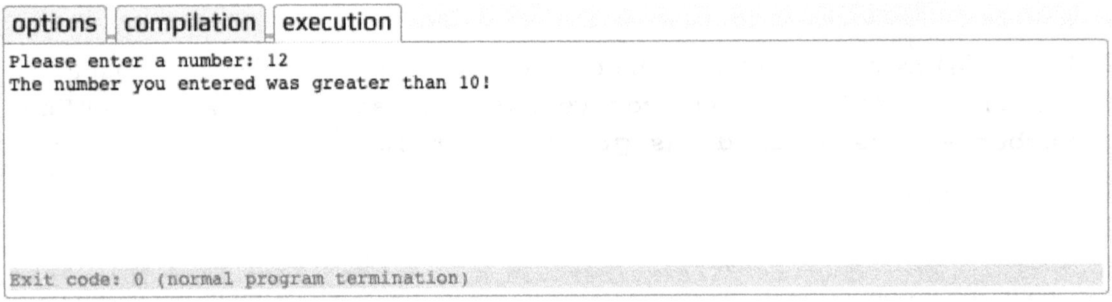

```
options   compilation   execution

Please enter a number: 12
The number you entered was greater than 10!




Exit code: 0 (normal program termination)
```

Figure 2.1: The if/else statement allows us to execute certain code based on conditions

In this preceding exercise, we used two **if** statements that both evaluate a condition, but what if we want a default action if neither condition is true? We can achieve this by using an **else** statement on its own:

```
if (condition1)
{
    // Do stuff.
}
else if (condition2)
{
    // Do different stuff.
}
else
{
    // Do default stuff.
}
```

In this case, if neither **condition1** nor **condition2** proves to be true, then the code in the **else** block will be executed as a default. This is because there's no **if** statement, so nothing has to be **true** to enter it.

Applying this to our simple number example, we currently check whether the number is less than or greater than 10, but not if it's exactly 10. We could handle this with an **else** statement, as follows:

```
if (number < 10)
{
    std::cout << "The number you entered was less than 10!\n";
}
else if (number > 10)
{
    std::cout << "The number you entered was greater than 10!\n";
}
else
{
    std::cout << "The number you entered was exactly 10!\n";
}
```

Ternary Operator

The ternary operator is a neat feature that allows us to quickly assign a value based on the outcome of an **if** statement. This is best shown with an example. Perhaps we have a float variable, the value of which depends on a Boolean. Without using the ternary operator, we could write this as follows:

```
if (MyBool == true)
{
    MyFloat = 10.f;
}
else
{
    MyFloat = 5.f;
}
```

Note

Here, we've used == instead of just =. The = operator assigns a value to a variable, whereas the == operator checks whether two values are equal, returning true if they are, and false otherwise. This will be covered in more detail in a later chapter on operators.

Using the ternary operator, we could also write this same code as follows:

```
MyFloat = MyBool ? 10.f : 5.f;
```

That's much more concise. Let's break down the syntax here and see what's happening. A ternary statement is written as follows:

```
variable = condition ? value_if_true : value_if_false;
```

> **Note**
>
> While ternary statements can be nested as we saw earlier with **if** statements, it's probably best to avoid it. They can be a real pain to read and understand at a glance.

We start by specifying the condition that we want to evaluate and follow it with the ? character. This sets our ternary statement in motion. We then define the different values we want to use if the value is **true** or **false**. We always start with the **true** value, followed by the **false** value, with them separated by the : character. This is a great way to concisely handle an **if/else** scenario.

Exercise 6: Creating a Simple Menu Program Using an if/else Statement

In this exercise, we're going to write a simple program that provides menu options for a food outlet. Users will be able to select multiple options from a menu, and we will present the price information based on that choice.

Here are the steps to complete the exercise:

> **Note**
>
> The complete code for this exercise can be found here: https://packt.live/35wflPd.

1. Create the template application, and output our three menu options to the user:

```
// if/else exercise - Menu Program
#include <iostream>
#include <string>

int main()
{
    std::string input;
```

```
        int number;

        std::cout << "Menu\n";
        std::cout << "1: Fries\n";
        std::cout << "2: Burger\n";
        std::cout << "3: Shake\n";
```

2. Next, we'll ask them to input their choice and store it:

```
        std::cout << "Please enter a number 1-3 to view an item price: ";
        getline (std::cin, input);
        number = std::stoi(input);
```

3. Now, we can use our **if/else** statements to check the user input and output the correct information:

```
        if (number == 1)
        {
            std::cout << "Fries: $0.99\n";
        }
        else if (number == 2)
        {
            std::cout << "Burger: $1.25\n";
        }
        else if (number == 3)
        {
            std::cout << "Shake: $1.50\n";
        }
        else
        {
            std::cout << "Invalid choice.";
        }

        return 0;
    }
```

4. The complete code looks like this:

```
    // if/else exercise - Menu Program
    #include <iostream>
    #include <string>

    int main()
    {
        std::string input;
```

```
    int number;

    std::cout << "Menu\n";
    std::cout << "1: Fries\n";
    std::cout << "2: Burger\n";
    std::cout << "3: Shake\n";
    std::cout << "Please enter a number 1-3 to view an item price: ";
    getline(std::cin, input);
    number = std::stoi(input);
    if (number == 1)
    {
        std::cout << "Fries: $0.99\n";
    }
    else if (number == 2)
    {
        std::cout << "Burger: $1.25\n";
    }
    else if (number == 3)
    {
        std::cout << "Shake: $1.50\n";
    }
    else
    {
        std::cout << "Invalid choice.";
    }

    return 0;
}
```

5. Run the application. When we input our menu option, we're presented with the correct information for that item, as shown in the following screenshot:

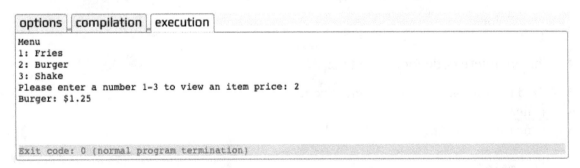

Figure 2.2: We can make menu selections and output the correct information

This ability to perform an action if a given condition is true really is at the heart of all programming. If you break down any system far enough, it will comprise "if x is true, do y." With this covered, the possibilities are endless.

switch/case

As we've seen, we can use **if/else** to perform certain actions based on which conditions are true. This is great when you're evaluating multiple conditional statements to determine flow, such as the following:

```
if (checkThisCondition)
{
    // Do something ...
}
else if (checkAnotherCondition)
{
    // Do something else ...
}
```

When we're evaluating the different possibilities of a single variable, however, we have a different statement available to us: the **switch** statement. This allows us to branch in a similar way to an **if/else** statement, but each branch is based on a different possible value of a single variable that we're switching on.

A good example of where this would be suitable is the menu application we created in the previous exercise. Currently, we chain **if/else** statements to handle the different possible values, but since we're switching on a single variable (the menu index), it would be more suitable as a switch statement.

A basic implementation of a **switch** statement block is as follows:

```
switch (condition)
{
    case value1:
        // Do stuff.
    break;

    case value2:
        // Do stuff.
    break;

    default:
        // Do stuff.
    break;
}
```

Applying this to the previous menu example, the condition would be the selected menu index that we read from our user, and the different values would be our supported possibilities (1-3). The default statement would then catch the cases where the user inputs an option that we're not handling. We could print an error message in those cases and have them select a different option.

A switch statement comprises a number of keywords:

- **switch**: This denotes the condition that we're evaluating. We're going to switch our behavior based on its value.

- **case**: Each case statement is followed by the value that we want to handle. We can then define our behavior for that scenario.

- **break**: This statement signals the end of our code for that given case. More on these in the next topic.

- **default**: This is the default case and is what will get called should none of the other cases match.

> **Note**
>
> A default case is not required but is recommended. It allows us to handle all other values, perhaps throwing an exception.

An important limitation of `switch` statements is that they can only be used with certain types. These are whole numbers and `enum` values. This means that, for example, we couldn't use either string or float types within a switch statement.

> **Note**
>
> Enumerated type, or `enum`, is a user-generated data type in C++. A detailed discussion on this is beyond the scope of this book. However, you can refer to the following documentation for further details: https://packt.live/35I6QWT.

It's also worth noting that not every case needs a `break` statement. They are optional, though will likely be required in the vast majority of cases. If the `break` statement is omitted, however, then the flow of execution will continue to the next `case` statement until a break is hit. Be careful here because missing `break` statements is a common cause of hard-to-find bugs; ensuring each case has a `break` statement where needed could save you lots of potential debugging time down the line.

Perhaps the best way to see the use of a **switch** statement is to convert some **if/else** chains to switch statements. This will be the objective of the following exercise.

Exercise 7: Refactor an if/else Chain into switch/case

In this exercise, we will reuse the code from the previous exercise and refactor it into a **switch** statement. This will clearly show how we can represent the same functionality using either method. Since we're only checking the different possible values of a single variable, however, a **switch** statement is preferred.

> **Note**
>
> Ensure that you have copied the code from the previous exercise (steps 1-2) in the compiler window. The complete code can be found here:
> https://packt.live/32ZZ5Ek.

We will break this down into a number of simple steps:

1. First, the variable we're checking here is **number**, so that's going to be the condition that we're switching on. Add that to a **switch** statement and open our curly brackets ready for the rest of the switch block:

    ```
    switch (number)
    {
    ```

2. Next, we'll convert our first **if** statement into a **case** statement. If we look at the first one, we're checking whether **number** is equal to 1. Add this as our first **case** value and copy the output into the **case** body:

    ```
    case 1:
        std::cout << "Fries: $0.99\n";
    break;
    ```

3. Now, repeat this for each of the **if** statements, apart from the last one. If you remember, this statement had no condition that it checked; it's simply the last option. This meant that if all other checks failed, execution would fall right through to that final default statement. This is exactly how the default case works, so we will end by moving that **else** statement into a default case. We should end up with the following **switch** statement, which will replace our **if/else** chain:

    ```
    switch (number)
    {
        case 1:
            std::cout << "Fries: $0.99\n";
    ```

```
        break;

    case 2:
        std::cout << "Burger: $1.25\n";
        break;

    case 3:
        std::cout << "Shake: $1.50\n";
        break;

    default:
        std::cout << "Invalid choice.";
        break;
    }
```

This statement is functioning the same as the chained **if/else**, so you could use either; however, you generally see switch statements over long **if** chains. Now, let's run this code and check that it's behaving how we'd expect.

4. The complete code looks like this:

```
// if/else to switch/case
#include <iostream>
#include <string>

int main()
{
    std::string input;
    int number;
    std::cout << "Menu\n";
    std::cout << "1: Fries\n";
    std::cout << "2: Burger\n";
    std::cout << "3: Shake\n";
    std::cout << "Please enter a number 1-3 to view an item price: ";
    getline(std::cin, input);
    number = std::stoi(input);

    switch (number)
    {
    case 1:
        std::cout << "Fries: $0.99\n";
        break;
```

```
        case 2:
            std::cout << "Burger: $1.25\n";
        break;

        case 3:
            std::cout << "Shake: $1.50\n";
        break;

        default:
            std::cout << "Invalid choice.";
        break;
        }

    }
```

5. Run the complete code. You will obtain an output that's similar to the following:

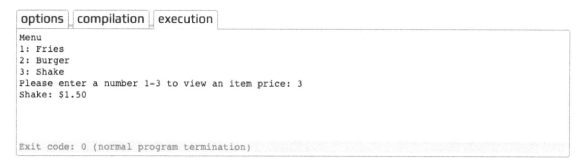

Figure 2.3: The code works the same, but this time presented as a switch statement

The program behaves in the same way but is arguably neater and easier to follow. We can clearly see each possible behavior branch and the case that will let it execute.

Loops

Alongside **if** statements, loops are among the most fundamental of programming concepts. Without loops, our code would execute by running through our logic statements one by one and then ending. That's how our applications have worked so far; however, in reality, this really isn't practical. Systems tend to consist of many moving parts, and code execution will jump all around the code base to where it's needed.

We've seen how this can be achieved by creating branches in our code where statements can be evaluated, and we do different things based on the outcome. Another way we do this is via loops. Loops allow us to rerun sections of code, either a set or indefinite number of times depending on which one we choose. We're going to be looking at three: **while**, **do while**, and **for** loops.

while

A **while** loop is one of the most basic loops in your arsenal and is usually the outermost loop in an application. When execution enters a while loop it typically won't leave until the condition is false. We say generally because multithreaded applications can break this rule; however, they're beyond the scope of this introductory book. Here is the basic implementation of a **while** loop:

```
while (condition)
{
    // Do stuff.
}
```

The following flowchart shows the structure and logic flow of a **while** loop:

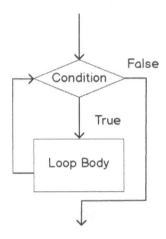

Figure 2.4: A while loop flowchart

A common thing to see in an application is an outmost **while** loop that will evaluate a **bool** such as **bIsRunning**. With this, you set an indefinite lifespan for your application, which is usually what we want. We want the software to run for as long as the user wants it to. As soon as we want the loop to stop running, we just change the bool to **false**. We need to be careful here, however, as it's easy to make a **while** loop that never ends as the condition never evaluates **false**. In this case, your loop will get stuck indefinitely with no way out.

The following code snippet shows this approach of using a **while** loop as an outermost loop to control the lifetime of the application. While **bIsRunning** is **true**, the application will run indefinitely:

```
int main()
{
    bool bIsRunning;
```

```
    // Do application setup.

    while (bIsRunning)
    {
        // Run application logic.
    }

    // Do application cleanup.

    return 0;
}
```

We've written a few example apps that accept user input, but generally stop after the first input. Let's take one of our existing applications and modify it so that it runs in a **while** loop; we'll continue with the menu application that we refactored into a switch. We want to put all of the code that we want to rerun inside the **while** loop. This includes the outputting of the menu items, the user selection, and the outputting of their answers.

Exercise 8: Implementing a while Loop

In this exercise, we will reuse the code from *Exercise 7, Re-factor an if/else Chain into switch/case*, and implement a **while** loop in our menu program.

> **Note**
>
> The complete code for this exercise can be found here: https://packt.live/35lj81p.

Follow these steps to complete the exercise:

1. Copy the code from the previous exercise into the compiler window.

2. Now, implement a **while** loop and pass the value **true** into it shown in the following:

```
#include <iostream>
#include <string>
int main()
bool bIsRunning = true;
{
    while (bIsRunning)
    {
        std::string input;
```

```
        int number;

        std::cout << "Menu\n";
        std::cout << "1: Fries\n";
        std::cout << "2: Burger\n";
        std::cout << "3: Shake\n";
        std::cout << "Please enter a number 1-3 to view an
                  item price: ";
        getline (std::cin, input);
        number = std::stoi(input);

        switch (number)
        {
            case 1:
                std::cout << "Fries: $0.99\n";
            break;

            case 2:
                std::cout << "Burger: $1.25\n";
            break;

            case 3:
                std::cout << "Shake: $1.50\n";
            break;

            default:
                std::cout << "Invalid choice.";
            break;
        }
    }
}
```

3. The complete code looks like this:

```
#include <iostream>

#include <string>

int main()
bool bIsRunning = true;
{
```

```cpp
    while (bIsRunning)
     {
         std::string input;
         int number;
         std::cout << "Menu\n";
         std::cout << "1: Fries\n";
         std::cout << "2: Burger\n";
         std::cout << "3: Shake\n";
         std::cout << "Please enter a number 1-3 to view an
                     item price: ";
         getline(std::cin, input);
         number = std::stoi(input);

         switch (number)
         {
             case 1:
                 std::cout << "Fries: $0.99\n";
             break;

             case 2:
                 std::cout << "Burger: $1.25\n";
             break;

             case 3:
                 std::cout << "Shake: $1.50\n";
             break;

             default:
                 std::cout << "Invalid choice.";
             break;
         }
     }
}
```

4. Run the program.

    For now, we just want this application to run indefinitely, hence we have used **true** as our expression. We can see that it loops, re-asking the user for their selection again, as shown in the following output:

```
 options   compilation   execution
Menu
1: Fries
2: Burger
3: Shake
Please enter a number 1-3 to view an item price: 1
Fries: $0.99
Menu
1: Fries
2: Burger
3: Shake
Please enter a number 1-3 to view an item price: 2
Burger: $1.25
Menu
1: Fries
2: Burger
3: Shake
Please enter a number 1-3 to view an item price: 3
Shake: $1.50
Menu
1: Fries
2: Burger
3: Shake
Please enter a number 1-3 to view an item price:
```

Figure 2.5: The application now loops and is able to process multiple user inputs

do while

The structure of a do while loop is very similar to that of a **while** loop, with one fundamental difference: the condition check is after the body. This subtle difference means that the body will always be executed at least once. The basic structure of a **do while** loop is as follows:

```
do
{
    // code
}
while (condition);
```

The following flowchart shows the structure and logic flow of a **do while** loop:

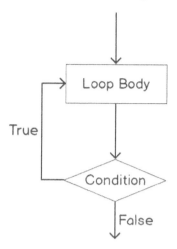

Figure 2.6: Diagram of a do while loop

Look at the following example:

```
while (false)
{
    // Do stuff.
}
```

The code inside this **while** statement will never be executed because we first evaluate the expression, **false**, and thus skip over that code. If we were to use the same condition with a **do while** loop, however, as shown in the following code snippet, we would see different behavior:

```
do
{
    // Do stuff.
}
while (false);
```

In this case, since the execution runs from top to bottom, the code is executed first, and then the condition; even though it's **false**, the code has already run once. We will see this with the help of our old friend—the **Hello World** program.

Exercise 9: Implementing while and do while Loops with a False Condition

In this exercise, we will edit our "Hello World" program to include a **while** and then a **do while** loop. For both of these loops, we will pass the **false** condition and observe the outputs.

> **Note**
>
> The complete code for this exercise can be found here: https://packt.live/2rc9vU2.

Follow these steps to complete the exercise:

1. Insert the following code, which includes a **while** loop only, in the compiler window, and then execute it:

```cpp
// While loop.
#include <iostream>
#include <string>

int main()
{
    while (false)
    {
        std::cout << "Hello World!";
    }

    return 0;
}
```

You will obtain the following output:

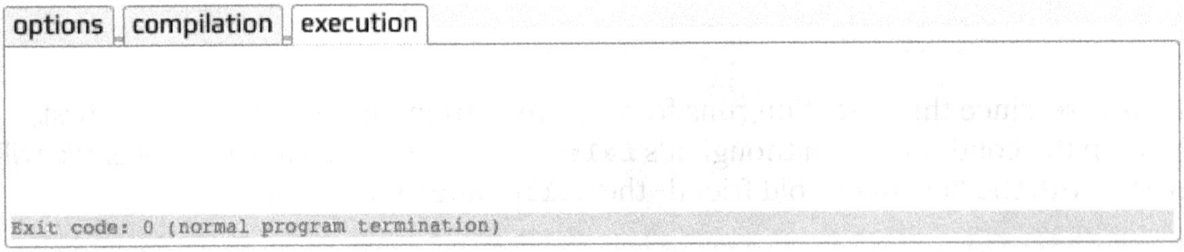

```
options   compilation   execution




Exit code: 0 (normal program termination)
```

Figure 2.7: Output when using the while loop

As can be seen in the output, we see nothing in the execution window. Since we did the evaluation first, the program never executed the code. This changes, however, if we replace the while loop with a do while loop.

2. Edit the code to include a **do while** loop, as shown in the following snippet:

```cpp
// do ... while loop.
#include <iostream>
#include <string>

int main()
{
    do
    {
        std::cout << "Hello World!";
    }
    while (false);

    return 0;
}
```

3. Run the code. You should obtain the following output:

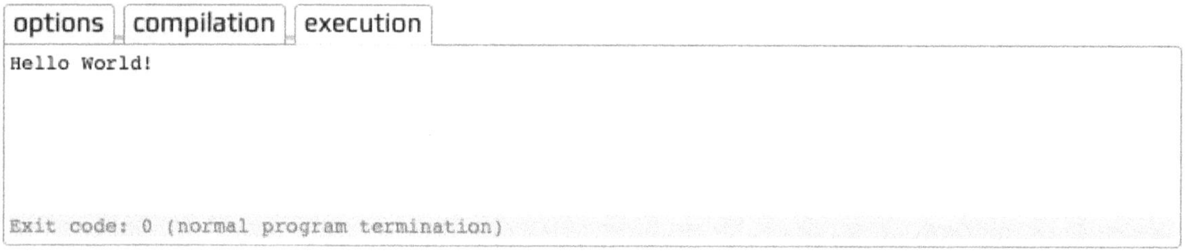

```
options  compilation  execution
Hello World!



Exit code: 0 (normal program termination)
```

Figure 2.8: A do while loop showing that the body is executed at least once

Now, we can see that we do indeed get the words **Hello World** printed to the console; so, while the two loops are similar in nature, they have a big difference. The **while** loop will evaluate the condition first, whereas the **do while** loop evaluates it after.

for

Both **while** and **do while** loops are indefinite loops, meaning they will only stop when their conditions evaluate **false**. Generally, when constructing these loops, we don't know how many iterations we need; we simply set it going and stop it at some later juncture. **for** loops, however, are used when we know how many iterations of something we need, and when we need to know what iteration we're currently on.

For example, let's say we have a collection of contacts and we want to run through them all, printing out their names and numbers. Since we know the size of this collection, we could write a for loop that would iterate the correct number of times, allowing us to visit every element in the collection sequentially. Since we also know which iteration we're currently on, we could use that to determine how we output the data. Perhaps, for the first half of the contact list, we want to output both the name and number, whereas, for the second half, we only require numbers. Or perhaps we want to do something special with the first and last contacts in the list. A **for** loop would allow us to do all of these things.

> **Note**
>
> One iteration is just a loop running once. If a loop is said to iterate five times, it just means it ran five times.

The basic structure of a **for** loop is as follows:

```
for (initialization; condition; iteration expression)
{
    statement(s);
}
```

The following flowchart shows the structure and logic flow of a **for** loop:

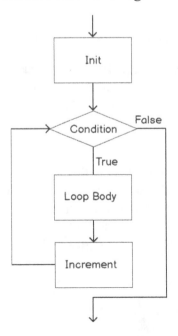

Figure 2.9: A for loop diagram

There are three clauses that are used in a **for** loop:

- **Initialization**: This is a statement that is run once at the very start of the loop. This is used to declare a variable that will be used as a counter.

- **Condition**: This is the condition that is checked each time before the loop runs. If the condition is **true**, the loop will run. If the condition is **false**, that's the end of the **for** loop. This is used to check that the counter variable is below a specified value. This is how we control how many times the loop will run.

- **Iteration Expression**: This is a statement that's run at the end of each loop. It's used to increment the counter variable.

Now, let's implement a basic **for** loop in the next exercise to cement our understanding.

Exercise 10: Implementing a for Loop

In this exercise, we will create a **for** loop that will run five times to print out a string of numbers: **01234**.

> **Note**
>
> The complete code for this exercise can be found here: https://packt.live/332boQl.

Perform the following steps to complete the exercise:

1. Begin with the main function:

```
#include <iostream>
#include <string>

int main()
{
```

2. Create a **for** loop with the variable **i** initialized to **0**, and **i** set to be less than **5**; increment the counter, and then finally print the output. You can use the following code for this:

```
for (int i = 0; i < 5; ++i)
{
    std::cout << i;
}
}
```

3. The complete code looks like this:

```cpp
#include <iostream>
#include <string>

int main()
{
    for (int i = 0; i < 5; ++i)
    {
        std::cout << i;
    }
}
```

4. Run the code. You will obtain the following output:

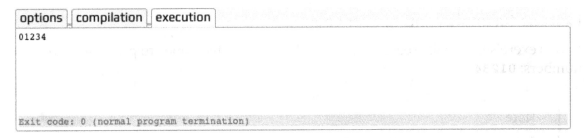

Figure 2.10: Output of the for loop

We can see that 5 numbers are printed out, 0 through 4, as shown in the preceding screenshot. Notice that the numbers are 0 through 4, as the increment runs after the main loop body, and **i** starts with a value of 0.

We can break the code down into the three statements we identified in the preceding section: **initialization**, **condition**, and **increment**. Our **initialization** statement in this loop is as follows:

```cpp
int i = 0
```

With this statement, we're creating our counter and setting its value to 0. This counter is what will be used to keep track of how many times we want our loop to run. Our **condition** statement in this loop is as follows:

```cpp
i < 5
```

This is the **condition** that we check to ensure that the loop can run, similar to how the `while` loop works. At the start of each iteration, this **condition** is checked. If `I` (our counter variable) is less than the value specified, then the loop will run. Our **increment** statement in this loop is as follows:

```
++i
```

This statement is called after each iteration of the loop and increments our counter so we can keep track of how many times the loop has run.

Range-based for loop

The last loop we're going to look at, and more briefly than the previous three, is the range-based loop. Introduced in C++ 11, this loop allows us to quickly iterate over all objects in a collection. We've not yet covered collections, so we will only address the basics here.

When iterating over collections using a `for` loop, we use the iterator. In our use cases, that's been the `i` variable to access the elements as shown in the following snippet:

```
int myVector[] {0, 1, 2, 3, 4};
for (int i = 0; i < myVector.size(); ++i)
{
    int currentValue = myVector[i];
    std::cout << "\n" << currentValue;
}
```

With a range-based `for` loop, however, we don't manually get the element via our incrementing value. Instead, the loop simply gives us each value in the collection:

```
int myVector[] {0, 1, 2, 3, 4};
for (int currentValue : myVector)
{
    std::cout << "\n" << currentValue;
}
```

Both these loops will produce the same output, but we can see that the second loop is more concise, less prone to error because we aren't manually fetching our elements, and is also very likely to be more efficient. Generally, if you don't need an index value, then this kind of loop will allow you to have cleaner, more solid code.

Exercise 11: Generating Random Numbers Using Loops

In this exercise, we're going to build an app that will generate a set of random numbers for the user. Our application will consist of a main outer loop and another loop within it to control the generation of our numbers.

For the outer loop, we're going to use a **while** loop—a common setup for an application. We know that this loop will run indefinitely, so it is perfect for controlling the outermost scope of an application. For the inner loop, we'll use a **for** loop, because we'll know how many numbers our user wants to generate.

> **Note**
>
> The complete code for this exercise can be found here: https://packt.live/2s4it6l.

Follow these steps to complete the exercise:

1. We'll start by creating our **main** function and defining our **main** variables. This includes the **bIsRunning bool**, which will control the lifetime of our application:

```
#include <iostream>
#include <string>
#include <cstdlib>
#include <ctime>

int main()
{
    bool bIsRunning = true;
    std::string input = "";
    int count = 0;
```

2. Next, we'll output our heading content and create the **main** loop. We're using a **while** loop, and our condition is going to be that **bool** we just defined:

```
std::cout << "***Random number generator***\n";
while (bIsRunning)
{
```

3. With our **while** loop in place, we can now add all the code that we want to run during each iteration of the **main** loop. This starts with outputting our instructions and reading the user input:

```
std::cout << "Enter amount of numbers to generate,
        or 0 to exit: ";
// Get count from user.
getline(std::cin, input);
count = std::stoi(input);
```

We've covered **break** in this chapter, and we can now use it to check whether the user wants to exit the application. If the user entered a **0**, indicating this, we can call **break**, exiting the main **while** loop and ending the application. We'll also set the seed for our random number generation.

> **Note**
>
> To generate our random numbers, we're using **rand** and **srand**. **rand** gives us our random number, and **srand** sets a seed for the random number generation. By using **time(0)**, time in seconds since the epoch, we get a seed and number random enough for our needs.

4. Input the following code to insert a **break** statement to allow the user to exit the application. We'll cover 'break' in more detail shortly:

```
// Check if user wants to quit application.
if (count == 0)
{
    break;
}
// Generate and output random numbers.
srand((unsigned)time(0));
```

5. Now, we can write the **main** loop that will generate our random numbers and output them to the user. Since we got a **count** variable from our user, we can use that to ensure we iterate the correct number of times. Within the loop, we'll generate a random number and do a bit of formatting. After each number, we want to print a comma to create a well-formatted list, but not after the last one. We can use a **continue** statement for this:

> **Note**
>
> The **continue** statement will be covered in the next topic. For now, note that it allows us to skip the rest of the current loop, starting the next one immediately.

```
        for (int i = 0; i < count; ++i)
        {
            std::cout << rand() % 10;
            if (i == count - 1)
            {
                continue;
            }
            std::cout << ", ";
        }
    }
```

> **Note**
>
> The modulus % operator returns the remainder after division. In the preceding step, we are using it, along with **rand()**, to generate numbers between 0 to 9. We'll cover this, and many other operators, in more detail in *Chapter 4, Operators*.

6. Finally, we'll output a couple of blank lines for presentation and add our final curly braces:

```
        std::cout << "\n\n";
    }
}
```

7. The complete code looks like this:

```
#include <iostream>
#include <string>
#include <cstdlib>
#include <ctime>

int main()
{
    bool bIsRunning = true;
    std::string input = "";
    int count = 0;
    std::cout << "***Random number generator***\n";
    while (bIsRunning)
    {
        std::cout << "Enter amount of numbers to generate,
                or 0 to exit: ";

        // Get count from user.
        getline(std::cin, input);
```

```cpp
        count = std::stoi(input);
        // Check if user wants to quit application.
        if (count == 0)
        {
            break;
        }

        // Generate and output random numbers.
        srand((unsigned) time(0));
        for (int i = 0; i < count; ++i)
        {
            std::cout << rand() % 10;
            if (i == count - 1)
            {
                continue;
            }

            std::cout << ", ";
        }
        std::cout << "\n\n";
    }
}
```

8. Run the application. When complete, the application should be able to generate the specified number of random integers, as shown here:

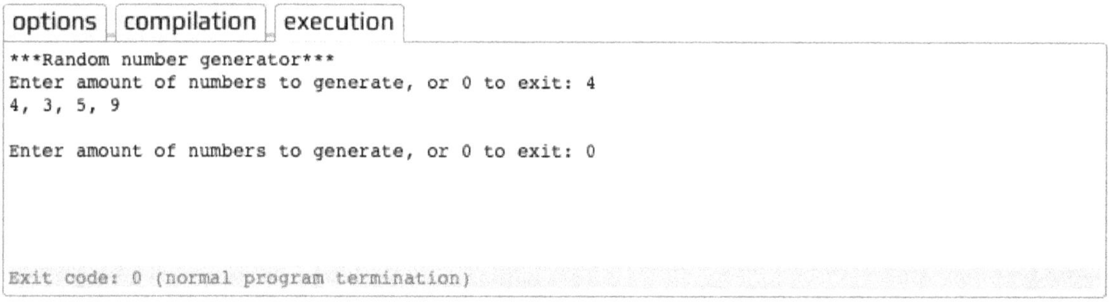

```
options   compilation   execution

***Random number generator***
Enter amount of numbers to generate, or 0 to exit: 4
4, 3, 5, 9

Enter amount of numbers to generate, or 0 to exit: 0



Exit code: 0 (normal program termination)
```

Figure 2.11: Program that will run indefinitely, outputting a series of numbers if the user doesn't quit

By using a **while** loop, we've been able to create an application that can be used for an indefinite amount of time. Imagine if every time you went to do something on your computer, you could only do one thing before it needed to be rebooted. This would not be very practical. Having the ability to loop code and manipulate program flow is essential.

break/continue

Having the ability to loop sections of code is very important, but it has to be used carefully. We've seen that it's possible to create loops that never end, and another concern is ensuring that they're used efficiently. So far, the loops we've looked at have been small, and we've been happy to see them run through in their entirety. But what if we needed more control over our loops, perhaps to end one early? Thankfully, we have two important keywords to help us with that—**break** and `continue`.

break

break is a C++ keyword that will exit the current loop, with execution jumping to the next section of code if there is any. This keyword works with the different types of loop that we've covered so far, and we can demonstrate it nicely using a simple counting application, as shown in the following snippet:

```cpp
// Break example.
#include <iostream>
#include <string>

int main()
{
    std::cout << "Loop Starting ...\n";

    int count = 0;

    while (count < 5)
    {
        ++count;
        std::cout << "\n" << count;
    }

    std::cout << "\n\nLoop finished.";
}
```

In this example, we're going to print out 5 numbers, 0-4. If we run this code as is, we can see that the loop runs in its entirety and gives us our expected outcome. We've also got statements at the start and end of the loop so we can see the flow execution more clearly:

Figure 2.12: Example counting application will print out numbers 0-4

Now, what if there was a condition that meant we wanted this loop to stop executing when the count was equal to 2? Well, we can put a **break** statement inside that check using an **if** statement:

```cpp
#include <iostream>

using namespace std;

int main()
{
    std::cout << "Loop Starting ...\n";
    int count = 1; // init
    while (count <= 5) // condition
    {
        std::cout << "\n" << count;
        if (count == 2)
        break;
        ++count; // increment
    }
    std::cout << "\n\nLoop finished.";

    return 0;
}
```

With that **break** condition in place, as soon as the count is equal to **2** (meaning we'll have had 2 iterations of the loop) then the break will be hit and we'll exit the loop. Now, let's run the application and see what we get:

```
options   compilation   execution
Loop Starting ...

1
2

Loop finished.


Exit code: 0 (normal program termination)
```

Figure 2.13: With the break statement in place, we only execute 2 loop iterations

We can now see, as soon as that condition is met and the **break** statement is hit, that the loop stops iterating, and code execution picks up immediately after the loop. The outcome of this will be exactly the same if we write it as a **do...while**:

```cpp
#include <iostream>

using namespace std;

int main()
{
    std::cout << "Loop Starting ...\n";
    int count = 1; // init
    do
    {
        std::cout << "\n" << count;
        if (count == 2)
        break;
        ++count; // increment
    }
    while (count <= 5); // condition

    std::cout << "\n\nLoop finished.";
    return 0;
}
```

And it will be the same if we write it as a **for** loop:

```cpp
#include <iostream>

using namespace std;

int main()
{
    std::cout << "Loop Starting ...\n";
    // init condition increment
    for (int count = 1; count <= 5; ++count)
    {
        std::cout << "\n" << count;
        if (count == 2)
        break;
    }

    std::cout << "\n\nLoop finished.";
    return 0;
}
```

Both these loops give the exact same behavior; two iterations before hitting the **break** statement and exiting the loop:

```
options   compilation   execution

Loop Starting ...

1
2

Loop finished.


Exit code: 0 (normal program termination)
```

Figure 2.14: All loops give the same outcome: two iterations before exiting

This shows that these loops are sometimes interchangeable, though some are more suited to certain use cases than others. For instance, with the counting example we're using here, a **for** loop is probably most suitable since it comes with an integer value that increments each loop–something we have to do manually with **while** and **do while** loops. When an incrementing integer is not required, however, a range-based **for** loop is recommended.

continue

The other keyword we have at our disposal is **continue**. This keyword allows us to skip over the current loop iteration but remain in the loop, in contrast with **break**. Again, the counting example will allow us to demonstrate this. In our example, we're printing the numbers 0-4; let's use the **continue** keyword to skip the printing of the number 3.

As we did with **break**, we can write a condition to check whether the count is equal to 3, and call **count** if so:

```
if (count == 3)
{
    continue;
}
```

We also need to change the location of this within our function. The **continue** keyword will skip the rest of the loop's body. Currently, this code is at the end of that body, so we won't actually be skipping anything. In order for **continue** to work as expected, it needs to come before any code that we want to skip but after any code we want to execute.

For this example, we will place the **continue** keyword with the **if** statement:

```cpp
// continue example.
#include <iostream>
#include <string>

int main()
{
    std::cout << "Loop Starting ...\n";

    int count = 0;

    while (count < 5)
    {
        ++count;

        if (count == 3)
        {
            continue;
        }

        std::cout << "\n" << count;
```

```
    }

    std::cout << "\n\nLoop finished.";
}
```

Here, we're always going to increment our **counter** variable and then check whether we want to skip the current iteration. If we do skip it, we'll just go back to the start of the next loop, and if we don't, we'll execute the remainder of the loop as usual. Once you run this code, you will obtain the following output:

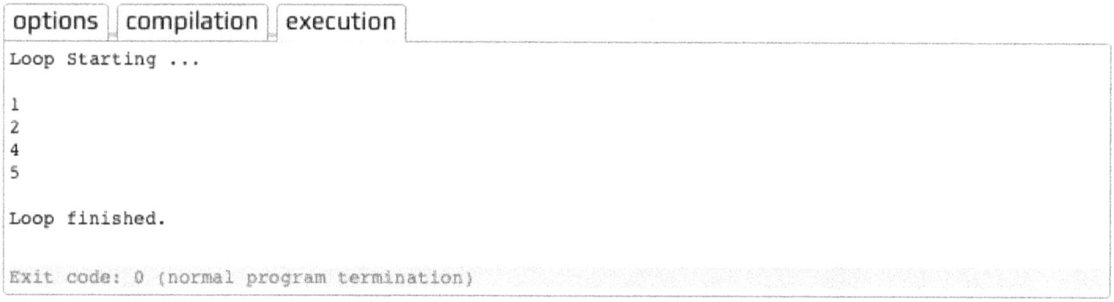

```
options  compilation  execution
Loop Starting ...

1
2
4
5

Loop finished.

Exit code: 0 (normal program termination)
```

Figure 2.15: The printing of number 3 has been skipped

We've skipped the printing of number 3 as we wanted, but the loop continued to execute the rest of the way. This can be extremely useful when searching for something. Imagine we have a list of names, and we only want to do things with those that start with the letter D. We could iterate over all our names, first checking whether or not the first letter is D; if not, we continue. In this way, we efficiently skip the use cases that don't interest us.

Exercise 12: Making a Loop More Efficient Using break and continue

In this exercise, we're going to make use of **break** and **continue** to make a loop more efficient. We'll create a loop that will run over the numbers 1-100, printing out only specific multiples of a given value.

> **Note**
>
> The complete code for this can be found here: https://packt.live/2KJrnN8.

Follow these steps to complete the exercise:

1. We'll first ask the user to choose the value whose multiples will be printed, as well as the maximum number of multiples to print:

```cpp
#include <iostream>
#include <string>

int main()
{
    int multiple = 0;
    int count = 0;
    int numbersPrinted = 0;
    std::string input = "";

    std::cout << "Enter the value whose multiples will be printed: ";
    getline(std::cin, input);
    multiple = std::stoi(input);

    std::cout << "Enter maximum amount of numbers to print: ";
    getline(std::cin, input);
    count = std::stoi(input);
```

2. Next, we'll create the **for** loop to iterate over the numbers 1-100:

```cpp
for (int i = 1; i <= 100; ++i)
{

}
```

3. Now, within the **for** loop, we can write the logic for determining our multiples. First of all, we have a set amount of numbers that we're going to print, so we can check that and **break** if that number has been reached:

```cpp
if (numbersPrinted == count)
{
    break;
}
```

4. We're only interested in numbers of our given multiple, so if that's not the case, we can use the **continue** statement to jump straight to the next iteration:

```cpp
if (i % multiple != 0)
{
    continue;
}
```

5. If the loop iteration makes it past both of these statements, then we've found a valid number. In this case, we'll print it, and then increment our **numbersPrinted** variable using the following snippet:

```cpp
        std::cout << i << "\n";
        ++numbersPrinted;
    }
```

6. The complete code looks like this:

```cpp
#include <iostream>
#include <string>

int main()
{
    int multiple = 0;
    int count = 0;
    int numbersPrinted = 0;
    std::string input = "";

    std::cout << "Enter the value whose multiples will be printed: ";
    getline(std::cin, input);
    multiple = std::stoi(input);

    std::cout << "Enter maximum amount of numbers to print: ";
    getline(std::cin, input);
    count = std::stoi(input);
    for (int i = 1; i <= 100; ++i)
    {
        if (numbersPrinted == count)
        {
            break;
        }
        if (i % multiple != 0)
        {
            continue;
        }
        std::cout << i << "\n";
        ++numbersPrinted;
    }
}
```

7. Run the application. You will obtain the following output:

```
options   compilation   execution
Enter the value whose multiples will be printed: 4
Enter maximum amount of numbers to print: 6
4
8
12
16
20
24

Exit code: 0 (normal program termination)
```

Figure 2.16: We use break and continue to control loop execution

By using the **break** and **continue** statements, we're able to control the execution of our loops, making them more efficient and controlled.

Activity 2: Creating a Number-Guessing Game Using Loops and Conditional Statements

For this chapter's activity, we're going to write a small number-guessing game. This will allow us to utilize the techniques that we've covered in this chapter. Thus, before attempting this activity, ensure that you have completed all the previous exercises in this chapter.

The program will allow the user to select a number of guesses: a minimum number and a maximum number. The application will generate a number within that range and then allow the user to guess the number. If they do so within the number of guesses they specified at the start, they win the game. Upon winning a game, the final output should be similar to the following:

```
options   compilation   execution
***Number guessing game***

Enter the number of guesses: 5
Enter the minumum number: 1
Enter the maximum number: 10

Enter your guess: 4
Your guess was too high. You have 4 guesses remaining
Enter your guess: 2
Well done, you guessed the number!

Enter 0 to exit, or any number to play again: 0

Exit code: 0 (normal program termination)
```

Figure 2.17: Number-guessing game output

> **Note**
>
> The complete code for this activity can be found here: https://packt.live/2pBYnPT.

Here are the steps to complete the activity, along with a few hints:

1. Declare all the variables we'll need. This includes **guessCount**, **minNumber**, **maxNumber**, and **randomNumber**.

2. Create a main outer loop that will run the application.

3. Present the user with some introductory text (**"Enter the number of guesses"**) and get from them the following: a number of guesses, a minimum number, and a maximum number.

   > **Note**
   >
   > You can pass the user input for the number of guesses, the minimum number, and the maximum number, to the variables.

4. Generate a random number within the range specified by the user.

   > **Note**
   >
   > In *Exercise 11, Generating Random Numbers Using Loops*, we've used **rand()** for generating random numbers between 0 to 9. Here, you can use a function similar to **rand () % (maxNumber - minNumber + 1)** to generate random numbers between two arbitrary limits.

5. Create a loop that will iterate the number of times that the user specified as their guess count.

6. Inside the **count** loop, fetch the user's guess.

7. Inside the **count** loop, check whether the user's guess is correct or too high/low. We can use **break** here to exit when the correct value has been guessed.

   Hint: Refer to *Exercise 7, Refactor an if/else Chain into switch/case*, to see how we used **break** to exit loops early.

8. When the number has been found, or the user has run out of guesses, present them with the option to either continue or exit the application.

> **Note**
>
> The solution to this activity can be found on page 516.

Within this application, we've used a number of techniques to control the flow of code to replicate a more complex scenario. We used a **while** loop for the main application loop, as we didn't know initially how many iterations were required. We then used a **for** loop to run the code a set number of times, and **if/else** statements to check the user's input and act accordingly.

Summary

In this chapter, we've learned about program flow and how we can manipulate the flow of execution through our applications. This is fundamental for representing logical systems.

We started by looking at basic **if/else** statements. These allow us to branch our code based on conditions and are one of the most fundamental ideas in programming. With this branching ability, we're able to replicate logical systems and behaviors by controlling the flow of execution through our application. We then looked at some alternatives to the basic **if/else** statement, such as **switch** and **ternary** statements.

Next, we looked at a number of different loops. We started with **while** and **do while** loops; loops that run indefinitely so long as the condition they're checking is true. We then looked at **for** loops, which run for a set number of iterations. Finally, we looked at **range-based** loops, which are useful for iterating over collections. We ended by looking at how we can ensure our loops are efficient, ending them early with the **break** statement, or by skipping iterations with the **continue** statement.

We put all of these new skills to practice by building a simple game that allowed the user to guess a number that had been randomly selected. We allowed the user to input a number of values in order to set up the game, and then gave them a number of guesses to try to find the number. We employed everything we learned in *Chapter 1, Your First C++ Application*, as well as if/else statements and a couple of the loops that we looked at in this chapter.

In the next chapter, we're going to take a closer look at the various data types that C++ offers. We'll start by looking at the various built-in types (**int**, **double**, **char**, and so on), moving onto looking at arrays and collections of these types. We'll then move onto ideas such as storage lifetime, scope, classes, and structs. With an understanding of C++ applications in general, controlling the flow of execution, and soon how to represent and store our data in various data types, we're well on our way to a functional understanding of the C++ language.

3

Built-In Data Types

Overview

This chapter presents the built-in data types provided by C++, including their fundamental properties and use within vectors and arrays. Well start by identifying and describing a selection of core data types, before moving onto their implementation both individually, and within containers such as vectors and arrays. We'll then look at their lifetime and scope before implementing them within a sign-up application we'll create as the final exercise of the chapter.

Introduction

In the previous chapter, we looked at control flow, learning a number of ways in which we can manipulate the flow of execution through our applications. In this chapter, we're going to take a closer look at how we represent that information using different data types; specifically, the built-in data types provided by C++.

We've used a few of them previously; for example, we know that integers represent numbers, and strings represent words and characters, but let's go into more detail. The core set of types provided by C++ are the building blocks for any and all user-defined types that we'll create later down the line, so a good understanding of what we have available to us is very important. We'll start by looking at the data they store, how they are assigned, and their sizes. We can then move onto looking at type modifiers—keywords that allow us to modify their properties. A chart will be provided for future reference.

Next, we'll move onto looking at creating arrays of those types. So far, the majority, if not all, of our variables have been singular—that is, a single number or a single string. As well as storing these individually we can store multiples of these together in collections. These are called arrays and are an important feature to understand and be comfortable with using.

After arrays, we'll be looking at storage lifetime or scope. This is the concept of where variables belong, and how long they're accessible for. This is a fundamental topic, so a strong understanding is key, and will lead us on to our final topic—classes and structs. These are objects that encapsulate our data and functions and are the heart of **Object-Oriented Programming** (**OOP**). These will be covered in detail in *Chapter 9, Object-Oriented Principles*, so our coverage here will merely constitute a brief introduction.

To finalize this chapter, we'll be putting what we've learned to the test by creating a real-world sign-up application. This will be the biggest application we've created so far and will allow users to both sign up to a system and to look up existing records via an ID. Not only will this make use of the concepts covered in this chapter, but all preceding ones too.

By the time this chapter has been completed, you will not only have a much greater understanding of the properties of the various types that we've used but also understand their lifetime and how they come in/out of existence within our applications.

Data Types

As we've seen throughout the book so far, we store data in variables—a user's name, age, or the price of food items. Given that these are different types of data—alphabetical, numerical, and so on, we store them in different variable types. It's these types that we're going to be taking a look at now, as it's important to use the correct variable type for the data you want to store.

Type Modifiers

Before we look at the fundamental data types themselves, however, let's quickly look at type modifiers. Initially mentioned in *Chapter 1, Your First C++ Application* when we looked at keywords, type modifiers allow us to change the properties of integer types. The following modifiers are available to us:

- `signed`: The `signed` keyword specifies that our variable can hold both positive and negative values. This increases the maximum lower value since we can now go negative, but doing so decreases the maximum upper value. This is because the range of values the variable can hold doesn't change; it just shifts, meaning half the range is now dedicated to negative numbers.

- `unsigned`: The `unsigned` keyword specifies that our variable should only hold positive values. This increases the upper range of the variable but decreases its lower range as it's capped at 0.

- `long`: The `long` keyword ensures that our variable will be at least the size of an `int`; typically, this will be 4 bytes. This will, in some cases, increase the range of the value that can be stored.

- `long long` (C++11): The `long long` keyword, added in C++11, ensures that our variable will be greater in size than `long`; typically, this will be 8 bytes. This will, in most cases, increase the range of the value that can be stored.

- `short`: The `short` keyword ensures that our variable has the smallest memory footprint it can, whilst ensuring a size less than `long`; typically, this will be 4 bytes.

> **Note**
>
> The exact size of data types depends on factors such as the architecture that you're working with and what compiler flags are set, though typical sizes will be shown in a reference chart shortly. It's important to note that the C++ standard does not guarantee absolute sizes for types but minimum ranges that they must be able to store. This then means that modified types may also differ between platforms.

Built-In Types

Now that we've had a primer on modifiers, we can look at the core set of fundamental data types that C++ provides us with. These types will serve your needs most of the time, and you don't need to do anything special to use them; they're part of the language. These built-in types are as follows:

- **bool**: The **bool** type stores either a **true** (non-zero) or **false** (0) value and has a size of one byte.

- **int**: The **int** type is used to store integers and is typically four bytes in size.

- **char**: The **char** type is used to store a single character. This is stored in the form of an integer and gets resolved into a character depending on which character set is used, typically ASCII. This data type is one byte in size.

- **float**: The **float** type represents single-precision floating-point numbers and is typically 4 bytes in size.

- **double**: The **double** type represents double-precision floating-point numbers and is typically 8 bytes in size.

- **void**: The **void** type is a special type that denotes an empty value. You cannot create objects of the **void** type. However, it can be used by pointers and functions to denote an empty value—for example, a **void** pointer that points to nothing, or a **void** function that doesn't return anything.

- **wide character**: The **wchar_t** type is used to store wide characters (Unicode UTF-16). The size of **wchar_t** is compiler-specific, although C++11 introduced the fixed size types, **char16_t** and **char32_t**.

Reference Table

Here is a table of the basic data types provided by C++ with a selection of type modifiers:

Type	Typical Size (Bytes)	Range (Based on Size)
bool	1	true (non-zero) or false (0)
int (signed)	4	-2,147,483, 648 to 2,147,483,647
unsigned int	4	0 to 4,294,967,295
short int (signed)	2	-32, 768 to 32,767
unsigned short int	2	0 to 65,535
long int (signed)	4	-2, 147, 483, 648 to 2, 147, 483, 647
unsigned long int	4	0 to 4, 294, 967, 295
long long int (signed) (C++11)	8	-9,223,372,036,854,775,808 to 9,223,372,036,854,775,807
unsigned long long int (C++11)	8	0 to 18,446,744,073,709,551,615
char (signed)	1	-128 to 127
unsigned char	1	0 to 255
float	4	+/- 1.4023x10-45 to 3.4028x10+38
double	8	+/- 4.9406x10-324 to 1.7977x10308

Figure 3.1: Table of C++ data types and their sizes

Note

The ranges of these types are dictated by their size and are not dependent on the data type. Also, the values in preceding table are only true for Microsoft Visual C++. The size of the fundamental types is different in gcc and clang than it is in visual studio.

Exercise 13: Declaring Data Types

For the chapters first exercise, we're going to declare a number of different variables, with and without type modifiers, and print out their size using the `sizeof` operator. Here are the steps to complete the exercise:

Note

If you're using a different compiler to the one in this book, don't be alarmed if your sizes are different. Remember, they can be sized differently on different platforms and architectures. The code files for this exercise can be found here: https://packt. live/2rdD8Em.

1. We'll start by defining a number of variables using three of the types from the preceding table:

```
int myInt = 1;
bool myBool = false;
char myChar = 'a';
```

2. The **sizeof** operator will give us the size of our variables in bytes. For each variable defined previously, add an **output** statement that will print its size:

```
std::cout << "The size of an int is " << sizeof(myInt) << ".\n";
std::cout << "The size of a bool is " << sizeof(myBool) << ".\n";
std::cout << "The size of a char is " << sizeof(myChar) << ".\n";
```

3. The complete code looks like this:

```
#include<iostream>

using namespace std;

int main()
{
    int myInt = 1;
    bool myBool = false;
    char myChar = 'a';
    std::cout << "The size of an int is " << sizeof(myInt) << ".\n";
    std::cout << "The size of a bool is " << sizeof(myBool) << ".\n";
    std::cout << "The size of a char is " << sizeof(myChar) << ".\n";

    return 0;
}
```

4. Run this code. You should see the sizes of our variables printed out:

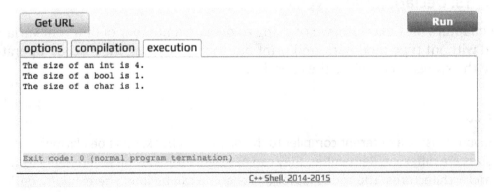

Figure 3.2: Using sizeof to determine the size of our variables

By using **sizeof**, we can quickly see the sizes of our variable. Again, your mileage may vary here depending on what platform and compiler configuration you're using. Continue this with some of the other data types that are listed in the preceding reference chart and see whether your sizes match those given. It's good to know this information about our data types so that we can be sure to use the most appropriate ones for a given scenario.

Containers

Now that we've looked at some of the built-in data types provided by C++, let's take a look at a couple of containers—objects that allow us to store multiple elements together. They come in many shapes and sizes depending on what data you're storing and how you wish to do so. For this early chapter, we're going to be focusing on two fundamental containers—arrays and vectors. Not all languages provide these types; Python, for example, has neither but provides lists instead. With C++, however, we're spoiled for choice. The standard library contains a myriad of collections to suit our needs, but these two are the ones we'll be focusing on in this chapter.

Arrays

Arrays are containers of objects, so instead of storing a single value in a variable, we can store many of them. These all sit next to one another in memory, so we access them through a single variable and an index. When we declare an array, we need to know its size at compile time since its memory is allocated upfront:

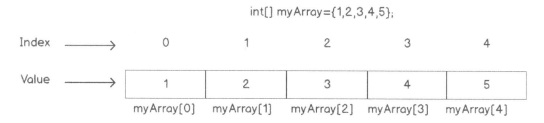

Figure 3.3: An array diagram

For example, perhaps we wanted to store some customers' ages; let's say five of them. We could do the following:

```
int customerAge1;
int customerAge2;
int customerAge3;
int customerAge4;
int customerAge5;
```

This gives us our five values, but it's taken five variable declarations, and each time we want to access a customer's age, we need to know which variable we need to use. With an array, however, we could store all this data in a single variable. Also, if you cast your mind back to *Chapter 2, Control Flow*, we saw how we can use loops to iterate over arrays, another really useful property to have. Let's, therefore, store this data in an array instead.

We declare arrays as follows:

```
type arrayName [numberOfElements]
```

So, in the case of our preceding example, we could do this:

```
int customerAges[5];
```

Note that this just creates the space in memory for five **int** values to sit nicely side by side. It hasn't yet given any of those integers a value, meaning they'll contain garbage at this point. We can see this if we try to access elements of the array before initializing it properly, as shown in the following snippet:

> **Note**
>
> We're going to cover accessing array values shortly, so don't worry if the following syntax is new to you.

```
int customerAges[5];
std::cout << customerAges[0] << std::endl;
std::cout << customerAges[1] << std::endl;
std::cout << customerAges[2] << std::endl;
std::cout << customerAges[3] << std::endl;
std::cout << customerAges[4] << std::endl;
```

If we were to run this code, we would get garbage data as we're yet to assign values to our individual integers within the collection:

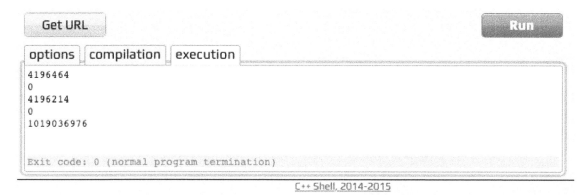

Figure 3.4: Since our array is uninitialized, our values hold garbage data

Let's look at remedying that.

Initialization

To initialize our arrays with values, C++ gives us a number of options, all of which make use of braces { }. When we define our array, we can give each element a value explicitly by placing them within braces and assigning them to our new array:

```
int customerAges[5] = {1, 2, 3, 4, 5};
```

This is a complete initialization as we're declaring an array with five elements in it and passing five values, one for each. If we rerun the preceding code, we will see that all values are now valid:

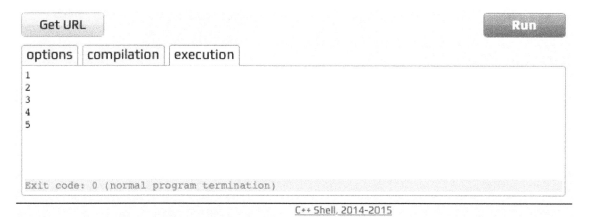

Figure 3.5: With the array properly initialized, we have valid data

When we initialize an array like this, passing in a value for each element, we can omit the size in the square brackets since the compiler is able to work it out for us. In this case, we're passing five elements in, so an array will be created of that size. This means that the following two array declarations are valid and result in the same array:

```
int customerAges[5] = {1, 2, 3, 4, 5};
int customerAges[] = {1, 2, 3, 4, 5};
```

We can also provide a partial initialization by providing values for some of our elements, but not all:

```
int customerAges[5] = {1, 2, 3};
```

Here's what we would expect if we were to make this change and then rerun the preceding code and our three initialized values, followed by the last two containing garbage:

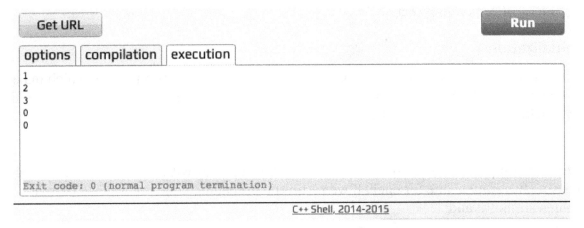

Figure 3.6: With partial initialization, we have a mix of our defined values and a default

We get a mix of our initialized values and default values. This is because C++ will treat empty braces as a default value, so the missing elements get treated as such. As an extension of this behavior, we could even initialize the array with just an empty set of brackets and all elements would be given this default value:

```
int customerAges[5] = {};
```

The output, in this case, would be as follows:

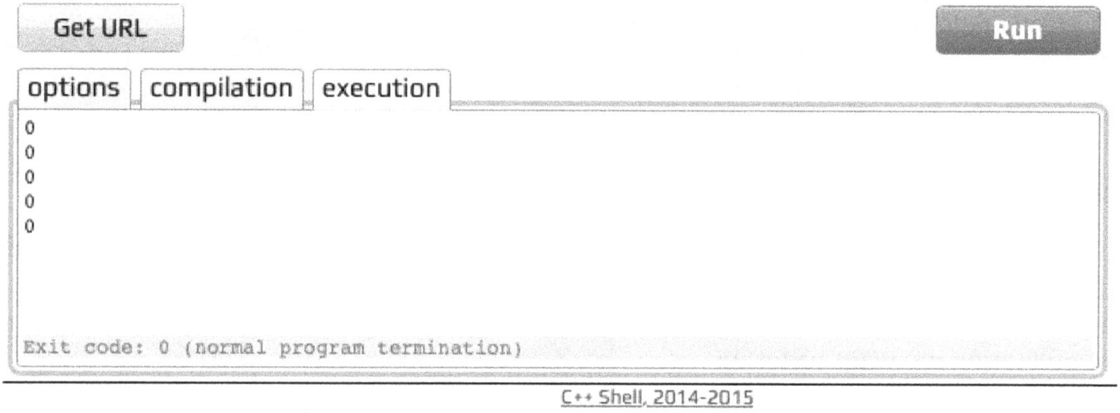

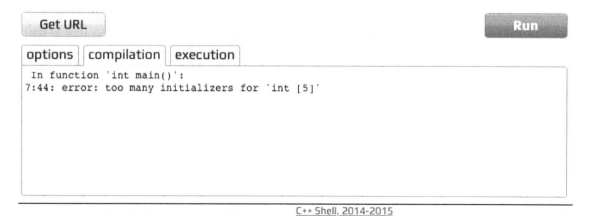

Figure 3.7: All our elements have default values since we used empty brackets

It's important here to note that while you can pass in fewer elements than the array can hold (in this case, three where we have an array of size five), this doesn't work the other way around. That is, you can't pass in more elements than the array can hold. Consider the following statement:

```
int customerAges[5] = {1, 2, 3, 4, 5, 6};
```

We're declaring an array of size five, but trying to initialize six elements. Thankfully, a compiler warning is thrown and our error can be corrected before we cause damage to something:

Figure 3.8: Trying to initialize too many elements throws a compiler error

Finally, since C++11, we've been able to initialize member arrays with braces directly, meaning the = symbol is no longer required. In practice, this means that the following two array declarations are identical and will produce the same array:

```
int customerAges[5] = {1, 2, 3, 4, 5};
int customerAges[5] {1, 2, 3, 4, 5};
```

Accessing Elements

Since we're now storing multiple values within a single collection, with a single variable name, we need a way of accessing the elements individually. For that, we use indices. Placed within square brackets after our variable name, they indicate which element in that collection we want to fetch:

```
int myArray[5] {1, 2, 3, 4, 5};
int mySecondValue = myArray[1];
```

It's important to note that in C++ and most other languages, indices start at **0**, not **1**. In our preceding example, that means that we'll output the number 2, not 1. It's also important to not attempt to access elements that don't exist. For example, in our preceding array, we have a total of 5 elements, meaning the indices 0-4 are valid. If we tried to access an element with index 5, our application would crash.

Let's look at the following snippet:

```
int myArray[5] {1, 2, 3, 4, 5};
int mySecondValue = myArray[5];
```

In this code, our array only has five elements, yet we try to access the sixth. This will read memory that doesn't belong to our array and will almost always result in a crash. We therefore have to make sure we use a valid index when accessing elements.

There are a couple of ways in which this can be done. A more classic approach is to find the size of the entire array, find the size of an element, and divide them to calculate how many elements it contains:

```
sizeof(myArray)/sizeof(myArray[0])
```

C++11 gives us **std::array**, which has its length accessible. This is accessed through the **<array>** header:

```
std::array<int, 5> myArray {1, 2, 3, 4, 5};
std::cout << myArray.size() << std::endl;
```

And finally, C++17 gives us **std::size()**, a function to return the element count of both standard containers or a C-style array:

```
std::array<int, 5> myArray {1, 2, 3, 4, 5};
std::cout << std::size(myArray) << std::endl;
int myArray[5] = {1, 2, 3, 4, 5};
std::cout << std::size(myArray) << std::endl;
```

> **Note**
>
> Your compiler will have to have C++17 support enabled for this to be available.

We usually have multiple options available to us for whatever it is we're trying to accomplish; it's all about finding the most suitable one for each scenario.

Array Memory

Given that all values in an array are stored side by side in memory, we can easily get to any of them by specifying an index. Our first index in an array in C++ is always 0 and in memory; this is the start of our array structure. Out next element has an index of 1. So, to get to it, we start at 0 and progress in memory by the size of our element multiplied by our index. In this case, an integer is 4 bytes, and we want index 1, so we'll look 4 bytes ahead of the start of the array and that's where we'll find our element:

Figure 3.9: Memory access

We can see this if we print out the memory addresses of the elements individually. We're not going to go into detail here—we'll cover it properly in later chapters—but the ampersand operator (**&**) in C++ fetches the memory address of the object that follows it. We can use this to see where in memory our elements lie.

The following code is an example:

```
int customerAges[] = {1, 2, 3, 4, 5};

std::cout << &customerAges[0] << std::endl;
std::cout << &customerAges[1] << std::endl;
std::cout << &customerAges[2] << std::endl;
std::cout << &customerAges[3] << std::endl;
std::cout << &customerAges[4] << std::endl;
```

If we run the preceding code, we will see the address of each of our elements:

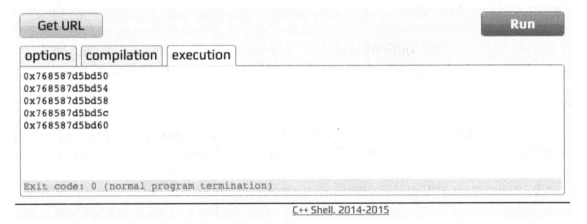

Figure 3.10: Printing the address of each element shows the addresses are incremented by 4 bytes

Memory addresses are stored in hexadecimal format (base 16), but we can see that the first address, element **0**, ends with **50**. If we then look to the next address, element 1, it ends in **54**, as its value has increased by 4 bytes. 4 bytes is the size of an integer, so this makes sense. If we look at the next one again, element 3, it's memory address ends in **58**. That's 4 bytes more than element 1, and 8 bytes more than element 0, showing how our indices let us navigate memory to address individual values in our array.

Exercise 14: Implementing Containers to Store Usernames

In this exercise, we'll write a small application that will store usernames in an array and allow them to be fetched once again later:

> **Note**
>
> The complete code for this exercise can be found here: https://packt.live/35kFKix.

1. We'll start by defining a macro that will determine how many names our system will hold, and we'll use that to initialize an array of the correct size:

```cpp
// Arrays exercise.
#include <iostream>
#include <string>

#define NAME_COUNT 5

int main()
{
    std::string names[NAME_COUNT];
```

2. Next, we have a bit of IO, where we want to ask our user for the correct number of names. We can use a **for** loop for this as we have in previous exercises. When we use **getline** to fetch input, we will put it directly into our array using the index of the **for** loop:

```cpp
std::cout << "Please input usernames." << std::endl;
for (int i = 0; i < NAME_COUNT; ++i)
{
    std::cout << "User " << i + 1 << ": ";
    std::getline(std::cin, names[i]);
}
```

3. Now that we have our usernames stored in our array, we want to allow the user to select as many as they like. We saw in *Chapter 2, Control Flow* how we can use a **while** loop to achieve this, and we'll employ the same approach here. The loop will allow users to continually select an index of a record to view, or to enter an index of **-1** should they want to quit the application.

```cpp
bool bIsRunning = true;
while (bIsRunning)
{
    int userIndex = 0;
    std::string inputString = "";
    std::cout << "Enter user-id of user to fetch or -1 to quit: ";
    std::getline(std::cin, inputString);
    userIndex = std::stoi(inputString);
    if (userIndex == -1)
    {
        bIsRunning = false;
    }
```

4. We're now at the final section of our application, where we want to fetch a user record based on the index. We need to be careful here to ensure that the index that the user has passed in is valid. We saw earlier in the chapter what happens if that's not the case.

For starters, we know the lowest index we can have is **0**, so any value lower than that is invalid. We also know the size of our array, **NAME_COUNT**, and since we start counting at **0**, our maximum valid index is going to be **NAME_COUNT – 1**. If the index that the user specified matches these two criteria, then great, we can use it. If not, we'll print an error and have them pick again:

```cpp
        else
        {
            if (userIndex >= 0 && userIndex < NAME_COUNT)
            {
                std::cout << "User " << userIndex << " = "
                    << names[userIndex] <<std::endl;
            }
            else
            {
                std::cout << "Invalid user index" << std::endl;
            }
        }
    }
}
```

That should be everything. We define our array, collect user records, and then allow our users to fetch them once again, ensuring that the index they've supplied us with is valid. Let's run the application and test it out:

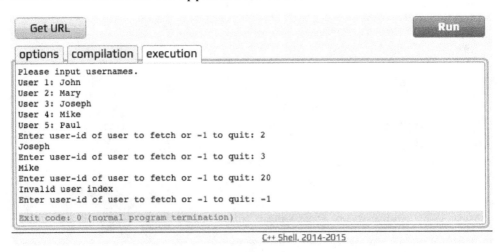

C++ Shell, 2014-2015

Figure 3.11: Our small name records application, which allows users to store and fetch name records

In this exercise, we've made use of an array for storing names in a dynamic way. We could have achieved something similar here by using individual string variables for each of our names, but that wouldn't be dynamic. We'd have to implement extra names individually, whereas with this approach, we need only change the macro defined at the top of the application. We've also been careful to check the sanity of the index that we're using with our array, and this is especially important in this case since it's supplied by the user.

Multidimensional Arrays

We've seen how arrays are used to store collections of objects, and there's nothing stopping us storing arrays of arrays. These are called multidimensional arrays and can be confusing at first, but they are incredibly useful.

The arrays we've used so far have all been one-dimensional (1D); that is, their elements are entirely linear and could be represented using a single row, as shown in the following diagram:

int[] myArray={1,2,3,4,5};

Index ⟶	0	1	2	3	4
Value ⟶	1	2	3	4	5
	myArray[0]	myArray[1]	myArray[2]	myArray[3]	myArray[4]

Figure 3.12: A 1D array

If we think of our array as a table of values (as above), to access a value, we only need to specify the column number. This is the single index we've used previously. It's possible, however, to increase the number of rows we use, and when we do this, we create a two-dimensional (2D) array:

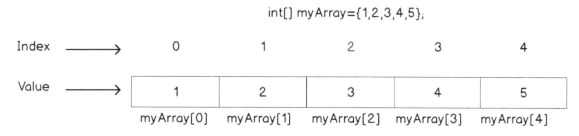

int myArray[3][5] = {{1,2,3,4,5}, {1,2,3,4,5}, {1,2,3,4,5}};

	Column 0	Column 1	Column 2	Column 3	Column 4
Row 0	myArray[0][0]	myArray[0][1]	myArray[0][2]	myArray[0][3]	myArray[0][4]
Row 1	myArray[1][0]	myArray[1][1]	myArray[1][2]	myArray[1][3]	myArray[1][4]
Row 2	myArray[2][0]	myArray[2][1]	myArray[2][2]	myArray[2][3]	myArray[2][4]

Figure 3.13: A 2D array

As we see here, instead of being able to map our data into a single row, we must now use multiple rows. This means that we're able to store much more data, but it introduces the need for a second index as we now need to specify both the row and the column.

Declaring a 2D array in code is very similar to a 1D array. The difference is that with a 2D array, we need to provide two size values: one for row count and another for column count. The array shown in the preceding diagram would therefore be defined as follows:

```
int myArray[3][5];
```

As with the 1D array, we can also initialize our values at the same time as we declare them. Since we now have multiple rows, we initialize each in its own nested set of curly braces. Initializing the array that we just defined would look like this:

```
int myArray[3][5] { {1, 2, 3, 4, 5}, {1, 2, 3, 4, 5}, {1, 2, 3, 4, 5}
};
```

In theory, arrays can be made of any number of dimensions; they're not just capped at two. It's not common, however, to see arrays with more than two dimensions in practice as their complexity and memory footprint become factors.

Exercise 15: Using Multidimensional Arrays to Store More Data

Let's extend the previous application to also store a user's surname. We'll achieve this using multidimensional arrays:

> **Note**
>
> The complete code for this exercise can be found here: https://packt.live/33cBVuE.

1. Copy the final output of *Exercise 14* into the code window.

2. We'll first update the array that's holding the names. We'll want this to be two-dimensional, where each record has two values—a forename and a surname:

```
std::string names[NAME_COUNT][2] {""};
```

3. Next, where we are currently fetching names from our user and reading them into **names[i]**, we need to ask instead for the forename. We also need to specify the second index, where we'll store this input. Since its **Forename**, that will be index **0**:

```
std::cout << "User " << i + 1 << " Forename: ";
std::getline(std::cin, names[i][0]);
```

4. We'll then do the same again, this time asking for the surname. Since we're now storing the second element, we'll want to use index **1** instead of **0**:

```
std::cout << "User " << i + 1 << " Surname: ";
std::getline(std::cin, names[i][1]);
```

5. The final **for** loop should now be as follows:

```
for (int i = 0; i < NAME_COUNT; ++i)
{
    std::cout << "User " << i + 1 << " Forename: ";
    std::getline(std::cin, names[i][0]);
    std::cout << "User " << i + 1 << " Surname: ";
    std::getline(std::cin, names[i][1]);
}
```

6. Finally, we need to update our output to include both names. We're currently just printing **names[userIndex]**, so we need to update this to use both the first and second indices—**Forename** and **Surname**, respectively:

```
std::cout << "User " << userIndex << " = " << names[userIndex][0]
          << " " << names[userIndex][1] << std::endl;
```

7. The complete code looks like this:

```
// Arrays exercise.
#include <iostream>
#include <string>

#define NAME_COUNT 5

int main()
{
```

```cpp
std::string names[NAME_COUNT][2] {""};
std::cout << "Please input usernames." << std::endl;
for (int i = 0; i < NAME_COUNT; ++i)
{
    std::cout << "User " << i + 1 << " Forename: ";
    std::getline(std::cin, names[i][0]);
    std::cout << "User " << i + 1 << " Surname: ";
    std::getline(std::cin, names[i][1]);
}
bool bIsRunning = true;
while (bIsRunning)
{
    int userIndex = 0;
    std::string inputString = "";
    std::cout << "Enter user-id of user to fetch or -1 to quit: ";
    std::getline(std::cin, inputString);
    userIndex = std::stoi(inputString);
    if (userIndex == -1)
    {
        bIsRunning = false;
    }
    else
    {
        if (userIndex >= 0 && userIndex < NAME_COUNT)
        {
            std::cout << "User " << userIndex << " = "
                      << names[userIndex][0] << "" ""
                      << names[userIndex][1] << std::endl;
        }
        else
        {
            std::cout << "Invalid user index" << std::endl;
        }
    }
}
```

8. Run the application. Enter some dummy names and check that we can access them properly, showing both names:

```
Get URL                                                    Run

options  compilation  execution

Please input usernames.
User 1 Forename: John
User 1 Surname: Smith
User 2 Forename: Mary
User 2 Surname: Jones
User 3 Forename: Joseph
User 3 Surname: Bank
User 4 Forename: Mike
User 4 Surname: Beck
User 5 Forename: Paul
User 5 Surname: Dean
Enter user-id of user to fetch or -1 to quit: 2
User 2 = Joseph Bank
Enter user-id of user to fetch or -1 to quit: 3
User 3 = Mike Beck
Enter user-id of user to fetch or -1 to quit: 20
Invalid user index
Enter user-id of user to fetch or -1 to quit: -1

Exit code: 0 (normal program termination)
```

Figure 3.14: We've stored more data by adding another dimension to our names array

By adding a second dimension to our names array, we've been able to store more information—in this case, a surname.

Vectors

Vectors are similar to arrays in that they store collections of elements continuously in memory, but vectors have dynamic sizes. This means that we don't need to know their size at compile time; we can just define a vector and add/remove elements at will. Given this, they manage their size carefully.

Each time a vector needs to grow, it has to find and allocate the correct amount of memory and then copy all elements from the original memory location to the new one—a heavy task. As a result, they do not grow with every insertion but will allocate more memory than they actually need. This gives them a buffer where a number of elements can be added without the need for another growth operation. However, when a limit is reached, they will have to grow again.

This dynamic sizing ability makes them preferable over arrays when the number of elements needed to be stored fluctuates. Take a sign-up application as an example, where the number of users who will sign up is unknown. If we were to use arrays here, we would have to pick an arbitrary upper limit and declare an array of that size. Unless the application was full, this would result in lots of wasted space. Likewise, if we set our upper limit at 1,000 users, and only register 100, that's lots of wasted space. We've also forced an absolute upper limit on the number of people that can register. These issues are mitigated if we use a vector in this scenario.

Declaring a vector is done as follows:

```
std::vector<int> myVector;
```

At this point, the vector contains no elements, but before we look at how we add them, we're going to look at how they're accessed. This will set us up for an exercise we're going to do shortly, where we'll iterate over the vector printing out each element.

Accessing Elements

To access the elements in a vector, we have a couple of options. First, since a vector stores its elements continuously in memory, the same way an array does, we can use the **[]** operator to access them:

```
int myFirstElement = myVector[0];
int mySecondElement = myVector[1];
```

Remember that elements start at index **0**, so for our second element, we'd want index **1**. We're also subject to the same considerations as we have with arrays, such as ensuring that we always use a valid index. Thankfully, vectors provide us with an **at** function, which behaves very much like the **[]** operator, augmented by an added check to ensure that the index is valid.

For example, to fetch the first and second elements as we just did, but using the **at** function, we would do the following:

```
int myFirstElement = myVector.at(0);
int mySecondElement = myVector.at(1);
```

The key difference here is that if we pass an out-of-bounds index to the **at** function, instead of undefined behavior, the function will throw an exception. Exceptions will be covered *Chapter 13, Exception Handling in C++*, but they allow us to catch and handle errors in a safe way without causing our applications to crash.

Now that we've seen how to access a vector's elements, let's write a small application that can loop through and print them all out. This will be useful moving forward, as we look at adding and removing elements.

Exercise 16: Looping over a Vector

Throughout this section, we're going to be interacting with a vector in various ways, so having the ability to visualize it through a single function call will be very useful. Let's write a small application to do this before moving forward. Here are the steps to complete the exercise:

> **Note**
>
> The code files for this exercise can be found here: https://packt.live/2QCGTxZ.

1. To start, initialize a vector of the **int** type:

```
// Vector example.
#include <iostream>
#include <string>
#include <vector>

std::vector<int> myVector;
```

2. Next, define a function named **PrintVector**. This is where we'll write the functionality to print the vector's contents:

```
void PrintVector()
{
}
```

3. To access elements in a vector, we can use an index, just like we did with arrays previously. Use a **for** loop for this, using the index to access the various elements in the vector. At the end of the function, we'll print out a couple of blank lines as spacers:

```
void PrintVector()
{
    for (int i = 0; i < myVector.size(); ++i)
    {
        std::cout << myVector[i];
    }

    std::cout << "\n\n";
}
```

4. Finally, add a call to our new **PrintVector** function within **main**:

```
int main()
{
    PrintVector();
}
```

5. The complete code looks like this:

```
// Vector example.
#include <iostream>
#include <string>
#include <vector>

std::vector < int > myVector;

void PrintVector()
{
    for (int i = 0; i < myVector.size(); ++i)
    {
        std::cout << myVector[i];
    }
    std::cout << "\n\n";
}

int main()
{
    PrintVector();
}
```

6. Run the program. We've not yet initialized **myVector** with any data, so there won't be any output, but we can confirm that it's compiling without errors:

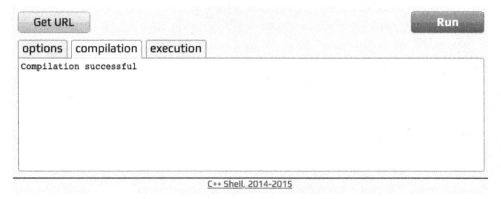

Figure 3.15: The program should compile without any errors

7. We'll use this application shortly, so keep it open in the compiler. For now, let's get some data added to our vector.

Initialization

As with arrays, there are a number of options available to us to initialize a vector with data. The first method we'll look at is specifying elements individually. The following initialization will give us a vector with five elements, the values of which are as follows: **1**, **2**, **3**, **4**, and **5**:

```
std::vector<int> myVector {1, 2, 3, 4, 5};
```

We can also specify the size of the vector, and the default value for each element. The following initialization will give us a vector with three elements, all with a value of **1**:

```
std::vector<int> myVector(3, 1);
```

Finally, it's possible to create vectors from both existing arrays and vectors. This is done by passing in their start- and end-memory locations. Respectively, this would be done as follows:

```
std::vector<int> myVector(myArray, myArray + myArraySize);
std::vector<int> myVector(myVector2.begin(), myVector2.end());
```

Modifying Elements

As with initialization, elements in a vector can be added/removed in a number of ways. To add an element to the end of the vector, we can use the **push_back()** function. And likewise, to remove an element from the end of a vector, we can use **pop_back()**:

```
myVector.push_back(1);
myVector.pop_back();
```

In this snippet, we would add the element **1** to the back of the vector and then remove it immediately.

We can also add and remove from our vector with more precision using the **insert** and **erase** functions. Both of these use iterators to determine where in the array the operation should take place. We're not going to cover iterators in detail at this point, but they're objects that allow us to traverse our collections.

To add and remove an element from a vector at a specific location, we would do the following:

```
myVector.erase(myVector.begin() + 1);
myVector.insert(myVector.begin() + 2, 9);
```

In this example, we use the **begin()** method, which returns an iterator pointing to the first element in the vector. We can then add an offset to get to our desired element. Remembering that indices start at **0**, we'd be erasing the element at index **1**, and then adding an element whose index would be **2**–the second and third elements in the vector.

> **Note**
>
> Iterators are objects that help us to iterate over our collections by "pointing" to items within them. They're covered in *Chapter 12, Containers and Iterators*. You can also refer to the following documentation for more details: https://packt.live/37rHIVA.

Let's use these functions to initialize a vector with data and then modify it by adding and removing elements at various locations.

Exercise 17: Modifying a Vector

In this exercise, we will modify a vector by adding and removing elements. We'll make use of the application we created in the previous exercise to print our vector out between steps so that we can clearly see what we're doing. Here are the files to complete the exercise:

> **Note**
>
> The code files for this exercise can be found here: https://packt.live/2QEZAB4.

1. Copy the program we created in *Exercise 16, Looping over a Vector*, into the compiler window if it isn't already there.

2. Replace the current vector definition with one that also initializes the vector with the following elements: **1**, **2**, **3**, **4**, and **5**:

```
std::vector<int> myVector {1, 2, 3, 4, 5};
```

3. Next, in the **main** function, after the call to **PrintVector**, remove the last element from the vector using **pop_back**. Follow immediately with another call to **PrintVector()**:

```
myVector.pop_back();
PrintVector();
```

4. Add a new element with the value **6** to the back of the vector using the **push_back** function. Again, follow this with a call to **PrintVector()**:

```
myVector.push_back(6);
PrintVector();
```

5. Remove the second element in the vector with the **erase** function. Follow this with another call to **PrintVector()**:

```
myVector.erase(myVector.begin() + 1);
PrintVector();
```

6. Finally, insert an element with the value **8** in the fourth position using the insert operator. Follow this with a final call to **PrintVector()**:

```
myVector.insert(myVector.begin() + 3, 8);
PrintVector();
```

7. The complete code looks like this:

```
// Vector example.
#include <iostream>
#include <string>
#include <vector>

std::vector<int> myVector {1, 2, 3, 4, 5};

void PrintVector()
{
    for (int i = 0; i < myVector.size(); ++i)
    {
        std::cout << myVector[i];
    }
    std::cout << "\n\n";
}

int main()
{
    PrintVector();
    myVector.pop_back();
    PrintVector();
    myVector.push_back(6);
    PrintVector();
    myVector.erase(myVector.begin() + 1);
```

```
        PrintVector();
        myVector.insert(myVector.begin() + 3, 8);
        PrintVector();
    }
```

8. Run the application and observe the state of the vector after each step.

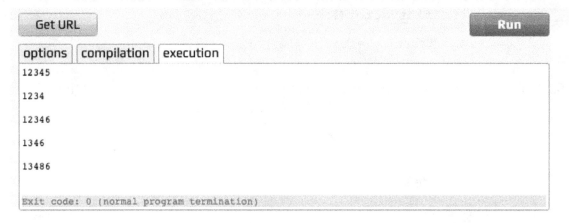

Figure 3.16: We've manipulated the elements in our vector by means of a number of methods

In this application, we've initialized an array with values and then modified them through a number of methods. We have our simple **push/pop** functions to add/remove items from the back of the array. We also have the ability to be more specific in terms of where we add/remove values by using the **insert/erase** functions. By iterating over the vector with a **for** loop, we were able to print out the elements at each stage so that we can clearly see the effects of the modifications we made.

There are other containers available, such as stacks, trees, and linked lists, and each has its pros and cons. Which of these you use will depend on your situation, as there's usually no single correct answer. Arrays and vectors are a good starting point and will give us the necessary tools to continue our learning. As you move forward do branch into some of these different containers, seeing how they behave and how they could best serve you in a given situation.

Classes/Structs

The basic types provided by C++ are a great starting point, but it's rare that these are the only variable types you'll need within an application. When we're representing real-world information, such as user records or the various properties of an object, we often need more complex data types to store our information. C++ allows us to create such types in classes and structs. Classes are going to be covered in greater detail in a later chapter, but for now, we're going to simply introduce a number of key concepts.

Classes

A class is a collection of variables and functionality, encapsulated neatly within a single object. When we define a class, we're creating a blueprint for that object. This means that every time we want to create an object of that type, we use that blueprint to construct our object. Classes are a core part of C++; after all, C++ was originally named *C with Classes*.

Members (variables and functions) declared in a C++ class are, by default, private. This means that they're only accessible to the class itself, so cannot be accessed by external classes. This can be changed, however, through the use of access modifiers; we'll cover these shortly. Classes can also inherit from one another, but this will be covered in *Chapter 8, Classes and Structs*.

The syntax for declaring a class in C++ is as follows:

```
class MyClassName:
{
Access Modifier:
    data members.
    member functions.
}
```

Using this syntax, let's define a simple class:

```
// Class example.
#include <iostream>
#include <string>

class MyClass
{
    int myInt = 0;
public:
    void IncrementInt()
    {
        myInt++;
        std::cout << "MyClass::IncrementInt: " << myInt;
    };
};

int main()
{
    MyClass classObject;
    classObject.IncrementInt();
}
```

In this code, we've defined a small class called **MyClass** that contains a variable and a function. The first is private, so can only be accessed via the class itself, and the other is public, so can be accessed from anywhere the class can be.

In our **main** function, we declare an instance of our class. This gives us an object, **classObject**, which contains all the properties and functionality that we defined within **MyClass**. Since we defined a **public** function, **IncrementInt**, we can call this through that class object:

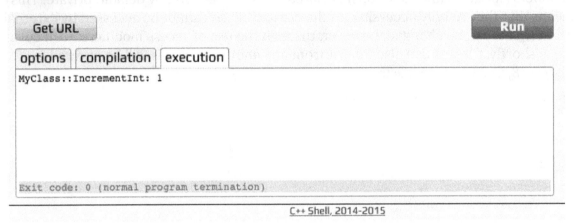

Figure 3.17: Running our code, we can see that our member function was called

Structs

Structs are very similar to classes. The difference between the two is that, by default, class members are private, and in a struct, they are public. Because of this, we tend to use structs to define objects whose purpose is mainly to store data. If we have an object that stores data but has a number of related functionalities, then that would usually be defined as a class.

A simple example of good use of a struct would be to store coordinates. Comprising an **x** and a **y** value, we could just define two individual float variables. This approach, however, requires two variables for each coordinate. We then have to manage them, keep them together, and so on. It's much easier to define a **struct** that encapsulates and contains those individual variables in a single logical unit.

Declaring a **struct** is almost identical to that of a class, but we replace the **class** keyword with **struct**:

```cpp
// Struct example.
#include <iostream>
#include <string>

struct Coordinate
{
    float x = 0;
    float y = 0;
};

int main()
{
    Coordinate myCoordinate;
    myCoordinate.x = 1;
    myCoordinate.y = 2;
    std::cout << "Coordinate: " << myCoordinate.x << ", "
              << myCoordinate.y;
}
```

Here, we've defined our coordinate in a **struct**, and since members are public by default, we haven't had to worry about access modifiers. We can simply declare an instance of that class and start using its members in our code without having to worry about this. Here is the output obtained by running the preceding code:

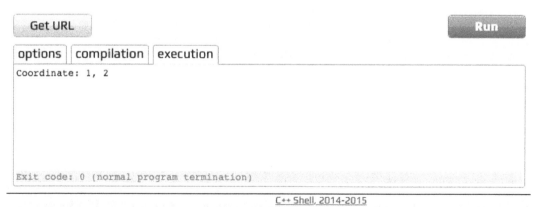

Figure 3.18: We're about to access our struct members by default as they're public

In terms of defining and instantiating classes and structs, we're going to leave it there. They'll be covered in detail in later chapters when we delve into OOP, so simply becoming familiar with their syntax will suffice. We also have a short exercise featuring them later in the chapter, but let's take a look at access modifiers.

Access Modifiers

As mentioned previously, the difference between a class and a struct is the default visibility of their member variables and functions. That's not to say that they can't be changed. When declaring these members, we have the following three access modifiers available to us:

- Public—Any members declared public are accessible from anywhere the class is.

- Private—Any members declared private are only available to the class in which they're defined and to friend functions.

- Protected—Protected members are similar to private members, with the addition that child classes can access them.

> **Note**
>
> Child classes are those that inherit from a base class. This will be covered in detail in *Chapter 10, Advanced Object-Oriented Principles*.

By defining our members with these keywords, we can control how visible they are to our application. The syntax for using these modifiers is as follows:

```
class MyClass
{
public:
    // Any members declared from this point forth will be public.

protected:
    // Any members declared from this point forth will be protected.

private:
    // Any members declared from this point forth will be private.
};
```

We define members in groups of accessibility by calling the **public/protected/private** keywords, and then subsequently declared members will have that visibility. You can use these modifiers more than once in a class definition; you're not limited to strict groups like this, but it makes your code more readable if members are grouped neatly.

Exercise 18: Using Accessibility Modifiers to Control Access

As a short exercise, let's add some members to the preceding class template and see how that affects how we can use them. For each of the visibility modifiers, we'll define an integer variable and then try to access it. This will show us how the different accessibility modifiers will affect our variables in practice:

> **Note**
>
> The complete code for this exercise can be found here: https://packt.live/35nNi4h.

1. Declare **myPublicInt**, **myProtectedInt**, and **myPrivateInt** as **public**, **protected**, and **private** variables, respectively:

```cpp
// Accessibility example.
#include <iostream>
#include <string>

class MyClass
{
public:
    int myPublicInt = 0;

protected:
    int myProtectedInt = 0;

private:
    int myPrivateInt = 0;
};
```

2. Next, instantiate an instance of the **MyClass** class and try to access each of the members we just defined in a **cout** statement:

```cpp
int main()
{
    MyClass testClass;

    std::cout << testClass.myPublicInt << "\n";
    std::cout << testClass.myProtectedInt << "\n";
    std::cout << testClass.myPrivateInt << "\n";
}
```

3. The complete code looks like this:

```cpp
// Accessibility example.
#include <iostream>
#include <string>

class MyClass
{

public:
    int myPublicInt = 0;

protected:
    int myProtectedInt = 0;

private:
    int myPrivateInt = 0;
};

int main()
{
    MyClass testClass;
    std::cout << testClass.myPublicInt << "\n";
    std::cout << testClass.myProtectedInt << "\n";
    std::cout << testClass.myPrivateInt << "\n";
}
```

4. Run the code and let's see what the compiler gives us:

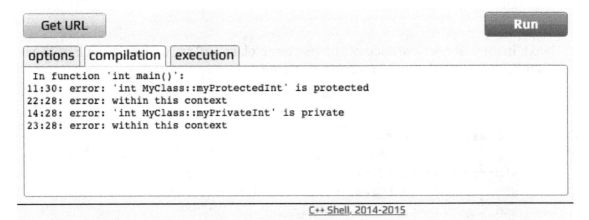

Figure 3.19: Only our public member variables are accessible; the others throw errors

We can see that only our public member variable was accessible. The other two threw errors, stating that they were protected and private; therefore, we couldn't use them as we were trying to. Having the correct accessibility for members is good practice when building applications so we can be sure that our data is used and accessed only in ways in which we intend it to be.

It can feel tempting at times to make variables and functions public for ease of use, especially as our applications become bigger and more complex; handling who can see what from where can become a bit of a task. However, proper access to our data and functions should not be compromised; this is paramount in creating secure systems that are not open to misuse. In *Chapter 9, Objected Oriented Principles*, we will cover the **getter/setter** paradigm, through which we define functions to allow access to private class members in a safe and controlled manner.

Constructors/Destructors

When we instantiate/destroy an object in C++, we may want to do certain things. For example, when an object is instantiated, we may want to do some setup for that object; maybe give some variables default values, or fetch some information from somewhere. Likewise, when we want to destroy an object, we may first want to do some cleanup. Perhaps we've created a temporary file that we want to get rid of or de-allocate some memory. C++ lets us achieve this by giving us constructors and destructors–functions that are run automatically, if defined, when an object is instantiated or destroyed.

An object's constructor is guaranteed to run as the object is being instantiated but before it's used anywhere. This gives us the opportunity to perform any setup that is required for the object to operate correctly. To define a constructor, we create a public function whose name is simply that of the class–for example, to define a constructor for our **MyClass** object:

```
public:
    MyClass()
```

To see our constructor in action, we can add a print statement and initialize our **myPublicInt** variable. With the addition of a print statement when our application starts, we can see the order in which things are being executed:

```
#include <iostream>
#include <string>

class MyClass
{
public:
    MyClass()
    {
```

```
        std::cout << "My Class Constructor Called\n";
        myPublicInt = 5;
    }
    int myPublicInt = 0;
};

int main()
{
    std::cout << "Application started\n";
    MyClass testClass;
    std::cout << testClass.myPublicInt << "\n";
}
```

> **Note**
>
> We can overload our constructors as we overloaded our normal functions in the previous chapter. We won't be covering that in this chapter, however. That's a task for further reading.

Once you run the preceding snippet, you will obtain the following output:

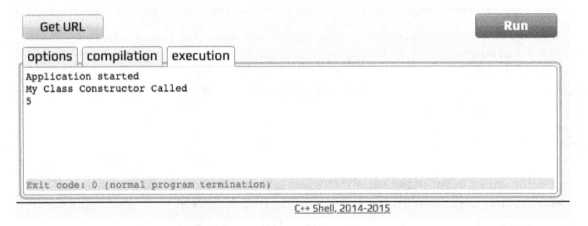

Figure 3.20: We can see that our constructor is called at the point our object is created

An object's destructor operates in a very similar manner to the constructor, just at the other end of the object's lifetime. This gives us the opportunity to perform any cleanup, such as de-allocating memory and so on. The syntax for a destructor is the same as that for the constructor, but is preceded by a tilde character:

```
~MyClass()
```

If we extend our preceding code to declare a destructor and, within it, print ourselves another statement, we can see when it's called. This happens when the main function ends; the application closes and cleans up after itself, therefore, our destructor is called and we see our statement:

```
~MyClass()
{
    std::cout << "My Class Destructor Called\n";
}
```

Get URL   Run

options	compilation	execution

```
Application started
My Class Constructor Called
5
My Class Destructor Called



Exit code: 0 (normal program termination)
```

C++ Shell, 2014-2015

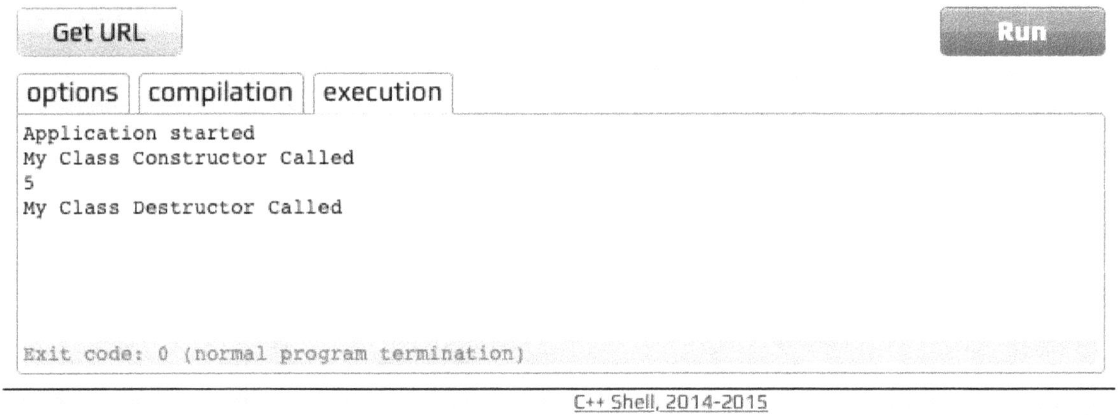

Figure 3.21: Our destructor is called at the end of the application as it performs cleanup, destroying the MyClass object

As mentioned at the start of this section, we're only taking a short tour of classes and structs here, by way of an introduction, before an in-depth examination in later chapters. The takeaways I hope you got from this are:

- Classes and structs encapsulate variables and behaviors.

- Class members are private by default, whereas they're public in a struct.

- We can modify the visibility of our members with access modifiers.

- Constructors and destructors can be used to call code at each end of an object's lifetime.

Exercise 19: Classes/Struct

As a brief exercise for this section, we're going to encapsulate the same data and functionality in both a **class** and a **struct** and observe once again how it affects their use. The data we're going to encapsulate is as follows:

- An integer variable

- A bool variable

- A function that will return a string

> **Note**
>
> The complete code for this exercise can be found here: https://packt.live/37rPd9B.

Here are the steps to complete the exercise:

1. Let's start by creating a class that will encapsulate this behavior and data:

```
class MyClass
{
    int myInt = 0;
    bool myBool = false;

    std::string GetString()
    {
        return "Hello World!";
    }
};
```

2. Next, do the same for the struct. The only change here will be replacing the **class** keyword with **struct**.

3. To test how accessible our variables are, instantiate an instance of our class and make calls to each member:

```
MyClass classObject;
std::cout << "classObject::myInt: " << classObject.myInt << "\n";
std::cout << "classObject::myBool: " << classObject.myBool
          << "\n";
std::cout << "classObject::GetString: " << classObject.GetString()
          << "\n";
```

We'll then do the same for the struct and run the application. We'll see some errors regarding the members in the class that has been inaccessible, but not with the struct:

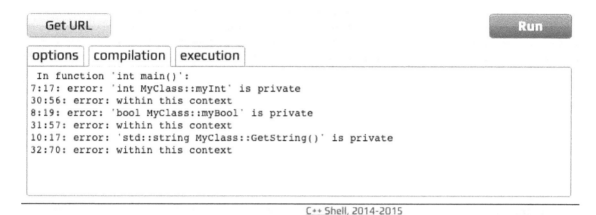

Figure 3.22: Inaccessible members due to the default private access that classes have

4. To fix this, we'll use the **public** access modifier to make our members accessible. The final code is as follows:

> **Note**
>
> It was stated earlier in this chapter that making everything public is generally bad practice, and that stands; this is for demonstration purposes. In later chapters, when we look at OOP properly, we'll cover getter/setter architecture, which allows us to access our variables in a more controlled way.

```cpp
// Classes/struct exercise.
#include <iostream>
#include <string>

class MyClass
{
public:
    int myInt = 0;
    bool myBool = false;
    std::string GetString()
    {
```

```
            return "Hello World!";
        }
    };

    struct MyStruct
    {
        int myInt = 0;
        int myBool = 0;
        std::string GetString()
        {
            return "Hello World!";
        }
    };

    int main()
    {
        MyClass classObject;
        std::cout << "classObject::myInt: " << classObject.myInt << "\n";
        std::cout << "classObject::myBool: " << classObject.myBool
                  << "\n";
        std::cout << "classObject::GetString: " << classObject.GetString()
                  << "\n";
        MyStruct structObject;
        std::cout << "\nstructObject::myInt: " << structObject.myInt
                  << "\n";
        std::cout << "structObject::myBool: " << structObject.myBool
                  << "\n";
        std::cout << "structbject::GetString: "
                  << structObject.GetString() << "\n";
    }
```

The final output is as follows:

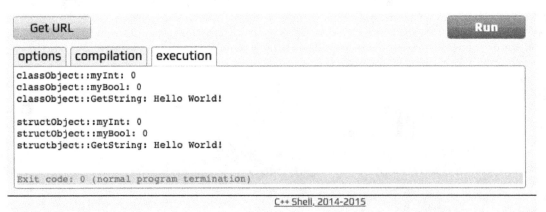

Figure 3.23: With the addition of the public access modifier, our class members become accessible

In this exercise, we've recapped how we can use classes and structs to encapsulate behaviors and made use of access modifiers to ensure their visibility. This understanding of the fundamental difference between the two will provide more context for when we reach the OOP chapters ahead.

Storage Lifetime

So far, in the applications and code we've been writing, we've been declaring all our variables in our **main** function. Since all our other code lives in this function also, we've had full access to all those variables. When we start to build bigger applications, however, and start making use of functions and classes, we need to understand *scope* and *storage lifetime.*

Object lifetime refers to how long an object is valid and accessible to us. With most of our variables having been declared in our **main** function so far, their lifetime has matched that of the application we've been writing, and there's nothing to worry about. Anytime we've wanted to use that variable, it's been there and valid as we're working within the same scope. Scope refers to a section of code that denotes the lifetime of objects declared within it, so we can see how these terms are related.

We use curly brackets to denote scope, be that in a function, or just on their own, as in the following code snippet:

```
void MyFunc()
{
    // scope 1
}

int main()
{
    // scope 2
    {
        // scope 3
    }
}
```

In this example, we have three different levels of scope: One in **MyFunc**, (**scope 1**), one in **main** (**scope 2**), and another in the curly brackets on their own (**scope 3**). The scope in which we declared variables in this example would directly impact where and when we could use that data and how long its lifetime would be. Let's see this in action.

Exercise 20: Storage Lifetime Example

To see clearly how scope affects our variables, let's perform a quick exercise. In each of the different scopes, we will define an integer variable and, at the end of the **main** function, attempt to print out the value of each. We can then examine the output to see the difference between scopes:

> **Note**
>
> The complete code for this exercise can be found here: https://packt.live/2XE9FzJ.

1. Copy the previous code snippet into the compiler, replacing the various comments regarding scope with integer variable definitions:

```cpp
#include <iostream>
void MyFunc()
{
    int myInt1 = 1;
}

int main()
{
    int myInt2 = 2;


    {
        int myInt3 = 3;
    }
```

2. Next, write three output statements, one for each of the variables just defined, that will print their value. Then, close the **main** function with a final '**}**':

```cpp
    // print values
    std::cout << myInt1 << std::endl;
    std::cout << myInt2 << std::endl;
    std::cout << myInt3 << std::endl;
}
```

3. The complete code is as follows:

```cpp
#include <iostream>

void MyFunc()
{
    int myInt1 = 1;
```

```
    }

    int main()
    {
        int myInt2 = 2;
        {
            int myInt3 = 3;
        }
        // print values
        std::cout << myInt1 << std::endl;
        std::cout << myInt2 << std::endl;
        std::cout << myInt3 << std::endl;
    }
```

4. Run the code. Our compiler will throw a number of errors and warnings at us, as follows:

Figure 3.24: Various variables we've tried to use are not within scope, so we get errors

If we read the errors in our compilation window, we can see we have two stating that **myInt1** and **myInt3** were not declared in this scope. When execution leaves a given scope (for example, when execution returns from the **MyFunc** function), the variables declared within it are destroyed and the memory is reclaimed. Once this has happened, the variable is no longer accessible.

> **Note**
>
> This is not always the case. We'll be looking at using pointers later, where it's possible for this not to happen, but for now, we can work on the premise that when the scope ends all variables within it are neatly tidied up for us.

With this in mind, we can see why we're unable to use these variables in the way we have. Our first variable, **myInt1**, is scoped to the **MyFunc** function, so outside of that, it's going to be inaccessible. The same goes for **myInt3**, since it's also declared in its own scope. The one variable we were able to use, **myInt2**, is declared within the same scope as the code that uses it, so that's fine.

As we move forward, it's important that we become familiar with scope and object lifetime. It can be tempting to put all our variables in the highest scope possible, and then not have to worry about where they are/aren't accessible from. This is bad design though. We should aim to have our variables declared in the smallest scopes possible, so we don't have memory sitting around that we're not using.

Static

Static is a special keyword in C++ that scopes an object's lifetime to that of the application. This means that static variables are only initialized once during the application, and therefore maintain their value throughout. Both variables and functions can be made static, so let's take a quick look at an example:

```
// Static example.
#include <iostream>
#include <string>

int MyInt()
{
    int myInt = 0;
    return ++myInt;
}
```

```
int main()
{
    for (int i = 0; i < 5; ++i)
    {
        std::cout << MyInt();
    }
}
```

In this example, we have a function that will return an integer it defines, and then we print its value. As you'd expect, if we run this code as is, we will get an output of five identical values. Each time the function is called, the variable is re-initialized to the value **0**, incremented, and then returned:

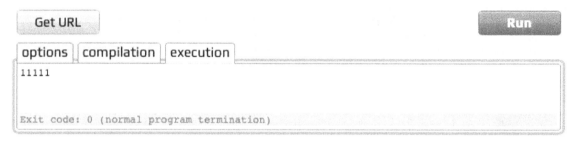

Figure 3.25: Since our variable is re-initialized each time the function is called, our output is the same

If we make a change to this application, however, and define our **myInt** variable as **static**, then our program will behave very differently:

```
static int myInt = 0;
```

Our variable will only be initialized once during the application's lifetime – the first time it is encountered. This means that although we initialize the value to **0**, that will only be observed once, allowing **myInt** to keep its value between different function calls. Let's run the application again:

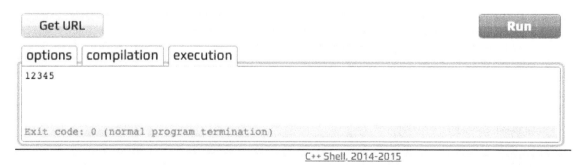

Figure 3.26: With the variable now declared static, its value persists between function calls

We can now see that the value is incrementing, confirming the fact that the variable is not being re-initialized each time we call the function thanks to the static keyword.

Activity 3: Sign-Up Application

In this third activity, we're going to be writing a user registration application. This will allow users to register with the system, providing both their name and age, and we'll store this information in our own custom type. We'll also provide the ability for a user to be looked up by an ID, retrieving their information.

Once you complete the activity, you should obtain an output similar to the following:

Figure 3.27: Our application allows the user to add records and then recall them via an ID

This activity will put everything you've learned in this chapter to the test, extending the exercise we did when looking at containers. You'll also lean on skills learned previously, such as looping, branching, and reading user input. Let's get started.

> **Note**
>
> At one point in this application, we'll be handling an exception. This is not something we've covered thus far, so don't worry if it seems alien to you. The complete code for this activity can be found here: https://packt.live/2KHdXRx.

Here are the steps to complete the activity:

1. Start by including the various headers that the application will need.

2. Next, define the class that will represent a record in the system. This is going to be a person, containing both a name and an age. Also, declare a vector of this type to store these records. A vector is used for the flexibility it gives in not having to declare an array size upfront.

> **Note**
>
> You can refer back to *Exercise 19, Classes/Struct,* for a reminder on how to define a struct, and *Exercise 16, Looping over a Vector,* for vector initialization.

3. Now, you can start adding some functions to add and fetch records; first, add. A record consists of a name and age, so write a function that will accept those two as parameters, create a record object, and add it to our record vector. Name this function **Add Record**.

4. Add a function to fetch a record. This function should accept one parameter (a user ID) and return the record for that user. Name this function **Fetch Record**.

5. Enter the **main** function and start the body of the application. Start with an outer **main** loop, as you used in the last chapter, and output some options to the user. You will give them three options: **Add Record**, **Fetch Record**, and **Quit**.

6. Present these options to the user and then capture their input.

7. There are three possible branches now, depending on user input, which we'll handle with a **switch** statement. Case 1 is adding a record, and to do so, you'll get the user's name and age from the user and then make a call to our **AddRecord** function.

8. The next case is the user wanting to fetch a record. For this, you need to get a user ID from the user and then make a call to **FetchRecord**, outputting its result. This is where you'll be catching an exception, something we've not covered before, so the following code is provided:

```
try
{
    person = FetchRecord(userID);
}
catch (const std::out_of_range& oor)
{
    std::cout << "\nError: Invalid UserID.\n\n";
    break;
}
```

> **Note**
>
> The names of the functions and variables in the preceding snippet may differ for you, depending on what you named them.

After calling this code, you just need to output the record details. Again, don't worry if this syntax is unfamiliar, as it will be covered in a later chapter.

9. The next case is when the user wants to exit the application. This one is fairly simple; you just need to exit our **main** loop.

10. Finally, add a default case. This will handle invalid options entered by the user. All you'll do here is output an error message and send them back to the start of the application.

11. With all of this in place, the application should be ready to go.

> **Note**
>
> The solution for this activity can be found on page 520.

Summary

In this chapter, we've focused on various data types provided by C++, and how we can create our own more complex objects to represent our data and encapsulate functionality. Starting with the built-in data types provided by C++, we looked at them more closely, investigating their memory footprint and the different keyword modifiers we have in order to extend and change their behavior and properties.

We then moved on to looking at arrays and vectors. These derived types allow us to store collections of different elements under a single variable name, yet still address them individually using an index. We looked at the fixed array (a collection that requires knowing its size at compile time) and at the more flexible vector, which can grow/shrink dynamically to match our needs. It's this latter container that we utilized in the final activity to create our user records application.

Next, we took a short tour of classes and structs. These will be the focus of their own chapter later, so we just covered the basics, looking at the differences between a class and a struct, how we declare them, and how constructors and destructors operate. Finally, we looked at storage lifetime and scope to get a better understanding of how long our objects are around for, and when/where we can access them.

In the first part of *Chapter 4*, *Operators*, we're going to be looking at operators. We've used a number of them throughout our work so far, but we'll take some time to close in on them and look at them more deeply. Operators are how we manipulate our objects and data, so a strong understanding of their operation is crucial.

4

Operators

Overview

This chapter presents a variety of operators provided by C++ describing what they do, and how they can allow us to manipulate our data. By the end of this chapter you will be able to describe and use various arithmetic, relational, and assignment operators. We'll then look at unary and logical operators, before ending with overloading operators for use with custom types. The chapter will close with a popular programming exercise, Fizz Buzz, that will implement the operators covered in the chapter.

Introduction

In the last chapter, we learned about the various data types provided by C++, and how we can use them to store and represent the data within our systems. In this chapter, we will take a look at operators, the mechanisms by which we assign and manipulate this data. We've been using them throughout our work so far—it's hard to write C++ and not use them to some extent, at least—but we've yet to address them head-on. That's what we'll be doing now.

Operators come in many shapes and sizes, but in general, their role is to allow us to interact with our data. Be it assigning a value, modifying it, or copying it, this is all done through operators. We'll start by looking at arithmetic and relational operators. These allow us to perform mathematical operations such as adding, subtracting, and dividing numbers, and to compare values to one another.

We'll then move on to looking at assignment operators. These allow us to assign data to our variables, and our variables to one another. This is the operator we've used the most so far, but there's certainly more to learn about this and the multiple variations that combine both assignment and arithmetic operators.

The final operator types that we'll be looking at are logical and unary operators. Logical operators allow us to check conditions, resulting in a Boolean value for us to check. Unary operators are operators that operate on a single value, changing it in some way.

We'll end the chapter by looking at overloading and assigning our own operators. While we have a wide range of operators available, it may sometimes be necessary for us to overload them, providing our own behavior for a certain type. C++ allows us to do that. It also allows us to define operators for our own user-defined types.

At the end of this chapter, we'll put our understanding of operators to the test in a final activity in which we create the **Fizz Buzz** application, which is a common activity that is used to test C++ proficiency. When complete, we'll have a well-rounded understanding of the operators that we have available, allowing us to confidently and competently interact with the data within our systems.

Arithmetic Operators

Arithmetic operators are those that allow us to perform mathematical operations on our data. These are very self-explanatory and straightforward to use as, aside from the modulus operator, they have the same symbol that we'd use for everyday mathematics. For example, in order to add a number, you simply use the "+" sign as you would anywhere. Generally, these operators are going to be used with numeric data types, however, there's nothing stopping a type from implementing this operator. This will be covered as the final topic of the chapter.

Let's take a quick look at our four basic operators: addition, subtraction, multiplication, and division. As stated previously, these four operators have the same symbols that you'd use day to day, so they should be familiar. The following example implements all four types of arithmetic operators:

```cpp
// Arithmetic operators.
#include <iostream>
#include <string>

int main()
{
    int addition = 3 + 4;
    int subtraction = 5 - 2;
    int division = 8 / 4;
    int multiplication = 3 * 4;

    std::cout << addition << "\n";
    std::cout << subtraction << "\n";
    std::cout << division << "\n";
    std::cout << multiplication << "\n";
}
```

If you run the preceding code, you should obtain the following output:

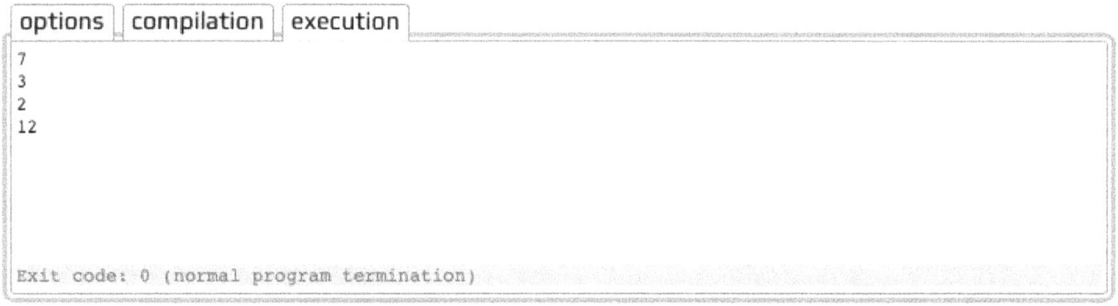

options	compilation	execution

```
7
3
2
12




Exit code: 0 (normal program termination)
```

Figure 4.1: Observing our simple arithmetic operators

We can use both variables and constants (that is, plain numbers) in these operations—they're interchangeable. Here is an example:

```cpp
int myInt = 3;
int addition = myInt + 4;
```

In this code snippet, we add the value **4**, a constant, to **myInt**, a variable. The outcome of this is that the **addition** variable will now have a value of 7.

The final arithmetic operator we'll look at is the modulus operator. This operator returns the remainder of an integer division and is represented by the % symbol:

```cpp
// Arithmetic operators.
#include <iostream>
#include <string>

int main()
{
    int modulus = 11 % 2;
    std::cout << modulus << "\n";
}
```

Once you run the preceding code, you will obtain the following output:

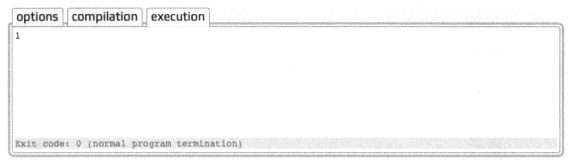

Figure 4.2: The modulo operator

In this example, we perform **11 % 2**. Here, 2 divides 11 five times, leaving a remainder of 1. This is the value that the modulus operator finds us. This operator is useful in a number of situations, such as determining whether a number is even or odd, doing something at a set increment, or within random number generation, as we saw in *Chapter* 3, *Control Flow*. Let's take a look at some examples of this:

```cpp
// Determine if a number is even.
bool isEven = myInt % 2 == 0;

// Print multiples of 5.
for (int i = 0; i < 100; ++i)
{
    if (i % 5 == 0)
    {
        std::cout << i << "\n";
    }
}
```

```
// Generate a random number between 1 and 10.
srand(time(0));
int random = (rand() % 10) + 1;
```

> **Note**
>
> In the preceding code, both the = and == operators are used. These will be covered in more detail shortly; however, = is the assignment operator, and == is an equality operator. The former assigns values to things, and the latter checks whether things are equal. There will be more on this later.

In this snippet, we first determine whether a number is even by checking whether there's a remainder after dividing by 2. If there's no remainder, then the number divides by 2 cleanly—so it is, therefore, even.

Next, we loop over the numbers from 0 to 99, printing only multiples of 5. This uses a similar method to the first example, but here, we're only dividing by 5. If we do this and there's no remainder, then it is indeed a multiple of 5.

In the last two lines of the snippet, we use the modulus operator to generate a random number within a range. The **rand() % 10** operation will result in an answer between 0 and 9, and then we add 1 to increase that range from 1 to 10.

It's important to be aware of operator precedence here, and thus the order of evaluation. Thankfully, the basic rules we learned in mathematics regarding the order of operations in a sum are maintained in C++; that is, addition will take precedence over subtraction. C++ contains many operators so a full list of operators and their precedence can be found at https://packt.live/2QO1j7t. Being aware of what has precedence over what will be very helpful.

If we want to manually specify the order of operations in our sums, however, we can make use of parentheses. Take the two following sums as an example:

```
//Example 1
int a = 3 * 4 - 2;      // a = 10
//Example 2
int b = 3 * (4 - 2);   // b = 6
```

In the first sum, we leave the order of operations to what they would be naturally. This means that the multiplication is done first, followed by the subtraction, giving us an answer of 10. In the second example, we wrap the subtraction in parentheses, so it's calculated first. 4 subtracted by 2 gives us 2, which we then multiply by 3 to get to our solution: 6. The proper use of parentheses is very important in allowing us to ensure our expressions are being evaluated in the manner in which we desire.

Let's now write an application that implements some of the operators covered here to determine whether a number is prime.

Exercise 21: The Prime Number Checker

In this first exercise of the chapter, we'll write an application that can determine whether a number is a prime or not. This will make use of the modulus operator; the other operators are trivial so there's not much that we need to cover again here. A prime number is a number that's whole, is greater than one, and is only divisible by one and itself; we can use the modulus operator to help us determine this. Take a look at the following steps:

> **Note**
>
> The complete code for this exercise can be found here: https://packt.live/2QDdILi.

1. To start, we'll ask our user to input the number that they want to check is a prime or not:

```cpp
// Prime number checker.
#include <iostream>
#include <string>

int main()
{
    int numberToCheck = 0;
    std::cout << "Prime number checker\n";
    std::cout << "Enter the number you want to check: ";
    std::cin >> numberToCheck;
```

2. We can now start the process of determining whether the number is prime. Part of our definition of a prime number was that it must be greater than 1, so we can omit any value below or equal to this straightaway:

```cpp
if (numberToCheck <= 1)
{
    std::cout << numberToCheck << " is not prime.";
    return 0;
}
```

3. 2 is an interesting prime number as it's the only even one. All even numbers greater than this are divisible by at least 1, 2, and their own value. Given this, we can now add a quick check to handle this case:

    ```
    else if (numberToCheck == 2)
    {
        std::cout << numberToCheck << " is prime.";
        return 0;
    }
    ```

4. Now we can get to the main section of the prime check. We've handled the "special" cases, where the number entered is 0, 1, or 2, so now we need to handle values greater than 2. To do this, we can determine whether any numbers greater than 1 and less than the value the user inputs, will divide exactly into the number we're checking.

    > **Note**
    >
    > There are more possible optimizations to this, such as only checking even values. However, in order to not detract too much from the modulus operation, we're going to omit them.

    We used the modulus operator earlier and saw how it fetches the remainder after division; if we use this with our user's input and a loop value, we can determine whether our input value has any factors other than 1 or itself. The factors of 1 and the number itself won't be checked, so we know that if we find any other factor, then the number can't be prime. If we find none, then it is:

    ```
    for (int i = 2; i < numberToCheck; ++i)
    {
        if (numberToCheck % i == 0)
        {
            std::cout << numberToCheck << " is not prime.";
            return 0;
        }
    }
    std::cout << numberToCheck << " is prime.";
    }
    ```

5. The complete program looks like this:

```cpp
// Exercise 21: Prime number checker.
#include <iostream>
#include <string>

int main()
{
    int numberToCheck = 0;
    std::cout << "Prime number checker\n";
    std::cout << "Enter the number you want to check: ";
    std::cin >> numberToCheck;
    if (numberToCheck <= 1)
    {
        std::cout << numberToCheck << " is not prime.";
        return 0;
    }
    else if (numberToCheck == 2)
    {
        std::cout << numberToCheck << " is prime.";
        return 0;
    }
    for (int i = 2; i < numberToCheck; ++i)
    {
        if (numberToCheck % i == 0)
        {
            std::cout << numberToCheck << " is not prime.";
            return 0;
        }
    }
    std::cout << numberToCheck << " is prime.";
}
```

6. We can now run this application and test its functionality. The first five prime numbers are 2, 3, 5, 7, and 11. We can check these, and the numbers around them too, in order to determine whether our application is working correctly:

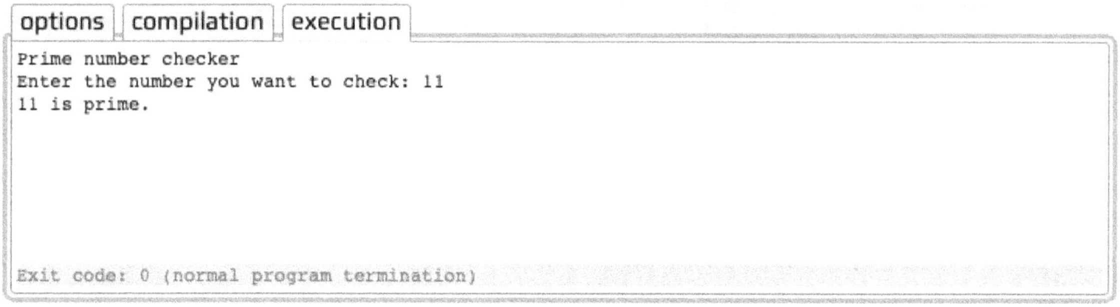

```
options   compilation   execution
Prime number checker
Enter the number you want to check: 11
11 is prime.




Exit code: 0 (normal program termination)
```

Figure 4.3: Determining whether a number is a prime

By using the modulus operator, we were able to determine whether a number was a prime or not. This is just one of many uses of the modulus operator, and of arithmetic operators in general.

Relational Operators

Relational operators allow us to compare values with one another. We could, for example, check whether one value was greater than another, or if two values were equal. These operators not only work on integer values but also on collections and objects. There are two fundamental relationships that are often checked for: **equality** and **comparison**.

Equality

The relational operators that are used to determine the equality of two values are **==** and **!=**; that is, equal and not equal, respectively. A value is placed on either side of the operators, referred to as LHS on the left and RHS on the right, and it's these two values that are compared. A single Boolean value is returned that denotes whether the equality check was true or not.

The two operators can be used as follows:

```
// Relational operators. Equality.
#include <iostream>
#include <string>

int main()

{
```

```
int myInt1 = 1;
int myInt2 = 1;
int myInt3 = 5;

if (myInt1 == myInt2)
{
    std::cout << myInt1 << " is equal to " << myInt2 << ".\n";
}

if (myInt1 != myInt3)
{
    std::cout << myInt1 << " is not equal to " << myInt3;
}
}
```

In this small program, we've declared a number of integers and determined which are equal using the two relational equality operators. The following output is obtained once you run the preceding code:

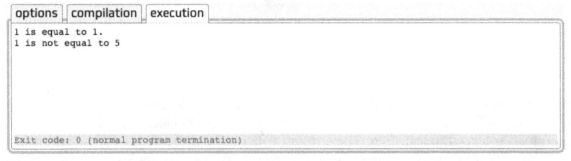

Figure 4.4: We can test the equality of two values or objects by using relational operators

Both of our equality checks returned true, so we executed both print statements. Note that just because they both returned true that doesn't mean they were both equal. In the first example, we're checking whether they are equal, and in the second example, we're checking whether they are not.

As well as working with simple integer values we can also use this to test the equality of floating-point types, objects, and lists, assuming that those operators have been defined. It's in that operator definition that the rules for determining whether two objects are equal are outlined; we'll look at this, and overloading operators, in more details toward the end of the chapter.

When comparing the equality of floating-point types, it's important to know that **==** might produce erroneous results. All floating-point operations have the potential for error as floating-point numbers are unable to be represented in binary exactly; instead, they're stored as very close approximations. This gives rise to the potential for error. To counteract this, it's common to instead check whether the difference between two floating-point numbers is below some very small value, such as epsilon. If the difference is below this small value, we might generally consider that the two are "close enough." Of course, this depends on your needs, but generally speaking, this will suffice. We're not going to go into floating-point errors in more detail as it's a large topic; however, just bear this in mind when working with floating-point comparisons.

> **Note**
>
> For further reading on floating-point comparisons, you can refer to https://packt. live/2s4njk2.

Comparison

The other subset of relational operators is comparison operators. These allow us to compare the values of our variables. We have four available to us: greater than (**>**), less than (**<**), greater than or equal to (**>=**), and less than or equal to (**<=**). These are used in the same way as the equality operators; that is, they have both left-side and right-side values, and will return true if the comparison is **true**, or **false** if the comparison is false.

An example of how these operators can be used is as follows:

```cpp
// Relational operators. Equality.
#include <iostream>
#include <string>

int main()
{
    int myInt1 = 1;
    int myInt2 = 1;
    int myInt3 = 5;

    if (myInt1 > myInt2)
    {
        std::cout << myInt1 << " is greater than" << myInt2 << ".\n";
    }
```

```
    if (myInt1 < myInt3)
    {
        std::cout << myInt1 << " is less than " << myInt3 << ".\n";
    }

    if (myInt3 >= myInt2)
    {
        std::cout << myInt3 << " is greater than or equal to " << myInt2
                  << ".\n";
    }

    if (myInt2 <= myInt1)
    {
        std::cout << myInt2 << " is less than or equal to " << myInt1;
    }
}
```

Similar to how we checked for equality, here, we're comparing two values together. The first two are fairly straightforward—we're simply checking whether one number is greater than the other, or less than the other. The last two statements make use of the "or equal to" operators. In these cases, the greater than or less than check will return true if the values are also equal. It's a mixture of the equality (==) operator we saw earlier and the first two comparison operators.

If we run this code in our compiler, we can see which statements were executed:

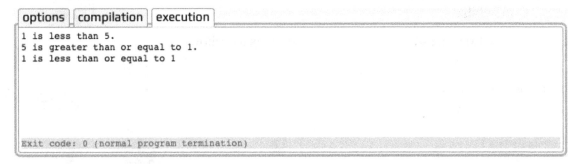

Figure 4.5: Using relational comparison operators to determine the relationship between values

We can see that all but one of our comparisons evaluated to true, so we executed three of our print statements.

Exercise 22: The Time-of-Day Calculator

For this exercise, we're going to write a small application that will determine the time of day based on the hour. We'll have our users input the time in military time format (for example, 1800), and will present them with a string representing the appropriate time of day. Here are the steps to complete the exercise:

> **Note**
>
> The complete code for this exercise can be found here: https://packt.live/2rg9ONu.

1. We'll start by outputting the instructions to our user, and then reading their answer into an integer:

```cpp
#include <iostream>
#include <string>

int main()
{
    std::cout << "***Time of Day Calculator***\n";
    std::cout << "Enter time in military format.
            eg. (1800, 1430)\n\n";
    std::cout << "Enter time: ";

    std::string input;
    getline(std::cin, input);

    int time = std::stoi(input);
```

2. Now we can start to evaluate our times. We start by ensuring that our value is within the valid range. If **time** is less than **0000** or greater than **2400**, then we print a message to the user informing them that their time was invalid:

```cpp
    if (time < 0000 || time > 2400)
    {
        std::cout << "Invalid time.";
        return 0;
    }
```

3. Before we get into defining time ranges, we can check specific times of day, starting with midnight. This will be the case when the time is equal to **0000**, and if so, we'll print the message **"It's currently midnight."**:

```
if (time == 0000)
{
    std::cout << "It's currently midnight.";
}
```

4. Next, we check whether the time is noon. This will be the case when the time is equal to **1200**, and if so, we'll print the message **"It's currently noon."**:

```
else if (time == 1200)
{
    std::cout << "It's currently noon.";
}
```

5. Now we will start defining some time ranges. We'll start with morning and we'll classify it as the time that falls between 6 a.m. and noon. If that's the case, we'll print the message **"It's currently morning."**:

```
else if (time >= 0600 && time < 1200)
{
    std::cout << "It's currently morning.";
}
```

6. Our next time range will be afternoon. This will be for times that fall between 12:01 and 5 p.m. When this is the case, we'll print the message **"It's currently afternoon."**:

```
else if (time > 1200 && time <= 1700)
{
    std::cout << "It's currently afternoon.";
}
```

7. Evening comes next, and we'll define this range as any time after 5 p.m. but before 8 p.m. When this is the case, we'll print the message **"It's currently evening."**:

```
else if (time > 1700 && time <= 2000)
{
    std::cout << "It's currently evening.";
}
```

8. Our final time range is night, and we'll define this as any time after 8 p.m. but before 6 a.m. When this is the case, we'll print the message **"It's currently night."**:

```
    else if (time > 2000 || time < 0600)
    {
        std::cout << "It's currently night.";
    }
}
```

9. The complete program looks like this:

```
// Time of Day Calculator.
#include <iostream>
#include <string>

int main()
{
    std::cout << "***Time of Day Calculator***\n";
    std::cout << "Enter time in military format.
                eg. (1800, 1430)\n\n";
    std::cout << "Enter time: ";
    std::string input;
    getline(std::cin, input);
    int time = std::stoi(input);

    if (time < 0000 || time > 2400)
    {
        std::cout << "Invalid time.";
        return 0;
    }

    if (time == 0000)
    {
        std::cout << "It's currently midnight.";
    }
    else if (time == 1200)
    {
        std::cout << "It's currently noon.";
    }
    else if (time >= 0600 && time < 1200)
    {
        std::cout << "It's currently morning.";
    }
```

```
        else if (time > 1200 && time <= 1700)
        {
            std::cout << "It's currently afternoon.";
        }
        else if (time > 1700 && time <= 2000)
        {
            std::cout << "It's currently evening.";
        }
        else if (time > 2000 || time < 0600)
        {
            std::cout << "It's currently night.";
        }
    }
```

10. If we run this application now, our users should be able to input a time and have the time of day presented to them:

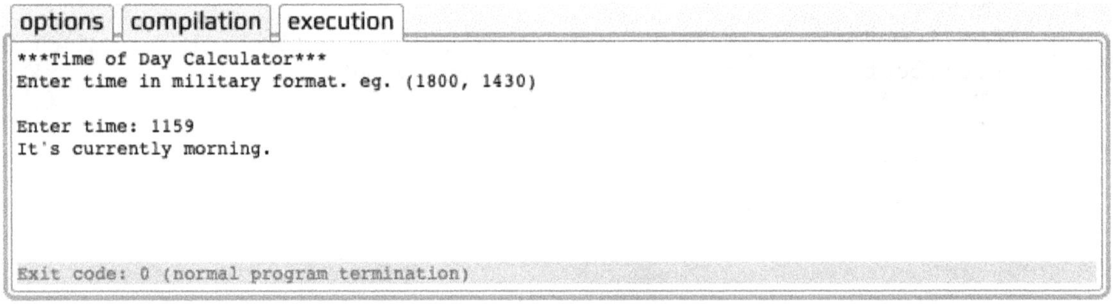

| options | compilation | execution |

```
***Time of Day Calculator***
Enter time in military format. eg. (1800, 1430)

Enter time: 1159
It's currently morning.
```

Exit code: 0 (normal program termination)

Figure 4.6: Using relational operators, we can determine what time of day it is

In this exercise, we've used a selection of relational operators to determine the current time of day. There's no input validation, so the user input has to match what we expect, or we'll get undefined behavior, but we can examine how we can use relational operators to compare and categorize the times entered.

Unary Operators

So far, the operators that we've used had a value, typically called an operand, on either side of them: rhs and lhs. Unary operators are those operators, however, that take only one value and modify that. We'll be taking a quick look at minus (-), increment (++), and decrement (--). There are a number of other unary operators (logical complement (!) and bitwise complement (~)), but we'll cover these in the following sections.

Let's start with the minus (-) operator; this allows us to manipulate the sign of a value. It is fairly straightforward—when placed in front of a value, it will turn a negative value positive, and a positive value negative.

Here is an example:

```cpp
// Negation example.
#include <iostream>
#include <string>

int main()
{
    int myInt = -1;
    std::cout << -myInt * 5 << std::endl;

    myInt = 1;
    std::cout << -myInt * 5 << std::endl;
}
```

We can see the effect that these operators have on our value if we run this application in our code editor:

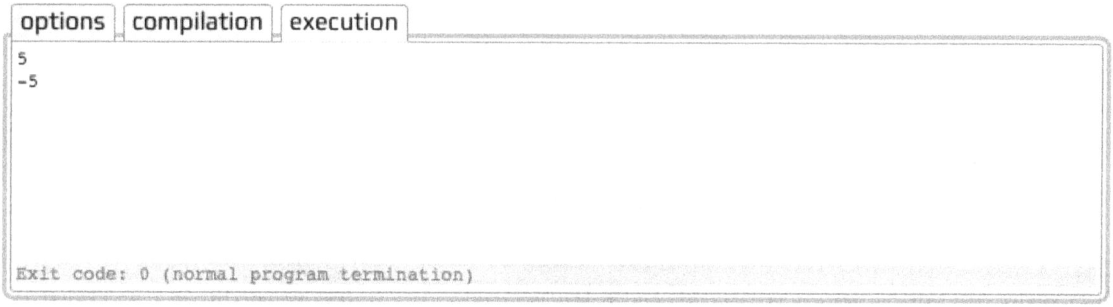

```
options  compilation  execution
5
-5




Exit code: 0 (normal program termination)
```

Figure 4.7: Using the minus operator to change sign

We can see from this output that the sign of our output is opposite to that of the variable since we're using it with the minus operator.

The other unary operators we're going to look at are increment (++) and decrement (--). These two operators allow us to increase or decrease a value by one, respectively. We've already used the increment (++) operator in **for** loops to increment the loop counter. Decrement (--) works in the same way but is reversed.

In the following code, we define a value, then increment or decrement it, and view its value:

```cpp
// Increment/Decrement example.
#include <iostream>
#include <string>

int main()
{
    int myInt = 1;
    std::cout << ++myInt << std::endl;
    std::cout << --myInt << std::endl;
}
```

In this simple snippet, we've defined a value as 1, incremented it, and then immediately decremented it again, printing its value at each stage. Once you run this in the code editor, you'll obtain the following output:

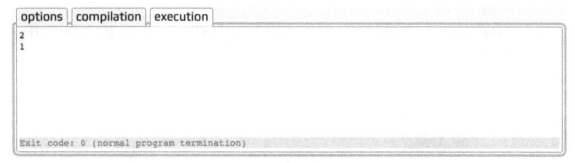

Figure 4.8: Using increment or decrement to modify a value

We can see that, after incrementing our value, it increased by one, and after decrementing the value, it returned back to normal. There are a couple of interesting things that we need to be aware of here. Unlike the minus operator, the increment and decrement operators actually change the value of the variable used with it. After incrementing, our variable didn't return to its original value as we saw with the minus operator; that is, once incremented, the incremented value becomes the new value.

It's also important to note that a value can be either pre-increment or post-increment. That is, the increment or decrement operator can be placed before or after the variable, and this changes how the value is returned. Let's move onto a small exercise that will highlight this subtle difference.

Exercise 23: A Pre-Increment/Post-Increment Example

We just saw that it's possible to either pre-increment or post-increment a value, and that they each have a subtle but clear difference in how they operate. Let's take a look at an example of this by writing an application that does both. Will you be able to guess the output? Take a look at the following steps:

> **Note**
>
> The complete code for this exercise can be found here: https://packt.
> live/2QADmQC.

1. Start by declaring our function title and **#include** statements:

```
// Pre/Post Increment Example.
#include <iostream>
#include <string>
```

2. Next, we'll define our **main** function and define an **int**, giving it a default value of **5**. We'll then pre-increment the value within a print statement and then print the value on its own:

```
int main()
{
    int myInt = 5;
    std::cout << ++myInt << std::endl;
    std::cout << myInt << std::endl;
```

3. Now, we'll reset our integer back to 5, and then increment it within a print statement again. This time, however, we'll be post-incrementing the value:

```
    myInt = 5;
    std::cout << myInt++ << std::endl;
    std::cout << myInt << std::endl;
}
```

4. The complete program looks like this:

```
// Pre/Post Increment Example.
#include <iostream>
#include <string>

int main()
{
```

```
        int myInt = 5;
        std::cout << ++myInt << std::endl;
        std::cout << myInt << std::endl;
        myInt = 5;
        std::cout << myInt++ << std::endl;
        std::cout << myInt << std::endl;
    }
```

5. Let's run this code and examine how the different types of increments have interacted with the **std::cout** statements. What do you think the output of each line will be? Make a note before running the application:

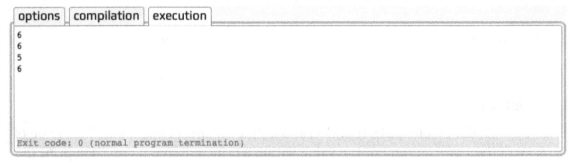

Figure 4.9: Pre-increment versus post-increment gives us different results

In the first case, we output **6** both times. This means that the increment took place before the value was printed. In the second case, however, we can see that we print the numbers **5** and **6**. This means that the value was first printed, and then the increment took place. It's important to keep the order of the operations in mind, as it's easy to see from this example how we could introduce a subtle bug that would be hard to trace. If you're incrementing a value and disregarding the expression result, however, such as incrementing a **for** loop, then either is fine.

Assignment Operators

Assignment operators allow us to assign values to our objects. We've used this operator many times throughout our chapters so far—it's one of the most fundamental operations in programming, but as always, there's more that we can learn about these operators.

The most basic assignment operator is where we take a value and assign it to an object, as follows:

```
    int myInt = 5;
```

We're familiar with this, but what we might not be familiar with is the concept of combining these with arithmetic operators. Let's imagine a scenario where we need to increment a value by 5. We could do this as follows:

```
myInt = myInt + 5;
```

We take the value of **myInt**, add **5** to it, and then assign it back to the original variable. We can do this in a more refined way, however, by combining the two operators together. The assignment operator can be preceded by an arithmetic operator to achieve this, as follows:

```
myInt += 5;
```

This is the case for any of the arithmetic operators; they can precede an assignment operator and their effects are combined. This can be seen in the following example application:

```cpp
// Assignment Operators Example.
#include <iostream>
#include <string>

int main()
{
    int myInt = 5;

    myInt += 5;
    std::cout << myInt << std::endl;

    myInt -= 5;
    std::cout << myInt << std::endl;

    myInt *= 5;
    std::cout << myInt << std::endl;

    myInt /= 5;
    std::cout << myInt << std::endl;

    myInt %= 5;
    std::cout << myInt << std::endl;
}
```

If we run this code in our editor, we can see how the assignment statement changes the value of `myInt`:

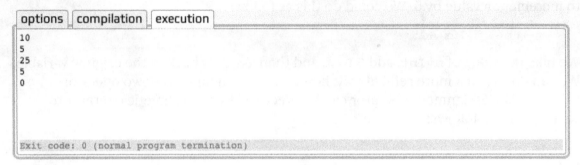

Figure 4.10: Combining the simple assignment operator with arithmetic operators

By combing the simple assignment operator with arithmetic operators, we're able to perform a mathematical operation and assignment in a single statement. This works for the various bitwise operators that we'll cover later too.

Logical Operators

Logical operators allow us to evaluate multiple Boolean values together in a single statement. We've seen previously that when we evaluate a condition, such as in an `if` statement, we end up with a Boolean value. We can, therefore, use logical operators to combine and evaluate two or more conditions at one time.

We have three such operators available to us:

- **AND (&&)**: This returns true when both conditions are true, and false otherwise.

- **OR (||)**: This returns true when either condition is true, and false otherwise.

- **NOT (!)**: This returns true if the condition is false, and true otherwise; essentially, it returns the opposite of the condition.

Let's take a look at how these operators work using an example.

Exercise 24: Logical Operators Example

To demonstrate how these logical operators work, let's create a quick example application. We'll take a number of inputs from the user, perhaps some names, and check them against one another using our operators:

> **Note**
>
> The complete code for this exercise can be found here: https://packt.live/2KGX0a2.

1. To start with, let's add a program title and add our **#include** statements:

```
// Logical Operators Exercise.
#include <iostream>
#include <string>
```

2. Now we can define our **main** function. To start with, we need to define three string variables and fetch three names from the user:

```
int main()
{
    std::string name1;
    std::string name2;
    std::string name3;

    std::cout << "Please enter name 1: ";
    std::cin >> name1;

    std::cout << "Please enter name 2: ";
    std::cin >> name2;

    std::cout << "Please enter name 3: ";
    std::cin >> name3;
```

3. Now we can do our first check. We'll first check to see whether all our names are the same. To do this, we'll check **name1** against **name2**, and **name2** against **name3**. We'll then use the **&&** operator to ensure both of these are true. If they are, we know all the names matched, so we can output a message:

```
    // Check if all or any of the names match.
    if (name1 == name2 && name2 == name3)
    {
        std::cout << "\nAll the names are the same.";
    }
```

4. If that fails, we'll check to see whether any of the names match. We'll check each **name** against the others and use the **||** operator to return true if either of the conditions is true:

```
    else if (name1 == name2 || name2 == name3 || name1 == name3)
    {
        std::cout << "\nSome of the names matched.";
    }
```

5. Finally, we'll use the **!** operator check whether **name1** and **name2** match. We're also going to use a ternary statement for this. First, we'll add the code, and then look at what it's doing:

```cpp
    // Check if names 1 and 2 are different.
    std::cout << "\nNames 1 and 2 are "
              << (!(name1 == name2) ? "different." : "the same.")
              << std::endl;
}
```

In this ternary statement, we check whether **name1** and **name2** match and then negate the result with the **!** operator. This means that the ternary statement condition will be true if the two names are different. We then use this to return the correct string.

Note that we've used brackets here, and this comes down to the order of precedence that we talked about earlier. For example, we want the evaluation of **name1** and **name2** to be carried out before we try to apply the **!** operator. Likewise, we want the whole ternary statement to be evaluated before using it with the **<<** operator; otherwise, we get an error. This is a good example of how we can use parentheses to control the order of precedence.

6. The complete program looks like this:

```cpp
    // Logical Operators Exercise.
    #include <iostream>
    #include <string>

    int main()
    {
        std::string name1;
        std::string name2;
        std::string name3;

        std::cout << "Please enter name 1: ";
        std::cin >> name1;

        std::cout << "Please enter name 2: ";
        std::cin >> name2;

        std::cout << "Please enter name 3: ";
        std::cin >> name3;

        // Check if all or any of the names match.
        if (name1 == name2 && name2 == name3)
```

```
    {
        std::cout << "\nAll the names are the same.";
    }
    else if (name1 == name2 || name2 == name3 || name1 == name3)
    {
        std::cout << "\nSome of the names matched.";
    }

    // Check if names 1 and 2 are different.
    std::cout << "\nNames 1 and 2 are "
            << (!(name1 == name2) ? "different." : "the same.")
            << std::endl;

}
```

7. Run the application and test it with a few different names:

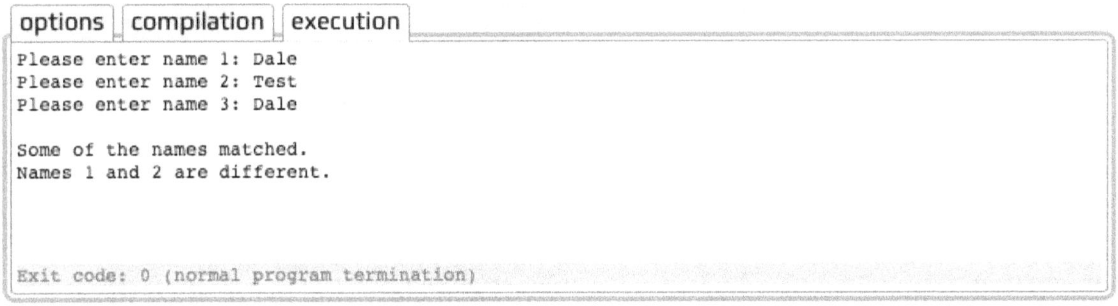

```
options    compilation    execution

Please enter name 1: Dale
Please enter name 2: Test
Please enter name 3: Dale

Some of the names matched.
Names 1 and 2 are different.


Exit code: 0 (normal program termination)
```

Figure 4.11: Using logical operators to test conditions

In this exercise, we've used a number of logical operators with various conditions. By doing so, we're able to evaluate multiple conditions as a collective, such as only doing something if all the values are true. We're also able to manipulate the conditions by flipping their logical value (using the ! operator to return the opposite value). This is very useful, and is just the tip of the iceberg in terms of how they can be employed.

Operator Overloading

All the operators we've seen so far have been defined by C++. That's not to say, however, that we can't overload them in our own classes just as we can with functions. Operator overloading is incredibly powerful and allows us to define our own behaviors, with our own types, for most operators available in C++. The syntax for overloading an operator is as follows:

```
returnType operator symbol (arguments)
```

Let's take a look at an example of this with a simple test class:

```cpp
// Operator Overloading Example
#include <iostream>
#include <string>

class MyClass
{
    public:
    void operator + (MyClass const & other)
    {
        std::cout << "Overloaded Operator Called" << std::endl;
        return;
    }
};

int main()
{
    MyClass A = MyClass();
    MyClass B = MyClass();
    A + B;
}
```

In this trivial example, we've created a small **MyClass** class, and overloaded the **+** operator, providing our own definition. All we do in there, for now, is print a message that lets us know our operator code has been run. However, you can imagine how we could put anything we wanted in here, defining custom behaviors for our objects. Let's run the code and confirm that we're using our overloaded operator:

```
options   compilation   execution
Overloaded Operator Called




Exit code: 0 (normal program termination)
```

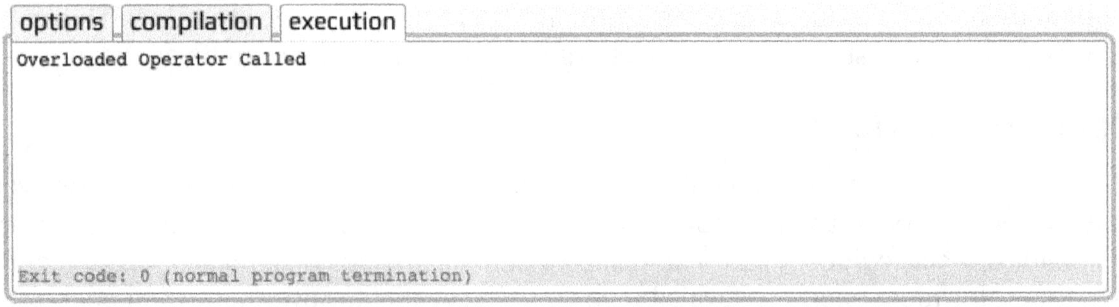

Figure 4.12: Overloading an operator with our own behavior

On running the application, we do indeed see our printed message, so we know we're running our overloaded operator behavior. By doing this, we're able to use the operators we've covered in this chapter with our own types. Let's take a look at a more real-world application of this by overloading the equality operator for a custom type.

Exercise 25: Operator Overloading Example

Let's override the equality operator for a simple **Person** class that encapsulates a name and age. We could conceivably have multiple references to the same person and want to check whether they're the same, such as checking whether the same person exists amongst multiple lists. The equality operator will let us check that. Take a look at the following steps:

> **Note**
>
> The complete code for this exercise can be found here: https://packt.live/2QyS4b0.

1. First, we'll add our **#includes**:

```
// Operator Overloading Example
#include <iostream>
#include <string>
```

2. Next, we'll declare our **Person** class. This will be a simple class that holds a name and an age. Start by defining the class name, our required member variables, and a constructor that will initialize them:

```
class Person
{
public:
    Person(int age, std::string name) : age(age), name(name)
    {
    };

    float age = 0;
    std::string name = "";
```

3. Now we can overload the **==** operator. We'll start with the initial declaration. We want to overload the **==** operator, and return a bool; we'll accept another object of the same type as the object we'll compare against:

```
    bool operator== (Person const& other)
    {
```

4. Now it's time for the body of the operator; two **Person** records can be considered the same if both the names and ages are exact matches. We can check for this and return the value as the result. This will also complete our class definition, so we'll add our closing brackets:

```
        return ((age == other.age) && (name == other.name));
    }
};
```

5. Now, to see our new operator in action, we'll declare three **Person** records. Two will be identical, and the third will differ in name but not age:

```
int main()
{
    Person PersonA = Person(27, "Lucy");
    Person PersonB = Person(27, "Lucy");
    Person PersonC = Person(27, "Susan");
```

6. Finally, we'll check which types are identical by using the new operator. Evaluate the equality of **PersonA** and **PersonB**, and **PersonB** and **PersonC**:

```
    std::cout << (PersonA == PersonB) << std::endl;
    std::cout << (PersonB == PersonC) << std::endl;
}
```

7. The complete program looks like this:

```
// Operator Overloading Example
#include <iostream>
#include <string>

class Person
{
public:
    Person(int age, std::string name): age(age), name(name) {};
    float age = 0;
    std::string name = "";
    bool operator == (Person const & other)
    {
        return ((age == other.age) && (name == other.name));
    }
};

int main()
{
```

```
        Person PersonA = Person(27, "Lucy");
        Person PersonB = Person(27, "Lucy");
        Person PersonC = Person(27, "Susan");
        std::cout << (PersonA == PersonB) << std::endl;
        std::cout << (PersonB == PersonC) << std::endl;
    }
```

8. Let's run this code and see what we get:

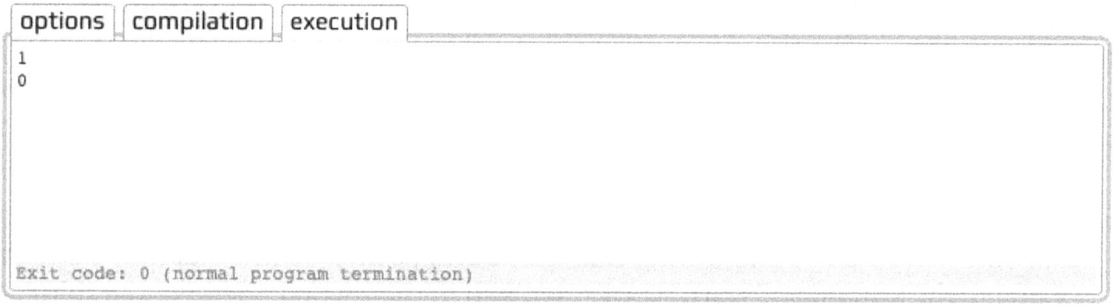

Figure 4.13: Person A and B were a match. Person B and C were not

Since both the names and ages match for persons A and B, our equality operator returns true, so we print the value. The name differs between persons B and C so it does not match, and we print 0 (that is, false). We can see that by defining these operators for our own user types, we give them lots of utility.

Bitwise Operators

Bitwise operations are those that work on individual bits, such as shifting a bit to the left, and for this, we have a suite of specialized operators known as bitwise operators. We're not going to go into too much detail here—a full discussion on bitwise operators is for another day. However, we will take a quick look at what bitwise operators we have available to us, along with some quick examples of their use. This will give you some preliminary understanding so that when you do come across them later, they'll be familiar.

Note

Remember, a bit (that is, a binary digit) is the most fundamental unit of data in a computer. With two possible values, either 1 or 0, all data is stored in bits. The smallest addressable unit of data on a machine is a byte, which is made up of 8 bits, so bitwise operations allow us to manipulate bits individually.

In the following examples, we're going to be working with bitsets. This is a simple collection of bits and will allow us to see the results of bitwise operators. Each example will be in the following format:

```
{lhs bitset} {operator} {rhs bitset} = {resulting bitset}
```

In principle, this is no different to a normal calculation (such as $a + b = c$) so don't let any potential unfamiliarity with bits cause confusion. With that preface, let's get on with it.

C++ provides us with six bitwise operators, as follows:

- **& Binary AND**: This operator copies only those bits that are present in both operands to the new value. Consider the following example: 00110 & 01100 = 00100. Here, only the third bit was present in both the two original values, so that's the only bit set in the result.

- **| Binary OR**: This operator copies bits that are present in either operand to the new value. Consider the following example: 00110 | 01100 = 01110. Here, in our first operand, the second and third bits are set, and in the second operand, the third and fourth bits are set. The result, therefore, has the second, third, and fourth bits set.

- **~ Binary Ones' Compliment**: This operator flips each of the bits in a value. Consider the following example: ~00110 = 11001. Here, in our first operand, the only bits that are set are the second and third. Our result therefore has all bits set except these.

- **<< Binary Left Shift Operator**: This operator will shift the bits in the left operand to the left by the number specified in the right operand. Consider the following example: 00110 << 2 = 11000. Here, our left operand has the second and third bits set, so after shifting them two places to the left, the fourth and fifth bits are now set.

- **>> Binary Right Shift Operator**: This operator will shift the bits in the left operand to the right by the number specified in the right operand. Consider the following example: 01100 >> 2 = 00011. Here, our left operand has the third and fourth bits set, so after shifting them two places to the right, the first and second bits are now set.

> **Note**
>
> In this context, the terms "bitwise" and "binary" are interchangeable. It's equally correct to say "binary AND" or "bitwise AND,".

Let's take a look at these examples in code. Provided, as part of the standard library, is the bitset class. This allows us to represent an integer value as its series of bits, allowing us to more easily see the results of our bitwise operations. The following code represents the examples given previously:

```cpp
// Bitwise Operator Examples.
#include <iostream>
#include <string>
#include <bitset>

int main()
{
    int myInt1 = 6; // 00110 when expressed in binary
    int myInt2 = 12; // 01100 when expressed in binary

    // Binary AND
    std::cout << std::bitset < 5 > (myInt1 & myInt2) << std::endl;

    // Binary OR
    std::cout << std::bitset < 5 > (myInt1 | myInt2) << std::endl;

    // Binary Ones Compliment
    std::cout << std::bitset < 5 > (~myInt1) << std::endl;

    // Binary Left Shift Operator
    std::cout << std::bitset < 5 > (myInt1 << 2) << std::endl;

    // Binary Right Shift Operator
    std::cout << std::bitset < 5 > (myInt2 >> 2) << std::endl;
}
```

> **Note**
>
> The value of **5** in **std::bitset<5>** denotes the number of bits in the bitset. For more information on bitsets, you can refer to https://packt.live/2QGLqzp.

If we run this code in our editor, we can see that the results of the bitwise operations match those of the exercises:

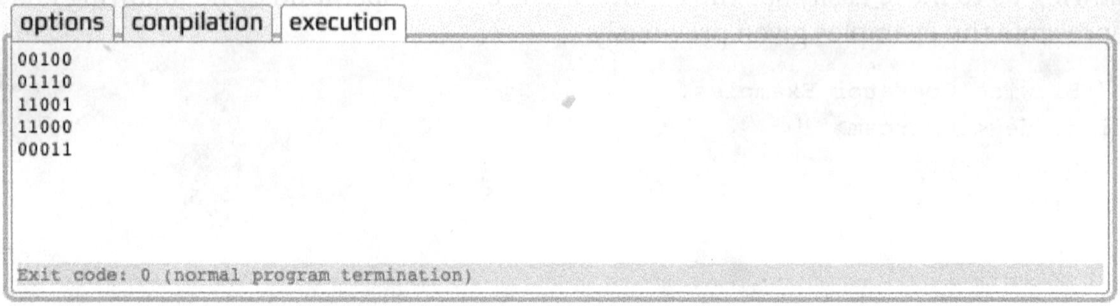

```
options    compilation    execution

00100
01110
11001
11000
00011




Exit code: 0 (normal program termination)
```

Figure 4.14: We can see the results of our bitwise operations by using the bitset class

While manipulating individual bits can seem intimidating at first, there are plenty of occasions where it's incredibly useful. One such occasion is with flags. Perhaps we want to keep track of multiple things, say, active layers in a game engine. We have multiple layers that can be active at any one time, so we can define an integer giving us a series of bits and use each bit to determine which layers are active:

```
int layer1 = 1;              // 00001
int layer2 = 2;              // 00010
int layer3 = 4;              // 00100
int layer4 = 8;              // 01000
// [...]
int activeLayers = 9;        // 01001
```

In the preceding example snippet, we define four layers, each with a different bit set to the value **1**. Since each layer requires a different bit, we can represent all of them in a single 4-bit group. For example, **layer 1** sets the first bit, and **layer 4** sets the fourth bit. If we wanted to denote that both of these layers were active, we could set both of their bit values to 1, resulting in the number 9 (01001 in binary, or the first and fourth bit). This is just the bitwise AND of their individual values. This is known as bit masking and has many potential applications—managing active layers, as in this example.

That's all for now on bitwise operations as it's a large topic. Hopefully, this short introduction has explained the basics so that when you do run across bitwise operations in the future it won't be totally alien. Let's now move on to a final activity in which we create a famous programming test: Fizz Buzz.

Activity 4: Fizz Buzz

The final activity of this first part will see us creating the Fizz Buzz application. This is a common activity that is used to test programming understanding across various languages, and makes use of many of the topics covered so far.

The idea behind the Fizz Buzz test is straightforward: write a program that will output the numbers 1 to 100. For multiples of 3, print the word "Fizz" instead of the number, and for multiples of 5, print the word "Buzz":

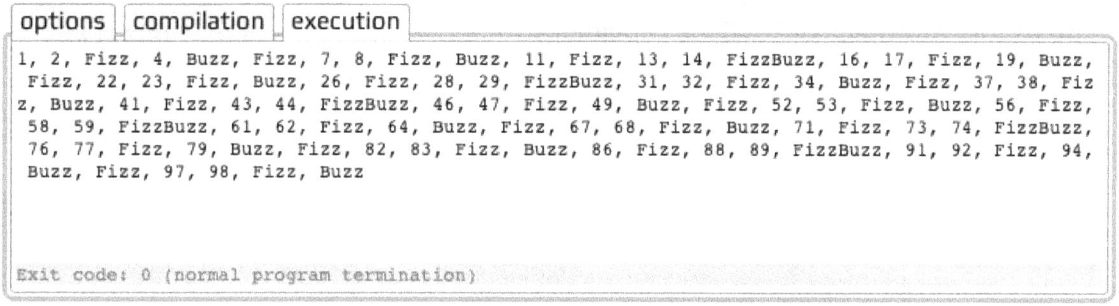

```
options   compilation   execution

1, 2, Fizz, 4, Buzz, Fizz, 7, 8, Fizz, Buzz, 11, Fizz, 13, 14, FizzBuzz, 16, 17, Fizz, 19, Buzz,
Fizz, 22, 23, Fizz, Buzz, 26, Fizz, 28, 29, FizzBuzz, 31, 32, Fizz, 34, Buzz, Fizz, 37, 38, Fiz
z, Buzz, 41, Fizz, 43, 44, FizzBuzz, 46, 47, Fizz, 49, Buzz, Fizz, 52, 53, Fizz, Buzz, 56, Fizz,
58, 59, FizzBuzz, 61, 62, Fizz, 64, Buzz, Fizz, 67, 68, Fizz, Buzz, 71, Fizz, 73, 74, FizzBuzz,
76, 77, Fizz, 79, Buzz, Fizz, 82, 83, Fizz, Buzz, 86, Fizz, 88, 89, FizzBuzz, 91, 92, Fizz, 94,
Buzz, Fizz, 97, 98, Fizz, Buzz

Exit code: 0 (normal program termination)
```

Figure 4.15: The Fizz Buzz application – a common coding test exercise

> **Note**
>
> The complete code for this activity can be found here: https://packt.live/2KHiSC7.

Here are some steps that will help you complete this activity:

1. As usual, we'll start by including the headers we need for the application and starting our main loop.

2. The Fizz Buzz application tells us that for multiples of 3, we'll print **Fizz**, and for multiples of 5, we'll print **Buzz** instead. However, both conditions can occur at the same time. For example, 15 is a multiple of both, so we'll next define a Boolean value (**multiple**) which will help us to keep track of this, and give it an initial value of **false**.

3. Next, we can check whether our current loop value, **i**, is a multiple of 3. If so, we'll print the word **Fizz** and set our multiple Boolean to **true**.

4. We can then do the same for **Buzz**, checking whether **i** is a multiple of 5 instead. Again, we'll set our multiple Boolean to true if so.

5. Now that we've checked whether our number is a multiple of either 3 or 5, and have a Boolean that will be **true** if so, we can use this to determine whether we print the normal number. If we've reached this point with our **multiple bool** still being **false**, then we know we need to print the normal number, **i**.

6. Finally, we'll do a little bit of formatting. If we're not on our final iteration of the loop, we'll print a comma followed by a space. This will just make our application a little neater when printed.

7. Let's run the application now and see it in action. We should see numbers leading up to 100. Multiples of 3 will be replaced with **Fizz**, multiples of 5 by **Buzz**, and multiples of both by **FizzBuzz**.

> **Note**
>
> The solution for this activity can be found on page 524.

This simple application allows us to use a number of common operators in a common coding exercise that applicants can be asked to do. Operators allow us to interact with the data in our programs, so having a strong understanding of their use is key.

Summary

In this chapter, we've taken a closer look at the operators provided by C++ and how we can use them to interact with our data. They were presented in groups—the first of which was arithmetic operators. These allow us to perform mathematical operations on our values (such as adding two numbers), or in the case of the activity we just completed, using modulus to determine whether one number is a multiple of another. We then moved on to looking at relational operators. These allow us to compare values with one another, such as determining whether two objects are equal, or whether one number is larger than another.

We then moved on to unary operators. These are operators that operate on a single operand, such as incrementing a value or negating a Boolean value. This led to looking at the assignment and logical operators. We explored how we can combine the simple assignment operator with arithmetic operators to more concisely multiply our values, and how we can evaluate multiple Boolean values in a single condition, such as checking whether two Booleans are true.

Finally, we took a quick look at some advanced bitwise operators, introducing the concept of bitwise operations. We then ended the chapter by looking at operator overloading, a means by which we can define our own behavior for these operators for our user-defined types.

The skills we learned in this chapter were employed in our final activity of the chapter, the **Fizz Buzz** challenge. This saw us printing the numbers 1 to 100, but printing words instead of numbers when certain criteria were met. This is a common coding exercise presented to applications across various disciplines and languages, so it is a great real-world example with which to test our skills.

This chapter wraps up our initial introduction to C++. The goal for the first four chapters was to introduce a handful of core topics and concepts and for us to start writing code as quickly as possible. Hopefully, you now feel confident with the basics and are comfortable opening up an editor and writing a simple C++ application. Now we move into the next set of chapters, where we'll be building on these fundamental skills, exploring C++ in more depth with topics such as inheritance, polymorphism, and object-orientated programming.

5

Pointers and References

Overview

This chapter presents C++ built-in pointer types and reference types in enough detail for you to use them effectively. Pointer and reference types are important raw materials out of which data structures are built, so understanding these simple, primitive types is crucial to your success as a C++ developer.

By the end of this chapter, you will be able to describe the memory address model used by C++; explain how pointers and references refer to other variables; declare, initialize, and use pointers and references; explain how pointers and arrays are similar; describe how a pointer can be stepped through the elements of an array; perform pointer arithmetic and use pointers and references as function arguments.

Introduction

So far, this book has examined several types of variables: integers, characters, floating-point numbers plus arrays and structs composed of these simple types. In previous chapters, you have been introduced to pointers and references. In this chapter, we will look at these variables in greater detail.

A pointer is a variable that *points* to another variable. Pointers have a type; that is, a pointer to **int** *points* to or refers to an **int**. A pointer to **char** refers to a **char**. A pointer to **int** can be assigned to another pointer to **int**, but not to a pointer to **char**. A pointer to class **foo** refers to an instance of class **foo**. A pointer can also be the special value **nullptr**, which means the pointer is not pointing to anything. A reference, which will be discussed in more detail later in this chapter, is a pointer, but with constraints that make it safer to use.

C++ pointers can point to any variable inside any data structure, and can iterate through arrays. To make pointers efficient, C++ does nothing to check whether a pointer refers to a valid memory location containing a variable of the same type as the pointer. This means that pointers can cause havoc, unexpectedly overwriting data in a program that does not use them carefully. The inventors of newer languages always name pointers as a reason to avoid C++. However, as we will see later, the risks of pointers are relatively easy to manage.

In the early days of C++, pointers gave it a tremendous speed advantage over other languages when iterating through arrays. Even simple compilers produced excellent code when the program used pointers. This particular advantage is less important in modern C++ implementations because compilers have become more sophisticated, but pointers still have advantages. Pointers are woven deeply into the fabric of the C++ language and into the culture of C++ programming.

Because pointers and references can point into other data structures, using a pointer is a shortcut that eliminates the need to repeatedly write code to access data. This can also give C++ a speed advantage over other languages.

Pointers and references can be used to link one part of a complex data structure to another. Pointers can iterate through arrays and also through linked data structures. Iterating through arrays is covered later in this chapter. Iterating through linked data structures is discussed in the next chapter.

Pointers and references are also useful because a pointer to a big array or class instance can be passed into a function, instead of copying the array or instance into the function's formal argument. Pointers have an important role referring to dynamic variables; This will be described in chapter 6.

Memory Addresses

The memory of a computer can be modeled as a very long array of bytes. Each byte has an address that has the same role as an array subscript. Every variable has an address that is the first of perhaps several byte addresses at which the bits of the variable are stored. Normal variables are known by a name that the compiler translates into an address. The following diagram shows a region of memory as a long tape extending from left to right. The hexadecimal numbers above the tape are memory addresses. For simplicity, we have only shown every fourth byte address:

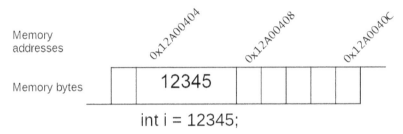

Figure 5.1: Visualizing computer memory as a long array of bytes

The bytes of memory have no fixed meaning until the program declares a variable. In the diagram, the program has declared an **int** variable named **i**, and initialized it to the integer value **12345**. The compiler reserves 4 bytes of storage for the **int** variable, which defines this particular storage to hold an integer value. The compiler puts **12345** in that storage initially, though the program can change it later. The name **i** is now a synonym for the memory address **0x12A00404**.

Pointers

A pointer is a variable that holds the address of another variable. That is, a pointer *points to* another variable. Pointers are declared with the type name and an asterisk *****; so, to declare a pointer called **ptr** to an **int** variable, the declaration looks like **int* ptr;**. C purists may prefer to put the asterisk with the variable name, as in **int *ptr;**. The reasons for this preference are not covered here.

The **&** address-of operator produces the address of its argument, converting a variable into a pointer to that variable. If **i1** is an **int** variable, then **&i1** is a pointer to **int** that points to **i1**. The **&** operator may be read as "take the address of...". The effect of the address-of operator can be understood by referring to the following diagram:

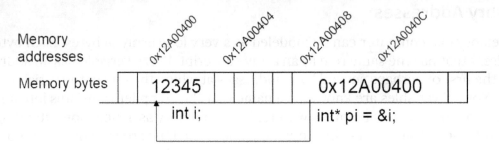

Figure 5.2: Pointer initialization

In this diagram, the pointer **pi** is initialized to point to the **int** variable, **i**, using the declaration **int *pi = &i;**. It points to memory address **0x12A00400**, which is the address at which the compiler placed **i**.

Like other basic types of variables in C++, if a pointer is not initialized and no value is assigned to the pointer, it contains the random bits that happened to be in memory when it was created. These random bits probably do not point to the address of any valid variable.

Because the value contained in a pointer has no decipherable meaning, it is hard to tell whether a pointer has been assigned a value. To help solve this problem, C++ defines the constant **nullptr** as a pointer value that is guaranteed not to point to any valid memory address. **nullptr** can be assigned to any type of pointer. The integer constant, **0**, has the same meaning as **nullptr** when assigned or compared to a pointer. In older C++ code, you may also see the preprocessor macro **NULL** assigned to pointers instead of **nullptr**. **NULL** is normally defined as zero. It's a good idea to assign **nullptr** to all pointer variables when they are declared.

The ***** (**dereference**) operator dereferences a pointer. That is, if a pointer **p** refers to an **int** variable, ***p** is the **int** variable to which it refers. If the program applies the ***** operator to dereference a pointer that is set to **nullptr**, the program will crash with a brief error message, because the program has tried to access a machine address that isn't mapped to any actual memory. If you dereference a pointer that was never set, it might crash, or it might continue running, but it won't produce a valid result.

With the basic functioning of pointers in mind, the first exercise provides a very brief example of how to put the pieces together in a functioning C++ program.

Exercise 26: Pointers

In this exercise, you will write a very simple program that creates a pointer, sets it to point to an `int`, and then changes the value of the `int` through the pointer. The program will illustrate the syntax of pointer declarations and assignments. The program will also print the value of the pointer and the address of the `int`, to demonstrate that they are the same, and the value of the `int` before and after changing it through the pointer, to verify that it has changed.

> **Note**
>
> The complete code for this exercise can be found here: https://packt.live/2qnUzCt.

Here are the steps to complete the exercise:

1. First, enter the skeleton of the `main()` function:

   ```
   #include <iostream>
   using namespace std;

   int main()
   {
       return 0;
   }
   ```

2. In function `main()`, declare an `int` variable, `i`, and initialize it to **12345**:

   ```
   int i = 12345;
   ```

3. Declare a pointer to `int` variable `p` and initialize it to point to the `int`:

   ```
   int *p = &i;
   ```

4. Output the value of the pointer and the address of the `int` variable:

   ```
   cout << "p = " << p << ", &i = " << &i << endl;
   ```

   The specific hexadecimal addresses printed may change from compiler to compiler, and from run to run, but the point is that the two numbers are the same; that is, the pointer points to the `int`.

5. Output the value of the `int` variable, `i`:

   ```
   cout << "i = " << i << endl;
   ```

6. Use the * operator to dereference the pointer, producing the pointed-to **int**. Then, add **2** to the value and save it again:

```
*p = *p + 2;
```

7. Finally, print out the value to prove that adding **2** to the dereferenced pointer also added **2** to the **int**:

```
cout << "i = " << i << endl;
```

8. The complete program looks like this:

```
#include <iostream>
using namespace std;

int main()
{
    int i = 12345;
    int *p = &i;
    cout << "p = " << p << ", &i = " << &i << endl;

    cout << "i = " << i << endl;
    *p = *p + 2;
    cout << "i = " << i << endl;

    return 0;
}
```

9. Compile and run the program. This is the output of one particular run of the compiled program:

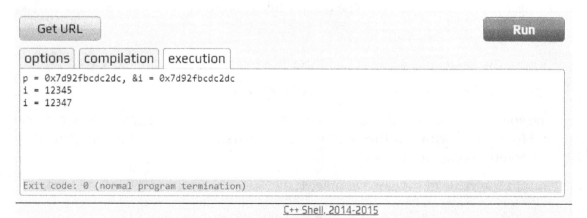

Figure 5.3: Output produced by exercise 26

The hexadecimal addresses displayed in this result may be different from the addresses printed in your run of the program. That is expected. What is important is that the two addresses will be the same. After assigning a new value to the dereferenced pointer, the value of the **int** changed, also as expected.

Exercise 27: Dereferencing nullptr

Dereferencing **nullptr** causes an error at runtime and stops the program. Dereferencing **nullptr** is not something a programmer does deliberately. It's something that happens by accident when some execution path through the program does not initialize the pointer to a valid machine address before the pointer is used. Initializing every pointer to **nullptr** produces a particular error message, whereas dereferencing an uninitialized pointer can cause more subtle errors. Here are some steps that you can perform to see this in action:

> **Note**
>
> The complete code for this exercise can be found here: https://packt.live/2pGNtZi.

1. Type in the following program:

```cpp
#include <iostream>
using namespace std;

int main()
{
    int *p1 = nullptr;
    cout << "p1 = " << p1 << endl;
    *p1 = 22;

    return 0;
}
```

You can enter it into one of the online C++ compilers, or use your editor of choice to create a file for a conventional C++ compiler.

2. Now run the program. The output of one particular run of the program looks like this:

```
$g++ -o main *.cpp
$main
p1 = 0
timeout: the monitored command dumped core
sh: line 1:  5714 Segmentation fault       timeout 10s main
```

Figure 5.4: The program crashes with an error message

> **Note**
>
> Not all online C++ compilers print messages from the operating system. Use a compiler such as tutorialspoint (https://www.tutorialspoint.com/compile_cpp_online.php) to be sure you see the preceding output.

As expected, the program crashed with an error message from the operating system. Both Windows and Linux produce an error message. If you are using an online compiler, and the particular online compiler used didn't show an error message, try a different online compiler.

Pointers to Arrays

Arrays and pointers are almost indistinguishable from each other in C++. A pointer to the beginning of an array, the address of the first element, and the bare array name all mean the same thing.

Array elements are variables. The **&** operator can be used to get the address of an array element to assign to a pointer. The expression **p** = **&a[2]**; updates **p** to point to the third entry in array **a** (remember, arrays start from zero).

A pointer works like an array in C++. It can be subscripted like an array. If **p** points to **a[2]**, then the expression **p[3]** fetches the sixth entry in the array (that is, the one at **a[5]**).

Exercise 28: Pointers to Arrays

This is the first of several exercises on pointers and arrays. In this simple exercise, you will set a pointer to point to an array element, and test that it points to the expected value. You will subscript a pointer, and see that it produces the expected array element. Remember that arrays start at zero in C++, so that **a[5]** is the sixth element.

> **Note**
>
> The complete code for this exercise can be found here: https://packt.live/2OA77yz.

Here are the steps to complete the exercise:

1. Enter the skeleton **main()** function, as follows:

```cpp
#include <iostream>
using namespace std;

int main()
{
    return 0;
}
```

You can compile and run each part of this program if you want; otherwise, you can wait until you have it all entered to run it.

2. Following the opening curly brace of **main()**, declare an array of **7 ints** called **a**, and initialize it. Then, declare a pointer to **int** named **p**, and set it to **nullptr** so that we know it is set to no known address:

```cpp
int a[7]{ 1, 3, 5, 4, 2, 9, -1 };
int *p = nullptr;
```

3. Now, set **p** to the address of **a[2]** using the **&** address-of operator to take the address of the array element:

```cpp
p = &a[2];
```

4. Output the dereferenced pointer, ***p**, and the value of **a[2]** to see that the pointer is actually pointing to **a[2]**:

```cpp
cout << "*p = " << *p << ", a[2] = " << a[2] << endl;
```

5. Next, output **p[3]** and **a[5]**. This shows that pointers can be subscripted like arrays, and that **p[3]** points to the same value as **a[5]**:

```cpp
cout << "p[3] = " << p[3] << ", a[5] = " << a[5] << endl;
```

6. The complete program looks like this:

```cpp
#include <iostream>
using namespace std;

int main()
{
    int a[7] {1, 3, 5, 4, 2, 9, -1};
    int * p = nullptr;

    p = & a[2];
    cout << "*p = " << * p << ", a[2] = " << a[2] << endl;
    cout << "p[3] = " << p[3] << ", a[5] = " << a[5] << endl;

    return 0;
}
```

7. Compile and run the program. Here is the output of this program:

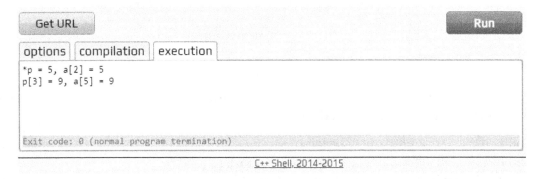

Figure 5.5: Output of program in exercise 28

The values printed are equal, as expected. They are both the same array element, as can be verified by looking at the array initializer. Subscripting a pointer works exactly like subscripting an array; however, since the address of **a[2]** was assigned to the pointer instead of the address of **a[0]**, the subscripts of the pointer are offset from those of the array.

Pointer Arithmetic

C++ converts the name of an array into a pointer to **a[0]**, the first entry of the array. The statement **p = a;** where **a** is an array, updates **p** to point to the first entry in **a**.

The program can add one to a pointer. If the pointer points into an array, the result of **p+1** is a pointer to the next array element. The pointer's hexadecimal address value changes by the size in bytes of an array element.

The program can add the value of any integral expression to a pointer, which produces a pointer that advances by that many elements. If **p** is a pointer and **k** is an **int**, then the pointer expression **p+k** is a pointer of the same type as **p**.

The program can subtract one pointer from another if they are pointing into the same array. The result is the number of array elements between the two pointers. The result of subtracting pointers cannot be interpreted if the two pointers don't point into the same array.

The program can compare two pointers if they point into the same array, using any of the relational operators (such as **==**, **!=**, **<**, **>**, **<=**, and **>=**). If the pointers point into different arrays, then a meaningless answer is produced.

Exercise 29: Pointer Arithmetic

This exercise demonstrates how pointer arithmetic and pointer relational operators work, and will also get you used to interpreting pointer expressions.

> **Note**
>
> The complete code for this exercise can be found here: https://packt.live/2KVIvPV.

Here are the steps to complete the exercise:

1. Enter the skeleton **main()** function. You can run the program after each step, or wait until it's all entered to run it:

```
#include <iostream>
using namespace std;

int main()
{
    return 0;
}
```

2. Following the opening curly brace of **main()**, declare an array of five **ints** called **numbers**. Declare a pointer to **int** called **pint**, and initialize it to **numbers**. Declare another pointer to **int** called **p2**, and initialize it to point to **numbers[3]**:

```
int numbers[5]{ 0, 100, 200, 300, 400 };
int* pint = numbers;
int* p2 = &numbers[3];
```

3. Next, output the value of **pint**, the value of the pointer expression **pint+1**, and **sizeof(int)**, which tells you how many bytes of memory an **int** occupies on this machine. Although the hexadecimal values printed for pointers are not normally interpretable by human beings, you will see that the two hexadecimal numbers printed differ by **sizeof(int)**. Adding **1** to a pointer adds the size of the pointed-to type:

```
cout << "pint = " << pint << ", pint+1 = " << pint+1
     << ", sizeof(int) = " << sizeof(int) << endl;
```

4. Output the expression ***(pint+1)** and the value of the subscripted pointer, **pint[1]**, to demonstrate that they are the same. Then, output ***(pint+4)** and **pint[4]**, which are also the same:

```
cout << "*(pint+1) = " << *(pint+1)
     << ", pint[1] = " << pint[1] << endl;

cout << "*(pint+4) = " << *(pint+4)
     << ", pint[4] = " << pint[4] << endl;
```

5. Output the pointer expression **p2 - pint**. The difference should be printed as **3**:

```
cout << "p2 - pint = " << p2 - pint << endl;
```

6. Output a couple of pointer comparisons using the **==** and **>** operators. The output manipulator **boolalpha** causes expressions of type **bool** to print as **true** or **false**. Otherwise, they are converted to **int**, and print as 1 or 0. Additionally, the comparison operators have lower operator precedence than the output inserter operator, **<<**. Comparison expressions must be parenthesized to avoid a compile error:

```
cout << "p2 == pint = " << boolalpha << (p2 == pint) << endl;
cout << "p2 > pint = " << boolalpha << (p2 > pint) << endl;
```

7. The complete program looks like this:

```
#include <iostream>
using namespace std;

int main()
{
    int numbers[5] {0, 100, 200, 300, 400};
    int * pint = numbers;
    int * p2 = & numbers[3];

    cout << "pint = " << pint << ", pint+1 = " << pint + 1
```

```
                    << ", sizeof(int) = " << sizeof(int) << endl;

        cout << "*(pint+1) = " << * (pint + 1)
             << ", pint[1] = " << pint[1] << endl;

        cout << "*(pint+4) = " << * (pint + 4)
             << ", pint[4] = " << pint[4] << endl;

        cout << "p2 - pint = " << p2 - pint << endl;
        cout << "p2 == pint = " << boolalpha << (p2 == pint) << endl;
        cout << "p2 > pint = " << boolalpha << (p2 > pint) << endl;
        return 0;
    }
```

8. Compile and run the program. The output of the program is as follows; note that the particular hexadecimal addresses may differ in another run of the program:

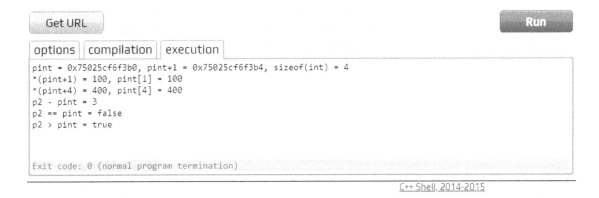

Figure 5.6: Output of program in exercise 29

This is the output we expected: **a[1]** == ***(pint + 1)** and **a[4]** == ***(pint + 4)**. Pointers behave just like arrays in C++, and pointer subtraction works as expected: **p2 - pint** == **3**. Finally, pointers can be compared using the six comparison operators as expected.

Exercise 30: Incrementing Pointers

This exercise puts together the previous exercises to do some useful work—that is, stepping a pointer through an array and printing each array element.

> **Note**
>
> The complete code for this exercise can be found here: https://packt.live/2CZzUHs.

Here are the steps to complete the exercise:

1. Enter the skeleton **main()** function again:

```
#include <iostream>
using namespace std;

int main()
{
    return 0;
}
```

2. Following the opening curly brace of **main()**, declare an array of five **int**s called **a** and initialize it. Declare an **int** pointer called **p**. The code looks like this:

```
int a[5]{ 10, 20, 30, 40, 50 };
int* p;
```

3. Now enter a **for** loop to iterate through each element of **a** by starting **p** at the first element of **a**, which in C++ is **a[0]**. Increment **p** so that it points to each entry in turn. Stop when **p** falls off the end of **a**, which is **a[5]**. Inside the loop, output each entry. Notice in the output expression that there is a space (" ") but no **endl** at the end, so these printed values appear on the same line. Don't forget to output an **endl** at the end of the loop. The code looks like this:

```
for (p = &a[0]; p < &a[5]; p = p + 1)
{
    cout << *p << " ";
}
cout << endl;
```

4. The complete program looks like this:

```
#include <iostream>
using namespace std;

int main()
{
    int a[5]{ 10, 20, 30, 40, 50 };
    int* p;
    for (p = &a[0]; p < &a[5]; p = p + 1)
    {
        cout << *p << " ";
```

```
        }
        cout << endl;
        return 0;
    }
```

5. Compile and run the program. Here is its output:

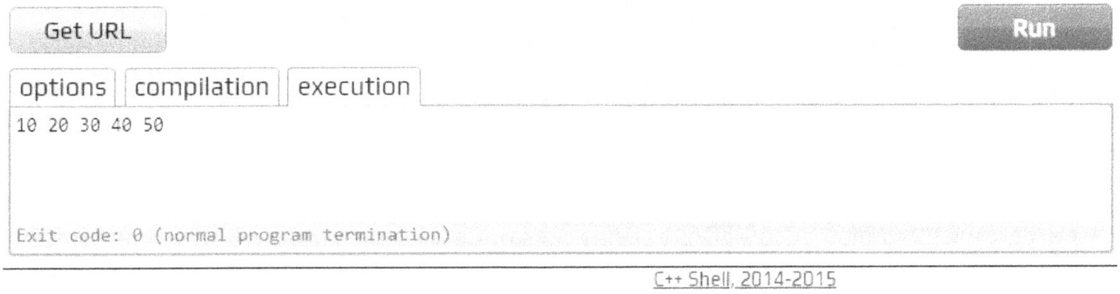

```
Get URL                                                        Run

options   compilation   execution
10 20 30 40 50



Exit code: 0 (normal program termination)
```

C++ Shell, 2014-2015

Figure 5.7: Output of the program in exercise 30

Refining the for Loop

This program could be better. Right now, it is untidy in several ways. The program relies on knowing that the array, **a**, is five items long. It's dangerous to rely on numeric constants because, if more elements are later added to array **a**, the developer must remember to change the constants everywhere they occur, and C++ offers no help there. The first thing to change is to let the size of **a** be set by its initializer. The declaration `int a[]{ 10, 20, 30, 40, 50 };` says to let the initializer of **a** declare its size.

The second thing to change is the **for** loop. The first element of **a** can be written as `&a[0]`, but it can also just be written as **a**, which looks simpler:

```
for (p = a; p < &a[5]; p = p + 1)
```

The end of the loop comes when **p** falls off the end of array **a**. There is a way to build this pointer expression without knowing the size of **a**. The expression `sizeof(a)/sizeof(a[0])` means take the size of **a** in bytes and divide by the size of one element of **a**. The result is the number of elements in **a**. So, the termination condition is a pointer expression that points to the first byte past the end of **a**. That looks like this:

```
for (p = a; p < a + sizeof(a)/sizeof(a[0]); p = p + 1)
```

The last thing to change is the **for** loop step expression. This was originally written as `p = p + 1`, but there is another operator in C++ that does the same thing. It's called the prefix increment operator, **++**. The prefix increment operator adds one to the pointer's value, saves the result in the pointer variable, and then produces the incremented pointer.

Additionally, there is a postfix ++ increment operator (**p++**), which works a little differently. The postfix increment operator first takes note of the pointer's value before incrementing it, adds one to the pointer and saves that result into the pointer variable, and then produces the saved value before incrementing it.

There are prefix and postfix -- decrement operators, which work like their ++ cousins, except that they subtract one from the pointer. So, the **for** statement finally looks like this:

```
for (p = a; p < a + sizeof(a)/sizeof(a[0]); ++p)
```

This looks like the kind of **for** loop you will encounter in commercial C++ code.

So, why is there a special ++ operator in C++? Well, it's because an obsolete minicomputer called the PDP-11 could do pre- and post-increment and decrement in a single instruction. Most modern processors, influenced by the existence of C and C++, also have instructions that do pre- and post-increment and decrement. And now, you can see how C++ got its name. It's a pun, the language that results from adding a minimal amount to C.

6. The complete updated program is as follows. Run the program and verify for yourself that it produces the same output as the previous version:

```
#include <iostream>
using namespace std;

int main()
{
    int a[]{ 10, 20, 30, 40, 50 };
    int* p;
    for (p = a; p < a + sizeof(a)/sizeof(a[0]); ++p)
    {
        cout << *p << " ";
    }
    cout << endl;
    return 0;
}
```

The idiom of incrementing a pointer through the elements of an array is one that recurs frequently in C++. There are many ways that this **for** loop could be written—some using pointers and some not.

Pointers to Pointers

A pointer can refer to another pointer. If **char* p;** is a pointer to **char**, then **char** q = &p;** is a pointer to a pointer to **char**. Where could this exotic type possibly be useful? When dealing with arrays of pointers, of course.

Exercise 31: Pointers to Pointers

In this exercise, you will manipulate an array of pointers by using a pointer to a pointer.

> **Note**
>
> The complete code for this exercise can be found here: https://packt.live/2O6jG5t.

Here are the steps to complete the exercise:

1. Type in the skeleton **main()** function:

    ```
    #include <iostream>
    using namespace std;

    int main()
    {
        return 0;
    }
    ```

2. Following the opening curly brace of **main()**, declare an array alphabet of literal character strings. **alphabet** is an array of pointers to **const char**:

    ```
    char* alphabet[26]
    {
        "alpha",
        "bravo",
        "charlie",
        "delta",
        "echo",
        "foxtrot"
    };
    ```

    The array alphabet is declared as having **26** entries, presumably corresponding to the 26 spoken words that form the NATO radio alphabet. However, only the first six array entries are initialized; the compiler sets the remaining 20 entries to **nullptr**. Making the last entry in an array of pointers **nullptr** is another way to provide a loop termination condition.

3. Next, enter a **for** loop to print the entries of **alphabet** until the program comes to one that is equal to **nullptr**:

```
for (char **p = alphabet; *p != nullptr; ++p)
{
    cout << *p << " ";
}
cout << endl;
```

The induction variable **p** is of type pointer to pointer to **char**. Now, **p** is initially set to **alphabet** (an array of pointers to **char**) which the compiler converts to a pointer to pointer to **char**. The **for** loop's continuation condition is if ***p** is not equal to **nullptr**. At the end of each iteration, the pointer **p** is incremented. Inside the **for** loop we print ***p**, which is a pointer to char, followed by a space.

By printing the entries with no trailing **endl**, they are all printed on the same line. The C++ output stream attempts to print a pointer to **char** as though it was a null-terminated string. Like in the previous exercise, output **endl** after the loop so that the line actually goes to the output.

4. The complete program looks like this:

```
#include <iostream>
using namespace std;

int main()
{
    char* alphabet[26]
    {
        "alpha",
        "bravo",
        "charlie",
        "delta",
        "echo",
        "foxtrot"
    };
    for (char **p = alphabet; *p != nullptr; ++p)
    {
        cout << *p << " ";
    }
    cout << endl;
    return 0;
}
```

5. Compile and run the program. The output of this program is as follows:

```
$g++ -o main *.cpp
main.cpp: In function 'int main()':
main.cpp:13:3: warning: ISO C++ forbids converting a string constant to 'char*' [-Wwrite-strings]
   };
   ^
main.cpp:13:3: warning: ISO C++ forbids converting a string constant to 'char*' [-Wwrite-strings]
main.cpp:13:3: warning: ISO C++ forbids converting a string constant to 'char*' [-Wwrite-strings]
main.cpp:13:3: warning: ISO C++ forbids converting a string constant to 'char*' [-Wwrite-strings]
main.cpp:13:3: warning: ISO C++ forbids converting a string constant to 'char*' [-Wwrite-strings]
main.cpp:13:3: warning: ISO C++ forbids converting a string constant to 'char*' [-Wwrite-strings]
$main
alpha bravo charlie delta echo foxtrot
```

Figure 5.8: Printing the first six entries of the array alphabet

In addition to the output, the compiler prints half a dozen lines of warning messages, each saying something to the effect of *warning: ISO C++ forbids converting a string constant to 'char*'*, or something similar. Some online compilers print these error messages in the same window as the output. For others, you must click on the compilation button to view the error messages. To make these error messages go away, change the type of **alphabet** to **char const* alphabet[26]**, and change the type of **p**, the **for** loop induction variable, to **char const** p;**. Compile and run the changed program and notice that the warning messages have gone away.

In C++, a literal string is of type pointer to **const char**. An array of literal strings, therefore, has type pointer to pointer to **const char**.

The declarator **const char** means that the program may not change the pointed-to characters. In C, literal strings were of type pointer to **char**. C++ was originally that way as well, but C++ was updated to make these strings pointers to **const char** instead. The topic of const-ness is an important one in C++, but the topic is too wide in scope to talk about in this book.

> **Note**
>
> Eliminating warning messages from your code is the mark of a professional developer.

References

A reference is a second kind of variable that holds the address of another variable. That is, the reference *points to* another variable. Unlike pointers, which can refer to a valid variable, an invalid memory location, or **nullptr**, a reference must be initialized to point to a variable when declared.

One difference between references and pointers is that a reference cannot be updated; once it is declared, it always points to the same variable. This means that a reference can't be incremented to step through an array the same way that a pointer can.

A second difference is that references are implicitly dereferenced in use. Arithmetic and relational operators applied to references affect the pointed-to variable. If `ir` is an `int` reference, then the statement `ir = ir - 10;` subtracts 10 from the referenced `int`. Mathematical expressions involving references, therefore, have a very natural appearance. A developer can use references to efficiently point to a variable with a numeric meaning, such as a complex number or matrix, and expressions such as `a = b * c;` have their expected meaning.

By contrast, arithmetic and relational operations on pointers refer to the machine addresses that are the values of the pointers themselves, not to the pointed-to variables. If numeric types such as matrices are pointed to by pointers, the resulting mathematical expressions require explicit dereference operators, so that they might look like `*a = *b * *c;` which clever students may notice contains many possibilities for misunderstanding.

In the next exercise, we will practice declaring and using references.

Exercise 32: References

This exercise involves a small program that creates some references to illustrate their syntax and demonstrate their properties.

> **Note**
>
> The complete code for this exercise can be found here: https://packt.live/33aollH.

Here are the steps to complete:

1. Type the skeleton `main()` function:

```
#include <iostream>
using namespace std;

int main()
{
    return 0;
}
```

2. Following the opening curly brace of **main()**, declare an **int** variable called **i**, and initialize it to **10**. Declare an **int** reference, **ir**, and initialize it to point to **i**. References are declared with the type name and **&** and are initialized to a variable, for example, **int& ir = i;** or **int& ir {i};**:

```
int i = 10;
int& ir = i;
```

3. Now assign **i + 10** to **i**, and **ir * 10** to **ir**. Notice that the arithmetic expression looks the same using **int**s as it does using **int** references:

```
i = i + 10;
ir = ir * 10;
```

4. Output the value of **i** to demonstrate that when the program changed **ir**, it really changed what was in **i** (hint: **(10 + 10) * 10 = 200**):

```
cout << "i = " << i << endl;
```

5. Declare a pointer called **ip** and initialize it to the address of **ir**. The address-of operator **&** affects the variable that **ir** points to, so **ip** now points to **i**. Dereference **ip** to change the value of the variable that **ip** points to **33**:

```
int* ip = &ir;
*ip = 33;
```

6. Now output **i**, ***ip**, and **ir** to demonstrate that changing ***ip** really changed **i**, and **ir** has also changed:

```
cout << "i = " << i << ", *ip = " << *ip
    << ", ir = " << ir << endl;
```

7. The complete program looks like this:

```
#include <iostream>
using namespace std;

int main()
{
    int i = 10;
    int & ir = i;
    i = i + 10;
    ir = ir * 10;
    cout << "i = " << i << endl;
    int *ip = & ir;
```

```
    *ip = 33;
    cout << "i = " << i << ", *ip = " << * ip
        << ", ir = " << ir << endl;
    return 0;
}
```

8. Compile and run the program. The output of the program looks like this:

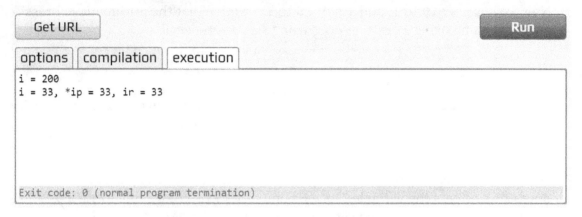

Figure 5.9: Output of program in exercise 32

The output shows that both references and pointers are types that point to another variable. When the program modifies references or dereferenced pointers, it modifies the pointed-to variable.

Exercise 33: Bad References

A reference always points to a variable when declared, and a valid reference always points to a variable. Unfortunately, a reference can become invalid. This exercise introduces you to one of the dark alleys of C++, where references can be null or invalid.

> **Note**
>
> The complete code for this exercise can be found here: https://packt.live/2KHdpes.

Here are the steps to complete the exercise:

1. Enter the following very short program:

```
int main()
{
    char* p = nullptr;
    char& r = *p;
```

```
    r = '!';
    return 0;
}
```

2. Run the program. If you are using an online compiler, use one such as **coliru**, which captures error messages output from the operating system:

```
bash: line 7: 14177 Segmentation fault        (core dumped) ./a.out
```

```
g++ -std=c++17 -O2 -Wall -pedantic -pthread main.cpp && ./a.out
```

Figure 5.10: Dereferencing nullptr causes the operating system to stop the program

Notice that it crashes with an error from the operating system. It's pretty clear what happened. The pointer points to **nullptr**. The reference is set to point to **nullptr**. Dereferencing **nullptr** causes the operating system to stop the program. This is called a null reference. C++ will smile at you when you compile it, and only at runtime will you discover your fatal mistake. Other programming languages might check each reference for **nullptr** before dereferencing it, but this would slow the execution down, and C++ is about performance. C++ will permit you to write code that crashes because it assumes you know what you are doing.

3. Examine the following function:

```
int& invalid_ref()
{
    int a = 10;
    return a;
}
```

This function returns a reference to a local variable on the function call stack. The variable goes out of scope and becomes invalid when the function returns, producing an invalid reference. The next function called will almost certainly overwrite the storage formerly occupied by **a**. The program won't necessarily crash, but it won't reliably produce a correct answer either.

Some pundits will tell you that references are safer than pointers. It would be smart to ignore this advice. It's true that a valid reference always points to a variable, but C++ allows the developer to create invalid references and null references. The difference between pointers and references should be considered a difference in style rather than safety.

Pointers and References as Function Arguments

When an expression is an argument to a function call, the value of the expression is copied into the function's local storage on the function call stack. The cost of copying is not a problem when the expression is a fundamental type such as **int** or **float**, but copying can consume significant amounts of time when the argument is a struct or class instance with many members. These objects may contain large arrays, or linked data structures (these are discussed in the next section).

Instead of passing a struct or class instance directly to a function, the program can pass a reference or pointer to the instance into the function. This allows large data structures to be passed efficiently. Pointers and references are equally efficient, so the choice of which to use comes down to style.

A pointer passed into a function should be checked for **nullptr**. Using a reference as a function argument documents that the programmer thinks the reference must be valid and is not going to be checked inside the function.

Because a pointer can be **nullptr**, it is useful when an argument is optional. That is, when an argument may or may not be required to compute the function. A value must always be provided for a reference argument.

A pointer argument is appropriate when an argument points to an array.

Because the storage pointed to by a pointer or reference comes from outside the function, a pointer or reference argument is also useful when a program wants to pass information out of a function, or when the purpose of the function is to modify a data structure.

Exercise 34: Pointers as Function Arguments

This program contains a function that copies an array of **char** into another array. Since the function's arguments are arrays, pointers are more appropriate than references for the function's formal arguments.

> **Note**
>
> The complete code for this exercise can be found here: https://packt.live/2D3sYcs.

Here are the steps to complete the exercise:

1. Enter the skeleton **main()** function:

    ```
    #include <iostream>
    using namespace std;

    int main()
    {
        return 0;
    }
    ```

2. Following **using namespace std;** enter the skeleton of the **copychars()** function. **copychars()** takes two **char** pointers, one to copy from and another to copy into. It also takes an **int count** of characters to copy:

    ```
    void copychars(char* from, char* to, int count)
    {
    }
    ```

3. Pointers should be compared to **nullptr** unless the developer is absolutely sure a caller has already checked them. The code for that should go right after the opening brace of **copychars()**. It looks like this:

    ```
    if (from == nullptr || to == nullptr)
        return;
    ```

4. Now enter the main copy loop, that copies **count** characters:

    ```
    while (count-- > 0)
    {
        *to++ = *from++;
    }
    ```

    Each character is copied from the location pointed to by **from** into the location pointed to by **to**. The heart of the loop is the statement ***to++ = *from++;** which copies one character and increments the two pointers so they are ready to copy the next character. This is a very common idiom in C++, so it's worth looking at in detail. The two **++** operators are called post-increment operators. They use the variable they will increment, and then increment it later as a side effect. You can imagine that this statement expands into the compound statement **{ *to = *from; to = to + 1; from = from + 1; }**. The compiler knows how to generate very efficient code for this idiom. The operator precedence works out so you don't have to put parentheses around anything to make this statement work.

Now type in the contents of the **main()** function. First, declare an array called **string[]** and initialize it to **"uvwxyz"**. When you compile this, you will notice that there are no messages about **string[]** not being **const char**. That's because the literal character string **"uvwxyz"** is copied into **string[]** when **string[]** is initialized. Notice how the program doesn't specify a size for array **string[]**. The C++ compiler knows that it is initialized with seven characters—seven, because a null character, **'\0'**, is appended to the end of the literal string to mark its end:

```
char string[] { "uvwxyz" };
```

5. Declare an array of **10** chars called **buffer[]**. This is the array that the program will copy into. Now the program can call **copychars()**, with **string[]** in the **from** argument position, and **buffer[]** in the **to** argument. **count** is set to **7**:

```
char buffer[10];
copychars (string, buffer, 7);
```

6. Finally, output **buffer[]** to prove that **string[]** was moved into **buffer[]**:

```
cout << buffer << endl;
```

7. The complete program looks like this:

```
#include <iostream>
using namespace std;

void copychars(char* from, char* to, int count)
{
    if (from == nullptr || to == nullptr)
        return;

    while (count-- > 0)
    {
        *to++ = *from++;
    }
}

int main()
{
    char string[] { "uvwxyz" };
    char buffer[10];
    copychars (string, buffer, 7);
    cout << buffer << endl;
    return 0;
}
```

8. Compile and run the program if you haven't already. The program output is as follows:

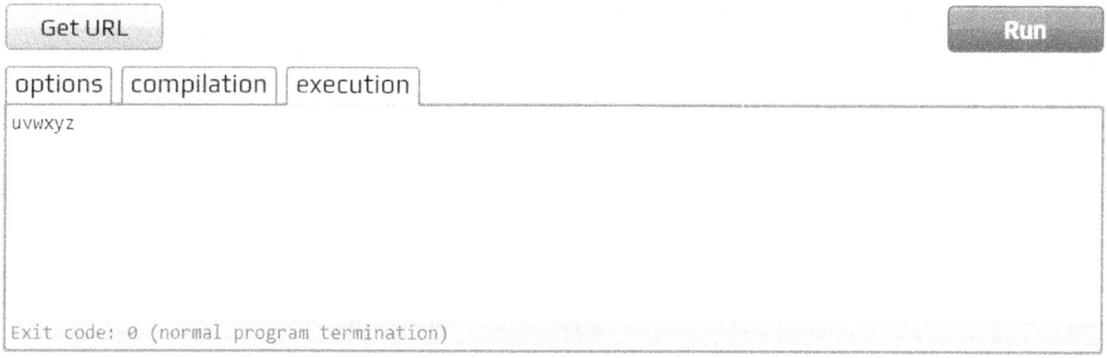

Figure 5.11: Output of the program in exercise 34

This proves that the characters were copied to the output buffer as expected.

> **Note**
>
> Buffer-copying functions are almost always fraught with security risks. A function that copies characters until it gets to the null termination of the **from** buffer risks copying more characters than the **to** buffer is declared to hold. This causes accidental overwriting of other variables. The standard library **strcpy()** function has this flaw. Specifying the length mitigates this risk only slightly, assuming the calling program has checked that the buffer **to** has sufficient space. A fully safe function would specify the maximum size of the buffer **to** and use either the null termination or yet another **count** to specify how many characters to copy.

Pointers to Classes or Structs

A member of a class or struct is selected using the . member access or dot operator–for example, **instance.membername**. When a pointer points to an instance, the pointer must first be dereferenced using the * operator. Because of operator precedence and associativity rules, this expression must be parenthesized–for example, **(*pinstance).membername**. The developers of C++ provided a streamlined notation.

pinstance->membername dereferences the pointer and then selects the named member.

Exercise 35: Pointers to Class Instance

In this exercise, the program will output the contents of an array of struct instances. Structs and classes are similar in C++. All the members of a struct are public, so the struct takes fewer lines to write. In production code, it is far more likely that a class would be used, as will be described in another chapter.

> **Note**
>
> The complete code for this exercise can be found here: https://packt.live/2Xw60Eb.

Here are the steps to complete the exercise:

1. Enter the skeleton **main()** function. It has the familiar form below:

```
#include <iostream>
using namespace std;

int main()
{
    return 0;
}
```

2. Enter **struct mydata**. It has a **char const*** field called **name_** and an **int** field called **hero_**. **mydata** is a struct, so the fields are automatically declared public and are, therefore, accessible from outside the struct. Note that the member names have a trailing underscore. We'll talk about that in a minute. Struct **mydata** looks like this:

```
struct mydata
{
    char const* name_;
    bool hero_;
};
```

3. Next, create an array of **mydata** instances called **cast**, and initialize it as shown below. You may recognize the entries in the array as the names of some comic book super heroes. Here, the **hero_** member is set to **true** if the character is a hero, and to **false** if the character is a villain. The array is not given an explicit size so the number of initializers sets its size:

```
mydata heroes[]
{
    { "Spider Man", true },
    { "The Joker", false },
    { "Doctor Octopus", false },
    { "Thor", true },
    { "Batman", true },
    { "Loki", false }
};
```

4. Next, type in the **printdata()** function. This function prints out a **mydata** instance:

```
void printdata(mydata * p)
{
    cout << "Hello. I am " << ( * p).name_ << ". ";
    if (p - > hero_)
        cout << "I am a hero." << endl;
    else
        cout << "I am a villain." << endl;
}
```

5. Inside **main()**, output the size of an instance of struct **mydata**, followed by the size of a pointer to **mydata**. The instance is bigger and thus more expensive to copy into functions as an argument than is the pointer. In production code, **mydata** might be hundreds or thousands of bytes long or have a constructor that performs expensive operations. Passing a pointer instead of copying the instance is therefore more efficient:

```
cout << sizeof(mydata) << " " << sizeof(mydata*) << endl;
```

6. Next, enter a **for** loop that prints out the **mydata** instances in the **heroes[]** array. You have seen code like this before: start at the first instance, step to each next instance, and terminate when you get past the end. And yes, this code has the same issue with using a hardwired constant to describe the size of the array:

```
for (mydata* p = heroes; p < heroes + 6; ++p)
{
    printdata(p);
}
```

7. The complete program looks like this:

```cpp
#include <iostream>
using namespace std;

struct mydata
{
    char const * name_;
    bool hero_;
};
mydata heroes[]
{
    {"Spider Man", true},
    {"The Joker", false},
    {"Doctor Octopus", false},
    {"Thor", true},
    {"Batman", true},
    {"Loki", false}
};

void printdata(mydata * p)
{
    cout << "Hello. I am " << ( * p).name_ << ". ";
    if (p - > hero_)
        cout << "I am a hero." << endl;
    else
        cout << "I am a villain." << endl;
}

int main()
{
    cout << sizeof(mydata) << " " << sizeof(mydata * ) << endl;
    for (mydata * p = heroes; p < heroes + 6; ++p) \
    {
        printdata(p);
    }
    return 0;
}
```

8. Compile and run the program. Here is the output of the program:

Figure 5.12: Output of the program in exercise 35

We can fix the hardcoded size problem. We did it once before using **sizeof(array) / sizeof(array[0])**. However, there's another way–using the **std::end()** function. **std::end()** does essentially the same thing as the **sizeof** trick, but it has to use heavy template magic to copy the whole array declaration into the function and keep it from decaying into a pointer. Here's what the **for** statement looks like with **std::end()**:

```
for (mydata* p = heroes; p < std::end(heroes); ++p)
```

9. **std::end()** works for arrays and pointers, and it also works for iterators that step through standard library container classes, which you will learn more about in *Chapter 10, Advanced Object-Oriented Principles*. There's another function, **std::begin()**, that produces a pointer to the beginning of the array (or an iterator to the beginning of a standard library container).

There is one more part to perfecting your **for** loops. **std::begin()** returns a pointer or iterator. However, the **for** statement declares a pointer. That is not completely general, but modern C++ offers a fix. It's called **auto**.

Now, **auto** declares a variable when its type is obvious in context, such as when it is the target of an assignment statement. **auto** is just perfect for declaring **for** loop induction variables. In our program, we've included **namespace std**, so we don't need to use the **std::** prefix. With all of these changes, our **for** statement looks very streamlined:

```
for (auto p = begin(heroes); p < end(heroes); ++p)
```

> **Note**
>
> A pointer member such as **mydata::name_** is risky to use unless it is initialized by a literal constant. The storage that **name_** points to must remain valid until the class instance goes out of scope, or the pointer will point to invalid memory and the program will misbehave.

We've had some practice dereferencing pointers to class instances now, and we've learned how to build beautiful and general **for** loops. The next exercise is about using references as function arguments.

References as Function Arguments

References contain a pointer to data, just like pointers do. However, as mentioned earlier, operators applied to a reference are applied to the pointed-to object. To select a member of a struct or class pointed to by a reference, use the . member access, or dot operator. The dot operator applies to the pointed-to variable; that is, the class instance. Using . with a reference generates the same code as if you had used **->** with a pointer.

Another difference between references and pointers is that you can initialize a reference with a variable. With pointers, you must explicitly take the address of the variable, converting it into a pointer, in order to assign it to the pointer. The same convention applies to function arguments. What happens under the hood is that the formal argument of type reference to instance is initialized to point to the actual argument instance.

There is a special form of the **for** loop that is suitable for iterating through an array when a program needs to have a reference to each element of the array. It is called a range-based **for** loop. The syntax looks like this: **for (mydata& ref : arr)**. The compiler recognizes the variable **arr** as an array and generates code to step through each element of the array. Each element, in turn, is assigned to **ref**. Remember we said that a reference variable can't be modified once it is set, but this reference variable is newly created each time through the loop.

A further refinement of this **for** loop is the use of the **auto** keyword, as in **for (auto& ref : arr)**. The **auto** keyword asks the compiler to deduce the type of **ref** by looking at the element type of **arr**. The **&** operator tells the **for** loop that each time through the loop it should initialize a reference to the array element rather than copying the array element into an instance variable.

Exercise 36: References as Function Arguments

This program is quite similar to the program in the previous exercise except it uses references instead of pointers. It prints an array of class instances.

> **Note**
>
> The complete code for this exercise can be found here: https://packt.live/2QBoj9l.

Here are the steps to complete the exercise:

1. Type the skeleton **main()** function you have seen many times before:

```
#include <iostream>
using namespace std;

int main()
{
    return 0;
}
```

2. Next, enter the definition of struct **mydata**. This example is **const-correct** and does not generate any warning messages from the compiler, like the previous exercise did:

```
struct mydata
{
    char const* name_;
    bool darkside_;
    mydata (char const* name, bool dark)
    {
        name_ = name; darkside_ = dark;
    }
}
```

Notice that the **name** argument of the constructor has type **char const***, and so does the **name_** member.

Why do the member variables of struct **mydata** have an underscore appended to their name?

It's to make the constructor on *line 8* work. If the constructor had an argument called **name**, and the struct had a member called **name**, you wouldn't be able to set that member inside the constructor because its name would be hidden by the argument's name. Most C++ coding standards call for class fields to have names with a specific format. The trailing underscore is one such form that is used in the C++ standard document. There are many others.

3. Initialize an array cast of three **mydata** instances:

```
mydata cast[3]
{
    { "Darth Vader", true },
    { "Luke Skywalker", false },
    { "Han Solo", false }
};
```

4. Type in the **printname()** function. It takes a reference to an instance of **mydata** as its argument. When using a reference to a struct or class instance, use the dot . member access operator to access a member. The dot operator applies to the referenced object, not to the reference:

```
void printname(mydata& data)
{
    cout << "Hello. I am " << data.name_ << endl;
    if (data.darkside_)
        cout << "I was seduced by the dark side" << endl;
}
```

5. Now enter the contents of function **main()**:

```
for (mydata& data : cast)
{
    printname(data);
}
```

Because the program uses references, the range-based version of the **for** loop can be used. It consists of a declaration for the induction variable, which looks like **mydata& data** in this example, followed by a colon, and then something that can produce a range of data. In this case, an array produces a range of data.

6. The complete program looks like this:

```
#include <iostream>
using namespace std;

struct mydata
{
    char const* name_;
    bool darkside_;
    mydata (char const* name, bool dark)
    {
        name_ = name; darkside_ = dark;
    }
}
```

```cpp
};
mydata cast[3]
{
    { "Darth Vader", true },
    { "Luke Skywalker", false },
    { "Han Solo", false }
};

void printname(mydata& data)
{
    cout << "Hello. I am " << data.name_ << endl;
    if (data.darkside_)
        cout << "I was seduced by the dark side" << endl;
}

int main()
{
    for (mydata& data : cast)
    {
        printname(data);
    }
    return 0;
}
```

7. Compile and run the program. Here is its output:

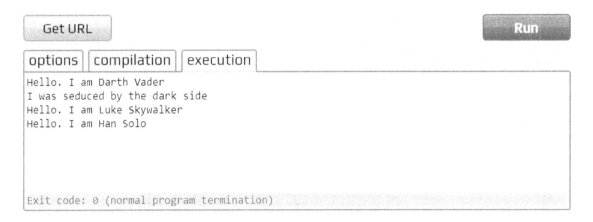

Figure 5.13: The output of the program in exercise 36

8. Edit the program to use **auto** in the **for** loop so that it says **for (auto& data : cast)**. Compile and run the program to see how it works.

9. Remove the **&** in the **for** loop so that it says **for (auto data : cast)**. Compile and run the program. **auto data** works, too, but it's less efficient because it copies elements of the array into **data**, which is of type **mydata**, rather than **mydata&**. If these elements have a lot of data in them, that's a lot of copying.

Activity 5: Using Pointers and References to Manipulate an Array of Strings

This is the summative activity for this chapter on pointers and references. In this activity, you will be asked to use both pointers and references to write a function that manipulates an array of strings, and to provide tests to ensure that the code works correctly. The function is like thousands of similar functions written every year by developers around the world.

The function is called **printarray()**. It takes two pointers as arguments into an array of null-terminated literal strings. One pointer points to the first entry of the array that **printarray()** will print, and the other points to one after the last entry to be printed. **printarray()** also takes as an argument a reference to **int** that is set by **printarray()** to a count of those strings that are not **nullptr**. Also, **printarray()** outputs strings that are not **nullptr** to the console, one string per line. **printarray()** returns 1 if it runs successfully, and 0 if it detects a problem with the arguments. The array has a maximum size of 26 elements.

> **Note**
>
> The complete code for this activity can be found here: https://packt.live/2XxhSWt.

The main program must test the function with various arguments, including invalid arguments.

Here are the steps to complete the activity:

1. Enter a skeleton **main()** function.

   Above **main()**, create an array of strings. The code will be easier to debug if you use strings that are in alphabetical order, such as **"alpha"**, **"bravo"**, **"charlie"** and so on, or **"alphs"**, **"bets"**, **"gamms"**, and so on.

2. Enter a skeleton of the **printarray()** function. Since we are printing an array of literal strings, the pointers are of the **char const**** type. The **count** argument is an **int** reference. Define the return type, which is specified as **int** in the assignment.

3. Inside **printarray()**, enter code to detect errors in the arguments to **printarray()**.

4. Clear **count**.

5. Enter a loop to control printing.

6. Inside **main()**, write some tests. The tests should check whether the returned value is correct for the arguments. You can also look at the count of arguments printed.

> **Note**
>
> The solution to this activity can be found on page 526.

Summary

Pointers and references are two C++ types that point to other variables. They are useful in overlapping situations, and the choice between pointers and references is mostly one of style. Pointers and references are examples of C++ features that are "unsafe," in the sense that they must be used knowledgeably to prevent bugs that cause programs to crash. Among the most important uses introduced so far for pointers and references are iterating through arrays and passing large arrays or class instances into functions efficiently.

The next chapter explores another very important use for pointers—that is, referring to dynamic variables. Dynamic variables don't have a name and are only known by a pointer that refers to them. **Dynamic variables** allow C++ programs to access the vast amount of memory in modern computers, and to build up complex containers.

Dynamic Variables

Overview

This chapter introduces dynamic variables—that is, variables that can be created when needed and can hold an arbitrarily large amount of data, limited only by the amount of memory available. By the end of this chapter, you will be able to describe why dynamic variables are important; create dynamic variables and arrays; describe the difference between the stack and the heap; refer to dynamic variables and arrays through pointers; delete dynamic variables and arrays and create linked data structures using pointers.

Introduction

All the basic kinds of variables, arrays, and structs introduced so far have a fixed size that is known at compile time. Fixed-size variables have many advantages; they can be laid end to end to use memory efficiently. Compiled machine code can access fixed-size variables very quickly, but fixed-size variables have a weakness. There is no way to hold an arbitrarily large data structure in fixed-sized variables. The developer must anticipate the largest problem a program will be asked to solve. Memory is wasted when a program solves a smaller problem, and a program will fail when it tries to exceed its capacity.

Imagine, for example, that a developer wants to store all the words in a book but can only make use of fixed-size variables. They could declare a two-dimensional array of **char** to hold the words, but how big should the array be?

The average book has between 75,000 and 100,000 words. The developer could pick the worst-case size of 100,000 words which would accommodate many, but perhaps not all, books. The average English word is about 8 characters long, but the longest word is much longer. The developer would have to pick the worst-case size for the words too – 20 characters, for example. The declaration for the array would therefore be as follows:

```
char book[100000][20];
```

The size of this array is 2 million bytes, which is modest by modern standards of comparison. But no matter how big you make the array, a book might not fit, either because it has long words or because it has too many words. The developer might invent more elaborate data structures than a plain array, but they would all suffer from one or both of these problems. The computer running the program might have gigabytes of available memory, but the program has no way to make use of it.

Fortunately, C++ offers a solution to this problem called **dynamic variables**.

Dynamic Variables

Global variables are laid out end to end in a single block of memory allocated when the program starts up. There is thus no runtime cost to declare a global variable, but all global variables continue to take up storage for the entire life of the program, even if they are not used.

Variables that are local to functions or other block scopes delimited by { and } are laid out end to end on top of a stack of local variables. The cost of allocating memory for local variables is negligible. When execution leaves the block, the storage for the local variables in that block is popped off the top of the stack. This storage is efficiently reused the next time execution enters a block scope.

Dynamic variables are constructed by an executable statement rather than being declared like other kinds of variables. The storage for each dynamic variable is allocated separately from a region of memory called the heap. Dynamic variables are not automatically destroyed when execution exits a block scope delimited by { and } or at the end of the program. Instead, each dynamic variable is explicitly deleted by another executable statement, and its storage is returned separately to the heap.

The heap is a collection of unused memory blocks. When the program requests a new dynamic variable, the C++ runtime system searches the heap for an appropriately sized block of memory. The C++ runtime system may return an available block from the heap, may break a larger memory block into two pieces and return one of them, or may request a new memory block from the operating system. When a program deletes a dynamic variable, the dynamic variable's storage is returned to the heap's collection of available memory blocks so that the storage can be reused for another dynamic variable.

There is no fixed limit to the number or size of dynamic variables that can be created. However, that doesn't mean the program can create an infinite number of dynamic variables. It just means that the computer, the operating system, and the pattern of previous requests all contribute to whether a particular request can be satisfied.

C++ throws an exception when a request to create a dynamic variable cannot be satisfied. Exceptions are covered in *Chapter 13*, *Exception Handling in C++*, of this book.

The power of dynamic variables does not come for free. Creating and deleting dynamic variables has a significant runtime cost. In fact, creating and deleting dynamic variables is by far the most expensive operation built into C++. This is due to the need to scan the heap of available memory blocks for an appropriately sized block.

A dynamic variable is created using a **new**-expression. The **new**-expression takes a type as its operand and returns a pointer to an instance of the named type. A dynamic variable is known by this pointer, not by a name like global and local variables. The **new**-expression doesn't just return some random bytes of storage; it constructs the variable into the returned storage, initializing it or calling its constructor depending on the type.

Here are some examples of creating dynamic variables using **new**-expressions:

```
char *p1 = new char;
int *p2 = new int{12345};
someclass *p3 = new someclass("testing", 123);
```

Here, **p1** is assigned a pointer to storage sufficient to hold a **char**. Because no initial value is specified, the **char** is not initialized to any value but contains the random bits that were in the storage when it was allocated to the new dynamic variable. **p2** is assigned a pointer to storage sufficient to hold an **int**. The **int** is initialized to **12345**. **p3** is assigned a pointer to storage sufficient to hold an instance of class **someclass**. The instance is constructed by calling the constructor **someclass::someclass(char const*, int)**. Creating a dynamic **char** or **int** variable is not very useful and is rarely seen in programs. However, programs frequently create dynamic **class** or **struct** instances.

Dynamic variables are deleted using a **delete**-expression. When a dynamic variable is deleted, the C++ runtime system calls its **destructor member function**, if any, and its storage is returned to the heap by the C++ runtime system. A **delete**-expression takes a pointer to an object created by a **new**-expression and returns **void**.

The three dynamic variables created above are deleted by the following three lines of code:

```
delete p1;
delete p2;
delete p3;
```

Although deleting a pointer destroys the pointed-to object and returns the storage it occupied to the C++ runtime system, it does not alter the value of the pointer. The pointer still contains a memory address; only now, this address is not the address of a dynamic variable. If the program tries to access this invalid address, the program is quite likely to crash, but maybe not right away.

Every dynamic variable created with a **new**-expression must be deleted by a matching **delete**-expression or the storage occupied by the variable will become inaccessible to the program; the memory will *leak* from the program. If a program with a memory leak runs for a long time, it can exhaust all the memory on the computer, causing the program, other programs, or the operating system to become unstable and crash.

The next four exercises cover the basics of creating and deleting dynamic variables and arrays.

Exercise 37: Creating and Deleting Dynamic Variables of Basic Types

The first exercise involves a brief program to create and destroy a couple of dynamic variables. It inspects the pointers to those variables and examines the variables' values, just to demonstrate that **new** and **delete** behave as expected.

> **Note**
>
> The complete code for the exercise can be found at https://packt.live/349pGjw.

Here are the steps to perform the exercise:

1. Enter the skeleton **main()** function, as follows:

```
#include <iostream>
using namespace std;

int main()
{
    return 0;
}
```

2. Following the opening curly brace of **main()**, enter the following code to create a dynamic **int** variable. Declare a pointer to **int** called **pint**, and initialize it to **nullptr**. Then, assign a new **int** to **pint**. The **new**-expression retrieves storage from the heap sufficient to hold an **int** and assigns a pointer to that storage into **pint**:

```
int* pint = nullptr;
pint = new int;
```

3. Output **pint** to show that it has a memory address and is no longer **nullptr**:

```
cout << "pint = " << pint << endl;
```

4. Delete **pint**. This returns the storage occupied by the dynamic **int** variable to the heap:

```
delete pint;
```

5. Finally, output **pint** again to demonstrate that it still holds a pointer to the invalid memory location that was formerly a dynamic **int** variable:

```
cout << "pint = " << pint << endl;
```

> **Note**
>
> Since the dynamic variable was not initialized, its value is random. We did not have the program print its value because some operating systems set new and deleted storage to zero to assist in debugging. It is a terrible idea to rely on this behavior, assuming that you don't have to set initial values for dynamic variables. One day, you will use a compiler with different behavior, and your program will malfunction mysteriously.

So far, the program looks like this:

```cpp
#include <iostream>
using namespace std;

int main()
{
    int* pint = nullptr;
    pint = new int;
    cout << "pint = " << pint << endl;
    delete pint;
    cout << "pint = " << pint << endl;
    return 0;
}
```

6. Compile and run the program and observe the result, which looks something like this:

Figure 6.1: Output of the program in exercise 37

The hexadecimal numbers are machine addresses. Your program will probably report a different hexadecimal number, but the two numbers will be the same.

After assigning a new **int** to **pint**, **pint** contains a memory address. This is the address of the dynamic **int** variable. After deleting **pint**, it still contains the same memory address, but this address is no longer valid. This means that it no longer points to a dynamic variable. Using pointers after deleting the variables they point to is a common cause of bugs in C++ programs.

7. Following the code you just added, create a new dynamic **int** variable and assign it to **pint**. **pint** can be reused because it doesn't point to anything valid. Notice that the **new**-expression has an initializer after the **int**, which sets the dynamic **int** variable to **33333**. Output the value of the dynamic **int** variable just to prove it was initialized as expected. Then, delete the dynamic **int** variable. The code looks like this:

```
pint = new int{33333};
cout << "*pint = " << *pint << endl;
delete pint;
```

8. The complete program looks like this.

```
#include <iostream>
using namespace std;

int main()
{
```

```
int * pint = nullptr;
pint = new int;
cout << "pint = " << pint << endl;
delete pint;
cout << "pint = " << pint << endl;

pint = new int {33333};
cout << "*pint = " << * pint << endl;
delete pint;

return 0;
}
```

9. Compile and run the completed program. The program has the following output:

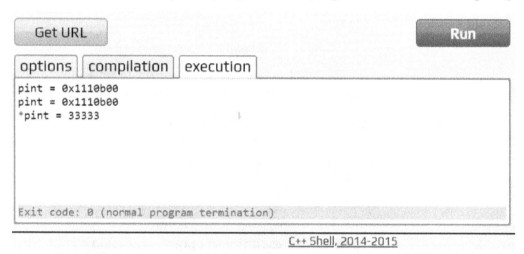

Figure 6.2: Output of the revised program of exercise 37

The dynamic variable pointed to by **pint** has been initialized as expected.

While it is relatively unusual to create dynamic instances of basic data types such as **int** or **char**, it is quite common to create dynamic **class** or **struct** instances. Class instances form the fundamental building blocks of linked data structures such as lists, trees, and graphs.

Exercise 38: Creating and Deleting Dynamic Class Instances

This exercise demonstrates the basics of creating dynamic class instances. Dynamic class instances, like **int** or **char** variables, are created with a **new**-expression. The only difference is that the class instance is initialized with a constructor argument list.

> **Note**
>
> The complete code for the exercise can be found at https://packt.live/35kwCKR.

Here are the steps to perform the exercise:

1. Type in the skeleton of the **main()** function. It looks like this:

    ```
    #include <iostream>
    using namespace std;

    int main()
    {
        return 0;
    }
    ```

2. Following **using namespace std;**, type in a definition of class **noisy**. Now, **noisy** is useful for illustrating the behavior of dynamic variables. Its constructor function, which runs when an instance of **noisy** is created, prints the message **constructing noisy X**, where **X** is the value of the constructor argument. The constructor uses a constructor initializer instead of a simple assignment in the body of the constructor. A constructor initializer list can set the value of any member variable, and may use constructor arguments or expressions containing constructor arguments.

    The destructor, which runs when an instance of **noisy** is deleted, prints the message **destroying noisy X**.

Since **noisy** is a class and not a **struct**, members are private by default, so a **public:** access control declaration is required. Here is the definition of **noisy**:

```
class noisy
{
    int i;
public:
    noisy(int i) : i_(i)
    {
        cout << "constructing noisy " << i << endl;
    }
    ~noisy()
    {
        cout << "destroying noisy " << i_ << endl;
    }
};
```

3. Following the opening curly brace of **main()**, declare an instance of **noisy** called **N**. Pass 1 to the constructor of **N**. When we run the program, N will print a message to demonstrate that local class instances are automatically destroyed on scope exit:

```
noisy N(1);
```

4. Declare a pointer to **noisy** called **p**, and initialize **p** to a new instance of **noisy**, initialized as **noisy(2)**. Then, delete **p**. This demonstrates that dynamic class instances must be destroyed using a **delete**-expression. The code looks like this:

```
noisy* p = new noisy(2);
delete p;
```

5. The complete program looks like this.

```
#include <iostream>
using namespace std;

class noisy
{
    int i_;
public:
    noisy(int i) : i_(i)
    {
        cout << "constructing noisy " << i << endl;
    }
```

```
    ~noisy()
    {
        cout << "destroying noisy " << i_ << endl;
    }
};

int main()
{
    noisy N(1);
    noisy* p = new noisy(2);
    delete p;

    return 0;
}
```

6. Compile and run the program. The output is as follows:

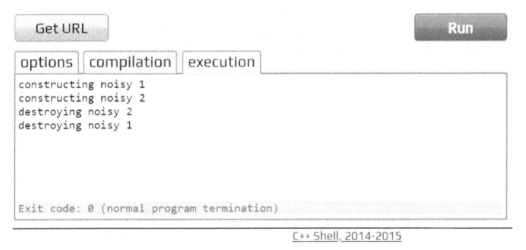

Figure 6.3: Output of the program for exercise 38

What's going on in this program? Well, when execution enters **main()**, an instance of **noisy** is constructed. The **noisy** constructor is called, printing the first message, **constructing noisy 1**.

The next statement creates a dynamic **noisy** instance. The **noisy** instance is constructed, causing the second message, **constructing noisy 2**, to be printed. The next statement deletes **p**, causing the destructor of **noisy 2** to print a message. Execution leaves the scope of **main()**, causing the local variable, **N**, to go out of scope, and triggering a call to the destructor of **noisy 1**. This is what you would expect for a variable with function scope.

Dynamic Arrays

Dynamic arrays of basic types or class or struct instances can be created. They follow the same rules as dynamic variables.

Dynamic arrays are created at runtime using a **new[]**-expression. Like dynamic variables, dynamic arrays are not destroyed when execution exits a scope or at the end of the program. They must be explicitly deleted by a **delete[]**-expression. Like other dynamic variables, a dynamic array is not known by a name but is instead known by a pointer to the dynamic array.

The size of a dynamic array can be specified at runtime by an expression when a new dynamic array is created. The size doesn't have to be a constant like the size in an array declaration. If a dynamic array has two or more dimensions, only the size of the leftmost dimension can be specified at runtime.

Exercise 39: Creating and Deleting Dynamic Arrays of Basic Types

This brief exercise creates and deletes a dynamic array of **char** and fills it with a null-terminated literal string. This is a very common idiom in C programming. In C++, a far more sophisticated string container class called **std::string** is available, with many useful functions for inserting and extracting substrings. There is more to say about **std::string** in *Chapter 12, Containers and Iterators* of this book.

> **Note**
>
> The complete code for the exercise can be found at https://packt.live/35nB0ZO.

Here are the steps to perform the exercise:

Type the skeleton **main()** function into the C++ compiler. The code looks like this:

```cpp
#include <iostream>
using namespace std;

int main()
{
    return 0;
}
```

1. This program will use standard library functions to handle null-terminated character strings, so it must include the **<cstring>** header. Add the following line after the **#include <iostream>** preprocessor directive:

```
#include <cstring>
```

2. In the function **main()**, declare a **char const** pointer called **cp**, and initialize it to any null-terminated string literal. Next, declare a pointer to **char** called **buffer**. Create a new dynamic **char** array sufficient to hold the null-terminated string pointed to by **cp**. The length may be determined by calling the function **strlen()**, from the standard library, which counts the number of characters in a string. Space must also be reserved for the null-termination mark, **\0**, which is not included in the count returned by **strlen()**:

```
char const* cp = "arbitrary null terminated text string";
char* buffer = new char[ strlen(cp)+1 ];
```

3. Copy the string pointed to by **cp** into **buffer**, using the standard library **strcpy()** function. **strcpy()** copies the characters from a null-terminated string source into the destination array until it copies the null-termination at the end of the source string:

```
strcpy(buffer, cp);
```

Some compilers issue a warning when a program uses **strcpy()** because it does nothing to ensure that there is enough space in the destination array to hold the source string. In this case, the code written so far computes the size of the destination array buffer, so there is no risk.

4. Output the contents of **buffer** to prove that the copy was successful:

```
cout << "buffer = " << buffer << endl;
```

5. Delete **buffer** using a **delete[]**-expression. The resulting code looks like this:

```
delete[] buffer;
```

The complete program looks like this:

```cpp
#include <iostream>
#include <cstring>
using namespace std;

int main()
{
    char const* cp = "arbitrary null terminated text string";
    char* buffer = new char[ strlen(cp)+1 ];
    strcpy(buffer, cp);
    cout << "buffer = " << buffer << endl;
    delete[] buffer;

    return 0;
}
```

6. Compile and run the program. Its output, which is a copy of **buffer**, is as follows:

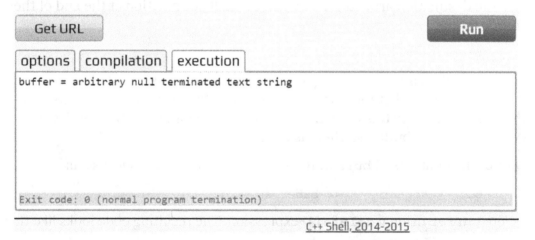

Figure 6.4: Output of the program in exercise 39

Apart from the slightly different syntax of the **new[]**- and **delete[]**-expressions, creating and deleting dynamic arrays follow the same rules as for dynamic variables of basic types.

Exercise 40: Creating and Deleting Dynamic Arrays of Classes

It's possible to create and delete dynamic arrays of class instances, too. The interesting thing to notice about dynamic arrays of class instances is that each instance in an array is constructed; that is, its constructor member function is called. Destroying an array of class instances calls the destructor of each instance.

> **Note**
>
> The complete code for the exercise can be found at https://packt.live/35o4BlL.

Here are the steps to perform the exercise:

1. Type the skeleton **main()** function into the C++ compiler. The code looks like this:

```
#include <iostream>
using namespace std;

int main()
{
    return 0;
}
```

2. Type in a definition of class **noisy** following the **using namespace** declaration. As you remember from *Exercise 38, Creating and Deleting Dynamic Class Instances*, **noisy** makes visible the construction and destruction of instances of **noisy** instances. This version of **noisy** is defined as a struct instead of a class, and its two small member functions are defined inline. This reduces the amount of space taken up by this familiar class:

```
struct noisy
{
    noisy() { cout << "constructing noisy" << endl; }
    ~noisy() { cout << "destroying noisy" << endl; }
};
```

3. Inside **main()**, output a message **getting a noisy array**. Declare a pointer to **noisy** called **pnoisy** and assign it a new dynamic array of three **noisy** instances:

```
    cout << "getting a noisy array" << endl;
    noisy* pnoisy = new noisy[3];
```

4. Output the message **deleting noisy array**. Then, delete the **noisy** array using a **delete[]**-expression whose argument is **pnoisy**. The resulting code looks like this:

```
cout << "deleting noisy array" << endl;
delete[] pnoisy;
```

5. The complete program looks like this.

```
#include <iostream>
using namespace std;

struct noisy
{
    noisy() { cout << "constructing noisy" << endl; }
    ~noisy() { cout << "destroying noisy" << endl; }
};

int main()
{
    cout << "getting a noisy array" << endl;
    noisy* pnoisy = new noisy[3];
    cout << "deleting noisy array" << endl;
    delete[] pnoisy;

    return 0;
}
```

6. Compile and run the program. The resulting output is as follows:

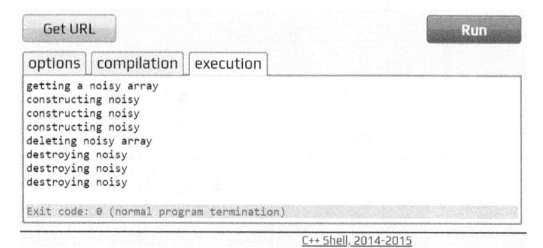

C++ Shell, 2014-2015

Figure 6.5: Creating and deleting dynamic arrays of classes

The important thing to notice is that each of the class instances in a dynamic array is constructed rather than being random bits that happened to be in memory. When the array is deleted, the instances are destroyed.

So that's it in a nutshell: how to create new dynamic variables and arrays, and how to delete them. Maybe you have heard how difficult C++ pointers and references are. Maybe you are wondering now what all the hullabaloo is about. Well, the next topic discusses some of the ways that programmers can go wrong when using dynamic variables.

Seven Dynamic Variable Sins

The next seven exercises illustrate seven ways that misusing dynamic variables can destroy your program, either by sending it to the chaos of heap corruption or invoking the sudden thunderbolt of an operating system trap.

Several of the following exercises were contrived to print error messages and terminate the program. The specific message produced depends both on the C++ runtime system version, and on the operating system on which the program runs. There is no guarantee you will see the same error message, so each example also contains a description of what happens.

Exercise 41: Using a Dynamic Variable before Creating It

The first deadly dynamic variable sin is using a pointer to a dynamic variable before creating the dynamic variable. It should be obvious that dereferencing a pointer to invalid storage will cause undefined behavior, which may include a crash, or simply producing the wrong result.

> **Note**
>
> The complete code for the exercise can be found at https://packt.live/2XAak52.

Here are the steps to perform the exercise:

1. Enter the following abbreviated skeleton **main()** function:

```
int main()
{
    return 0;
}
```

2. Inside **main()**, create a char pointer called **p**:

```
char* p = nullptr;
```

3. Set **p[10]** to **'!'**.This symbol is known to typesetters as "bang":

```
p[10] = '!';
```

The complete program looks like this:

```
#include<iostream>
using namespace std;

int main()
{
    char * p = nullptr;
    p[10] = '!';
    return 0;
}
```

4. Compile and run the program. If you are using an online compiler, use a compiler that displays the output from the operating system, such as Coliru; cpp. sh does not. The output of the program is an error message (depending on the operating system):

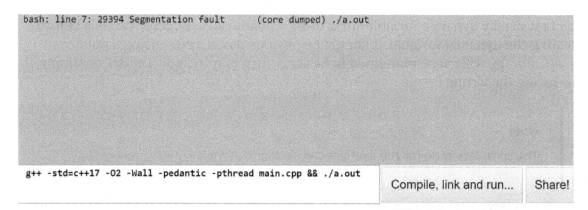

Figure 6.6: Error message resulting from running the program in exercise 41

The error is obvious in this brief example; no dynamic variable was ever assigned to **p**. In a bigger program, the pointer may be set in one place, used in another, and deleted in a third. It may not be obvious at the point where the error occurred what code path led to using the variable without creating it. Embedded operating systems may not catch a write to an invalid address, and may instead overwrite critical system information, making the embedded program unstable instead of crashing immediately.

The relatively informative **segmentation fault** error message happens because this particular pointer was initialized to **nullptr**. The operating system trapped the access to unmapped memory. If the pointer had some other invalid address, it might overwrite variables or damage the heap's free block list, resulting in a different error message at a point in the program that is far from the source of the problem. That's just one reason why initializing pointers to **nullptr** is such a good idea.

Exercise 42: Using a Dynamic Variable after Deleting It

The second deadly dynamic variable sin is deleting a dynamic variable and then continuing to use the pointer as though it still refers to that dynamic variable.

> **Note**
>
> The complete code for the exercise can be found at https://packt.live/338B65K.

Here are the steps to perform the exercise:

1. Enter the skeleton of the **main()** function:

```
#include <iostream>
using namespace std;

int main()
{
    return 0;
}
```

2. Inside **main()**, create a **char** pointer called **p** that is initialized to the result of a **new[]**-expression, creating an array of 10 **char**s:

```
char* p = new char[10];
```

3. Set **p[0]** to **'!'**:

```
p[0] = '!';
```

4. Delete **p** using a **delete[]**-expression, because **p** points to an array:

```
delete[] p;
```

5. Print the value of **p[0]**. Remember, **p** doesn't point to anything valid at this point:

```
cout << "p[0] = " << p[0] << endl;
```

6. The complete program looks like this.

```
#include <iostream>
using namespace std;

int main()
{
    char * p = new char[10];
    p[0] = '!';
    delete[] p;
    cout << "p[0] = " << p[0] << endl;
    return 0;
}
```

7. Compile and run the program. Its output on one particular compiler and operating system is as follows:

```
p[0] = p
```

```
g++ -std=c++17 -O2 -Wall -pedantic -pthread main.cpp && ./a.out        Compile, link and run...    Share!
```

Figure 6.7: Output of the program in exercise 42

You might expect the value of **p[0]** to be **'!'** because you can see the line of code that set it to **'!'**. However, when the program deleted **p**, it signaled to the C++ runtime system that the program was done using the storage **p** pointed to. After that, C++ did something else with it. The C++ runtime system probably put a pointer to the next item on the list of free memory blocks into the beginning of **p**. However, it could have done anything. The fact that the program printed the character **'p'** is purely coincidence. It certainly didn't print **'!'**.

A special circle of hell is reserved for programs that commit this sin, because the program doesn't crash immediately. Symptoms of this error include variables changing value unexpectedly or a crash on a subsequent **new**-expression or **delete**-expression that may occur on a line that is far from the line in the program where the error occurred.

Exercise 43: Not Deleting a Dynamic Variable

The next deadly dynamic variable sin is creating a dynamic variable and then forgetting to delete it.

> **Note**
>
> The complete code for the exercise can be found at https://packt.live/2CZPSRU.

Here are the steps to perform the exercise:

1. Enter the skeleton **main()** function:

    ```
    #include <iostream>
    using namespace std;

    int main()
    {
        return 0;
    }
    ```

2. Inside **main()**, create a char pointer called **p**, initialized to the result of a **new[]**-expression, creating an array of 10 chars:

    ```
    char* p = new char[10];
    ```

3. Set **p[0]** to **'!'**:

    ```
    p[0] = '!';
    ```

4. Print the value of **p[0]**:

    ```
    cout << "p[0] = " << p[0] << endl;
    ```

5. The complete program looks like this.

    ```
    #include <iostream>
    using namespace std;

    int main()
    {
    ```

```
char * p = new char[10];
p[0] = '!';
cout << "p[0] = " << p[0] << endl;
return 0;
}
```

6. Compile and run the program. The output is as you expected. It looks like this:

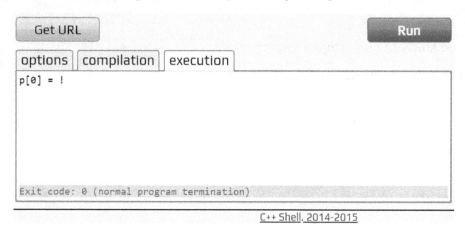

Figure 6.8: Output of the program in exercise 43

There are also no error messages. So, why is this a deadly sin? The problem is that every dynamic variable created with a **new**-expression or **new[]**-expression must be deleted by a matching **delete**-expression or **delete[]**-expression. Otherwise, the storage occupied by the variable will become inaccessible to the program; that is, the memory will *leak* from the program.

If a program with a memory leak runs for a long time, then it will send the whole computer on which it runs to the hell of memory exhaustion, causing the running program, other programs, or the operating system itself to become unstable and crash. Some operating systems reclaim leaked memory when the program terminates. Others do not. Relying on the operating system to reclaim your un-deleted dynamic variables is a bad habit of old Unix programmers that you would be well-advised to avoid.

Exercise 44: Overwriting a Pointer to a Dynamic Variable

If you overwrite a valid pointer to a dynamic variable, you may destroy the last reference to the variable, causing it to leak. This is a deadly dynamic variable sin.

> **Note**
>
> The complete code for the exercise can be found at https://packt.live/2KD5DSU.

Here are the steps to perform the exercise:

1. Retype the code from *Exercise 38: Creating and Deleting Dynamic Class Instances*. The code is as follows:

```cpp
#include <iostream>
using namespace std;

class noisy
{
    int i_;
public:
    noisy(int i): i_(i)
    {
        cout << "constructing noisy " << i << endl;
    }
    ~noisy()
    {
        cout << "destroying noisy " << i_ << endl;
    }
};

int main()
{
    noisy N(1);
    noisy * p = new noisy(2);
    p = new noisy(3);
    delete p;

    return 0;
}
```

2. Just before deleting **p**, add a statement assigning another new instance of **noisy**, initialized as **noisy(3)**, to **p**. The code looks like this:

```cpp
    p = new noisy(3);
```

3. The complete program looks like this:

```cpp
#include <iostream>
using namespace std;

class noisy
{
    int i_;
```

```
public:
    noisy(int i) : i_(i)
    {
        cout << "constructing noisy " << i << endl;
    }
    ~noisy()
    {
        cout << "destroying noisy " << i_ << endl;
    }
};

int main()
{
    noisy N(1);
    noisy* p = new noisy(2);
    p = new noisy(3);
    delete p;

    return 0;
}
```

4. Compile and run the completed program. The output of this program is as follows:

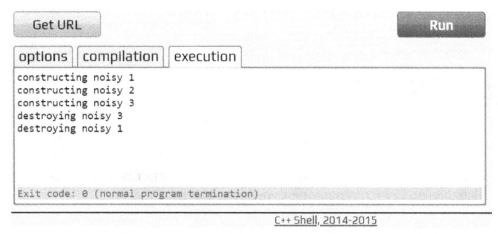

Figure 6.9: Output of the program in exericse 44

When execution enters **main()**, an instance of **noisy** is created. The **noisy** constructor is called, printing the first message, **constructing noisy 1**.

The next statement creates the first dynamic noisy instance, causing the second message, **constructing noisy 2**, to be printed. The next statement constructs another **noisy** instance, **noisy 3**, and assigns a pointer to that instance to **p**, replacing the pointer to **noisy 2**.

The next statement deletes **p**, causing **noisy 3**'s destructor to print a message. Then **main()** returns, causing the local variable, **N**, to go out of scope, and triggering a call to the destructor of **noisy 1**.

What happened to **noisy 2**? A dynamic variable must be deleted, but there is no pointer left in the program that points to **noisy 2** because it was overwritten by the pointer to **noisy 3**, so **noisy 2** cannot be deleted. However, **noisy 2** doesn't just cease to exist. The operating system doesn't know where **noisy 2**'s storage is. The operating system handed over the management of **noisy 2**'s storage to the program, but the program has forgotten where **noisy 2** is; **noisy 2** has *leaked* out of the program.

What happens after that depends on the operating system. Linux lets you off easy, freeing up all the memory used by a program. On embedded systems and on Windows, however, the leaked memory may be gone until the next time the computer reboots. Every time the program is run, another instance of **noisy 2** becomes inaccessible. If this happens enough times, the operating system won't have enough memory to run programs. It will become unstable and cause an operating system kernel panic.

Exercise 45: Deleting a Dynamic Variable Twice

The next deadly dynamic variable sin is deleting a dynamic variable more than once—that is, using the same pointer in more than one **delete**-expression.

When a program deletes a dynamic variable, the dynamic variable's storage goes back on the heap's list of available storage blocks. The pointer, however, is not changed; it still points to the beginning of what used to be the dynamic variable. If the program deletes the same pointer again, the C++ runtime system tries to call the destructor of the already destroyed former dynamic variable, which may crash the program all by itself.

Then, C++ tries to put the former dynamic variable's storage, already on the available storage list, onto the list of available storage blocks again, which will very likely corrupt the list of available storage blocks.

> **Note**
>
> The complete code for this exercise can be found at https://packt.live/330kHjW.

1. Enter this simplified skeleton **main()** program:

```
#include <iostream>
using namespace std;
int main()
{
    return 0;
}
```

2. Inside **main()**, declare a new pointer to char called **p**. Initialize it to a new 10 **char** dynamic array:

```
char* p = new char[10];
```

3. Add two lines that each say **delete[] p;**:

```
delete[] p;
delete[] p;
```

The complete program is as follows:

```
#include <iostream>
using namespace std;

int main()
{
    char * p = new char[10];
    delete[] p;
    delete[] p;
    return 0;
}
```

4. Compile and run the program. If you are using an online compiler, use a compiler that displays the output from the operating system, such as coliru. The output may contain an error message that looks something like this on Linux:

```
*** Error in `./a.out': double free or corruption (fasttop): 0x00000000011bac20 ***
======= Backtrace: =========
/lib/x86_64-linux-gnu/libc.so.6(+0x777e5)[0x7fdbddda87e5]
/lib/x86_64-linux-gnu/libc.so.6(+0x8037a)[0x7fdbdddb137a]
/lib/x86_64-linux-gnu/libc.so.6(cfree+0x4c)[0x7fdbdddb553c]
./a.out[0x40051e]
/lib/x86_64-linux-gnu/libc.so.6(__libc_start_main+0xf0)[0x7fdbddd51830]
./a.out[0x400559]
======= Memory map: ========
00400000-00401000 r-xp 00000000 ca:01 852422                              /tmp/1565244746.5693452/a.out
00600000-00601000 rw-p 00000000 ca:01 852422                              /tmp/1565244746.5693452/a.out
011a9000-011db000 rw-p 00000000 00:00 0                                   [heap]
7fdbd8000000-7fdbd8021000 rw-p 00000000 00:00 0
7fdbd8021000-7fdbdc000000 ---p 00000000 00:00 0
7fdbddd31000-7fdbddef1000 r-xp 00000000 ca:01 606342                      /lib/x86_64-linux-gnu/libc-2.23.so
7fdbddef1000-7fdbde0f1000 ---p 001c0000 ca:01 606342                      /lib/x86_64-linux-gnu/libc-2.23.so
7fdbde0f1000-7fdbde0f5000 r--p 001c0000 ca:01 606342                      /lib/x86_64-linux-gnu/libc-2.23.so
7fdbde0f5000-7fdbde0f7000 rw-p 001c4000 ca:01 606342                      /lib/x86_64-linux-gnu/libc-2.23.so
7fdbde0f7000-7fdbde0fb000 rw-p 00000000 00:00 0
7fdbde101000-7fdbde119000 r-xp 00000000 ca:01 606340                      /lib/x86_64-linux-gnu/libpthread-2.23.so
7fdbde119000-7fdbde318000 ---p 00018000 ca:01 606340                      /lib/x86_64-linux-gnu/libpthread-2.23.so
```

Figure 6.10: Error output of the program in exercise 45

The message goes on for many more lines. Not all C++ compilers produce a runtime error message for this program; it depends on the compiler and the compile options. This compiler's runtime system checks for deletion of an already deleted dynamic variable and prints a warning. There is no guarantee that the C++ runtime system will print this error message, especially if you command the compiler to perform optimization. Instead, the operating system may cast the program into the fiery pit at some point in the future when the program tries to execute a **new**-expression or **delete**-expression.

Exercise 46: Deleting a Dynamic Array with delete instead of delete[]

Deleting a dynamic array using **delete** is the next deadly dynamic variable sin.

> **Note**
>
> The complete code for this exercise can be found at https://packt.live/2OAtSlO.

1. Enter the skeleton **main()** function and the definition of struct **noisy**. It looks like this:

```
#include <iostream>
using namespace std;

struct noisy
{
    noisy() { cout << "constructing noisy" << endl; }
    ~noisy() { cout << "destroying noisy" << endl; }
```

```
};

int main()
{
    return 0;
}
```

2. Inside **main()**, declare a **noisy** pointer called **p**, initializing it to a dynamic array of three **noisy** instances using a **new[]** expression:

```
noisy* p = new noisy[3];
```

3. Delete **p** using a **delete**-expression instead of a **delete[]**-expression:

```
delete p;
```

4. The complete program looks like this.

```
#include <iostream>
using namespace std;

struct noisy
{
    noisy() { cout << "constructing noisy" << endl; }
    ~noisy() { cout << "destroying noisy" << endl; }
};

int main()
{
    noisy* p = new noisy[3];
    delete p;
    return 0;
}
```

5. Compile and run the program. If you are using an online compiler, use a compiler such as coliru, which displays the output from the operating system. Here is a representative output of the operating system:

```
constructing noisy
constructing noisy
constructing noisy
destroying noisy
*** Error in `./a.out': munmap_chunk(): invalid pointer: 0x000000000164dc28 ***
======= Backtrace: =========
/lib/x86_64-linux-gnu/libc.so.6(+0x777e5)[0x7f7f6f3607e5]
/lib/x86_64-linux-gnu/libc.so.6(cfree+0x1a8)[0x7f7f6f36d698]
./a.out[0x400b30]
/lib/x86_64-linux-gnu/libc.so.6(__libc_start_main+0xf0)[0x7f7f6f309830]
./a.out[0x400bd9]
======= Memory map: ========
00400000-00402000 r-xp 00000000 ca:01 852422                               /tmp/1565244823.7642927/a.out
00601000-00602000 rw-p 00001000 ca:01 852422                               /tmp/1565244823.7642927/a.out
0163c000-0166e000 rw-p 00000000 00:00 0                                    [heap]
7f7f6f2e9000-7f7f6f4a9000 r-xp 00000000 ca:01 606342                       /lib/x86_64-linux-gnu/libc-2.23.so
7f7f6f4a9000-7f7f6f6a9000 ---p 001c0000 ca:01 606342                       /lib/x86_64-linux-gnu/libc-2.23.so
7f7f6f6a9000-7f7f6f6ad000 r--p 001c0000 ca:01 606342                       /lib/x86_64-linux-gnu/libc-2.23.so
7f7f6f6ad000-7f7f6f6af000 rw-p 001c4000 ca:01 606342                       /lib/x86_64-linux-gnu/libc-2.23.so
7f7f6f6af000-7f7f6f6b3000 rw-p 00000000 00:00 0
7f7f6f6b9000-7f7f6f6d1000 r-xp 00000000 ca:01 606340                       /lib/x86_64-linux-gnu/libpthread-2.23.so
```

Figure 6.11: Error message when deleting a dynamic array with delete instead of delete[]

Looking at the output, there is an excellent symptom of this problem beyond the crash report. Three **noisy** instances were constructed, but only one **noisy** instance was destroyed, instead of three.

On this particular compiler and operating system, the C++ runtime system detects a problem, prints a message, and then terminates the program. There is no guarantee that another C++ runtime system will detect a problem. There is a guarantee that the other two instances of **noisy** were not destroyed, so they leaked any dynamic variables they contained. At least some of the storage for the **noisy** array was not returned to the free storage list, so it leaked, too. There is also a possibility that the heap's list of free memory blocks has been corrupted, so, eventually, the program will become unstable.

Exercise 47: Deleting a Dynamic Variable with delete[] instead of delete

This final deadly dynamic variable sin is the reverse of the previous one: deleting a non-array dynamic variable with **delete[]**, which is intended for deleting arrays.

> **Note**
>
> The complete code for this exercise can be found at https://packt.live/2qwT8l3.

1. Enter the skeleton **main()** function and the definition of the struct **noisy**. It looks like this:

```
#include <iostream>
using namespace std;

struct noisy
{
    noisy() { cout << "constructing noisy" << endl; }
    ~noisy() { cout << "destroying noisy" << endl; }
};

int main()
{
    return 0;
}
```

2. Inside **main()**, declare a **noisy** pointer called **p**, initializing it to a new dynamic **noisy** instance using a **new**-expression:

```
noisy* p = new noisy;
```

3. Delete **p** using a **delete[]**-expression instead of a **delete**-expression:

```
delete[] p;
```

4. The complete program looks like this.

```
#include <iostream>
using namespace std;

struct noisy
{
```

```
        noisy() { cout << "constructing noisy" << endl; }
    ~noisy() { cout << "destroying noisy" << endl; }
};

int main()
{
    noisy* p = new noisy;
    delete[] p;
    return 0;
}
```

5. Compile and run the program. Example operating system output from Linux is reproduced below:

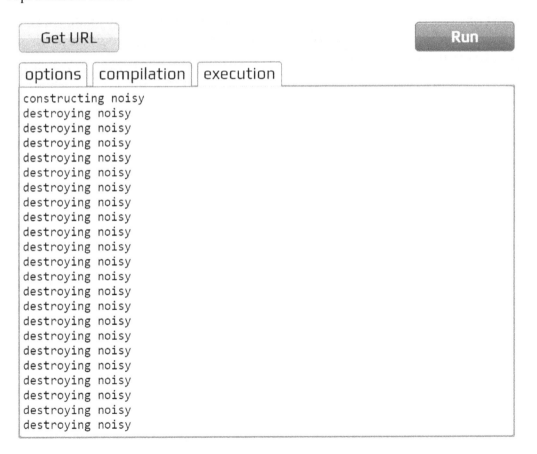

Figure 6.12: Error message when deleting a dynamic variable with delete[] instead of delete

So, what happened here? Well, one noisy instance was constructed, but an apparently endless number of instances were deleted.

A **new[]**-expression saves the size of the array it allocates so it can call a destructor for each instance in the array. A **new**-expression doesn't save this value. The **delete[]**-expression looks for the secret count of instances and reads garbage. Unless the garbage happens to be equal to one, which is quite unlikely, **delete[]** will try to delete instances that don't exist. The program will then descend into the chaotic circle of hell called **undefined behavior**.

C++ provides very powerful, very efficient tools. However, the efficiency comes at the price of vigilance. C++ doesn't check everything the programmer does to make sure they did it right. Forget to do the right thing, and C++ has a terrible fate in store for your program. C++ will let the developer do great things. However, it will not coddle them. If that wasn't obvious before, studying dynamic variables has hopefully made this clear. As already mentioned in the first chapter, if C++ had a philosophy, it would be *With great power comes great responsibility.*

Managing dynamic variables is hard enough that modern C++ defines something called a *smart pointer*; that is, a class that automatically deletes its dynamic variable when the smart pointer goes out of scope. Smart pointers are covered in *Chapter 7, Ownership and Lifetime of Dynamic Variables.* Smart pointers are the only good way to handle dynamic variables. Until we get to smart pointers, you must deal with dynamic variables in the old-fashioned way.

Dynamic Containers

A **container** is a data structure consisting of multiple instances of the same data type. For instance, a C++ array is a simple kind of container. The type of array says what kind of data it contains. An array has a fixed size specified at compile time. A dynamic array is a container that has a fixed type and an arbitrary size, but the size is fixed when the container is created.

Linked Lists

Using dynamic class instances, each containing a single pointer, a program can create a container that can grow to a size that is not predetermined. Each entry in a container is a class (or struct) instance. The class has a payload (a member called **value_**, an **int** in the following example) and a pointer member (called **next_** in the following example), which refers to the next instance in the container. The class definition looks like this:

```
struct numeric_item
{
    int value_;
    numeric_item* next_;
};
```

Dynamically created instances of this class can be chained together using their **next_** member. A pointer variable, called **head** in the following diagram, points to the whole container. The **next_** pointer at the end of the chain is set to **nullptr**:

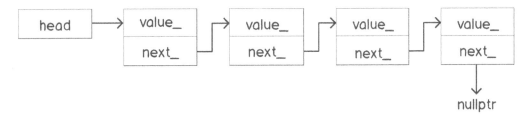

Figure 6.13: Visualizing linked lists

Such a container is called a **linked list**.

Binary Search Trees

Using dynamic class instances, each containing two pointers, a program can create another kind of container that can grow to a size that is not predetermined. Each entry in a container is a class instance. The class has a payload (an **int** member called **value_** in the following example) and two pointer members (called **left_** and **right_** in this example). The class definition looks like this:

```
struct numeric_tree
{
    int value_;
    numeric_tree* left_;
    numeric_tree* right_;
};
```

Dynamically created instances of this class can be linked together using their **left_** and **right_** members. A pointer variable, called **root** in the following diagram, points to the whole container. **left_** and **right_** pointers that do not point to instances are set to **nullptr**. The resulting data structure resembles a tree growing upside down:

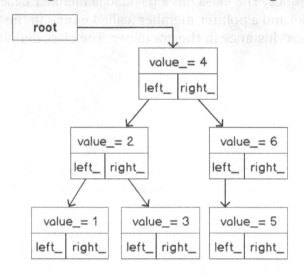

Figure 6.14: A binary search tree growing upside down

Such a container is called a binary tree.

Recursive Data Structures

Linked lists and binary trees are examples of recursive data structures—that is, data structures that are defined in terms of themselves. For instance, a linked list can be defined as either **nullptr** or as an item with a single link pointing to a linked list. A binary tree is a data structure that is either **nullptr** or else consists of an item with two links, called the **left subtree** and the **right subtree**, that point to binary trees. A data structure that is defined recursively is interesting because it can be manipulated by functions that are themselves recursive, although this is not guaranteed to be efficient.

A **binary search tree** is a binary tree with the additional property that the values of all items on the left subtree of an item are less than the value of that item, and the values of all items on the right subtree are greater than the value of that item. The binary tree in the preceding diagram is a binary search tree. One advantage of a binary search tree is that there is an algorithm to efficiently visit the nodes of the binary search tree in ascending or descending sorted order.

Visiting Items in a Recursive Data Structure

The recursive definition of a linked list tells us how to write a function to visit all the items in a linked list and print each one. If a linked list is empty, there's nothing to print but **endl**. Otherwise, print the item and then recursively print the **next_** pointer as a linked list. The function looks like this:

```
void print_recursive(numeric_item* p)
{
    if (p == nullptr)
    {
        cout << endl;
    }
    else
    {
        cout << p->value_ << " ";
        print_recursive(p->next_);
    }
}
```

The only problem with recursively printing a linked list is that if there are n items in the list, there will be n nested calls to the recursive function before it begins to return. This is no problem if **n = 10**, but it is a very big problem indeed if n is 1,000,000. Fortunately, there is a non-recursive way to print a linked list. A **while** loop prints the current list item while it is not **nullptr**, and then prints the **endl** after the loop. This resembles the recursive function, with the loop substituting the recursive call. The iterative (that is, non-recursive) **print** function looks like this:

```
void print(numeric_item* p)
{
    while (p != nullptr)
    {
        cout << p->value_ << " ";
        p = p->next_;
    }
    cout << endl;
}
```

To visit and print the items of a binary search tree recursively, the function returns immediately if the tree is empty; otherwise, it recursively visits the left subtree, prints the current item, and recursively visits the right subtree. Such a **print** function looks like this:

```
void print(numeric_tree* item)
{
    if (item == nullptr)
    {
        return;
    }
    print(item->left_);
    cout << item->value_ << " ";
    print(item->right_);
}
```

There is an iterative way to print a binary tree, but it uses a stack that simulates the function call stack. It doesn't offer any advantage over the recursive function. If the order in which items are inserted in a binary search tree is random, a million-item tree will only have about 20 levels of recursive calls. This is less likely to cause problems than a million nested calls. The insertion order for the tree in *Figure* 6.2 is **4, 2, 1, 3, 6, 5**. There are insertion orders that would create deeper trees. For instance, the insertion order **1, 2, 3, 4, 5, 6** would generate a tree all of whose left subtrees were empty, and which had a worst-case recursive depth.

Finding Items

An item can be found in a list or tree by comparing items to a key value and returning a pointer to the found item, or **nullptr** if no item is found. This pointer gives the developer access to the fields of the found item, but it doesn't give access to the pointer that led to the item, which would be very handy for inserting or removing an item. A slightly different function steps through the pointers to each item using and returning a pointer-to-pointer so that a new item can be inserted before the found item, if desired.

An iterative solution for linked lists uses a **while** loop. The initial condition (before the **while** loop) sets **pp** to the address of **head**. The loop terminates if ***pp** is **nullptr** (reached the end of list), or if **(*pp)->value_** is equal to **v**. The loop step expression sets **pp** to the address of **(*pp)->next_**:

```
numeric_item** pp = &head;
while((*pp) != nullptr && (*pp)->value_ != v)
{
    pp = &((*pp)->next_);
}
```

Initially, **pp** points to **head**'s address, so that **(*pp)** points to the first list item, or **nullptr**. If **(*pp)** is **nullptr** or the list item's **value_** is equal to the target value **v**, execution breaks out of the loop. Otherwise, the pointer to pointer **pp** is stepped to point to the address of the list item's **next_** pointer, which points to the next list item. After the loop, either **(*pp)** points to the item whose value is **v**, or **(*pp)** is equal to **nullptr**. **pp** points to the pointer where a new item should be inserted just before **v**; otherwise, it points to the last pointer in the list if **v** was not found.

A recursive function using the same pointer-to-pointer idiom finds the insertion point in a binary search tree. The first arm of the **if** block ends the recursion if the pointer is **nullptr**. Otherwise, **find()** uses the binary search tree property, recursing down the left subtree if the key is less than the value of the current node, or down the right subtree if not:

```
numeric_tree** find(int v, numeric_tree** pp)
{
    if (*pp == nullptr)
    {
        return pp;
    }
    else if (v < (*pp)->value_)
    {
        return find(v, &((*pp)->left_));
    }
    else
    {
        return find(v, &((*pp)->right_));
    }
}
```

Adding Items

To add an item into a linked list, the list is conceptually divided into a head part, which will come before the inserted item, and a tail part, which will come after the inserted item. The head part may be as short as only the list pointer (that is, the variable **head** in the diagram) or as long as the whole list. The inserted item is added first to the front of the tail of the list, and then to the back end of the head part of the list.

The back end of the head of the list is represented by the address of the last pointer in the head of the list–that is, by a pointer to a pointer, which is called **pp** in the code below. The last pointer in the head of the list points to the tail part. The list item to be inserted is pointed to by **newp**.

The pointer to the tail is copied from the last pointer in the head of the list to the inserted item's **next_** pointer. This links the inserted item to the tail of the list. Then the last pointer in the head of the list is updated, through the pointer to the pointer, to point to the inserted item. This appends the inserted item to the head part of the list. If **pp** is a pointer to pointer that refers to the end of the head part, and **newp** is a pointer to the new item to be inserted, this looks like the following:

```
newp->next_ = *pp;
*pp = newp->next_;
```

The following diagram shows how to add items to a linked list:

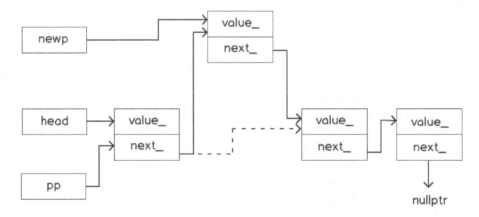

Figure 6.15: Adding items to a linked list

This code can add an item at any position, even at the front, because **pp** can be set to the address of **head**. The preceding diagram shows the list before adding an item (dotted line) and after (solid lines).

Inserting into a binary search tree is even easier. The value returned by **find()** always points to the insertion point, so assigning a pointer to the new item to the dereferenced pointer returned by **find()** inserts the new item.

Deleting Dynamic Items

Dynamically created items must be deleted to avoid a memory leak. A common idiom for deleting a linked list is to remove each item from the head of the list and then delete that item. A common mistake made by users is deleting the dynamic variable **head** points to, and then saying **head = head->next_ ;**. The problem with this code is that after deleting **head**, it no longer points to anything valid. Depending on your compiler, this incorrect idiom may seem to work, but will probably fail unexpectedly at some future time.

Instead, use a pointer variable, called **p** in the code below, to temporarily save the value of **head**, set **head** to **head->next_**, and then delete **p**:

```
while (head != nullptr)
{
    numeric_item* p = head;
    head = head->next_;
    delete p;
}
```

These idioms are worth memorizing. You are going to use them many times while programming in C++.

Exercise 48: Creating Linked Lists of Class Instances

In this exercise, you'll create a container for storing a sequence of numbers. You will need functions to add an item in a list, to find an item in a list, and to print a list, so this exercise will be a little longer than some of the previous exercises:

> **Note**
>
> The complete code for this exercise an be found at https://packt.live/2QqiWJO.

1. To begin the exercise, enter the skeleton of the **main()** program:

```
#include <iostream>
using namespace std;

int main()
{
    return 0;
}
```

2. Above **main()**, add a definition for struct **numeric_item**. **numeric_item** has an int member named **value_** and a pointer to **numeric_item** called **next_**:

```
struct numeric_item
{
    int value_;
    numeric_item* next_;
};
```

3. Declare the **numeric_item** list pointer **head**. Initialize **head** to **nullptr** because that's how the program can tell that the list is empty:

```
numeric_item* head = nullptr;
```

4. So far, the program looks like this; you can compile the program, but it doesn't do anything yet:

```
#include <iostream>
using namespace std;

struct numeric_item
{
    int value_;
    numeric_item* next_;
};

numeric_item* head = nullptr;

int main()
{
    return 0;
}
```

Iterating through a linked list

The next function iterates through the list, printing the value of each **numeric_item** struct in the list:

5. Following the declaration of **head**, define a **void** function **print()**. The skeleton of **print()** looks like this:

```
void print()
{
}
```

6. **print()** contains a **for** loop to print each list entry. The initialization clause declares a pointer to **numeric_item** called **p**, initialized to **head**, which is the pointer to the first item of the list. The termination clause exits the loop if **p** is **nullptr**, and the step clause advances **p** to the next list item by assigning **p->next** to **p**. The **for** statement looks like this:

```
for (numeric_item* p = head; p != nullptr; p = p->next_)
```

7. If the list is empty, **head** will be equal to **nullptr**, so **p** will initially be set equal to **nullptr** and the loop will terminate. Otherwise, the value of the list entry will be printed. When the function is done printing the item, **p** is set to **p->next_** –that is, the next list item. This repeats for each list item. The final list item's **next_** pointer is equal to **nullptr**. When **p->next_** is assigned to **p**, it becomes equal to **nullptr**, and the **for** loop terminates. The code looks like this:

```
for (numeric_item* p = head; p != nullptr; p = p->next_)
{
    cout << p->value_ << " ";
}
```

This exercise shows that a **for** loop can do much more than count up integer values or increment through arrays. You can compile the code, but it won't do anything yet if you run it.

8. The list items were output with a separating space and without an **endl**, to flush the line out to the terminal. At the end of the **for** loop, output **endl** so the output line becomes visible:

```
cout << endl;
```

9. The complete **print()** function looks like this:

```
void print()
{
    for (numeric_item* p = head; p != nullptr; p = p->next_)
    {
        cout << p->value_ << " ";
    }
    cout << endl;
}
```

You can compile the program at this point if you wish, but it still won't do anything.

Inserting items into a linked list

The next function inserts an item at any position in the list:

10. Add the function **add()** below **print()**. Now, **add()** takes two arguments: an **int** value, **v**, which will initialize a new dynamic **numeric_item**; and a pointer to pointer called **pp**, which will be the insertion point. **add()** is a **void** function since it returns nothing at all. The skeleton of **add()** looks like this:

```
void add(int v, numeric_item** pp)
{

}
```

11. **add()** defines a **numeric_item** pointer called **newp** and assigns the result of creating a dynamic **numeric_item** instance to **newp**. The **value_** member of **newp** is set to the **v** argument:

```
numeric_item* newp = new numeric_item;
newp->value_ = v;
```

12. The new item is made to point to the tail of the list, currently given by ***pp**. Now, ***pp** is updated to point to the new item, **newp**:

```
newp->next_ = *pp;
*pp = newp;
```

13. The completed **add()** function looks like this:

```
void add(int v, numeric_item** pp)
{
    numeric_item* newp = new numeric_item;
    newp->value_ = v;
    newp->next_ = *pp;
    *pp = newp;
}
```

14. There is now enough machinery in the program to actually do something. Inside **main()**, write a **for** loop to add some **numeric_item** instances to the list. Use the **for** loop induction variable to set the values of these **numeric_item** instances. Start the loop at 1, and add 2 during each iteration to create an instance containing the values 1, 3, 5, 7, and 9:

```
for (int i = 1; i < 10; i = i + 2)
{
    insert_at(i, &head);
}
```

15. After the **for** loop, call **print()** to output the list that was just created:

```
print();
```

The contents of **main()** look like this:

```
int main()
{
    for (int i = 1; i < 10; i = i + 2)
    {
        insert_at(i, &head);
    }

    print();

    return 0;
}
```

16. Compile and run the program. Its output should look like this:

Figure 6.16: Output of the first version of the program in exercise 48

Note that the program we just ran committed one of the seven deadly sins of dynamic variables—that of not deleting a dynamic variable when finished with it. We'll fix that soon.

Finding an item in a list

17. Define a function called **find()**. This function finds an item in the linked list given by the pointer-to-pointer **pp**, whose value is equal to the **int** argument, **v**. It returns the address of the pointer to the found item—in other words, a pointer to a pointer. The pointer to a pointer is needed in order to insert an item into the list at the found position. If no item is found, it returns a pointer to the end of the list. Enter the skeleton of **find()**, which looks like this:

```
numeric_item** find(int v, numeric_item** pp)
{

}
```

18. Iterate the pointer to pointer through the list looking for an item whose **value_** member is equal to the function argument **v**. Initially, **pp** is set to the address of **head**. The loop terminates if **pp** is **nullptr** (that is, has reached the end of the list) or if **(pp)->value_** is equal to **v**. The step sets **pp** to the address of **(*pp)->next_**. The completed **find()** function looks like this:

```
numeric_item** find(int v, numeric_item** pp)
{
    while ((*pp) != nullptr && (*pp)->value_ != v)
    {
        pp = &((*pp)->next_);
    }
    return pp;
}
```

19. To continue implementing **main()**, use **find()** to find some items, and insert new items before them. Declare a pointer to a pointer to **numeric_item** and call it **pp**. Set **pp** to the result of finding item 7. **pp** now points to the pointer to item 7. Add an item numbered 8 in front of item 7, using the **add()** function. Output the result using **print()**. The code looks like this:

```
numeric_item** pp;
pp = find(7, &head);
add(8, pp);
print();
```

20. Now insert another item. You can use **find()** to get a pointer to the end of the list by searching for an item that is known not to be in the list. Search for -1. Insert an item, 0, at the end of the list. Output the result using **print()**. The code below is another way to do that:

```
add(0, find(-1, &head));
print();
```

Deleting dynamic items in a linked list

The dynamically created list items must be destroyed to avoid a memory leak:

21. Enter a **while** loop. The loop continues while **head** is not equal to **nullptr**:

```
while (head != nullptr)
{
}
```

22. Inside the loop, create a pointer, **p**, to remember the first item in the list:

```
numeric_item* p = head;
```

23. Assign **head** to point to the next list item:

```
head = head->next_;
```

24. Delete **p**:

```
cout << "deleting " << p->value_ << endl;
delete p;
```

The completed **while** loop looks like this:

```
while (head != nullptr)
{
    numeric_item* p = head;
    head = head->next_;
    cout << "deleting " << p->value_ << endl;
    delete p;
}
```

25. Compile and run the program. The output of this program is as follows:

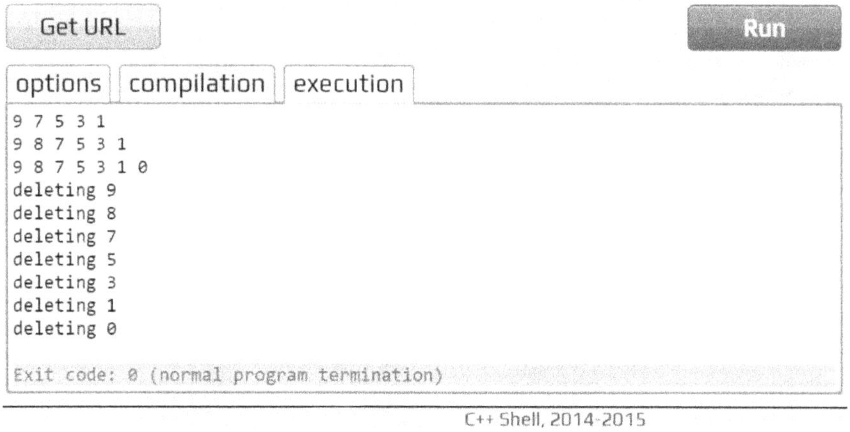

Figure 6.17: Output of the program in exercise 48

The advantage of this linked dynamic data structure is that the only thing that limits how big it gets is how much memory is available. To look back at our book example, we could create an item in this list for every word in the book, but the value of the item would be a dynamic array containing a word. We could create 70,000 words, or 100,000, or 120,000–that is, whatever the book requires.

Building dynamic data structures is what makes pointers and dynamic variables so powerful.

Activity 6: Creating Binary Search Trees of Class Instances

Write a program to construct binary search trees. There should be a function **add()** to add an item to a tree, a function **delete_tree()** to delete a tree, a function **find()** to find an insertion point in the tree, and a function **print()** to print the tree.

> **Note**
>
> The complete code for this activity can be found at https://packt.live/33116Bu.

Here are the steps to complete the activity:

1. Start with a skeleton **main()** function.

2. Add a definition for struct **numeric_tree**. It needs an int **value_** member, and pointers to the left and right subtrees, which are themselves **numeric_tree** instances.

3. Add a variable called **root** as the root of the tree. It's a pointer to **numeric_tree**.

4. Add a skeleton of the function **add()**. **add()** takes as its arguments an **int** value to be added, and a pointer to the address of a pointer to the tree–that is, a pointer to pointer. This is similar to the **add()** function for linked lists. For the **add()** function, realize that the added item will always be added to a subtree that is equal to **nullptr**.

5. Add a skeleton for the **delete_tree()** function. **delete_tree()** takes a pointer to tree as its argument. **delete_tree()** is most easily implemented as a recursive function.

6. Add a skeleton of the **find()** function. **find()** takes as arguments, an **int** value to be added, and a pointer to the address of a pointer to tree–that is, a pointer to pointer. **find()** returns a pointer to pointer. **find()** can be implemented either recursively or iteratively. The recursive version was defined earlier in this chapter.

7. The **print()** function was previously described. It is best implemented recursively.

8. Inside **main()**, items can be added one item at a time, but we chose to automate the process, using a **for** loop to insert each item from an array of **int** values. The **for** loop calls **add()** for each value.

9. Print the newly constructed tree (or the program may not have any output at all).

10. The tree is a dynamic data structure. When you're done with it, it must be deleted.

Here are some hints:

1. The functions are the same functions you implemented to build the linked list.

   The functions can either be defined recursively, using the recursive definition of a binary search tree above as a guide, or can be defined iteratively.

   All the functions take a tree as argument.

2. The function to add an item can use the pointer-to-pointer idiom used in the function **add()** for linked lists.

   The order in which you add items makes a difference. If you add items in the order **1, 2, 3, 4, 5, 6**, the tree will only use the right subtree pointer. It will, in effect, be a linked list. The insertion order of **4, 2, 1, 3, 6, 5** will make a nice symmetrical tree resembling *Figure 6.14*, which will test more of your program.

> **Note**
>
> The solution to this activity can be found on page 529.

Lists and trees are two simple-to-define data structures, but they only scratch the surface of what you can do with dynamic variables. For the first 20 years of C++, developers built data structures quite similar to these.

Chapter 12, Containers and Iterators explores the container classes of the C++ standard library. Originally introduced in the late 1990s, these containers provide standardized, sophisticated versions of lists, trees, and other data structures that can satisfy the majority of users' needs with pre-written code, which is customizable through templates. Modern C++ developers almost always use the standard library containers instead of writing their own custom container classes.

Summary

In this chapter, you learned that there is no fixed limit to the number of dynamic variables or arrays that a program can create. The only limit is the amount of available memory. You learned that dynamic variables are created by an explicit statement, and destroyed by another explicit statement. There are two kinds of **new**-expressions and two kinds of **delete**-expressions—one each for ordinary variables and one each for arrays, respectively. You learned that mistakes made while creating, using, and deleting dynamic variables have consequences that vary depending on the operating system and compiler, but generally cause the program to crash. You learned that dynamic variables are referred to by pointers and that they can be linked together by pointers into lists, trees, and other data structures.

The next chapter discusses the ownership and lifetime of dynamic variables. Understanding these concepts allows the developer to more reliably manage dynamic variables, so that they are deleted when they are no longer needed and do not leak.

Ownership and Lifetime of Dynamic Variables

Overview

This chapter provides tools and strategies to make the use of pointers and dynamic variables in C++ programs safer and easier to understand. By the end of this chapter, you will be able to describe the weaknesses of C++ with respect to dynamic variable ownership and lifetime; explain the use of owned and unowned pointers; embed pointers into class instances to establish ownership and control the lifetime of dynamic variables; use smart pointer classes **unique_ptr<>** and **shared_ptr<>** to automate the ownership and lifetime of dynamic variables.

Introduction

In the previous chapter, we learned how to create and delete dynamic variables and dynamic arrays. We also learned at least seven ways to make a mistake using dynamic variables that will crash your program. Obviously, these powerful tools require some discipline in order to use correctly. In this chapter, we describe ways to manage dynamic variables that reduce the chances of making a mistake when working with them, beginning with the concepts of lifetime and ownership.

Lifetime and ownership are key concepts that experienced developers use to tame the complexity of dynamic variables so that memory leaks do not occur. The concepts of lifetime and ownership of dynamic variables are not fully expressed by C++ syntax. They are things that the developer must manage.

The result of each **new**-expression must be assigned to a pointer variable, or else the new dynamic variable becomes inaccessible. This pointer variable may be said to own the dynamic variable when it is created. Each **delete**-expression takes a pointer to a dynamic variable as argument. This pointer may be said to own the dynamic variable when it is deleted.

The Lifetime of Dynamic Variables

Most variables have a well-defined lifetime. At the beginning of their life the variable is constructed or initialized. At the end of its life, the variable is destroyed. Global (**static** or **extern**) variables are constructed, in a particular order, before **main()** begins. They are destroyed automatically, in reverse order to their construction, after **main()** exits. Function-local and block-local variables, which are also called automatic variables, are constructed at the point where they are declared. They are destroyed when execution leaves the scope (delimited by curly braces) in which the variables were declared. Class member variables are destroyed when the class instance that contains them is destroyed.

Dynamic variables, including dynamic arrays, are frustrating exceptions to these simple rules. Dynamic variables live from the time they are created by an executable statement until they are destroyed by another executable statement. The program can explicitly control the lifetime of data structures built from dynamic variables. This is a double-edged sword because, if the program forgets to destroy a dynamic variable, its memory becomes inaccessible.

Ownership of Dynamic Variables

Responsibility for destroying dynamic variables is shared by the entire program. C++ is generous in permitting any line of the program to create or destroy additional pointers to a dynamic variable and generous in allowing the program freedom to define the lifetime of the dynamic variable. However, C++ exacts a harsh penalty if the developer forgets to delete or double-deletes a dynamic variable: a memory leak or an error trap from the operating system that halts the program. Moreover, hunting these bugs down might involve tracing all execution paths in the program. This situation, with diffuse responsibility for managing dynamic variables and a significant cost of failure, is almost intolerable.

Developers may attempt to tame the raw power of dynamic variables informally by documenting the *ownership* of dynamic variables. A pointer variable is designated to *own* a dynamic variable during its lifetime. The pointer is called an *owned* pointer. The designated pointer variable is used to delete the dynamic variable. Any other pointer to the dynamic variable is called an *unowned* pointer. This is not something the C++ compiler helps with. It's something developers do that may be subject to error because the compiler does not enforce the developer's rules of ownership.

C++ is full of unowned pointers. Standard library iterators and `std::string_view` instances are unowned pointers. Many functions return unowned pointers into standard library data structures. Champions of programming languages that are not C++ may cite how dangerous unowned pointers are as sufficient reason to abandon C++. This concern is valid to an extent. But don't abandon all hope; there are good ways to cope with ownership and lifetime.

One of the most powerful ways to manage ownership of a dynamic variable is to make the owned pointer to a dynamic variable a class member variable, and delete the dynamic member variable when the class instance is destroyed. Then the developer can declare a global, function-local, or block-local instance of the class, and the dynamic variable contained in the class instance will have the same lifetime as the class instance. This technique makes the lifetime of dynamic variables as easy to understand as the lifetime of other kinds of variables.

Resource Acquisition Is Initialization (RAII)

Class instances that own pointers to dynamic variables and delete the dynamic variables when the instance is destroyed are one instance of a broader idiom, where a class instance acquires some resource, owns that resource, and releases the resource when the class instance is destroyed. This idiom is called **RAII (Resource Acquisition Is Initialization)**.

RAII is a powerful idiom in C++ that is used for many resources: dynamic variables, open files, window handles, semaphores and mutexes (which are multithreaded synchronization primitives that are not discussed in this book). What makes RAII classes so useful is that they manage the lifetime of the resource they own. The developer doesn't have to think about how to release the resource. It's all automatic.

Exercise 49: Lifetime Demonstration

The program in this exercise creates and destroys some class instances to illustrate the lifetime of global, function-local, and block-local variables:

> **Note**
>
> The complete code for this exercise can be found here: https://packt.live/2Dd3qJD.

1. Enter the skeleton of the program:

```
#include <iostream>
using namespace std;

int main()
{
    return 0;
}
```

2. Enter a definition of **class noisy**. In this case, **noisy** takes a null-terminated string constructor argument that provides a comment on the scope where the instance was declared:

```
class noisy
{
    char const* s_;
public:
    noisy(char const* s)
    { cout << "constructing " << s << endl; s_ = s; }
    ~noisy()
    { cout << "destroying " << s_ << endl; }
};
```

3. Enter the definition of the function **func()**, which declares a function-local **noisy** instance and then returns:

```
void func(char const* s)
{
    noisy func(s);
}
```

4. Enter two global declarations of **noisy** instances at file scope:

```
noisy f("global 1");
noisy ff("global 2");
```

Before control is transferred to **main()**, all the file-scope variables are constructed, one by one, in the order in which they are declared. After execution returns from **main()**, they are destroyed in reverse order. If you declare file-scope variables in multiple files, there is a rule that tells you the order in which they are constructed. You can look that up in a copy of the standard if you ever need to know it.

5. In **main()**, create an instance of **noisy** called **n1**:

```
noisy n1("main() function local 1");
```

n1 is a function-local variable that is alive for all of **main()**. This is effectively the same lifetime as a global variable. The difference is that the definition of **n1** is only visible within **main()**, while the definitions of **f** and **ff** are visible everywhere in the file.

6. Call **func()** with an argument saying **"function local 2"**. **func()** will print a pair of messages as it creates and then immediately destroys a **noisy** instance:

```
func("function local 2");
```

7. Next, enter a block scope consisting of curly braces. This is legal C++ syntax, and it allows the developer to create a scope with its own local declarations:

```
{
}
```

8. Inside the empty curly braces goes a declaration of another **noisy**, and a call to **func()**. So, the block-local **noisy** is constructed, then **func()** is called, which constructs a **noisy** instance at function scope. Then **func()** returns, destroying the function scope **noisy** instance. When execution leaves the curly-brace block, it pauses just long enough to destroy the **noisy** instance on its way past:

```
noisy n("block local");
func("function local 3");
```

9. After the block, **main()** returns, which also destroys the **noisy** instance in **main()**'s scope.

There isn't any visible code corresponding to this, but the two global **noisy** instances are destroyed, in the reverse order of construction.

10. The completed program is reproduced below.

```
#include <iostream>
using namespace std;

class noisy
{
    char const* s_;
public:
    noisy(char const* s)
    { cout << "constructing " << s << endl; s_ = s; }
    ~noisy()
    { cout << "destroying " << s_ << endl; }
};

void func(char const* s)
{
    noisy func(s);
}

noisy f("global 1");
noisy ff("global 2");

int main()
{
    noisy n1("main() function local 1");
    func("function local 2");

    {
        noisy n("block local");
        func("function local 3");
    }

    return 0;
}
```

11. Compile and run the program. Its output is as follows, along with a description of what you are seeing:

constructing global 1	Before main() starts, constructing f
constructing global 2	Before main(), constructing ff
constructing main() function local 1	main() function scope
constructing function local 2	inside the call to func() in main()
destroying function local 2	before func() exits
constructing block local	inside the block in main
constructing function local 3	in the call to func() in the block
destroying function local 3	exiting the call to func() in the block
destroying block local	exiting the block
destroying main() function local 1	end of main()
destroying global 2	after main(), destroying ff
destroying global 1	after main, destroying f

Figure 7.1: Output of the program in exercise 49 with corresponding description

So, here's what we learned from this exercise:

- The lifetime of a variable—which also means a dynamic variable if suitably wrapped in a class instance—can extend for all of a program's execution, or all of **main()** and any functions called from within **main()**, or all of any other function, or a block within a function.

- We can use curly braces to create block scopes within the scope of a function where different declarations have effect. This is useful for much more than dynamic variables.

- Since the lifetime of a variable begins when it is declared, we can further constrain a variable's lifetime by declaring the variable in the middle of a block where we want its lifetime to begin.

Any place you see an instance of **class noisy** say **constructing**..., remember that it is also an opportunity to create a dynamic variable whose pointer is owned by a class such as **noisy** and has the same lifetime as that **noisy** instance.

When an instance of **class noisy** says **destroying**..., that is an opportunity to destroy a dynamic variable with the same lifetime as that **noisy** instance.

It is just barely possible to imagine a need for a dynamic variable to have a lifetime other than what is possible using the RAII class illustrated by this example, but the cost in terms of code review and debugging to maintain total freedom is rarely worth it because RAII is so powerful.

Exercise 50: Owned Pointers in Data Structures

The program in this exercise shows how to manage the lifetime and ownership of dynamic variables in a data structure. Data structures that own their dynamic content are a frequently occurring pattern in C++ development. In this exercise, the **numeric_list** class owns all the dynamically created **numeric_item** instances that make up the list.

> **Note**
>
> The complete code for this exercise can be found here: https://packt.live/2QIrBYG.

A common C++ idiom is that one class defines the data structure while another class defines the items in the data structure. In languages that are not so object-oriented, it's common for programmers to declare a record structure for the data structure items while a simple pointer points to the root of the data structure.

In C++, you can attach member functions that act on the whole data structure, for example to print or delete it. **numeric_list::head_** is an owned pointer to **numeric_item**. When an instance of **numeric_list** is destroyed, the destructor deletes each dynamic variable in the list. The **next_** pointers in the individual **numeric_item** instances are not owned pointers; all the instances are owned by the **head_** pointer in **numeric_list**:

1. Enter the default **main()** function and the definition of struct **numeric_item**. You have seen these before, at the end of the *Chapter 6, Dynamic Variables*:

```
#include <iostream>

using namespace std;

struct numeric_item
{
    int value_;
    numeric_item* next_;
};
int main()
{
    return 0;
}
```

2. Enter a definition of class **numeric_list**:

```
class numeric_list
{
    numeric_item* head_;
public:
    numeric_list() : head_(nullptr) {}
    ~numeric_list();
    void print();
    void add(int v);
    numeric_item* find(int v);
};
```

numeric_list has a private member variable–a pointer to **numeric_item** called **head_**. Its public interface has a constructor, a destructor, a **void** function called **print()**, a **void** function called **add()**, and a function called **find()** that takes an **int** argument and returns an unowned pointer to **numeric_item**, which might be **nullptr**.

3. The functions in **numeric_list** are declared in the class definition for **numeric_list** but are defined outside the class definition, the way you would do if the class definition was in a header file while the member functions were defined in a **.cpp** file. When defined in this way, the compound function name with **numeric_list** and **::**, must be added to the front of the function name as it appears inside the class definition.

> **Note**
>
> In Java, all member functions must be defined inside the class definition. This syntax works in C++ too, but it is not a familiar style to most C++ developers. C++ developers are used to the class definition being a concise overview of the class and the member function definitions appearing elsewhere. Most developers put template member functions in the class definition. Some developers put short member functions in the class definition.

The destructor function is called implicitly by the C++ runtime system, but if you were to call it explicitly, its name would be **~numeric_list()**. Because **head_** is an owned pointer, the destructor must delete any dynamic variables owned by the pointer which, in this case, is each element of the list. The destructor walks the list, repeatedly removing the first item from the list, and then deleting that removed item.

The destructor looks like this:

```
numeric_list::~numeric_list()
{
    while (head_ != nullptr)
    {
        numeric_item* p = head_;
        head_ = head_->next_;
        cout << "deleting " << p->value_ << endl;
        delete p;
    }
}
```

It is a common mistake to delete **head_**, and then say **head_ = head_->next_;**. The problem with this seemingly simple notation is that after you delete **head_**, it no longer points to anything. I've seen code with this error run. I've also seen it fail.

4. The **print()** function is the same as in the exercise in the last chapter. It is reproduced here:

```
void numeric_list::print()
{
    for (numeric_item* p = head_; p != nullptr; p = p->next_)
    {
        cout << p->value_ << " ";
    }
    cout << endl;
}
```

5. The **add()** function creates a new **numeric_item** instance and adds it to the head of the list:

```
void numeric_list::add(int v)
{
    numeric_item* newp = new numeric_item;
    newp->value_ = v;
    newp->next_ = head_;
    head_ = newp;
}
```

6. The **find()** function iterates through the list looking for an item that has the same value as the **v** argument. It returns an unowned pointer to the found item, or **nullptr** if no item is found:

```
numeric_item* numeric_list::find(int v)
{
    for (numeric_item* p = head_; p != nullptr; p = p->next_)
    {
        if (p->value_ == v)
            return p;
    }
    return nullptr;
}
```

Why is this pointer returned by **find()** unowned? Deleting this pointer would damage the list. The previous list item would point to something that was no longer valid, so the program's behavior would be undefined. Even if the program didn't crash before then **numeric_item**'s destructor would eventually double-delete the already deleted item, leaving the program a flaming wreck.

How does a developer who did not write this list class know that the pointer returned by **find()** is unowned? Well, they don't know, unless the developer who wrote the class documents it. A comment with the function's declaration in the class definition might say, **// returns unowned pointer to list_item, or nullptr**.

Any time a member function of a container class, such as **numeric_list**, returns an unowned pointer is an opportunity for errors. The developer must ensure that unowned pointers are not used after the container class is destroyed. As will be shown later, both the unowned pointer variable and the list container are destroyed at the same time—as execution leaves **main()**—so in this case, the use of the unowned pointer does not cause a problem.

7. The next step is to begin entering the body of **main()**. First, declare an instance of **numeric_list** called **l**. This function-local variable will be destroyed when **main()** returns:

```
numeric_list l;
```

8. Create a **for** loop to add five items to the list, and then print out the list:

```
for (int i = 1; i < 6; ++i)
{
    l.add(i);
}
l.print();
```

9. Declare a **numeric_item** pointer called **p**, and assign to **p** the value returned by **l.find(4)**. The value in **p** is an unowned pointer. We already know **find()** will discover an item with this value because we added it moments ago. Output a message if the returned pointer is not **nullptr**, just to be sure:

```
numeric_item* p = l.find(4);
if (p != nullptr)
    cout << "found numeric_item 4" << endl;
```

That's it. When **main()** returns, **p** is still pointing to an item in **l**. **p** isn't deleted, but that's fine because **p** is an unowned pointer.

As **main()** returns, **l**'s destructor is called. Since **l** has an owned pointer, **l**'s destructor must delete anything it points to, which is the entire list.

10. Compile and run the program. Its output is reproduced here:

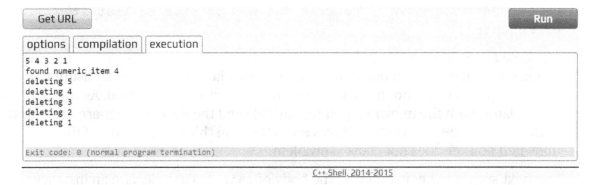

Figure 7.2: Output of the program in exercise 50

As expected, the program inserted five items into the list, and five items were output by **print()**. Item **4** was found in the list, and the list's destructor deleted the five items.

An unowned pointer is an unsafe pointer. There is absolutely nothing *preventing* a developer from holding onto an unowned pointer after the owned pointer that refers to it has been destroyed and the dynamic variable has been deleted. C++ developers must accept the responsibility to ensure that this doesn't happen in exchange for fast execution of their code.

But how does the developer know that this unowned pointer isn't pointing to garbage? We can easily see the lifetime of the owned pointer inside **l**. It is the whole of **main()**. That's essentially the whole program. What about the lifetime of the unowned pointer, **p**? It goes from its point of declaration, where it is initialized to a value, to the end of **main()**. There is no chance of using **p** when it points to garbage. The analysis would be the same if **l** and **p** were declared in function or block scope.

> **Note**
>
> You will find people who don't like to write comments who will claim that the code should be its own documentation. This dangerous advice ignores the fact that the program itself does not document things such as lifetime and ownership of dynamic variables.

Sometimes, a function reads a file, accepts an input, or in some other way collects data that becomes a dynamic variable. When this happens, the owning pointer may be function-local. A transfer of ownership occurs when a pointer to the dynamic variable is returned. Nothing in the C++ code tells you when the raw pointer returned by a function is an owned pointer. You read the documentation or comments with the function, or you realize that since the function is returning a zillion-byte buffer that was not an argument, it must be an owned pointer.

Exercise 51: Transfer of Ownership

This exercise provides an example where a program must transfer ownership of a raw pointer. Here are the steps to complete the exercise:

> **Note**
>
> The complete code for this exercise can be found here: https://packt.live/2s0Kvzs.

1. Enter the skeleton **main()** program:

```
#include <iostream>

using namespace std;

int main()
{
    return 0;
}
```

2. Add an **include** directive for **<cstring>** because this program uses string functions:

```
#include <cstring>
```

3. Define a **noisy** class called **noisy_and_big**. It differs from the usual **noisy** class by having a 10,000-byte **char** array, simulating a **struct** so big that it has to be allocated dynamically:

```
struct noisy_and_big
{
    noisy_and_big() { cout << "constructing noisy" << endl; }
    ~noisy_and_big() { cout << "destroying noisy" << endl; }
    char big_buffer_[10000];
};
```

4. Define a function to create **noisy_and_big** instances:

```
noisy_and_big* get_noisy_and_big(char const* str)
{
    noisy_and_big* ownedp = new noisy_and_big;
    strcpy(ownedp->big_buffer_, str);
}
```

In real code, the buffer would be filled by reading a file or getting a network packet, but for this brief demonstration, just write a string into the buffer. Also in real code, we would have to check the length of **str** before we used **strcpy()** to copy it into **big_buffer**.

When the **noisy_and_big** instance is created, **ownedp** is its owner. However, **ownedp** only lives until the end of the function. **get_noisy_and_big()** must either delete **ownedp** (which doesn't make sense) or conceptually transfer ownership to the caller.

5. Enter the body of **main()**. The first statement declares a pointer called **newownedp** and assigns it the result of calling **get_noisy_and_big()**. Now, **newownedp** is the owner. Output a message to show that the contents of the buffer have arrived:

```
noisy_and_big* newownedp = get_noisy_and_big("a big, big buffer");
cout << "noisy and big: " << newownedp->big_buffer_ << endl;
```

6. Production code does something useful with the **noisy_and_big** instance, and then it's time to delete the owned pointer:

```
delete newownedp;
```

7. The completed program is reproduced below.

```
#include <iostream>
#include <cstring>

using namespace std;

struct noisy_and_big
{
    noisy_and_big() { cout << "constructing noisy" << endl; }
    ~noisy_and_big() { cout << "destroying noisy" << endl; }
    char big_buffer_[10000];
};

noisy_and_big* get_noisy_and_big(char const* str)
{
    noisy_and_big* ownedp = new noisy_and_big;
    strcpy(ownedp->big_buffer_, str);
}

int main()
{
    noisy_and_big* newownedp = get_noisy_and_big("a big, big buffer");
    cout << "noisy and big: " << newownedp->big_buffer_ << endl;

    delete newownedp;

    return 0;
}
```

8. Compile and run the program. Its output is reproduced here:

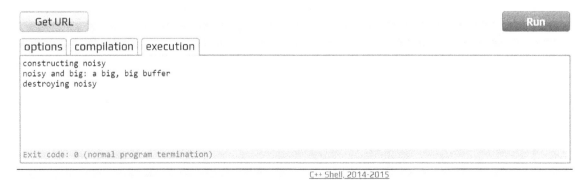

Figure 7.3: Output of the program in exercise 51

The `noisy_and_big` instance is constructed in `get_noisy_and_big()` and destroyed in `main()`. Ownership was transferred from one owning pointer to another. It is important that there is nothing about C++ that indicates the transfer. It's all about documentation and convention.

The discipline of tracking ownership of dynamic variables is one of the things that separated experienced C++ developers from novices for the first 20 years of C++ development. Most people agree that lack of automated support for tracking ownership was far from optimal. Fortunately, there are better solutions, which we will examine next.

Smart Pointers — Automated Ownership of Dynamic Variables

Previous exercises have demonstrated that an owned pointer can be wrapped in a class instance, which can delete the dynamic variables owned by the pointer when the class is destroyed. It is possible to take this design a step further and create a class consisting only of an owned pointer to a dynamic variable. Such an object is called a smart pointer.

The design of the smart pointers in the C++ standard library takes advantage of most of the advanced features of C++, including operator functions, template metaprogramming, move semantics, variadic templates, and perfect forwarding. The design is too advanced to cover in this brief course. However, the result is a thing that looks and acts much like a raw pointer but deletes its owned dynamic variable when the smart pointer is destroyed.

unique_ptr<>

`unique_ptr<>` is a smart pointer template class that owns a dynamic variable. In C++, a template class is a kind of macro that can generate a family of classes. Templates are an important topic in C++ programming. They are covered in *Chapter 11, Templates*. For now, what's most important is that you include a library of template classes with an `include` directive, then specialize the template for a specific type by naming the type in angle brackets in a template class declaration as shown in the following:

```
#include <memory>

unique_ptr<MyClass> pMyClass;
```

The declaration creates a smart pointer to a dynamic MyClass variable. `unique_ptr<>` generates code that is just as fast as code for a raw pointer. It is called `unique_ptr` because it does not share ownership.

Among the many advantages of **unique_ptr<>** over raw pointers are:

- **unique_ptr<>** owns its dynamic variable and deletes the dynamic variable when the **unique_ptr<>** is destroyed.

- **unique_ptr<>** never contains random bits. Either it contains **nullptr** or it contains a pointer to a dynamic variable.

- **unique_ptr<>** does not contain a dangling pointer after its dynamic variable is deleted. It deletes the dynamic variable on destruction, or **unique_ptr::reset()** deletes the dynamic variable and sets the pointer inside of **unique_ptr<>** to **nullptr**.

- **unique_ptr<>** documents ownership. Raw pointers are unowned pointers in a program that uses **unique_ptr<>** for owned pointers.

Exercise 52: Working with unique_ptr<>

This exercise constructs and destroys some **unique_ptr<>** instances pointing to dynamic variables and dynamic arrays, and shows how to transfer ownership of a dynamic variable from one **unique_ptr<>** to another:

> **Note**
>
> The complete code for this exercise can be found here: https://packt.live/2D3A1lk.

1. Enter the skeleton **main()** program:

   ```
   #include <iostream>

   using namespace std;

   int main()
   {
       return 0;
   }
   ```

2. The **<memory>** header is where the **unique_ptr<>** template is defined. Include **<memory>** below **#include <iostream>**:

   ```
   #include <memory>
   ```

3. This program uses one of the string functions from the **<cstring>** header. Include **<cstring>**:

   ```
   #include <cstring>
   ```

4. Enter a definition for **class noisy**. This version of **noisy** has two different constructors: a default constructor and one that takes an int argument. In this exercise, we will show off some of the options of the **new**-expression by constructing **noisy** in both ways:

```
struct noisy
{
    noisy() { cout << "default constructing noisy" << endl; }
    noisy(int i) { cout << "constructing noisy: arg " << i << endl; }
    ~noisy() { cout << "destroying noisy" << endl; }
};
```

5. Inside **main()**, first declare a **unique_ptr<noisy>** instance called **u1** and initialize it to a new **noisy** instance. This **new**-expression calls **noisy**'s default constructor.:

```
unique_ptr<noisy> u1(new noisy);
```

6. Declare a **unique_ptr<noisy>** instance called **u2**. The default constructor for **unique_ptr<>** sets this pointer to **nullptr**. Then, set **u2** to a new **noisy** instance initialized to **100**. using the **noisy** constructor that takes an **int** argument. The member function **unique_ptr::reset()** deletes any dynamic variable the **unique_ptr** currently refers to, and then sets the **unique_ptr** to point to the argument of **reset()**. In this case, **u2** points to **nullptr**, so the effect of **reset()** is to set **u2** to the new **noisy** instance:

```
unique_ptr<noisy> u2;
u2.reset(new noisy(100));
```

7. Declare a **unique_ptr<>** instance to a **noisy** array called **u3**, and initialize it to a new dynamic array of three **noisy** instances:

```
unique_ptr<noisy[]> u3(new noisy[3]);
```

There are several things to notice about this declaration. For one thing, a **unique_ptr<>** to an array is declared differently to a **unique_ptr<>** to an ordinary variable so that the template will select the **delete[]**-expression appropriate for deleting arrays. Another thing to notice is that **unique_ptr<>** never creates a dynamic variable itself, but rather accepts ownership of a dynamic variable created outside of **unique_ptr<>**. In the next exercise, we will see the **make_unique()** function, which creates both the **unique_ptr<>** instance and the dynamic variable at the same time.

8. Declare a **unique_ptr** instance to a **noisy** array called **u4**. Initialize it to a new dynamic array of two **noisy** instances, the first initialized to 1, and the second default-initialized because there are not enough initializers in the initializer list:

```
unique_ptr<noisy[]> u4(new noisy[2]{1});
```

9. Declare a **unique_ptr<noisy>** instance called **u5**. It is default-initialized to **nullptr**:

```
unique_ptr<noisy> u5;
```

10. Output the raw pointer values of **u1** and **u5**, using the **get()** member function to get a raw, unowned pointer:

```
cout << "before transfer of ownership u1 = " << u1.get()
     << ", u5 = " << u5.get() << endl;
```

11. Transfer ownership of the dynamic variable in **u1** to **u5**. Use the **release()** member function to release ownership of the dynamic variable of **u1** and return an owned raw pointer. This becomes the argument to **reset()**, which deletes the dynamic variable owned by **u5** and then accepts ownership of the owned raw pointer from **u1**. Since **u5** was constructed by default, its previous value was **nullptr**:

```
u5.reset(u1.release());
```

12. Output the raw pointers of **u1** and **u5** following the transfer of ownership:

```
cout << "after transfer of ownership u1 = " << u1.get()
     << ", u5 = " << u5.get() << endl;
```

13. Transfer ownership of **u5** back to **u1** by a different method. Use the function **std::move()** to move **u5** to **u1** using move semantics. Move semantics is an advanced C++ concept that is too complex to cover in this book, but it's one that is worth your attention in the future. A **unique_ptr<>** instance returned by a function also transfers ownership by move semantics. At the end of this statement, **u5** is **nullptr**:

```
u1 = move(u5);
```

14. Output **u1** and **u5** after the transfer:

```
cout << "after second transfer u1 = " << u1.get()
     << ", u5 = " << u5.get() << endl;
```

15. Create a **unique_ptr<>** instance to a **char** array. This is a common idiom for creating dynamically sized buffers without having to worry about deleting them later. This buffer will be automatically deleted as **main()** returns. Put a short string in the buffer and use **get()** to output the **char** pointer as a string:

```
unique_ptr<char[]> buf(new char[20]);
strcpy(buf.get(), "xyzzy");
cout << "buf = " << buf.get() << endl;
```

When **main()** returns, all the **unique_ptr<>** instances are destroyed, and their dynamic contents are deleted. The completed program looks like this.

```cpp
#include <iostream>
#include <memory>
#include <cstring>

using namespace std;

struct noisy
{
    noisy() { cout << "default constructing noisy" << endl; }
    noisy(int i) { cout << "constructing noisy: arg " << i << endl; }
    ~noisy() { cout << "destroying noisy" << endl; }
};

int main()
{
    unique_ptr<noisy> u1(new noisy);
    unique_ptr<noisy> u2;
    u2.reset(new noisy(100));
    unique_ptr<noisy[]> u3(new noisy[3]);
    unique_ptr<noisy[]> u4(new noisy[2]{1});
    unique_ptr<noisy> u5;

    cout << "before transfer of ownership u1 = " << u1.get()
         << ", u5 = " << u5.get() << endl;

    u5.reset(u1.release());
    cout << "after transfer of ownership u1 = " << u1.get()
         << ", u5 = " << u5.get() << endl;

    u1 = move(u5);
    cout << "after second transfer u1 = " << u1.get()
         << ", u5 = " << u5.get() << endl;

    unique_ptr<char[]> buf(new char[20]);
    strcpy(buf.get(), "xyzzy");
    cout << "buf = " << buf.get() << endl;
    return 0;
}
```

16. Compile and run the completed program. Its output looks as shown below. Of course, different runs of the program may print out different hexadecimal pointer addresses:

```
Get URL                                                                    Run

options  compilation  execution
default constructing noisy
constructing noisy: arg 100
default constructing noisy
default constructing noisy
default constructing noisy
constructing noisy: arg 1
default constructing noisy
before transfer of ownership u1 = 0x3484d90, u5 = 0
after transfer of ownership u1 = 0, u5 = 0x3484d90
after second transfer u1 = 0x3484d90, u5 = 0
buf = xyzzy
destroying noisy
destroying noisy
destroying noisy
destroying noisy
destroying noisy
destroying noisy
destroying noisy

Exit code: 0 (normal program termination)
```

C++ Shell, 2014-2015

Figure 7.4: Output of the program in exercise 52

The first line of output is from **u1**. Then, **u2** is constructed with **100** as the constructor argument. The next three lines are the three members of the noisy array in **u3**. The next two lines are the noisy array in **u4**. The transfer from **u1** to **u5** and back appears as expected. The buffer is output. Then, the **noisy** instance in **u1**, the **noisy** instance in **u2**, the three **noisy** instances in **u3**, and the two **noisy** instances in **u4** are deleted. **u5** was **nullptr**.

What is notable about this is that the developer did not have to delete anything. The smart pointers kept track of things and deleted the dynamic variables they owned automatically.

> **Note**
>
> The **delete**-expression that disposes of the dynamic variable owned by a **unique_ptr<>** instance is hidden inside the definition of **unique_ptr<>**. Some software teams take advantage of this to run automated tools over a large code base, looking for instances of the **delete** keyword to flag for special attention during code reviews. Eliminating all explicit **delete**-expressions in favor of using smart pointers is likely to improve the quality of a code base.

`unique_ptr<>` does not solve every problem. For instance, the default version of `unique_ptr<>` isn't smart enough to delete all the members of a linked list data structure when the list head is destroyed. The `unique_ptr<>` template has a seldom-used optional second argument, called a `deleter`, which is a function to be called when the `unique_ptr` instance is destroyed. This allows the extension of `unique_ptr<>` to delete whole data structures and allows it to do other things, such as close files that are open.

The widespread adoption of smart pointers in C++ marked a significant improvement in the reliability of C++ programs versus older C and C++ code bases. Even though C++ is an "unsafe" language, teams following modern C++ practices have few problems with memory leaks. We will discover in a future chapter that smart pointers are particularly powerful when combined with C++ exception handling.

make_unique()

`make_unique()` is a template function that creates a dynamic variable and assigns it to a `unique_ptr` instance of the appropriate type, which is then returned. Just as `unique_ptr<>` hides the `delete` expression in its definition, `make_unique()` does the same for the `new` expression. This allows teams to use a coding standard that forbids "naked" `new`- and `delete`-expressions to improve code quality.

Exercise 53: Using make_unique()

This exercise demonstrates how to use `make_unique()` to hide new expressions. Here are the steps to complete the exercise:

> **Note**
>
> The complete code for this exercise can be found here: https://packt.live/35nhLiQ.

1. Enter the skeleton `main()` program:

```
#include <iostream>
using namespace std;

int main()
{
    return 0;
}
```

2. The **<memory>** header is where the **unique_ptr<>** template is defined. Include **<memory>** below **#include <iostream>**:

   ```
   #include <memory>
   ```

3. Enter a definition for class **noisy**:

   ```
   struct noisy
   {
       noisy() { cout << "constructing noisy" << endl; }
       ~noisy() { cout << "destroying noisy" << endl; }
   };
   ```

4. Inside **main()**, declare a **unique_ptr<noisy>** instance called **u1**, and initialize it to a new **noisy** instance:

   ```
   unique_ptr<noisy> u1(new noisy);
   ```

5. Declare a **unique_ptr<noisy>** called **u2**. Assign it the value returned from a call to **make_unique<noisy>()**:

   ```
   unique_ptr<noisy> u2 = make_unique<noisy>();
   ```

6. Declare a **unique_ptr<>** instance to a **noisy** array called **u3**, using the **auto** keyword to avoid re-entering the type of the variable, then assign the value returned by **make_unique<noisy[]>(4)**, which creates an array of four **noisy** instances:

   ```
   auto u3 = make_unique<noisy[]>(4);
   ```

   Compare the declaration of **u3** to the previous line declaring **u2**: The **auto** keyword in the declaration of **u3** allows the developer to omit the type name because it can be deduced from the initializer. The advantage of this modern C++ syntax becomes clear the first time the developer declares something with a long type-name or a bunch of template parameters.

7. The completed program looks like this.

   ```
   #include <iostream>
   #include <memory>

   using namespace std;

   struct noisy
   {
       noisy() { cout << "constructing noisy" << endl; }
       ~noisy() { cout << "destroying noisy" << endl; }
   ```

```
};

int main()
{
    unique_ptr<noisy> u1(new noisy);
    unique_ptr<noisy> u2 = make_unique<noisy>();
    auto u3 = make_unique<noisy[]>(4);
    return 0;
}
```

8. Compile and run the completed program. Its output looks like this:

Figure 7.5: Output of the program in exercise 53

The first declaration creates one **noisy** instance. The second creates one more. The third creates four. As **main()** exits, all six are deleted as the **unique_ptr<>** instances are destroyed.

make_unique() isn't perfect. For instance, the array version can only default-initialize a dynamic array. **make_unique()** has the valuable property of hiding the **new** keyword. **make_unique()** exists partly for stylistic compatibility with **make_shared()**, which is covered later.

In the next exercise, we'll see how smart pointers help to simplify the implementation of classes, often eliminating the need to write destructors.

unique_ptr<> as a Class Member Variable

When a class is destroyed, its destructor function is called, destroying the class instance; then the destructors of each member variable are called, destroying the members. The destructors for basic types, such as **int** or **char**, don't do anything. But, when a member is a class instance, the member's destructor is called.

When a class member is a smart pointer, the smart pointer's destructor is called automatically when the class instance containing it is destroyed. The developer need not write any code to delete the dynamic variable owned by the smart pointer.

If all the class members that contain dynamic variables are smart pointers, the class destructor may be empty. Even if the destructor is empty, the member destructors run when a class instance is destroyed. Smart pointers make your class's code look simple and streamlined, and make the code easier to review. Once you start using smart pointers, you'll never want to go back.

Exercise 54: Using unique_ptr<> as a Class Member Variable

This exercise involves creating a simple class whose members are smart pointers to illustrate the simplified class syntax that results when smart pointers are class members:

> **Note**
>
> The complete code for this exercise can be found here: https://packt. live/2DaBO7W.

1. Enter the skeleton **main()** program:

    ```
    #include <iostream>
    using namespace std;

    int main()
    {
        return 0;
    }
    ```

2. The **unique_ptr<>** template is defined in the **<memory>** header. Include **<memory>** following **#include <iostream>**:

    ```
    #include <memory>
    ```

3. This program uses one of the string functions from the **<cstring>** header. Include **<cstring>** as follows:

    ```
    #include <cstring>
    ```

4. Enter the usual definition for class **noisy**:

```
struct noisy
{
    noisy() { cout << "constructing noisy" << endl; }
    ~noisy() { cout << "destroying noisy" << endl; }
};
```

5. Enter a definition for class **autobuf**, which is intended to model a class containing a very large buffer, as if the data were read in from a file or a network packet:

```
class autobuf
{
    unique_ptr<noisy> np_;
    unique_ptr<char[]> ptr_;
public:
    autobuf(char const* str);
    char* get();
};
```

The class has two member variables. One member, called np, is a **unique_ptr<>** to an instance of class **noisy** . The presence of this noisy instance prints a message that makes it easier to see when an instance of **autobuf** is being constructed or destroyed. The other is a **unique_ptr<>** instance to a **char** array, called **ptr_**. Now, **autobuf** has a default constructor and an accessor function called **get()** which returns an unowned pointer to the buffer. The destructor of **autobuf** is automatically generated by the compiler. The compiler gets it right and we don't have to think about it at all.

6. Next, define the two member functions of **autobuf**. The two lines after the : are the constructor initializer list. This provides initial values for the two member variables. **np_** gets a new dynamic **noisy** instance, and **ptr_** gets a **char** buffer big enough to hold the constructor's **str** argument:

```
autobuf::autobuf(char const* str)
  : np_(make_unique<noisy>()),
    ptr_(make_unique<char[]>(strlen(str) + 1))
{
    strcpy(ptr_.get(), str);
}
```

7. The **get()** function returns an unowned pointer to the buffer using **unique_ptr<>**'s **get()** member function:

```
char* autobuf::get()
{
    return ptr_.get();
}
```

8. Inside **main()**, declare an **autobuf** instance called **buffer**. Initialize it to any handy literal string. Output the string in **buffer** using the **get()** member function of **buffer** to return a pointer to the **char** array:

```
autobuf buffer("my favorite test string");
cout << "Hello World! " << buffer.get() << endl;
```

9. The complete program is reproduced below.

```
#include <iostream>
#include <memory>
#include <cstring>

using namespace std;

struct noisy
{
    noisy() { cout << "constructing noisy" << endl; }
    ~noisy() { cout << "destroying noisy" << endl; }
};
class autobuf
{
    unique_ptr<noisy> np_;
    unique_ptr<char[]> ptr_;
public:
    autobuf(char const* str);
    char* get();
};

autobuf::autobuf(char const* str)
    : np_(make_unique<noisy>()),
      ptr_(make_unique<char[]>(strlen(str) + 1))
{
    strcpy(ptr_.get(), str);
}
char* autobuf::get()
```

```
    {
        return ptr_.get();
    }

    int main()
    {
        autobuf buffer("my favorite test string");
        cout << "Hello World! " << buffer.get() << endl;

        return 0;
    }
```

10. Compile and run the program. Its output is reproduced here:

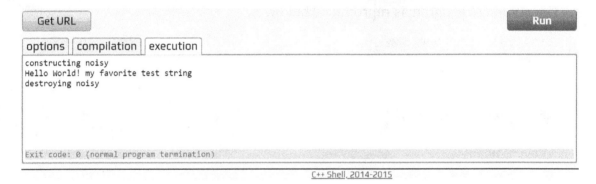

Figure 7.6: Output of the program in exercise 54

When **main()** begins to execute, the constructor for **autobuf** creates a new **noisy** instance, printing the first line of output. The output statement writes the second line of output, which includes the contents of **buffer**. Then, the execution leaves **main()**, which causes **buffer** to be destroyed. The destructor for **buffer**, which was generated by the compiler, destroys **np_** (the smart pointer to **noisy**), which deletes **noisy** and prints the third line of output, and **ptr_** (the smart pointer to the **char** array), which deletes the **char** array.

In this brief example, it might not seem like a big deal that the developer didn't have to write a destructor for **autobuf**. However, multiplied by many classes—some of which have several more member variables—it makes a difference because the developer didn't have to remember to add code to each destructor for every dynamic variable.

unique_ptr<> in Function Arguments and Return Values

It is typical to pass an unowned pointer to a function as a function argument because the pointer in the caller generally lives for the duration of the called function. A **unique_ptr<>** is dangerous to use as a function argument. If the actual argument is a **unique_ptr<>** instance, the function's formal argument will steal the value of the actual argument, leaving the actual argument equal to **nullptr**. If the function's actual argument is an unowned pointer, the **unique_ptr<>** argument will take ownership of the pointer and delete it when the function exits. This is almost never what the developer wants. Instead, make the function's formal argument an unowned pointer and use the **get()** member function of **unique_ptr<>** to get an unowned pointer to use as the function argument.

unique_ptr<> can be used when a function returns to indicate that the caller must take ownership of the returned dynamic variable.

Exercise 55: Using unique_ptr<> in Function Return Values

This exercise shows how to transfer ownership of a dynamic variable by returning a **unique_ptr<>** instance to it:

> **Note**
>
> The complete code for this exercise can be found here: https://packt. live/2OB8ZHm.

1. Enter the skeleton **main()** program:

    ```
    #include <iostream>
    using namespace std;

    int main()
    {
        return 0;
    }
    ```

2. **unique_ptr<>** is defined in the **<memory>** header. Include **<memory>** following **#include <iostream>**:

    ```
    #include <memory>
    ```

3. Define class **noisy**. We've seen this class before:

```
struct noisy
{
    noisy() { cout << "constructing noisy" << endl; }
    ~noisy() { cout << "destroying noisy" << endl; }
};
```

4. Create a function called **func()** which simulates a function that creates an owned pointer to a large data structure, perhaps by reading a file or receiving a network packet. **func()** takes no arguments and returns a **unique_ptr<>** instance:

```
unique_ptr<noisy> func()
{
    return make_unique<noisy>();
}
```

5. In **main()**, call **func()**, capturing the returned value. Use the **auto** keyword to avoid having to look up the exact type of the pointer returned by **func()**. Notice how streamlined this modern C++ syntax is:

```
auto u1 = func();
```

6. The completed program looks like this.

```
#include <iostream>
#include <memory>

using namespace std;

struct noisy
{
    noisy() { cout << "constructing noisy" << endl; }
    ~noisy() { cout << "destroying noisy" << endl; }
};

unique_ptr<noisy> func()
{
```

```
        return make_unique<noisy>();
    }

    int main()
    {
        auto u1 = func();
        return 0;
    }
```

7. The output of this program is reproduced here. A single instance of **noisy** is created inside **func()**, transferred to **u1**, and then deleted when **main()** returns, signaling the successful transfer of ownership:

Figure 7.7: Output of the program in exercise 55

In the vast majority of programming cases, a single owning pointer to a dynamic variable is appropriate. For the remaining cases, C++ offers a reference-counted **shared_ptr<>** for shared ownership.

Shared Ownership of Dynamic Variables

Prior to C++11, a more limited smart pointer called **auto_ptr<>** was available in the standard library. Among the many limitations of the **auto_ptr<>** template class was the fact that it could not be used as the element type in C++ standard library container classes or to transfer ownership of a dynamic variable out of a function. The standard library contained a reference-counted smart pointer class called **shared_ptr<>** that could be used in function arguments, return values, and standard library containers. For a few years, some teams used **shared_ptr<>** exclusively and forbade the use of raw pointers.

The problem with **shared_ptr<>** is that it is expensive in terms of runtime instructions. In addition to the dynamic variable that **shared_ptr<>** owns, it creates a second dynamic variable to hold a reference count, as shown in *Figure 7.8*, and deletes the reference count when the last reference is deleted. Every call into the memory allocator is quite expensive:

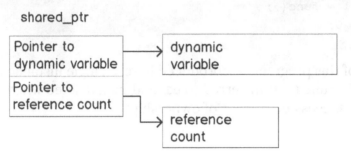

Figure 7.8: Simplified memory layout of shared_ptr

The code to increment and decrement the reference count uses expensive thread-safe interlocked increments and decrements. These are about 10 times slower than a simple increment or decrement. Each function argument that is a **shared_ptr<>** instance must be incremented as the function is called, and decremented as the function returns. For frequently called functions, the cost can become significant. The implementation of **shared_ptr<>** is made even more complex to support rarely used custom deleters and **weak_ptr<>** instances, which are not described in this chapter.

Exercise 56: Using shared_ptr<>

In this exercise, we create a few shared pointers and call a function that takes a shared pointer as an argument and returns a shared pointer. The idea of this program is that a function conditions a dynamic variable to never be **nullptr**, so the program doesn't have to test for **nullptr**:

> **Note**
>
> The complete code for this exercise can be found here: https://packt.live/2ObtwDb.

1. Enter the skeleton **main()** program:

```
#include <iostream>

using namespace std;

int main()
```

```
{
    return 0;
}
```

2. The **shared_ptr<>** template is defined in the **<memory>** header. Include **<memory>** below **#include <iostream>**:

```
#include <memory>
```

3. Define a function **func()** that takes a **shared_ptr<>** to a **char** array as argument and returns a **shared_ptr<>** to a **char** array:

```
shared_ptr<char[]> func(shared_ptr<char[]> str)
{
}
```

4. Inside **func()**, test whether **str** is equal to **nullptr**. The expression **!str** returns **true** if **str** is **nullptr**:

```
if (!str)
{
}
```

5. If **str** is **nullptr**, reset its value to a new one-character array. Set the value of the character to the null-terminator character, **'\0'**:

```
str.reset(new char[1]);
str[0] = '\0';
```

6. Inside **main()**, create a **shared_ptr<>** instance to a **char** array called **null**. The default constructor of **shared_ptr<>** sets **null** initially to **nullptr**:

```
shared_ptr<char[]> null;
```

7. Test whether **null** is equal to **nullptr**. This time we perform the test by getting the unowned pointer and comparing it to **nullptr** instead of using the expression **!null**. If **null** is equal to **nullptr**, print a message:

```
if (null.get() == nullptr)
    cout << "null is equal to nullptr" << endl;
```

8. Call **func()** with **null** as the argument. Create an **auto** variable called **result1** to receive the value returned by **func()**:

```
auto result1 = func(null);
```

9. Output a message if **result1** is equal to **nullptr**:

```
if (result1.get() == nullptr)
    cout << "result1 is equal to nullptr" << endl;
```

10. Call **func()** again with **result1** as the argument. Then, capture the return value in **result1**:

```
result1 = func(result1);
```

11. The resulting program looks like this:

```cpp
#include <iostream>
#include <memory>

using namespace std;

shared_ptr<char[]> func(shared_ptr<char[]> str)
{
    if (!str)
    {
        str.reset(new char[1]);
        str[0] = '\0';
    }
    return str;
}

int main()
{
    shared_ptr<char[]> null;
    if (null.get() == nullptr)
        cout << "null is equal to nullptr" << endl;
    auto result1 = func(null);
    if (result1.get() == nullptr)
        cout << "result1 is equal to nullptr" << endl;
    result1 = func(result1);

    return 0;
}
```

12. Compile and execute the program on a C++ compiler that supports C++17. Online compilers supporting C++17 include **Coliru** and **Tutorialspoint**. Unfortunately, cpp.sh is only a C++14 compiler and will not compile this code. The output looks like this:

```
ıl Result

$g++ -o main *.cpp
$main
null is equal to nullptr
```

Figure 7.9: Output of the program in exercise 56

This program looks simple, but there is a lot going on. We can't instrument **shared_ptr** to see it in action, so here is a description of the program execution:

- Create **shared_ptr** instance **null**. Its pointer is set to **nullptr**. Since it does not point to a dynamic variable, no allocation is needed for the dynamic variable or the reference count.

- Prove that **null** is empty by getting the raw pointer and verifying that it is equal to **nullptr**.

- Call **func()**. The actual argument, **null**, is copy-constructed into the formal argument, **str**. Since **null** is equal to **nullptr**, **str** also contains **nullptr**.

- Test whether **str** is equal to **nullptr**. Since it is, create a new dynamic **char** array and reset **str** to this value. **str** also creates a new dynamic variable to hold the reference count and sets the reference count to 1.

- Set the dynamic variable owned by **str** to the null terminator, **'\0'**.

- Return **str**. Now, **str** is copy-constructed into **result1**, which copies the pointers to the dynamic char array and the reference count into **str**, and increments its reference count to 2, since both **str** and **result1** are pointing to the dynamic array. Then, the destructor of **str** is called, which decrements the reference count of **str** to 1, and the function returns.

- Test whether **result1** is equal to **nullptr**. It is not equal to **nullptr** because it has just been set to a one-character dynamic array, so nothing is printed.

- Now call **func()** again.

- **result1** is copy-constructed into **str**. Since **result1** is not **nullptr**, its reference count is incremented to 2.

- **str** is tested for **nullptr**. Since **str** is not **nullptr** (it is a one-character array), the test fails.

- Return **str**. **str** is copy-constructed into **result1**. Remember that **str** and **result1** already point to the same **char** array and the same reference count. So, first, the reference count of the object about to be assigned is incremented to 3. Then, the reference count of the object about to be overwritten is decremented to 2. Then, **str** is destroyed, decrementing the reference count to 1. Since no reference count went to 0, nothing is deleted.

- Now **main()** returns. **result1** is destroyed, so the reference count of the object it owns is decremented to 0. The **char** array is deleted. The reference count is deleted.

- **null** is destroyed. It is already equal to **nullptr**, so nothing happens.

make_shared()

make_shared() is a template function that creates a dynamic variable and assigns it to a **shared_ptr<>** instance of the appropriate type. Just as **unique_ptr<>** and **shared_ptr<>** hide the **delete** expression in its definition, **make_shared()** does the same for the **new**-expression:

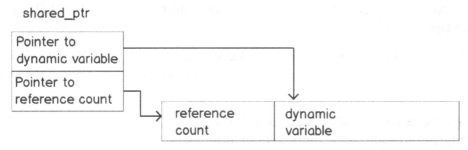

Figure 7.10: Simplified memory layout of a dynamic object and reference count after make_shared()

make_shared() has an additional capability of note. It allocates storage for both the dynamic variable and the reference count in a single object. Since creating dynamic objects is the most expensive C++ operation, cutting down the number of allocations can significantly improve the performance of code that uses **shared_ptr<>** heavily.

make_shared() has limitations. A dynamic array cannot be created as of C++17, though it is proposed for C++20. A deleter can't be specified.

Exercise 57: Using make_shared()

This exercise constructs a few dynamic variables using **make_shared()**:

> **Note**
>
> The complete code for this exercise can be found here: https://packt.live/2OyeFBO.

1. Enter the skeleton **main()** program:

```
#include <iostream>
using namespace std;

int main()
{
    return 0;
}
```

2. The **make_shared()** template function is defined in the **<memory>** header. Include **<memory>** following **#include <iostream>**:

```
#include <memory>
```

3. Enter a definition for class **noisy**:

```
struct noisy
{
    noisy() { cout << "constructing noisy" << endl; }
    ~noisy() { cout << "destroying noisy" << endl; }
};
```

4. Inside **main()**, declare a **shared_ptr<noisy>** instance called **u1**, and initialize it to a new **noisy** instance:

```
shared_ptr<noisy> u1(new noisy);
```

5. Declare a **shared_ptr<noisy>** instance called **u2**. Assign it the value returned from a call to **make_shared<noisy>()**:

```
shared_ptr<noisy> u2 = make_shared<noisy>();
```

6. Declare a **shared_ptr<noisy>** instance called **u3** and assign **u2** to it. Ownership of the **noisy** instance is shared between **u2** and **u3**:

```
shared_ptr<noisy> u3 = u2;
```

7. Release ownership of **u2**. Now, **u3** is the sole owner:

```
u2.reset();
```

8. The completed program looks like this.

```cpp
#include <iostream>
#include <memory>

using namespace std;

struct noisy
{
    noisy() { cout << "constructing noisy" << endl; }
    ~noisy() { cout << "destroying noisy" << endl; }
};

int main()
{
    shared_ptr<noisy> u1(new noisy);
    shared_ptr<noisy> u2 = make_shared<noisy>();
    shared_ptr<noisy> u3 = u2;
    u2.reset();
    return 0;
}
```

9. Compile and run the completed program. Its output looks like this:

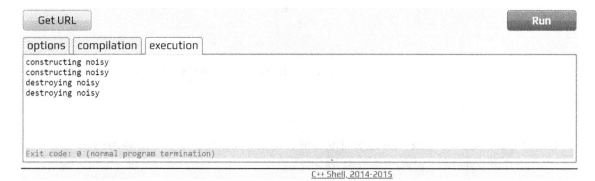

Figure 7.11: Output of program in exercise 56

As expected, two instances of **noisy** are created and two are destroyed.

Activity 7: Storing the Words of a Book Using Dynamic Variables

At the beginning of *Chapter 6, Dynamic Variables*, we looked at a data structure for storing all the words in a book without using dynamic variables. It was impossible to store every book, either because individual words might be too long or because the number of words might be too great, or both. With dynamic variables, these problems can be overcome.

In this activity, you will implement a program to store the words of a book that is not subject to either of the limitations just mentioned. This problem is similar to problems faced in the design of book readers, web browsers, and text editors.

The program must be able to reconstruct the input exactly. That is, it needs to record the number of spaces around each word and collect the words together on each line. The program shall have a function to print the book exactly as input.

The input to a book reader program would probably be a file containing the text in question. However, for this activity, the input to the program is an array of pointers to literal character strings. The literal character strings consist of non-space words separated by one or more spaces or string terminator characters (`'\0'`), each string representing one line of the book.

The C++ standard library defines container classes that might easily solve this problem, but please do not use them, even if you already know them. **std::string** would also be helpful, but don't use that either. The point of this activity is to test your knowledge of pointers and dynamic variables.

This sample input, a brief quotation from Hamlet, is enough to test your design without taxing your patience:

```
"What a piece of work is man, "
"   How noble in reason, how infinite in faculty,"
"In form and moving how express and admirable, "
"   In action how like an Angel, In apprehension how like a god."
"The beauty of the world.  The paragon of animals."
```

> **Note**
>
> The complete code for this activity can be found here: https://packt.live/339ahi6.

Here are some hints to help you complete the activity:

1. This is a big assignment, but it can be decomposed into parts. You need a data structure to hold a word containing a buffer containing the word string and a count of spaces. It must be able to output the word and spaces. You could just put them to **cout**, but putting them on to a string can make testing easier.

2. Then, you need a data structure that can hold a line of words. It must also be able to output the line. Finally, you need a data structure that can hold a whole book of lines, and you need to output the book. Making the classes you create similar to one another will help you find the structure in this assignment, which will make your work go faster.

3. Every word can be stored, along with the number of spaces that follow that word. How do you represent leading spaces? Consider a zero-length word.

4. What data structure should be used to hold a word? The text of the word should be a dynamic array of **char**. The number of trailing spaces can be an **int**. A smart pointer to the dynamic array would make deletion easy.

5. What data structure should be used to hold a line? A linked list of words would be an obvious choice, so a next pointer should be added to the two other fields that hold a word. The head node of the list should be a class containing a raw pointer with a destructor that deletes all the words of a line.

6. What data structure should be used to hold the entire book? A linked list of lines would be an appropriate choice. A dynamic array could be used, but then there would have to be code to copy the array to a larger array if the initial guess for the array's size was wrong. The head node of the book should be a class containing a raw pointer with a destructor that deletes all the lines of a book. You will want to add a next pointer to the line class.

7. How should a null-terminated string of characters be converted to a list of words? There are only three characters of interest in separating the string. Spaces come after each word. The null terminator comes at the end of the line. In a loop, you can set a pointer to the beginning of the word, and then step a second pointer looking for a space or null terminator. The difference between these pointers is the size of the word. Don't forget to add 1 for a null terminator.

8. You will need a function to produce a string representing the line from the list of words. You will need to know how many characters to allocate. You can find this out by counting the size of the word, plus the number of spaces for each word, and adding 1 for a null terminator at the end of the line. Then, you can copy words and spaces into this array. Since you need to know the length of each word, it is appropriate to store the number of characters of each word as another `int` in the word class.

> **Note**
>
> The solution to this activity can be found on page 534.

Summary

Pointers and dynamic variables are two of the most valuable tools in the basic C++ toolkit. They are worth the effort it takes to understand them and use them well. We learned that C++ does not enforce any discipline regarding the creation or deletion of dynamic variables. Developers can document the ownership of dynamic variables to bring some order to this chaos. We learned that a powerful way to manage ownership of dynamic variables is through the use of smart pointers, which tie the dynamic variable to an ordinary variable that is destroyed in a well-defined place. C++ is a powerful programming language because it offers a spectrum of choices, from bare-bones unsafe programming to expensive, automated smart library classes.

In the next chapter, we're going to take a deeper dive into the class type and object-oriented programming.

Classes and Structs

Overview

This chapter presents the fundamentals of structs and classes with the aid of practical examples and exercises. By the end of this chapter, you will be able to describe the differences between the class, struct and union types as well as how to correctly initialize and dispose of them using constructors and destructors.

Introduction

C++ is an extensive language, and each feature or paradigm you come to learn about will require in-depth knowledge to unlock its full potential. C++ has two kinds of types: built-in types and class types. Built-in types are any types that make up the core of the language, such as **int**, **float**, and **char**. Class types can be thought of as user-defined types; these are the types we create by declaring classes, structs, unions, and so on. Features and types from the C++ standard library (such as vectors and queues) are all class types built using C++, this shows the true power of the language and its ability to create types that feel as easy to use as the built-in types. Classes are the basis of object-oriented programming and covering them in more detail will help give you the required foundation to build upon. Having the ability to create robust types with solid interfaces is paramount to becoming a strong C++ programmer.

In *Chapter 6*, *Dynamic Variables* you learned about constructors and destructors and the use of **new** and **delete**, along with **new[]** and **delete[]**. In this chapter, you will learn how to use constructors to initialize class member variables, and how to use the destructor to clean up when a class is destroyed. Furthermore, you will learn about copy constructors and assignment operators, and how they relate to each other. Finally, you will learn how to declare and use the **union** type—an additional way to encapsulate data.

Classes versus Structs

In C++, you have a choice between declaring an object as a struct or a class. Both can utilize member functions and inheritance and have a mixture of public, protected, and private fields (more on these in later chapters). The main difference between a class and a struct is that a struct's member variables and methods are public, while a class's member variables and methods are private. In the following example, two equivalent data types are declared to show how a struct defaults (doesn't use public, private or protected keywords) its members to public while a class defaults to private:

```cpp
struct MyStruct
{
    int myInt = 0; // this defaults to public
};

class MyClass
{
```

```
    int myInt = 0; // this defaults to private
};

int main()
{
    MyStruct myStruct;
    MyClass myClass;

    // allowed - public
    int i = myStruct.myInt;

    // not allowed - private - compiler error
    int j = myClass.myInt;

    return 0;
}
```

These objects are identical except for this detail. An instance of a struct in C++ is exactly the same as an instance of a class. In compiled code, they are identical; memory usage, access time, and memory alignment are exactly the same, and there is no overhead associated with one over the other. A struct is traditionally used as a **Plain Old Data (POD)** type to help with backward compatibility with C libraries. A POD type is a class or struct that has no constructors, destructors, or virtual member functions. Structs are often used in this instance to indicate this intention, even though it does not fundamentally make any difference.

Unions

Classes and structs store data members in separate chunks of memory, while union types only allocate enough memory to store the largest data member. All members of a union share the same memory location; consequently, one chunk of allocated memory can be used to access different data types if they were to be laid out the same in memory. Unions are a data type that you don't see a lot of, but it is worth having some understanding of how they work. One useful advantage is being able to read data in one format and then access it in another.

The following example shows a union type called **Backpack**. This has an array of four integers and a struct named **data** that has four **int** members. Look closely at how the data can be set and read using both the array and the struct:

Example08_1.cpp

```cpp
1   #include <iostream>
2
3   using namespace std;
4
5   union Backpack
6   {
7       int contents[4];
8       struct
9       {
10          int food, water, key, flashlight;
11      }
12      data;
13  };
14
15  void DisplayContents(Backpack& backpack)
16  {
17      cout << "Has Food = " << backpack.data.food << endl;
18      cout << "Has Water = " << backpack.data.water << endl;
19      cout << "Has Key = " << backpack.data.key << endl;
20      cout << "Has Flashlight = " << backpack.data.flashlight << endl;
21  }
22
23  void UpdateBackpack(Backpack& backpack, int contents[4])
24  {
25      for(int i = 0; i < 4; i++)
26      {
27          backpack.contents[i] = contents[i] > backpack.contents[i]
28          ? contents[i] : backpack.contents[i];
29      }
30  }
31
32  void RemoveFromBackpack(Backpack& backpack, int idx)
33  {
34      backpack.contents[idx] = 0;
35  }
```

The complete example can be found here: https://packt.live/362LT3j

As demonstrated, unions can allow data to be stored and accessed in different ways. This isn't always the best idea, as we cannot guarantee that the size of a struct of integers is the same as that of an array of integers. Keep this in mind if unions crop up in some work you need to do.

Constructors and Destructors

Constructors are class functions used to initialize an object. Whenever an object is created, a constructor is called. Conversely, a destructor is called whenever an object is destroyed. Constructors differ from normal member functions in that they have the same name as the class they belong to. They do not have a return type and, as mentioned previously, they are called automatically whenever an instance of the class they belong to is created.

Constructors

This section will cover three different types of constructors:

- Default constructors
- Parameterized constructors
- Copy constructors

These types of constructors will be covered in order by creating a simple song track listing class that holds various information about a particular track.

Default Constructors

A default constructor is a constructor that takes no parameters, or a constructor where all parameters have default values. Let's look at a very simple class with a couple of member variables. The class is called **Track**, and it represents a music track (in other words, a song):

```cpp
#include <iostream>
#include <string>

using namespace std;

class Track
{
public:
    float lengthInSeconds;
    string trackName;
};
```

Here is the declaration of a class named **Track** with some data that might be included in relation to it: its name and length. Notice that there is no constructor defined for this class yet; at the very least, a default constructor is required to initialize an instance of a class.

As there is no explicitly defined default constructor in the preceding declaration of the **Track** class, the compiler will implicitly generate one for us. The following code will create an instance of the **Track** class:

```cpp
#include <iostream>

#include <string>

using namespace std;

class Track
{
public:
    float lengthInSeconds;
    string trackName;
};

int main()
{
    Track track;
    cout << "Track Name = " << track.trackName << endl;
    cout << "Track Length = " << track.lengthInSeconds << endl;

    return 0;
}
```

Running this code will output an empty string and a random float value, as shown in the following:

Figure 8.1: Output of the code

The compiler for **cpp.sh** initialized our float value to 0, and yet we cannot always guarantee that this will be the case for different compilers. The reason for this is that a compiler-generated default constructor will initialize the data members to a default value; in the case of a string that is a class type (more on that in later chapters), this has its own default constructor that initializes to **empty**, and in the case of a float, any random float value. This behavior is obviously not intended for even a default **Track** object; after all, whoever heard of a track that was **-4.71077e-33** (it is random, remember) seconds long and, outside of some obscure arthouse music, was called nothing?

Now, let's remedy this in the following exercise and create an explicit default constructor, initializing the member variables to something "sensible" or, at the very least, logical.

Exercise 58: Defining a Default Constructor

A default constructor has the same name as a class, has no parameters, and has no return type. In this exercise, we will create a constructor to be public so that we can call it from outside our class:

> **Note**
>
> The complete code for this exercise can be found here: https://packt.live/2KG6Icx.

1. First, we can create the stub of our constructor under the **public** keyword of our **Track** class:

```
Track()
{

}
```

2. We now must fill in our constructor in order to set our member variables to something sensible once the class is constructed. We will set the track length to **0** and the track name to **not set**:

```
Track()
{
    lengthInSeconds = 0.0f;
    trackName = "not set";
}
```

3. Now, we can use the **main** function from the last example to test that our constructor is being called:

```
int main()
{
    Track track;

    cout << "Track Name = " << track.trackName << endl;
    cout << "Track Length = " << track.lengthInSeconds << endl;

    return 0;
}
```

4. The complete code looks like this:

```
#include <iostream>
#include <string>

using namespace std;

class Track
{
public:
    float lengthInSeconds;
    string trackName;
    Track ()
    {
        lengthInSeconds = 0.0f;
        trackName = "not set";
    }
};

int main()
{
    Track track;
    cout << "Track Name = " << track.trackName << endl;
    cout << "Track Length = " << track.lengthInSeconds << endl;

    return 0;
}
```

5. Run the code. As can be seen from the following, our output reflects the values in our constructor:

Figure 8.2: Output reflecting the value from the constructor

This makes more sense and gives more control over what a default initialization of a **Track** instance should be. The definition of a default constructor also stated that it could be defined using parameters that all had default values. This type of constructor can be used as both a default and a parameterized constructor, and shall therefore be covered along with parameterized constructors.

Parameterized Constructors

Constructors can take parameters like any other function. A parameterized constructor is a constructor that takes at least one parameter. This is an extremely important concept and one that you will constantly take advantage of in C++. The current **Track** class constructor looks like this:

```
Track()
{
    lengthInSeconds = 0.0f;
    trackName = "not set";
}
```

Whenever an instance of **Track** is created, its member variables will be set to the values inside this constructor. Clearly, this isn't especially useful; song tracks invariably have different names and lengths. Parameterized constructors allow us to set what the **Track** object's member variables should be at initialization through the passing of parameters into the constructor.

You will recall that a default constructor can also take parameters as long as all of the parameters have default values. This enables a hybrid approach, where a constructor can be used as a default constructor or have parameters passed into it depending on the situation.

Exercise 59: Defining a Parameterized Constructor

A parameterized constructor has essentially the same syntax as a default constructor, with the difference being that, naturally, it takes parameters. Let's look at creating a parameterized constructor by adding parameters to the **Track** constructor:

> **Note**
>
> The complete code for this exercise can be found here: https://packt.live/35kthvj.

1. Write the existing **Track** constructor into the compiler:

```
Track()
{
    lengthInSeconds = 0.0f;
    trackName = "not set";
}
```

2. First, let's add some parameters that can set **lengthInSeconds** and **trackName**; we will need a **float** parameter and a **string** parameter:

```
Track(float lengthInSeconds, string trackName)
{
```

3. At this point, we want to be clearer on which variables are our class members and which are the passed-in parameters. To do this, we will prepend our variable names with **m_** (prepending variables with **m_** is a common way to denote a variable as a member variable):

```
// m_ prefix added to member variables, to avoid naming conflicts
//with parameter names

float m_lengthInSeconds;
string m_trackName;
```

4. And finally, we can set these member variables to the value of the passed-in parameters:

```
Track(float lengthInSeconds, string trackName)
{
    m_lengthInSeconds = lengthInSeconds;
    m_trackName = trackName;
}
```

5. Now, let's test this with a new **main** function. We will use the same code as we did for the default constructor exercise, but now, when creating our **Track** instance, we must use the parameterized constructor. We no longer have a default constructor because, as we have defined our own constructor, the compiler won't generate a default for us:

```cpp
int main()
{
    Track track(200.0f, "Still Alive");

    cout << "Track Name = " << track.m_trackName << endl;
    cout << "Track Length = " << track.m_lengthInSeconds << endl;

    return 0;
}
```

6. The complete code looks like this:

```cpp
#include <iostream>
#include <string>

using namespace std;

class Track
{
public:
    // m_ prefix added to member variables, to avoid naming conflicts
    //with parameter names

    float m_lengthInSeconds;
    string m_trackName;

    Track(float lengthInSeconds, string trackName)
    {
        m_lengthInSeconds = lengthInSeconds;
        m_trackName = trackName;
    }
};

int main()
{
    Track track(200.0f, "Still Alive");

    cout << "Track Name = " << track.m_trackName << endl;
```

```
        cout << "Track Length = " << track.m_lengthInSeconds << endl;

        return 0;
}
```

7. Run the program. The program should output **200** and **Still Alive** for length and name, respectively, as can be seen here:

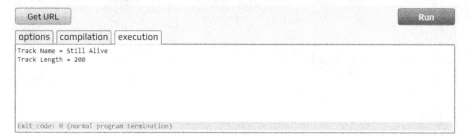

Figure 8.3: Track name and length output

Parameterized constructors can have default values. This means that we can use them just like default constructors (without parameters). This kind of default value parameterized constructor can be very useful in a case where the majority of the time the value passed into the constructor is the same, yet we would like to have the option to change it when the need arises. You can mix and match default and non-default parameters, but any default parameters must come after non-default parameters. Here is an example of a **Track** class constructor with default parameters:

```
// set default values to parameters
Track(float lengthInSeconds = 0.0f, string trackName = "not set")
{
    m_lengthInSeconds = lengthInSeconds;
    m_trackName = trackName;
}
```

We will now move onto more advanced constructors. They are equally as important when writing robust classes that behave as we expect in all situations.

Copy Constructors

A copy constructor is a constructor that creates a copy of an existing class instance. In addition to a default constructor, the compiler will also automatically create a copy constructor for each class type if one is not defined.

A copy constructor will be called in a number of situations, but the most important thing to keep in mind is that a copy constructor is used when a variable or object is created from another object. The copy constructor creates a copy of the existing object—hence, copy constructor.

The syntax of a copy constructor, using our **Track** class as an example, is as follows:

```
Track(const Track& track)
{
    lengthInSeconds = track.lengthInSeconds;
    trackName = track.trackName;
}
```

Looking at this syntax, we can see that a copy constructor is declared almost in the same way as the constructors covered previously, but with an important difference; it takes a reference to a **const** parameter. Making the parameter **const** ensures that the copy constructor will not alter the passed-in parameter. A reference to a parameter is used in the case of a copy constructor as a result of one of the situations where a copy constructor would be called; a copy constructor is called when an object is passed to a function by a value.

Consequently, if the parameter is not a reference, then passing it into the copy constructor would require calling the copy constructor to make a copy. This copy constructor would make a copy which would continue to invoke the copy constructor, and so on and so on (an infinite loop).

Shallow Copy or Deep Copy

As previously mentioned, the compiler will create a copy constructor for our types. This compiler-generated copy constructor is likely to be the same as the one shown in the example in the preceding section. This is known as a shallow copy, and it runs through each member variable and assigns them the corresponding value of the object currently being copied. This compiler-generated copy constructor is likely to be fine in a lot of cases, and we do not have to define one ourselves. A copy constructor will be called when a new object is created from an object that already exists.

The following example shows another situation where a copy constructor will be called (in this case, a compiler-generated copy constructor):

```
#include <iostream>
#include <string>

using namespace std;

class Track
{
public:
    Track(float lengthInSeconds = 0.0f, string trackName = "not set")
    {
        m_lengthInSeconds = lengthInSeconds;
```

```
        m_trackName = trackName;
    }

    // m_ prefix added to member variables, to avoid naming conflicts with
    //parameter names
    float m_lengthInSeconds;
    string m_trackName;
};

int main()
{
    Track track(200.0f, "Still Alive");

    Track track2 = track; // copy constructor is called

    cout << "Track Name = " << track.m_trackName << endl;
    cout << "Track Length = " << track.m_lengthInSeconds << endl;

    cout << "Track Name = " << track2.m_trackName << endl;
    cout << "Track Length = " << track2.m_lengthInSeconds << endl;

    return 0;
}
```

The preceding code should output the following:

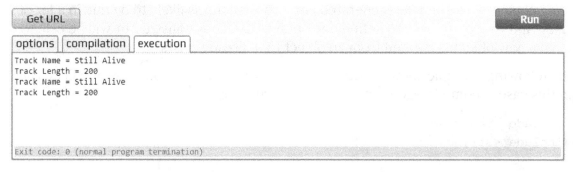

Figure 8.4: Output from the compiler-generated copy constructor

The **track2** object is created from the **track** object; the compiler-generated copy constructor creates a shallow copy. A shallow copy of an object copies all the members. This is usually fine when all the members are values. So, when is a shallow copy not enough? When a class has dynamically allocated memory, a deep copy is usually needed.

When a shallow copy is enacted on a pointer to dynamic memory, only the pointer is copied, not the memory it points to. The **Track** class could have a sample playable clip, possibly a few seconds of sound. For the sake of brevity, let's say we can store this playable clip's data in an array of characters to be parsed and played by some other sound software. Here is the sample **Track** class with this concept in place:

```
#include <iostream>
#include <string>
#include <cstring>

using namespace std;

class Track
{
public:
    Track(float lengthInSeconds = 0.0f, string trackName = "not set", const
    char * data = NULL)
    {
        m_lengthInSeconds = lengthInSeconds;
        m_trackName = trackName;

        // create the sample clip from data
        m_dataSize = strlen(data);
        m_data = new char[m_dataSize + 1];
        strcpy(m_data, data);
    }

    // definitely need a destructor to clean up the data
    ~Track()
    {
        delete[] m_data;
    }

    // m_ prefix added to member variables, to avoid naming conflicts with
    //parameter names
    float m_lengthInSeconds;
    string m_trackName;
```

```
    // sample clip data
    int m_dataSize;
    char * m_data;
};

int main()
{
    Track track(200.0f, "Still Alive",
    "f651270d6011098375db09912b03e5e7");
    Track track2 = track;

    cout << "Track 1" << endl;
    cout << "Track Name = " << track.m_trackName << endl;
    cout << "Track Length = " << track.m_lengthInSeconds << endl;
    cout << "Track Data = " << track.m_data << endl;
    cout << endl;
    cout << "Track 2" << endl;
    cout << "Track Name = " << track2.m_trackName << endl;
    cout << "Track Length = " << track2.m_lengthInSeconds << endl;
    cout << "Track Data = " << track2.m_data << endl;

    return 0;
}
```

The preceding code will yield the following output:

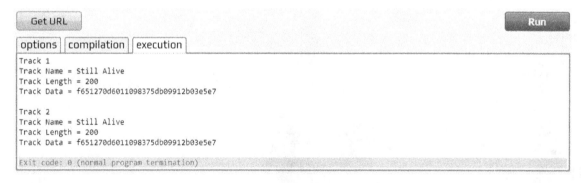

Figure 8.5: Shallow copy

The class at this point is still using the compiler-generated copy constructor, and this means **track2** is a shallow copy of **track**. The problem here is that shallow copies just copy over the addresses of pointers. In other words, the **m_data** variable for **track** and **track2** both point to the same memory address. This can be demonstrated by adding additional functionality to the **Track** class to allow the **m_data** variable to be changed through a function, as shown in the following snippet:

```
#include <iostream>
#include <string>
#include <cstring>

using namespace std;

class Track
{
public:
    // added additional artist name constructor parameter
    Track(float lengthInSeconds = 0.0f, string trackName = "not set",
          string artistName = "not set", const char * data = NULL)
    {
        m_lengthInSeconds = lengthInSeconds;
        m_trackName = trackName;
        m_artistName = artistName;

        // create the sample clip from data
        m_dataSize = strlen(data);
        m_data = new char[m_dataSize + 1];
        strcpy(m_data, data);
        }
    ~Track()
    {
        delete[] m_data;
    }
    void SetData(float lengthInSeconds = 0.0f, string trackName = "not
                 set", const char * newData = NULL)
    {
        m_lengthInSeconds = lengthInSeconds;
        m_trackName = trackName;
```

```
        // delete the array so it can be recreated
        delete[] m_data;

        // create the sample clip from data
        m_dataSize = strlen(newData);
        m_data = new char[m_dataSize + 1];
        strcpy(m_data, newData);
    }

    // m_ prefix added to member variables, to avoid naming conflicts with
    //parameter names
    float m_lengthInSeconds;
    string m_trackName;

    // additional artist name string member variable
    string m_artistName;

    // sample clip data
    int m_dataSize;
    char * m_data;
};
```

A logical step could be to allow the creation of **Track** objects and then create copies of those objects with the same artist name, in order to create an album of sorts. The added **SetData** function takes a new length, track name, and playable clip data as parameters, and if a new track is just a copy of another, then the artist's name no longer needs to be set on each track. It's genius. The following snippet shows this idea in practice:

```
int main()
{
    Track track(200.0f, "Still Alive", "GlaDos",
    "f651270d6011098375db09912b03e5e7");

    // copy the first track with the artist name
    Track track2 = track;

    // set the new needed data
    track2.SetData(300.0f, "Want You Gone",
    -"db6fd7d74393b375344010a0c9cc4535");
    cout << "Track 1" << endl;
```

```
    cout << "Artist = " << track.m_artistName << endl;
    cout << "Track Name = " << track.m_trackName << endl;
    cout << "Track Length = " << track.m_lengthInSeconds << endl;
    cout << "Track Data = " << track.m_data << endl;
    cout << endl;
    cout << "Track 2" << endl;
    cout << "Artist = " << track2.m_artistName << endl;
    cout << "Track Name = " << track2.m_trackName << endl;
    cout << "Track Length = " << track2.m_lengthInSeconds << endl;
    cout << "Track Data = " << track2.m_data << endl;

    return 0;
}
```

The preceding snippet should yield the following output:

Figure 8.6: Updated track data for a given artist using the SetData function

Unfortunately, this genius idea has a fatal flaw if we do not also add an explicit copy constructor. Notice that although the **m_data** variable on **track2** has indeed changed, this also affected the **m_data** variable on the copied **track** object because they point to the same place. This will cause a runtime error when the program finishes and calls the destructor for both tracks, attempting to free memory that has already been destroyed. This is known as a double-free error. The following is a seemingly innocuous function:

```
void PrintTrackName(Track track)
{
    cout << "Track Name = " << track.m_trackName << endl;
}
```

What happens when an object is passed by value to a function?

A copy constructor is called. When this function is called, the **Track** object whose value is printed is actually a local variable that is a copy of the passed-in **Track** object, and once this local variable goes out of scope, its destructor will be called. The **Track** class deletes the **m_data** array in its destructor, and, since the **Track** class does not have a user-defined copy constructor that correctly executes a deep copy, it deletes the same **m_data** variable used by the passed-in object. Here is an example of a variable going out of scope:

```
void PrintTrackName(Track track)
{
    cout << "Track Name = " << track.m_trackName << endl;
}

int main()
{
    Track track(200.0f, "Still Alive", "GlaDos",
    "f651270d6011098375db09912b03e5e7");

    PrintTrackName(track);
    cout << "Track 1" << endl;
    cout << "Artist = " << track.m_artistName << endl;
    cout << "Track Name = " << track.m_trackName << endl;
    cout << "Track Length = " << track.m_lengthInSeconds << endl;
    cout << "Track Data = " << track.m_data << endl;

    return 0;
}
```

The preceding code would yield the following output:

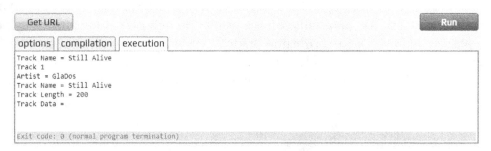

Figure 8.7: Output in the case when an object is passed by value

The data from the track was deleted as a result of the function being passed by value to the print track function and then going out of scope. Both issues can be resolved by adding a copy constructor that performs a deep copy.

We need a way to correctly handle the copy of our dynamically allocated memory, and we know that the compiler-generated copy constructor will not do this for us; we need to write our own. We can start by looking at how our **Track** class constructs itself in its usual constructor. Here is the **Track** constructor using the dynamically allocated data outlined in the examples presented in the *Shallow Copy or Deep Copy* section:

```
// added additional artist name constructor parameter
Track(float lengthInSeconds = 0.0f, string trackName = "not set",
        string artistName = "not set", const char* data = NULL)
{
    m_lengthInSeconds = lengthInSeconds;
    m_trackName = trackName;
    m_artistName = artistName;

    // create the sample clip from data
    m_dataSize = strlen(data);
    m_data = new char[m_dataSize + 1];
    strcpy(m_data, data);
}
```

Now that we have gone through a few examples of copy constructors, we will implement our learning in the following exercise by defining a copy constructor. We will use the preceding snippet as a reference and then build upon it.

Exercise 60: Defining a Copy Constructor

In this exercise, we will define a copy constructor. For this purpose, we can use constructor from the preceding snippet as a reference but use values from the new constructor passed in the **Track** object:

> **Note**
>
> The complete code for the exercise can be found here: https://packt.live/2rX6ozE.

1. First, we create the stub of our copy constructor. You will recall that we need to pass in a **const** reference to a **Track** object to our copy constructor:

```
Track(const Track& track)
{
}
```

2. Now we can assign our member variables to the values from the passed-in **Track** object in a similar way to the regular constructor:

```
Track(const Track& track)
{
    // these can be shallow copied
    m_lengthInSeconds = track.m_lengthInSeconds;
    m_trackName = track.m_trackName;
    m_artistName = track.m_artistName;
    m_dataSize = track.m_dataSize;
}
```

3. Now, we cannot just assign the data array to the track data array because, as we have discussed, this will only copy the pointer address and lead to both data arrays pointing to the same place. So, we must initialize the data array using **new[]** (we already know the size from the stored value in **m_dataSize**):

```
Track(const Track& track)
{
    // these can be shallow copied
    m_lengthInSeconds = track.m_lengthInSeconds;
    m_trackName = track.m_trackName;
    m_artistName = track.m_artistName;
    m_dataSize = track.m_dataSize;

    // allocate memory for the copied pointer
    m_data = new char[m_dataSize + 1];
```

4. Finally, we use the **strcpy** function just like the constructor, but pass in the data from the **track** object we are copying from:

```
Track(const Track& track)
{
    // these can be shallow copied
    m_lengthInSeconds = track.m_lengthInSeconds;
    m_trackName = track.m_trackName;
    m_artistName = track.m_artistName;
    m_dataSize = track.m_dataSize;

    // allocate memory for the copied pointer
    m_data = new char[m_dataSize + 1];
```

```
        // copy the value from the old object
        strcpy(m_data, track.m_data);
    }
```

We now have a working copy constructor that correctly handles our data.

5. Run the program. You should obtain the following output:

```
Get URL                                                      Run

options  compilation  execution
Track Name = Still Alive
Track 1
Artist = GlaDos
Track Name = Still Alive
Track Length = 200
Track Data = f651270d6011098375db09912b03e5e7

Track 2
Artist = GlaDos
Track Name = Want You Gone
Track Length = 300
Track Data = db6fd7d74393b375344010a0c9cc4535

Exit code: 0 (normal program termination)
```

Figure 8.8: Output when using the copy constructor

The copy constructor copies any members that are value types directly, but, in the case of the **char** array that was dynamically created to hold our data, it has to create a new **char** array for the new class and then copy the data from the other instance. We now know that this is required as we want a copy of the data, not a pointer to the other instance's data.

Copy Assignment Operator

A general rule to follow, known as the **Rule of Three** (now known as the **Rule of Five** due to additional special member functions in C++11, covered in more detail in later chapters), is that if a destructor, copy constructor, or assignment operator is explicitly defined, then all three should probably be explicitly defined (remember that the compiler will implicitly define any of these that have not been explicitly defined). The assignment operator is called when an existing object is assigned to another existing object.

When this copy assignment operation happens, it behaves much like the copy constructor, except that it must handle the cleanup of existing variables rather than assign values to uninitialized variables. The assignment operator must also handle self-assignment correctly.

Just like a copy constructor, the compiler will generate a copy assignment operator if not explicitly declared and, just like a copy constructor, this will only be a shallow copy. The following example shows this in practice:

```
{
    Track track(200.0 f, "Still Alive",
    "GlaDos","f651270d6011098375db09912b03e5e7");

    PrintTrackName(track);

    // construct another track with new values
    Track track2(300.0 f, "Want You Gone", "GlaDos",
    "db6fd7d74393b375344010a0c9cc4535");

    // here the assignment operator is called
    track2 = track;

    // set the new needed data
    track2.SetData(300.0 f, "Want You Gone",
    "db6fd7d74393b375344010a0c9cc4535");

    cout << "Track 1" << endl;
    cout << "Artist = " << track.m_artistName << endl;
    cout << "Track Name = " << track.m_trackName << endl;
    cout << "Track Length = " << track.m_lengthInSeconds << endl;
    cout << "Track Data = " << track.m_data << endl;
    cout << endl;
    cout << "Track 2" << endl;
    cout << "Artist = " << track2.m_artistName << endl;
    cout << "Track Name = " << track2.m_trackName << endl;
    cout << "Track Length = " << track2.m_lengthInSeconds << endl;
    cout << "Track Data = " << track2.m_data << endl;

    return 0;
}
```

The preceding code should yield the following output:

Figure 8.9: Output when overloading the assignment operator

The same issues we covered with copy constructors occur with a compiler-generated copy assignment operator; our dynamic data is not correctly copied.

When creating an overloaded assignment operator, we can again look at previous code we have written to help us. The copy constructor from the previous exercise (*step* 2) is a good starting point:

```
Track(const Track& track)
{
    // these can be shallow copied
    m_lengthInSeconds = track.m_lengthInSeconds;
    m_trackName = track.m_trackName;
    m_artistName = track.m_artistName;
    m_dataSize = track.m_dataSize;

    // allocate memory for the copied pointer
    m_data = new char[m_dataSize + 1];

    // copy the value from the old object
    strcpy(m_data, track.m_data);
}
```

We will implement this to overload the assignment operator in the following exercise.

Exercise 61: Overloading the Assignment Operator

In this exercise, we will overload the assignment operator to create copies of objects in the **Track** class. Here are the steps to complete the exercise:

> **Note**
>
> The complete code for this exercise can be found here: https://packt.live/2KHv3ij.

1. Create the stub of our overloaded assignment operator:

```
Track& operator=(const Track& track)
{

}
```

Just like with a copy constructor, we will pass in a **const** reference to a **track**, but since this isn't a constructor, we will need a return value. This return value will be a non-const **Track** reference (this isn't required, but it is the way in which the compiler generates the assignment operator).

2. An important check with an assignment operator is to verify that we are not attempting to assign an object to itself. This is known as self-assignment, and we do not need to execute our copying if this is the case.

```
Track& operator=(const Track& track)
{
    // check for self assignment
    if(this != &track)
    {
```

3. Next, we can do the shallow copying of member variables:

```
        // these can be shallow copied
        m_lengthInSeconds = track.m_lengthInSeconds;
        m_trackName = track.m_trackName;
        m_artistName = track.m_artistName;
        m_dataSize = track.m_dataSize;
```

4. Now we come to a step that is not the same in function as a copy constructor. Since we are assigning to an existing object, we need to delete the dynamically allocated array so that we can copy our new values over to it. First, we create a new **char*** array and copy the passed-in track reference objects data into it:

```
// allocate new memory and copy the existing data from the
//passed in object
char* newData = new char[m_dataSize];
strcpy(newData, track.m_data);
```

5. Now delete the existing **m_data** array:

```
// since this is an already existing object we must deallocate
//existing memory
delete[] m_data;
```

6. Finally, we can assign the **newData** array to the now-deleted **m_data** array. Note that we could not just assign the passed-in track reference **m_data** to the existing **m_data** array, because then we would just be making them point to the same place, which we know is not the behavior we want. To remedy this, we create a new array and make the **m_data** array point to that instead:

```
// assign the new data
m_data = newData;
```

7. And now, we can return a reference to the track we are assigning to; using the **this** keyword:

```
    }
    return *this;
}
```

8. Now that we have a working assignment operator, we can test it using the same example as the copy constructor. Run the code, and you will obtain the following output:

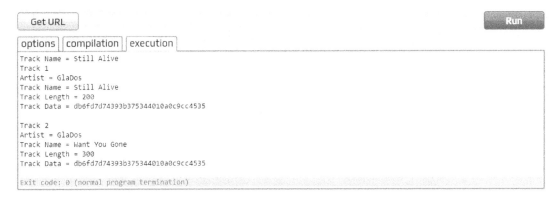

Figure 8.10: Output for the overloaded assignment operator

Although slightly more involved than a copy constructor, the principle is largely the same, and it stands to reason that if you need to define an explicit copy constructor, then you will almost always need to also define an explicit copy assignment operator.

Destructors

Destructors are special member functions that are called when the lifetime of an object ends. Objects are destroyed when they go out of scope or a pointer to them is deleted. Just as a constructor is responsible for the creation of an object, a destructor is responsible for the destruction of an object. If any memory has been dynamically allocated, then the destructor of an object must free this memory by using **delete** or **delete[]**, depending on the data type. Destructors have the same name as a class, take no parameters, have no return value, and are denoted with the tilde symbol, **~**. The following example shows the syntax required to define a destructor:

```
~Track()
{
    delete[] m_data;
}
```

When dealing with member variables that dynamically allocate memory, a destructor can be used to ensure that this memory is freed when the object is destroyed. The problem of dynamically allocated memory associated with the previous concepts applies to destructors also. If a class allocates memory dynamically, an explicit destructor should be created to ensure that this memory is freed correctly.

We do not need to do anything to non-dynamically allocated member variables and built-in types; they will destroy themselves.

Activity 8: Creating a VideoClip Class

The **Track** class has taught us a lot about writing classes. We will now implement something very similar to help solidify our understanding. We are going to write a class that represents a video clip. This will largely be the same as our **Track** class, requiring constructors, destructors, a copy constructor, and a copy assignment operator overload. Our desired outcome for this activity is to have a **VideoClip** class that behaves similarly to a **Track** class. Once you have successfully completed the activity, the output should contain information such as the video track length, name, and year of release. One such possible output is as follows:

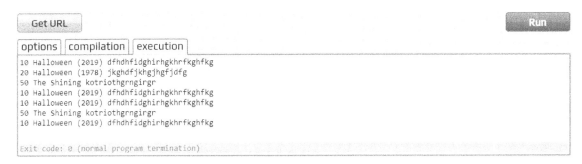

Figure 8.11: A possible output from the VideoClip class

Here are the steps that will help you complete the activity:

> **Note**
>
> The complete code to the activity can be found here: https://packt.live/2KHMwXP.

1. Open **cpp.sh** and get started with a blank project.

2. Create the **VideoClip** class outline.

3. Create member variables for video length and video name.

4. Write a default constructor that initializes the video length and name to a default value.

5. Write a parameterized constructor that sets the video length and name to the passed parameters.

6. Create a data char array and data size member variables and initialize them in both constructors.

7. Create a copy constructor that correctly handles the copying of the data array.

8. Create a copy assignment operator overload that correctly handles the copying of the data array.

9. Write a destructor that deletes the allocated data array.

10. Update the **main** function to create three different **videoClip** instances and output their values.

11. Test the copy constructor and copy assignment operators within the **main** function by initializing a video clip using an existing instance and initializing an instance of a video clip with its constructor and then later assigning it to another existing instance.

> **Note**
>
> The solution for this activity can be found on page 542.

Summary

We have covered several concepts in this chapter. We looked at unions and structs and how they differ from classes (and how they don't). We then went into detail about different types of constructors and discussed possible problems when copying objects and how to solve them. We learned about the rule of three and how important it is. Finally, we had a quick look at destructors.

We found that C++ has some very specific things we must keep in mind when defining our own types and found out that we must handle dynamic memory very carefully and design our classes accordingly. So long as we follow the guidelines laid out in this chapter, we can see that C++ gives us all the tools needed to create robust and easy-to-use types.

All this information has armed us with the necessary knowledge to step further into object-oriented concepts, confident that we have the basics covered. The coming chapter will discuss how best to design our classes from a front-facing perspective to ensure that they will be used only in the way we intend.

Object-Oriented
Principles

Overview

This chapter presents best practices for designing classes and will give you an overview of abstraction and encapsulation, where to use them, and how they can benefit your custom C++ types. More details about classes in general and how they fit into the object-oriented programming paradigm will also be covered.

Introduction

The previous chapter provided detailed information on the construction of objects along with information on the different keywords that C++ provides to define these objects. We learned that we must be careful when creating our own types and ensure that they are constructed and destroyed appropriately. This chapter delves further into object-oriented programming, explaining important principles for designing classes that should be kept in mind to most efficiently utilize the **object-oriented programming (OOP)** paradigm.

In this chapter, we will take things a step further and introduce best practices for defining our own types. Through this knowledge, we can write classes that insulate themselves against unintended use, and, using public and private functions and member variables, we can make it clear how we do intend a class to be used.

Encapsulation allows us to hide data we do not want a user to access directly, while abstraction provides the user of a class with an interface that exposes all of its important uses yet hides the details. Both topics will be covered in this chapter, along with some more detailed explanations of classes.

Classes and OOP

Classes are a way to group data and provide the functionality to manipulate that data. A class type is the C++ representation of an object. A class is essentially synonymous with an object. In the previous chapter, the **Track** class was an archetype of an object of type **Track**.

> **Note**
>
> The term archetype is a descriptive term to facilitate explanation, and is not an official term.

The word archetype is important to note as it implies the concept of reusability, one of the main benefits of an object-oriented design approach. Once an object has its archetypal foundations, then the specifics can be exposed to manipulation without changing the underlying description. An object built with its own specifics (**data**) from an archetype (**class**) is known as an instance of an object or class.

Here is the **Track** class that was used in the preceding chapter:

```cpp
#include <iostream>
#include <string>

using namespace std;

class Track
{
public:
    Track(float lengthInSeconds, string trackName)
    {
        m_lengthInSeconds = lengthInSeconds;
        m_trackName = trackName;
    }
    float m_lengthInSeconds;
    string m_trackName;
};
```

If asked to describe the **Track** object on a fundamental level, chances are you would describe it as a thing that has a name and a length. This describes the member variables that make up a class. When asked to describe a specific track, such as **Track track(180.0f, "Still Alive")**, it is likely that you would describe it as **a track called Still Alive that is 3 minutes long**. This is clearly a description of an instance of an object. Fundamentally, it is still a track that has a name and a length, but now the description is more detailed because the specifics have been set. What about another **Track**, constructed using the following snippet?

```cpp
Track anotherTrack(260.0f, "Want You Gone");
```

Again, it is quite likely that we would describe it as **a track called "Want you gone" that is 4 minutes and 20 seconds long**. Knowing what is expected when describing an object makes describing it (i.e. implementing it) much simpler. The same concept applies in an OOP-designed class because we know how to store the details of an object and what the names of the specifics we want to access are. This also extends to creating classes that can be used in multiple programs instead of just within the same program, essentially creating a "code library" that can be used to perform tasks that have been previously written—for example, a math class or file parsing class. This is the basis of **reusability**.

In the next part of the chapter, we are going to cover one of the concepts included in a set of ideas known by the acronym **SOLID**. This acronym and its ideas were created by Robert C. Martin, popularly known as Uncle Bob **[Martin 97]**. This acronym is shorthand for the first five object-oriented design principles, which are as follows:

- **S** – Single-responsibility principle

- **O** – Open-closed principle

- **L** – Liskov substitution principle

- **I** – Interface segregation principle

- **D** – Dependency inversion principle

- We will not be covering all of these but the **S** (for single-responsibility principle) is especially important to this chapter.

S in SOLID

The **S** in the SOLID acronym stands for **single-responsibility principle (SRP) [Martin 97]**. The SRP states that "*A class should have one and only one reason to change, meaning that a class should have only one job.*"

Returning to the concept of **reusability** can shed some light on the importance of this principle. If trying to reuse some code for some purpose, it should not bring along a bunch of additional responsibilities requiring maintenance or possibly redundant code. Furthermore, these additional responsibilities could have dependencies on other classes. Hence, they will need to be moved into the new project too. Clearly, this cycle of dependent classes is not desirable. Any class that has some functionality that we need should probably be able to be used on its own ("*...a class should have only one job*"). Sometimes, it may seem harmless to give a class a small additional responsibility. Yet, careful consideration should be given to abstracting and handing that responsibility to another class that can then be reused by other classes that need the functionality it provides.

Exercise 62: Creating a Class that Prints Values

In this exercise, we will create a class that can be used to print values from our classes. The preceding paragraph on the SRP stated that classes should only have one job—a single responsibility—so let's demonstrate one way we can implement this by removing the responsibility of printing to the console from the class itself and giving that responsibility to another class. Although this exercise may be trivial, it would be extremely useful for us to be able to easily swap out the class that prints to the console and replace it with a class that outputs to a file if we so wish. Here are the steps to complete the exercise:

> **Note**
>
> The complete code for this exercise can be found here: https://packt.live/2pD3LlP.

1. Add the **ValuePrinter** class to an empty file in **cpp.sh**. It is very simple and only consists of overloaded functions to print a message plus a **float**, an **int**, or a **string**. It will look like the following:

```cpp
#include <iostream>
#include <string>

using namespace std;

class ValuePrinter
{
public:
    void Print(string msg, float f)
    {
        cout << msg << " : " << f << endl;
    }
    void Print(string msg, int i)
    {
        cout << msg << " : " << i << endl;
    }
    void Print(string msg, string s)
    {
        cout << msg << " : " << s << endl;
    }
};
```

Now let's create a class that can utilize this **ValuePrinter**.

2. Create a class named **Article** and give it member variables for the title, page count, word count, and author. We will also write a constructor to initialize our member variables and add **ValuePrinter** as a member variable. This class should be like the following:

```
class Article
{
public:
    Article(string title, int pageCount, int wordCount, string author)
    {
        m_title = title;
        m_pageCount = pageCount;
        m_wordCount = wordCount;
        m_author = author;
    }
    string m_title;
    int m_pageCount;
    int m_wordCount;
    string m_author;
    ValuePrinter valuePrinter;
```

3. Next we want to create a function inside **Article** that prints our member variables using the **ValuePrinter** member object. We will call this function **ShowDetails** and it should look like the example that follows:

```
    void ShowDetails()
    {
        valuePrinter.Print("Article Title", m_title);
        valuePrinter.Print("Article Page Count", m_pageCount);
        valuePrinter.Print("Article Word Count", m_wordCount);
        valuePrinter.Print("Article Author", m_author);

    }
};
```

4. We can now test this in a **main** function to see our values printed out using **ValuePrinter**:

```
int main()
{
    Article article("Celebrity Crushes!", 2, 200, "Papa Ratsea");

    article.ShowDetails();

    return 0;
}
```

5. Run the complete program. You should obtain the following output:

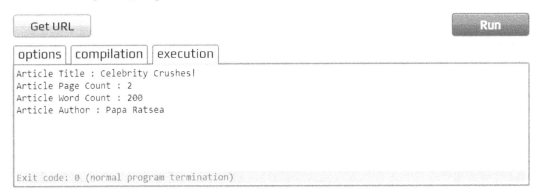

Figure 9.1: Printing values using ValuePrinter

As an additional exercise to really cement this concept, try and implement a **Shape** class that has a **string** member variable for its type and a **float** that holds its area, and then reuse **ValuePrinter** to write a **Shape ShowDetails** function.

We can see how the kind of pattern presented in the preceding exercise could be very useful. We have taken the responsibility of printing to the console away from the **Article** class and have given it to a different class. If we needed to change how **ValuePrinter** works internally, then **Article** would not need to be changed at all. Using **ValuePrinter** in this way segues nicely into our next two topics: **encapsulation** and **abstraction**.

Encapsulation

As a fundamental concept in OOP, encapsulation is very important to understand and should be applied to most classes you design. Encapsulation combines a class's data and the member functions to act on that data. Operations on data in a class should only be possible through the members that class provides; member data should not be directly accessible.

This is known as **data-hiding** and C++ gives us a few keywords to utilize when writing classes that make this possible. These keywords are known as **access modifiers**. The following table (*Figure* 9.2) shows these keywords and their meanings:

keyword	Description
public	Accessible within and anywhere outside the class
protected	Accessible to the class and any derived class types (more on this in subsequent chapters)
private	Only accessible within the class

Figure 9.2: Table describing the different keywords

Using the preceding table and the explanation of encapsulation, consider the following **Track** class, which we have been using:

```
#include <iostream>
#include <string>

using namespace std;

class Track
{
public:
    Track(float lengthInSeconds, string trackName)
    {
        m_lengthInSeconds = lengthInSeconds;
        m_trackName = trackName;
    }
    float m_lengthInSeconds;
    string m_trackName;
};
```

Does it fit with this principle? No, it does not. Both the member variables holding the data are under the **public** keyword and so, as shown in *Figure 9.2*, can be accessed from within and anywhere outside the class. It would be perfectly possible for another piece of code to grab a **Track** instance and mess with it, with the only restriction being the type. The following **main** function uses the **Track** class and shows how easy it is to grab data out of the **Track** class and alter it:

```
int main()
{
    // create
    Track t(260.0f, "Still Alive");
    cout << "My Favourite Song is: " << t.m_trackName << endl;

    // mess with it
    t.m_lengthInSeconds = 9405680394634.4895645f;
    // Song is now pretty much 300 millennia long!

    t.m_trackName = "S-Club Party"; // OH NO!!
    cout << "My Favourite Song is: " << t.m_trackName;

    return 0;
}
```

Our definition of encapsulation states that **member data should not be directly accessible**. *Figure 9.2* shows us that to make a member variable inaccessible from outside a class, we can use the **private** keyword. The following snippet shows that the **private** keyword is used to stop member variables from being accessed from outside a class, and then shows the **main** function that attempts to alter them:

> **Note**
>
> The constructor is still **public**. **Private** constructors are a topic for another chapter.

```
#include <iostream>
#include <string>

using namespace std;

class Track
{
public:
    Track(float lengthInSeconds, string trackName)
```

```
    {
        m_lengthInSeconds = lengthInSeconds;
        m_trackName = trackName;
    }

private:
    float m_lengthInSeconds;
    string m_trackName;
};

int main()
{

    // create
    Track t(260.0f, "Still Alive");

    cout << "My Favourite Song is: " << t.m_trackName << endl;

    // mess with it - Agh! thwarted, compiler error: these variables are
private
    t.m_lengthInSeconds = 9405680394634.4895645f;
    t.m_trackName = "S-Club Party";

    cout << "My Favourite Song is: " << t.m_trackName;

    return 0;
}
```

Running this code will give compiler errors along the following lines:

```
'float Track::m_lengthInSeconds' is private within this context
'std::string Track::m_trackName' is private within this context
```

Now that the member variables are **private**, anyone attempting to set those variables directly will instead be faced with a compiler error. This data is now hidden, and once the variables are set within the constructor, they cannot be changed or accessed directly. However, this presents a new problem; now that the variables are inaccessible from outside the class, they cannot be printed to the console or read into somewhere they might need to be used. For example, the following line of code in the preceding snippet will no longer compile:

```
    cout << "My Favourite Song is: " << t.m_trackName << endl;
```

Member functions can also be **private**, as there may be functions that we want to remain internal to the class. Functions are important to split up code or to implement functionality that can be reused in other functions within the class. By making these functions **private**, we ensure that they will only be used by the class itself and not exposed to users of the class; they are not part of the **public** interface.

Exercise 63: Creating a Position Class with Private Member Variables

In this exercise, we will create a class called **Position** that holds 2D Cartesian coordinates: x and y. Both x and **y** will be **private** member variables that will be set in the constructor, and we will create a **public** member function that takes another set of floats (**x**, **y**) and returns the Euclidian distance between them and our position as a **float** type. Here are the steps to perform the exercise:

> **Note**
>
> The complete code for this exercise can be found here: https://packt.live/2OwnHPU.

1. First, we can create the stub of our class by declaring **Position** as a class. Create a new project in **cpp.sh** and type out the following class stub and the **#include** statements that we are going to use. We are going to need **cmath** for its square root function:

```
#include <iostream>
#include <cmath>

class Position
{
};
```

2. Next, we can create the member variables that make up our coordinates, **x** and **y**. We want these member variables to be private, so we will use the **private** keyword above them. Both variables will be floats, and we will prefix them with **m_**, which is used to denote that a variable is a member variable:

```
#include <iostream>
#include <cmath>

class Position
{
private:
    float m_x;
    float m_y;
};
```

3. We need a way to set these variables when they are created. We will do this in the constructor using an initialization list syntax. Our constructor needs to be **public**, so we will use that keyword above our constructor, as shown in the following snippet:

```
#include <iostream>
#include <cmath>

class Position
{
public:
    Position(float x, float y) : m_x(x), m_y(y) {}
private:
    float m_x;
    float m_y;
};
```

4. We now need to create our **distance** function. This is a **public** member function that will take another **x** coordinate and any **y** coordinate as parameters, and return the distance from that coordinate to the position stored in our class as (**m_x**, **m_y**). Before we implement the functionality, we can first create the stub of this member function:

```
#include <iostream>
#include <cmath>

class Position
{
public:
```

```
        Position(float x, float y) : m_x(x), m_y(y) {}
        float distance(float x, float y)
        {
            // we must return something at this point if we want it to
            //compile
            return 0;

        }
    private:
        float m_x;
        float m_y;
    };
```

5. We can now implement the **distance** function by using a derivation of the Pythagorean Theorem:

$$Distance = \sqrt{(x_2 - x_1)^2 + (y_2 - y_1)^2}$$

Figure 9.3: Pythagorean theorem

6. This will be our straight-line distance between our two positions:

```
    float distance(float x, float y)
    {
        float xDiff = x - m_x;
        float yDiff = y - m_y;

        return std::sqrt(((xDiff * xDiff) + (yDiff * yDiff)));
    }
```

7. We are all set now to test our new class. Create a **main** function that creates a **Position** object that is set to (**10**, **20**) and print the distance from that to (**100**, **40**). Here is the code to do this:

```
int main()
{
    Position pos(10.0f, 20.0f);

    std::cout << "The distance from pos to (100, 40) is:"
              << pos.distance(100.0f, 40.0f) << std::endl;

    return 0;
}
```

8. Run the complete code. You will receive the following output:

Figure 9.4: Distance output

In this exercise, we have encapsulated our position data by making it **private** to our **Position** class. Anyone wishing to use those values must do so through the **public** function we provide. How do we give access to **private** data members while still keeping some semblance of control? The next part of this chapter will cover a common pattern that can provide a solution.

Getters and Setters

Classes are made to be utilized in some way, and yet the concept of **encapsulation** states that member data should not be directly accessible. Making member variables **private** ensured this was the case in our example, but we ended up rendering the **Track** class mostly useless for its most obvious purpose: holding readable data about tracks. A common technique for protecting data while still allowing sensible access is to use **getters and setters**. Unsurprisingly, a getter gets data and a setter sets data. Getters are commonly prefixed with the word **get** and setters with the word **set**. Here is the **Track** class with getters for its member data:

```
#include <iostream>
#include <string>

using namespace std;

class Track
{
public:
    Track(float lengthInSeconds, string trackName)
    {
```

```
        m_lengthInSeconds = lengthInSeconds;
        m_trackName = trackName;
    }

    float getLength()
    {
        return m_lengthInSeconds;
    }

    string getName()
    {
    return m_trackName;
    }

private:
    float m_lengthInSeconds;
    string m_trackName;
};

int main()
{
    // create
    Track t(260.0 f, "Still Alive");

    cout << "My Favourite Song is: " << t.getName() << endl;
    cout << "It is :" << t.getLength() / 60.0 f << " minutes long";

    return 0;
}
```

In the preceding code, **getLength** returns the **m_lengthInSeconds** variable and **getName** returns the **m_trackName** variable. These functions are both **public** and so can be used outside of the class to allow us to print their values while leaving the variables themselves **private** and therefore safe from being accessed directly from outside the class.

Setters allow the setting of some data. It is worth noting that a direct setter will essentially break encapsulation as it exposes the variable to be changed again. One thing that a setter allows that a publicly exposed member variable does not is the validation of the data to be set. Consider this with the help of the following code:

Example09_1.cpp

```
23      string getName()
24      {
25          return m_trackName;
26      }
27
28      void setName(string newTrackName)
29      {
30          // if S-Club is not found set the track name - otherwise do nothing
31          if (newTrackName.find("S-Club") == string::npos)
32          {
33              m_trackName = newTrackName;
34          }
35      }
36
37      void setLength(float newTrackLength)
38      {
39          if (newTrackLength < MAX_TRACK_LENGTH && newTrackLength > 0)
40          // no prog metal for us!
41          {
42              m_lengthInSeconds = newTrackLength;
43          }
44      }
```

The complete code for this example cam be found at: https://packt.live/2DLDVQf

In the preceding example, **setName** and **setLength** have been added. The **setName** function takes a string as a parameter to set **m_trackName** to, but first, it checks whether that parameter is equal to **S-Club** and does not set the variable if this is the case. The **setLength** function takes a float as a parameter and uses this to set the **m_trackLengthInSeconds** variable, but before it sets this variable it verifies that it is both greater than zero and not greater than **MAX_TRACK_LENGTH**.

Running the preceding example snippet will yield the following output:

Figure 9.5: Output using the setter method

In the example discussed here, the attempt to set the data to something not valid (in this context) did not work, thus satisfying the criteria for encapsulation outlined previously. Our data is safer now and can only be set in a way that we have approved using our public interface.

> **Note**
>
> These checks could also be performed in the constructor to ensure the data is valid at that point.

Exercise 64: Getters and Setters in a Position Class

In *Exercise 63*, *Creating a Position Class*, with **Private** member variables, we created a **Position** class and a **distance** function. The problem with our **distance** function is that we could not pass object values of another **Position** class to it as parameters because the variables needed to compute the distance were not available to us; they were private. One way around this would be to pass a **Position** object as a parameter, which raises an important point to note about private elements in C++: they can actually be accessed by a class of the same type because this access control is on a per-class basis, not a per-object basis.

For now, though, we will not pass in a **Position** object because, for the sake of argument, we'll assume we don't know how big a **Position** object is and we do not want to needlessly copy it when all we need are its **x** and **y** values. So, in this exercise, we will implement some getters for our **Position** class and create an example program that uses the **distance** function to ensure that two positions don't get too far apart.

> **Note**
>
> The complete code for this exercise can be found here: https://packt.live/2O63D7O.

Here are the steps to complete the exercise:

1. First, we can look at the **Position** class from *Exercise 63, Creating a Position Class,* and copy it into our new example:

```cpp
#include <iostream>
#include <cmath>

class Position
{
public:
    Position(float x, float y) : m_x(x), m_y(y) {}
    float distance(float x, float y)
    {
        float xDiff = x - m_x;
        float yDiff = y - m_y;
        return std::sqrt(((xDiff * xDiff) + (yDiff * yDiff)));
    }

private:
    float m_x;
    float m_y;
};
```

2. To this class, we can add some getters for our private member variables called **getX()** and **getY()**. All they will do is return our **m_x** and **m_y** variables. Add them after our **distance** function, but ensure that they are still under the **public** keyword:

```cpp
    float getX() { return m_x; }
    float getY() { return m_y; }
```

3. At this point, we can construct a new **Position** object and access its variables to pass through to the distance check. Let's see how this would look in an updated **main** function:

```cpp
int main()
{
    Position pos(10.0f, 20.0f);
    Position pos2(100.0f, 200.0f);

    std::cout << "The distance between pos and pos2 is: "
```

```
            << pos.distance(pos2.getX(), pos2.getY());

        return 0;
    }
```

4. Before we move onto our **main** function, we are going to create setters for our member variables. Add the setters below our getters, as shown:

```
    void setX(float x) { m_x = x; }
    void setY(float y) { m_y = y; }
```

5. Now, for our **main** function, we are going to define the maximum distance that our positions can be apart (in this case, it will be 500 units). Then, we will update our positions in a loop, stopping if we hit this maximum distance. To do this, we will make use of our getters and setters, and also the **distance** function. We will move one of our positions in the opposite direction of the other by first getting the direction between the two positions by subtracting their x and y values ($direction(x,y) = (pos2X - pos1X, pos2Y - pos1Y)$) and then normalizing it. We can normalize by dividing x and y between the two positions (we got this in the previous step) by the distance. You may recognize this as vector math, but if not, don't worry; the important part is the usage of our getters and setters. Here is the **main** function with our **distance** check:

```
int main()
{
    float maxDistance = 500.0f;
    Position pos(10.0f, 20.0f);
    Position pos2(100.0f, 200.0f);
    bool validDistance = true;
    int numberOfTimesMoved = 0;

    while(validDistance)
    {
        float distance = pos.distance(pos2.getX(), pos2.getY());

        if(distance > maxDistance)
        {
            validDistance = false;
            break;
        }

        // get direction
        float xDirection = pos2.getX() - pos.getX();
```

```
                float yDirection = pos2.getY() - pos.getY();

                // normalize
                float normalizedX = xDirection / distance;
                float normalizedY = yDirection / distance;
                pos.setX(pos.getX() - normalizedX);
                pos.setY(pos.getY() - normalizedY);
                numberOfTimesMoved++;
            }


        std::cout << "Too far apart." << " Moved " << numberOfTimesMoved
                << " times" ;

        return 0;
    }
```

6. Run this **main** function to get the output:

Figure 9.6: Printing the count to the console

Notice that this program also outputs the number of times the position changed before it hit the maximum distance.

Return Value or Reference

Deciding how the value from a getter should be returned is important and requires some knowledge about the options available. In C++, we can return variables by value, by pointer, and by reference along with their **const** counterparts, which we will discuss soon; however, we won't cover pointers in this chapter. The choice of how to return a variable largely depends on its use case, and this part of the chapter will cover this in the context of our **Track** class, and specifically, how it applies to our getters and setters.

Return by Value

Look at the following **getLength** method from the **Track** class:

```
float getLength() { return m_lengthInSeconds; }
```

This is **returning by value**. In other words, this method returns a copy of the value of **m_lengthInSeconds**. If this value is assigned to another variable, then any modifications to **m_lengthInSeconds** will not be reflected in the new variable (and vice versa) since it was a copy of the value that was returned. Here is an example:

```
int main()
{
    // create
    Track t(260.0f, "Still Alive");
    cout << "My Favourite Song is: " << t.getName() << endl;
    cout << "It is :" << t.getLength() / 60.0f << " minutes long" << endl;

    // create a new variable and assign to it
    // the value of the track length
    float tLength = t.getLength();

    // modify it
    tLength = 100.0f;
    cout << "My Favourite Song is: " << t.getName() << endl;
    cout << "It is :" << t.getLength() / 60.0f << " minutes long";

    return 0;
}
```

The preceding code will yield the following output:

Figure 9.7: Printing duration of the song

Modifying **tLength** did not modify the value of **m_lengthInSeconds** (the reverse also applies). This is safe and, more often than not, is desirable behavior. We don't want stuff from outside the class to be able to modify the **private** member variables.

Return by Reference

In addition to returning the value of data or an object, methods can also return a reference to data or an object. Returning a reference won't copy the value of data; it will return a reference to it, allowing that data to continue to be modified. Returning by reference is fast as it does not have to perform a **copy** operation. Typically, it is used to return large structs or classes where copying would be detrimental to performance. The following method is the **getLength** function, modified to return a reference:

```
float& getLength() { return m_lengthInSeconds; }
```

This allows modification of the data in the following way:

```
int main()
{
    // create
    Track t(260.0f, "Still Alive");
    cout << "My Favourite Song is: " << t.getName() << endl;
    cout << "It is :" << t.getLength() / 60.0f << " minutes long" << endl;

    // getLength now returns a reference and can be modified
    t.getLength() = 100.0f;

    cout << "My Favourite Song is: " << t.getName() << endl;
    cout << "It is :" << t.getLength() / 60.0f << " minutes long";

    return 0;
}
```

The preceding code would yield the following output:

Figure 9.8: Modifying data to print the song duration

As can be seen in the output, the track length has been modified. Encapsulation and **data-hiding** have been thrown out of the window. Our data should not be able to be modified in this way. **Operations on data from a class should only be possible through the methods that class provides. Member data should not be directly accessible.** The preceding example breaks this concept entirely.

It is worth noting that assigning the returned reference to a non-reference type variable will actually just assign a copy, not the reference. Take the following snippet, for example:

```cpp
int main()
{
    // create
    Track t(260.0f, "Still Alive");
    cout << "My Favourite Song is: " << t.getName() << endl;
    cout << "It is :" << t.getLength() / 60.0f << " minutes long" << endl;

    // getLength returns a reference but this actually is a copy
    float tLength = t.getLength();
    tLength = 100.0f;
    cout << "My Favourite Song is: " << t.getName() << endl;
    cout << "It is :" << t.getLength() / 60.0f << " minutes long";

    return 0;
}
```

The snippet yields the following output:

Figure 9.9: Printing duration of the song

The preceding snippet used the **getLength** function, which returns a reference. However, as we can see from the output, it did not actually assign a reference to **tLength**. This may seem obvious due to **tLength** not actually being a reference type, but it is worth knowing so you don't get caught out in the future.

When assigning a reference to another reference type, any modifications will be reflected in the class member data because the new reference is essentially just another name for the same thing. Here is an example:

```cpp
int main()
{
    // create
    Track t(260.0f, "Still Alive");
    cout << "My Favourite Song is: " << t.getName() << endl;
    cout << "It is :" << t.getLength() / 60.0f << " minutes long" << endl;

    // getLength now returns a reference and can be modified
    float& tLength = t.getLength();
    tLength = 100.0f;
    cout << "My Favourite Song is: " << t.getName() << endl;
    cout << "It is :" << t.getLength() / 60.0f << " minutes long";

    return 0;
}
```

The preceding snippet yields the following output:

Figure 9.10: Printing duration of the song

Notice that modifying **tLength** also modifies the **Track** object's length.

Another important thing to keep in mind when returning by reference is not to return variables that are local to a function by reference as, once that variable goes out of scope (local variables go out of scope at the end of a function and are destroyed), the reference will be a reference to garbage. Here is an example to see this in action:

```cpp
float& getLengthInMinutes()
{
    float lengthInMinutes = m_lengthInSeconds / 60.0f;

    return lengthInMinutes;
} // lengthInMinutes out of scope here
```

Thankfully, running the preceding code will usually result in a warning or an error. This advice also applies to **temporary** variables. For example, when evaluating expressions, the compiler will generate a temporary variable to store that expression result:

```
float& getLengthInMinutes()
{
    // creates a temporary
    return m_lengthInSeconds / 60.0f;
}  // temporary out of scope here
```

> **Note**
>
> Both these examples would be fine to return by value.

const

As explained earlier, there are situations where a class might want to return a reference, such as when the object it's returning is large and copying it would have an impact on performance. The problem with returning a reference is that it breaks encapsulation. In a case where a reference needs to be returned but is not modifiable, we can use the C++ **const** keyword. This keyword marks the data as read-only. Explaining the various uses of **const**, how it is used, and what can be marked as **const** takes a long time and can be quite confusing, but keep in mind that basically it is a way of being explicit about how a piece of data can be used.

Returning const References

We know how and when to return by reference, but we can return variables from a function in a different way, and that is in the form of a **const** reference. We know that **const** marks data as read-only and so a **const** reference is a reference that is marked as read-only–a non-modifiable reference.

Here is the **getLength** function that we used in the references example, now marked with **const**:

```
const float& getLength() { return m_lengthInSeconds; }
```

The following snippet attempts to use this data in the same way as the examples in the section on references:

```
int main()
{
    // create
    Track t(260.0f, "Still Alive");
    cout << "My Favourite Song is: " << t.getName() << endl;
    cout << "It is :" << t.getLength() / 60.0f << " minutes long" << endl;

    // getLength now returns a const reference
    float& tLength = t.getLength();
    tLength = 100.0f;

    cout << "My Favourite Song is: " << t.getName() << endl;
    cout << "It is :" << t.getLength() / 60.0f << " minutes long";

    return 0;
}
```

If we run this code, we will receive the following error:

```
error: binding 'const float' to reference of type 'float&' discards
qualifiers
```

This compiler error is telling us that the **const** reference returned from **getLength()** can only be bound to another **const** reference. We can take advantage of this; since that reference will be **const**, it will also be read-only, thereby protecting the data.

Here is an example of how we can remove the preceding compiler error by assigning the returned **const** reference to another **const** reference:

```
int main()
{
    // create
    Track t(260.0f, "Still Alive");
    cout << "My Favourite Song is: " << t.getName() << endl;
    cout << "It is :" << t.getLength() / 60.0f << " minutes long" << endl;

    // getLength now returns a const reference
    const float& tLength = t.getLength();
    tLength = 100.0f;
    cout << "My Favourite Song is: " << t.getName() << endl;
```

```
cout << "It is :" << t.getLength() / 60.0f << " minutes long";

return 0;
}
```

Note that the example also attempts to assign a new value to the **const** reference, resulting in another compiler error—which is exactly as we intended it:

```
error: assignment of read-only reference
```

> **Note**
>
> The same error would be thrown using the following syntax: **t.getLength() = 100.0f;**.

Const Functions

Member functions can also be declared as **const**. Member functions declared as **const** are not allowed to modify member data even though they are a part of the class itself. This allows programmers to be clear about the intention of the function, and that anyone who modifies the class should be aware that the function was intended to be **const** and so should not modify member data as this could have consequences for the overall application. Here is the **getLength** function marked as **const**. Note that **const** is after the declaration denoting the function itself as **const**, not the returned **float** value:

```
float getLength() const
{
// modify member data in const function
m_lengthInSeconds = 10.0f;
return m_lengthInSeconds;
}
```

Running this would yield the following error:

```
error: assignment of member 'Track::m_lengthInSeconds' in read-only object
```

The compiler error generated by this snippet is a consequence of the **const** **getLength** member function attempting to modify some member data.

Take note that **const** member functions can be called on non-const and **const** objects, whereas non-const member functions can only be called on non-**const** objects.

Say we have the following non-const member function in the **Track** class :

```
float getLength() { return m_lengthInSeconds; }
```

And the **main** function creates a **const Track** object and attempts to call the non-**const** function:

```
int main()
{
    // create
    const Track t(260.0f, "Still Alive");
    cout << "It is :" << t.getLength() / 60.0f << " minutes long" << endl;

    return 0;
}
```

This would cause the following compiler error because the **Track** object, **t**, is **const** and attempts to call a non-**const** member function:

```
error: passing 'const Track' as 'this' argument discards qualifiers
```

const is an important and occasionally confusing part of C++. The preceding examples and paragraphs are just a small example. Test out creating **const** objects and returning by **const** reference to get a feel for the syntax.

Abstraction

Abstraction and **encapsulation** are two sides of the same coin. Encapsulating data inside a class allows functionality on that data to be abstracted away, only exposing the methods the class design needs to make the class functional to a user and hiding all the nitty-gritty implementation details the class performs on its member data. **Abstraction provides only an essential interface to the user and hides the background details**.

The upcoming example will illustrate this using a **Playlist** class that can hold **Track** objects along with the following functionality:

- Add tracks and remove them by name
- Sort tracks in alphabetical or reverse alphabetical order
- Sort tracks by shortest or longest track
- Print the names of the current tracks along with their lengths

The **Playlist** class will not be responsible for creating **Track** objects. As in the previous examples, the **main** function will create these **Track** objects. The **Track** objects have been simplified from the previous examples to be **immutable** (they cannot change after creation). This is achieved through the use of **const**, as shown in the following snippet, which is the declaration of our **Track** class in the context of this part of the chapter:

```
#include <iostream>
#include <string>
#include <vector>
#include <algorithm>

using namespace std;

class Track
{
public:
    Track(float lengthInSeconds, string trackName)
    {
        m_lengthInSeconds = lengthInSeconds;
        m_trackName = trackName;
    }

    float getLength() const
    {
        return m_lengthInSeconds;
    }

    string getName() const
    {
        return m_trackName;
    }

private:
    float m_lengthInSeconds;
    string m_trackName;
};
```

The **Playlist** class is rather long and uses some features of the STL (sorting and **vector**) that have not been covered in this book so far. It is not important to understand every line of code in the class (although we would urge you to look a little further and try to understand some of the code to broaden your knowledge); it is more important to understand the concept of hiding all of these details from the end-user. Here is the definition of the **Playlist** class:

Example9_02.cpp

```
1   class Playlist
2   {
3   public:
4       void AddTrack(const Track* track)
5       {
6           if(!any_of(m_tracks.begin(), m_tracks.end(), [&track](const Track* t){
             return t->getName() == track->getName(); }))
7           {
8               m_tracks.push_back(track);
9               return;
10          }
11          cout << "Track: " << track->getName()
                 << " Not added as already exists in playlist";
12      }
13
14      void RemoveTrack(const string trackName)
15      {
16          m_tracks.erase(remove_if(m_tracks.begin(), m_tracks.end(),
17          [&trackName](const Track* t){ return t->getName() == trackName; }));
18      }
19
20      void PrintTracks() const
21      {
22          for (auto & track : m_tracks)
23          {
24              // round seconds
25              int seconds = static_cast<int>(track->getLength());
26              std::cout << track->getName() << " - " << seconds / 60 << ":"
                     << seconds % 60 << endl;
27          }
28      }
```

The complete code can be found at: https://packt.live/3a4XPVa

There is a lot in this class, but that is the point here. It is clear that all this functionality does not need to be known to the user of a **Playlist** class, only the methods that have been provided as a public interface. A sample use case of this **Playlist** class follows. From the perspective of someone using the class, as shown in the following snippet, there is not much to the **Playlist** class. All the detail has been abstracted away and is now presented to the user in the form of a simple **public** interface:

```
int main()

{

    Track t(100.0f, "Donut Plains");
    Track t2(200.0f, "Star World");
```

```
    Track t3(300.0f, "Chocolate Island");

    Playlist p;
    p.AddTrack( &t);
    p.AddTrack( &t2);
    p.AddTrack( &t3);
    p.SortAlphabetically(false);
    p.PrintTracks();
    p.SortAlphabetically(true);
    p.PrintTracks();
    p.SortByLength(false);
    p.PrintTracks();
    p.SortByLength(true);
    p.PrintTracks();

    return 0;
}
```

Once you run the preceding snippet, you will obtain the following output:

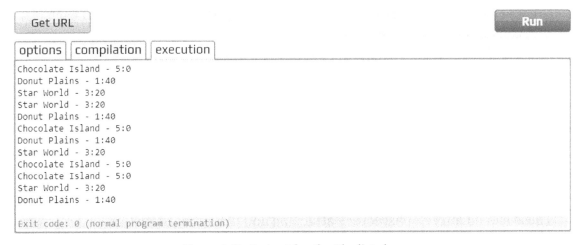

Figure 9.11: Output for the Playlist class

On the outside, the **Playlist** class is simple to use. All the gritty details are inside the class itself, along with the **Track** objects, thus ensuring that the **Playlist** class' own data is kept safe from outside interference. This type of abstraction of details means those details can be changed without anything using the class even needing to know that the change happened. Good **encapsulation** and **abstraction** decouple code from needing to know anything specific about the object being used, and if the specifics are unimportant, then they can be changed easily. For example, **Track** objects could be stored in a completely different way in the **Playlist** class than in the preceding example, and anything using **Playlist** would not need to know anything about it.

Activity 9: A Basic RPG Combat System

Now that you have learned about encapsulation and abstraction, we can combine this with our knowledge about creating classes, getters and setters, and constructors and their various forms. To help cement our knowledge about classes, we will now create a class from scratch while trying to keep everything we have learned about best practices in mind. We are going to create a very simple **RPG combat system**. An RPG is a role-playing game, and in these games, there are usually battles in which the hero and monsters take turns to stage attacks and use items. These attacks and items have stats that affect them in some way; we will implement the beginnings of a very simple version of this battle system. Once you have completed the activity, the names of characters along with the statistics of their items should be displayed on the screen.

> **Note**
>
> The complete code for this exercise can be found here: https://packt.live/3312hzy.

Here are some steps that will help you complete the activity:

1. Create classes for characters, attacks, and items with a **name** variable in each class that can be set in the constructor.

2. Give attacks an attack statistic (**attackStat**) variable and items a heal statistic (**healStat**) variable. Add appropriate getters and setters and constructor additions.

3. Let characters accept an array of attacks and items in their constructor and store them to be looked up by name when they need to be used.

4. Create functions to attack other characters, use items, and react to attacks.

5. Create member variables called **strengthMultiplier** and **defenseMultiplier**. These should affect a character's attacking and defending statistics.

6. Create a function to print a character's name and other statistics to the console.

7. Test everything in a **main** function with a few different characters.

Here are some hints that will help you complete the activity:

1. Remember the rule of three.

2. Look back to previous chapters to remind yourself how to create a dynamic **char** array when storing character names.

3. Feel free to use any containers that you may already be familiar with, but if intending to keep working with arrays (the solution uses arrays), then **memcpy** is the equivalent function to **strcpy** that you will need if the array is not a **char** array.

> **Note**
>
> The solution to this activity can be found on page 549. However, the solution is only one way of creating this system and should not be thought of as the definitive answer.

Summary

The topic of best practices when defining types in C++ is vast, and we have covered a great deal in this chapter to help you move toward creating classes that are robust and maintainable. We covered encapsulating data by using the **private** keyword to ensure that we decide how that data is accessed. We looked at getters and setters to give access to data and modify it in a way that can be validated. We also looked at how references can be used to give access to our data and modify it directly, and at how we can return data by value when we only want it to be read or used elsewhere without changing the object's internal data. We found that **const** can be used to ensure that any member variables we do not wish to be changed can be marked as such, along with member functions.

In the next chapter, we will look at what can be used to ensure that any dynamic objects we create can be properly destroyed using smart pointers. Pointers are a major part of C++ and come with their own pitfalls and best practices. You will learn the difference between plain pointers and smart pointers and why they are important.

10

Advanced Object-Oriented Principles

Overview

This chapter presents a number of advanced object-oriented principles, including inheritance and polymorphism, which will allow us to build more complex, dynamic, and powerful C++ applications. You will create new objects by inheriting functionality from base classes, implement virtual functions and abstract classes, use polymorphism to create versatile code, cast safely between types, and build a complex application using advanced OOP principles.

Introduction

Throughout *Chapter 8, Classes and Structs* and *Chapter 9, Object-Oriented Principles* we covered object-oriented principles in C++. We started by looking at classes and structs, creating our own user-defined objects to encapsulate our members. We then moved on to some basic object-oriented principles.

In this chapter, we're going to tackle some of the more advanced concepts of **object-oriented programming (OOP)**, such as inheritance, virtual member functions, abstract classes, polymorphism, and casting between types. With an understanding of these principles, we can really start making use of the great features that make C++ the versatile and powerful language it is.

We'll start by looking at inheritance, a feature through which we can define common functionality in a single base class, then extend it in unique child classes; this is one of the fundamental concepts in OOP. This will lead us on to looking at virtual member functions. These allow us to define functions in these common base classes that can be overridden in inheriting classes.

Next, we'll turn our attention to polymorphism. Through polymorphism, we gain the ability to call different implementations of the same function depending on which inheriting object we're calling the function on. We'll then look at casting between types using both **static_cast** and **dynamic_cast**, observing the differences between the two.

To finish our work on advanced object-oriented principles, we're going to complete an activity in which we create a small encyclopedia application that will display various bits of information on a selection of animals. A base class will be created to define an underlying structure, then we'll extend this with individual animal records, making use of polymorphism to fetch their data. When this chapter is complete, you'll have a strong understanding of these core principles of OOP.

Inheritance

When declaring a class in C++, we have the ability to inherit from another class. In fact, we can inherit from multiple classes at the same time—a feature of C++ that not all object-oriented languages share. When we inherit from another class, we gain all its members that have either public or protected privacy modifiers. Private members remain visible only to the class in which they're defined, not the inheriting class. This is one of the fundamental concepts in OOP and allows us to build flexible, maintainable objects where common functionality can be declared only once, then implemented and extended where needed.

Let's use vehicles and look at a quick example. We might define a base class, **Vehicle**, that defines some common properties, such as the maximum speed or the number of doors. We could then inherit from this class to create specialized vehicle classes such as **Car**, **Bike**, or **Lorry**. We create multiple classes that share a common base class and therefore share common members.

To inherit from a class, we would use the following syntax:

```
class DerivedClassName : [access modifier] BaseClassName
```

We define our class as normal then follow it with the : operator to start declaring the class(es) we want to inherit from. First, we provide an access modifier. We're going to cover what effect the different modifiers have on inheritance shortly, but the upshot is they determine the visibility of inherited members. Next, we simply declare the name of the class we wish to inherit from:

```
class MyBaseClass
{
};

class MyDerivedClass : public MyBaseClass
{
};
```

Our derived class will now have access to all the public and protected members declared in the base class. Remember, private members are only accessible to the class within which they're declared and friend classes.

> **Note**
>
> Private and protected members of a class can be accessed by other classes that are declared as friends of that class. Friend classes are beyond the scope of this book. More information, however, can be found here: https://packt.live/37vA8ns.

This relationship, a derived class inheriting from a base class, can be seen in the following simple diagram:

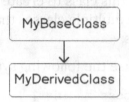

Figure 10.1: Single inheritance diagram

If we want to prohibit a class from being inherited from, C++11 provides us with the **final** keyword:

```cpp
class MyBaseClass final
{
};


class MyDerivedClass : public MyBaseClass
{
};
```

In this case, the code will fail to compile, giving us an error stating that **MyBaseClass** is **final**:

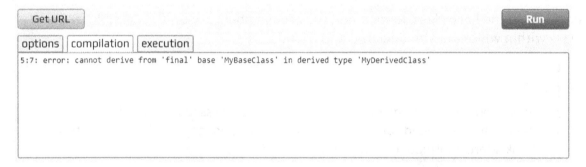

Figure 10.2: Compilation error since MyBaseClass is declared final

One of the main reasons to make classes final is so you can ensure that they are not inherited from and are thus the exact implementation that you intend. If you were writing a public library, for example, you might have a **Record** class. It might be vitally important that the implementation of this class is exactly as it should be, so you could mark the class as final to stop anybody from inheriting from it and using their user-defined version instead. Whatever your reason, marking a class as final means no class can inherit from it.

Let's take a look at an example of inheritance in code. Imagine we have three objects that all have a common member; say shapes and their areas. If we were to define these three classes individually, we'd end up with something like this:

```
class Square
{
public:
    int area = 10;
};

class Circle
{
public:
    int area = 10;
};

class Triangle
{
public:
    int area = 10;
};
```

We can see that there's common code here. We've declared the same member for each shape, which is unnecessary. Since it's common between each of the classes, we can move it into its own class and have the others inherit from it. This creates a relationship between the two. The class with the common functionality becomes known as the **base** class, and the class that inherits this behavior is known as the **derived** class.

Let's take these classes and move their common member into a base class.

Exercise 65: Inheritance

In the previous code snippet, we saw how we ended up with code repetition when we declared three shape classes, each with a member variable for area. Let's make use of inheritance to refactor this code:

> **Note**
>
> The complete code for this exercise can be found here: https://packt.live/2XE3HyT.

1. Declare a base class, **Shape**, that will contain the shared member. We'll also add a function to return it:

```cpp
#include <iostream>


class Shape
{
public:
    int area = 10;
    int GetArea() { return area; }
};
```

> **Note**
>
> The **get** function here isn't strictly necessary since our **area** variable is public. It's just here to demonstrate inheritance with a function.

2. Next, declare our three individual shape classes. This time, however, instead of declaring the **area** member in each as we did previously, inherit it from our new **Shape** class:

```cpp
class Square : public Shape
{
};
class Circle : public Shape
{
};
class Triangle : public Shape
{
};
```

3. Instantiate one of each of these classes in our **main** function:

```cpp
int main()
{
    Square mySquare;
    Circle myCircle;
    Triangle myTriangle;
```

4. Now, here's where we see inheritance at play. For the **Square** class we just created, we'll set a value for the **area** member, then call the **GetArea()** method to print it to the console:

```
mySquare.area = 5;
std::cout << "Square Area: " << mySquare.GetArea() << std::endl;
```

5. Do the same for the **Circle** class, but not the **Triangle** class. We'll just print this value, without giving the inherited member a new value:

```
myCircle.area = 15;
std::cout << "Circle Area: " << myCircle.GetArea() << std::endl;
std::cout << "Triangle Area: " << myTriangle.GetArea()
          << std::endl;
}
```

6. Run the application:

Figure 10.3: Accessing the area member defined in the base Shape class

We can see from the output and the fact that our program compiled without error, that our three classes, **Square**, **Circle**, and **Triangle**, all inherited the two members from the **Shape** class. In **Square** and **Circle**, we gave the inherited member variable a new value, and that was reflected when we called **GetArea**. In **Triangle**, where we didn't, we can see the original value defined in **Shape** was output.

We could go on to define any further shared properties or functionality in this base class, leaving any derived classes free to give them unique values. This is the main principle behind inheritance; we define shared members in the base class, leaving the inheriting class to make its specializations.

Multiple Inheritance

In the previous example, we created a derived class that inherited from a single base class, but one of the many great features of C++ is that multiple inheritance is supported. This means that a single derived class can inherit variables and functionality from multiple base classes to create a more complex object. Everything we learned about single inheritance remains true, the only difference is that the inherited members would come from multiple sources.

The syntax to inherit from multiple classes is as follows:

```
class DerivedClassName : [access modifier] BaseClassName, [access modifier]
AnotherBaseClassName
```

The following inheritance diagram shows how the directed class has two base classes from which it will inherit members:

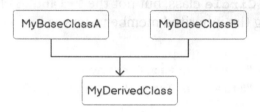

Figure 10.4: Multiple inheritance diagram

C++ doesn't implement a hard limit on the number of classes that can be inherited from; it's implementation-specific, though the C++ standard does provide recommended minimums:

- Direct and indirect base classes [16,384]

- Direct base classes for a single class [1,024]

- Direct and indirect virtual bases of a class [1,024]

Let's have a look at multiple inheritance in action:

```
class MyClassA
{
protected:
    int myInt;
};

class MyClassB
{
protected:
    std::string myString;
};

class MyClassC: public MyClassA, public MyClassB
{
    MyClassC()
    {
```

```
        myInt = 1;
        myString = 2;
    }
};
```

In the preceding code snippet, we define two base classes, **MyClassA** and **MyClassB**. We then create the derived type, **MyClassC**, and inherit from them both. **MyClassC** now has access to the members from both. This can be useful in letting us inherit values and behaviors from multiple sources, but there are a couple of things to be aware of.

The first is known as the diamond problem, so named for the shape of its inheritance diagram, and is the result of a class inheriting from two base classes that share a common base themselves. This can be seen more clearly in a diagram:

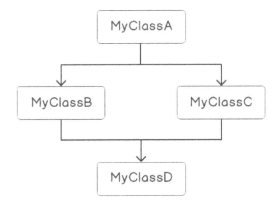

Figure 10.5: Diamond problem

In this diagram, we can see that **MyClassB** and **MyClassC** both inherit from **MyClassA**. **MyClassD** then goes to inherit from both **MyClassB** and **MyClassC**. This results in **MyClassD** having two copies of everything within **MyClassA** as it was instantiated twice, once from **MyClassB** and once from **MyClassC**. In code, this would be as follows:

```
// Diamond problem example.
#include <iostream>
#include <string>

class MyClassA
{
protected:
    int myInt;
};

class MyClassB: public MyClassA
{
```

```
};

class MyClassC: public MyClassA
{
};

class MyClassD: public MyClassB, public MyClassC
{
    MyClassD()
    {
        myInt = 1;
    }
};

int main()
{
}
```

If we try to run this code, we'll get an error stating that **myInt** is ambiguous. That's because **MyClassA** was instantiated twice, so there're two versions. The compiler doesn't know which one to use:

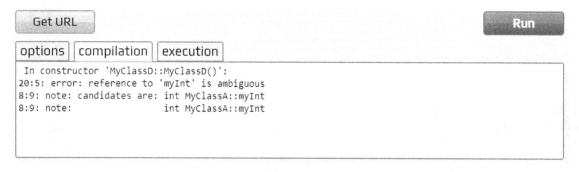

Figure 10.6: Properties accessed in scope

This can be avoided in two ways. The first is to qualify which version of the variable you want to access:

```
class MyClassD : public MyClassB, public MyClassC
{
    MyClassD()
    {
        MyClassB::myInt = 1;
    }
};
```

This would be fine because we've qualified which version of **myInt** we want to use by prefacing it with **MyClassB::**. This ensures we access the **MyClassB** version of it.

The second solution is through the use of virtual inheritance. When we use the **virtual** keyword when inheriting from a class, we ensure that only one copy of our base class's member variables will be inherited by any derived classes:

```
class MyClassB : public virtual MyClassA
{
};

class MyClassC : public virtual MyClassA
{
};
```

Now that **MyClassB** and **MyClassC** inherit from **MyClassA** virtually, its constructor will be called directly from **MyClassD** only once. This avoids duplicate properties and mitigates the diamond problem.

Exercise 66: Multiple Inheritance

Let's extend *Exercise 65, Inheritance*, to make use of multiple inheritance. We inherited from the **Shape** base class to provide area members, so let's inherit from a second class to inherit some color members:

> **Note**
>
> The complete code for this exercise can be found here: https://packt.live/2OBiGFB.

1. Copy the code of *Exercise 65, Inheritance*, into the compiler window.

2. Add a new class, **Color**, that defines a **color** variable, and a method to return it:

   ```
   class Color
   {
   public:
       std::string color = "";
       std::string GetColor() { return color; }
   };
   ```

3. Next, update all our derived classes to also inherit from this new class, as well as the original **Shape** class:

```
class Square : public Shape, public Color

//[...]

class Circle : public Shape, public Color

//[...]

class Triangle : public Shape, public Color
```

4. As the code stands we set the **Square** area variable, then return it within a **cout** statement. Let's do the same with our new **color** member:

```
mySquare.area = 5;
mySquare.color = "red";
std::cout << "Square Area: " << mySquare.GetArea() << std::endl;
std::cout << "Square Color: " << mySquare.GetColor() << std::endl;
```

5. Repeat these steps for the other two derived classes:

```
myCircle.area = 10;
myCircle.color = "blue";
std::cout << "Circle Area: " << myCircle.GetArea() << std::endl;
std::cout << "Circle Color: " << myCircle.GetColor() << std::endl;
myTriangle.area = 15;
myTriangle.color = "green";
std::cout << "Triangle Area: " << myTriangle.GetArea()
          << std::endl;
std::cout << "Triangle Color: " << myTriangle.GetColor()
          << std::endl;
```

6. Run the application. You will obtain the following output:

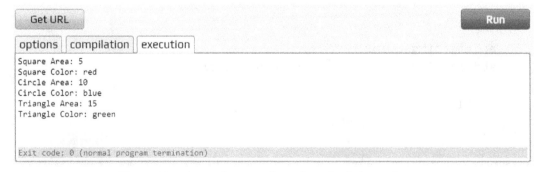

Figure 10.7: Accessing members from both base classes

Now that we've inherited from two classes, we have access to two sets of members: **area** and **GetArea** from the **Shape** class, and **color** and **GetColor** from the **Color** class.

In our examples so far, we've used public accessibility for everything because it means all members are visible everywhere. This was for demonstration purposes, however, and is not typically what we want in our systems because it leads to the potential misuse of things. As a general rule, our members should have the most restrictive visibility that they can. Have a look at how accessibility works with inheritance in the next section.

Access Modifiers and Inheritance

There are two areas of accessibility we need to be aware of when making use of inheritance. The first is the accessibility of the members in our base class, and the second is the access modifier we define when inheriting from a class. We'll start by looking at the first because it's been mentioned in previous chapters.

When declaring members, we have three access modifiers available to us that determine their visibility:

- **Public**: Visible anywhere
- **Protected**: Visible to the class in which they're defined and any derived classes
- **Private**: Visible only to the class in which they're defined

This means that if we want a variable to be accessible to a derived class, it must have either public or protected visibility. This only determines whether the member is visible to the derived class itself, however—not to others. For that, we turn to the access modifier we declare when inheriting from a class.

If you remember, the syntax to inherit from a class is as follows:

```
class DerivedClassName : [access modifier] BaseClassName
```

The access modifier we provide here is used in conjunction with the modifier on individual base members to determine their visibility; the most restrictive modifier wins. The following table shows how different inheritance types interact with access modifiers of base class members:

Base class access	Derived access with public inheritance	Derived access with protected inheritance	Derived access with private inheritance
Public	Public	Protected	Private
Protected	Protected	Protected	Private
Private	Private	Private	Private

Figure 10.8: Access modifier combinations

If we look at this table of all possible combinations, the earlier statement, "the most restrictive modifier wins" should become clearer. Whenever two different modifiers are combined (such as a protected base class variable being inherited privately) it's the most restrictive modifier that sticks; in that case, it would be private.

Exercise 67: Access Modifiers and Inheritance

To best see how access modifiers affect things, let's create a program that makes use of a variety of them. We'll create a base class with three members: one public, one protected, and one private. We'll then inherit from this class using various access modifiers to see each affect visibility of the members:

> **Note**
>
> The complete code for this exercise can be found here: https://packt.live/2D97LxH.

1. We'll start by declaring our base class. We'll continue with the shape example (it's a tried and tested analogy) and declare three members, giving each one of the three possible access modifiers:

```
#include <iostream>
#include <string>

class Shape
{
public:
    int area = 0;

protected:
    std::string color = "";

private:
    bool hasOutline = false;
};
```

2. Next, we'll inherit from this class, creating the derived **Square** class. For this first example, we'll use public inheritance:

```
class Square : private Shape
{
public:
    Square()
    {
```

```
        area = 5;
        color = "red";
        hasOutline = true;
    };
};
```

3. To test the visibility of the members, we'll instantiate this derived class and attempt to access each of its members in a **cout** statement:

```
int main()
{
    Square mySquare;

    std::cout << "Square Area: " << mySquare.area << std::endl;
    std::cout << "Square Color: " << mySquare.color << std::endl;
    std::cout << "Square Has Outline: " << mySquare.hasOutline
              << std::endl;
}
```

4. Let's run this application and see what our compiler gives us:

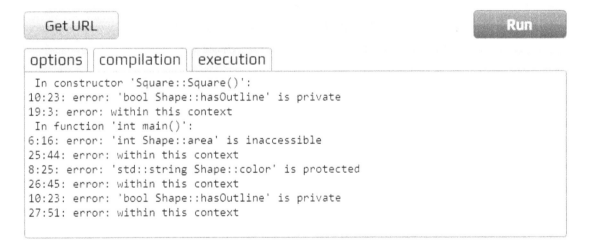

Figure 10.9: Errors to the accessibility of the members

In this case, we've created a derived class with public inheritance. For starters, we're unable to access the **hasOutline** member in our **Square** constructor. We're presented with the following error:

```
error: 'bool Shape::hasOutline' is private
```

This member was private in the base class, so it isn't accessible to derived classes.

Next, if we look at the code within the **main** function, we can see no errors accessing the **area** variable. This member was public in the base class, so it remains public and free to access. Accessing the **color** member, however, gives us the following error:

```
'std::string Shape::color' is protected
```

Even though we used public inheritance, the base class's protected modifier is more restrictive, so this is the one that gets used. This means that we're unable to publicly access this variable. We also get an error when trying to access **hasOutline**:

```
'bool Shape::hasOutline' is private
```

This is again due to the base class giving this variable private access. It's not visible to even the derived class, so certainly can't be publicly accessed.

5. Now, change the access modifier used in the inheritance to **protected**. Run the application and read through the compiler output, as we did earlier.

6. Finally, change the access modifier used in the inheritance to **private** and do the same again. You should hopefully have an idea of what errors this will result in. Refer to the chart given previously for clarification, if needed.

Understanding how different access modifiers affect inheritance is important, and often, a cause of confusion. For starters, all variables, regardless of the access modifier, are fully visible to the class in which they are defined. Derived classes (those that inherit from a base class) can access public and protected members. Finally, the access modifier used when inheriting from the base class determines the final visibility of the members, and therefore, how all other classes can access them. The previous chart shows all possible combinations, but just remember that the most restrictive modifier will always be chosen.

Virtual Functions

When we inherit from a base class, we've seen that we gain access to any public and protected members. With member variables, we've then gone on to give them unique values in our derived classes; but with functions, we've simply gained access to them and called them. It's possible, however, to specialize a function in a derived class, much like giving a member variable a unique value. We do this through the use of virtual functions.

In C++, a virtual function is one that can have its functionality overridden by a derived class. To mark a function as virtual, we simply use the **virtual** keyword at the start of its declaration:

```
virtual return_type function_name();
```

This then allows the function to be overridden in a deriving class. This is done, first, by declaring a function with the same signature, return type, name, and the override keyword and then by defining it. Let's look at an example of this:

```cpp
class MyBaseClass
{
public:
    virtual void PrintMessage()
    {
        std::cout << "Hello ";
    }
};

class MyDerivedClass: public MyBaseClass
{
public:
    void PrintMessage() override
    {
        std::cout << "World!";
    }
};
```

In this code, we've defined two classes: **MyBaseClass** and **MyDerivedClass**. In **MyBaseClass**, we declare a virtual **PrintMessage** function that will print the word **Hello** to the console. We then inherit from this class in **MyDerivedClass** and override the function to instead print the word **World**. If we instantiate **MyDerivedClass** and call its **PrintMessage** function, what do you think we'll see?

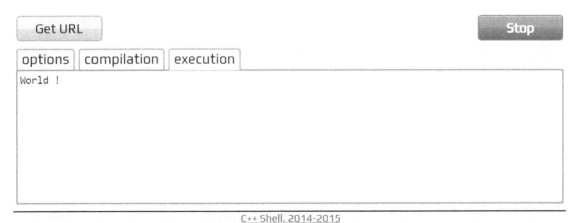

Figure 10.10: The output from our overridden virtual function

We see the word **World!**, which shows that the base function wasn't called, but the overriding function in the derived class was. If we look at that source code, you can see the 'override' keyword after our function definition in the derived class. This optional identifier not only makes it clear to a programmer that this is an overridden virtual function but also results in compile-time checks to ensure it's a valid override of a base function. Overriding virtual functions will work just fine without this identifier, but it's good practice to include it.

> **Note**
>
> Unlike **virtual**, override is not a keyword. It is instead an identifier with special meaning. It has no special meaning outside of the context of virtual functions.

So, when we override a virtual function and then call it, it will call the version defined in the derived class. But what if we want to call the base definition as well? Thankfully, this is possible. In our overridden **virtual** functions, it's possible to call the base implementation as well. This is done through the following syntax:

```
void MyFunction()
{
    BaseClass::MyFunction();
}
```

In our overriding function, we can make a call to the base function through our base class type. This will run the logic defined in the base version of the function before running that of the overriding function. Let's update our example to see this:

```
class MyDerivedClass : public MyBaseClass
{
public:
    void PrintMessage() override
    {
        MyBaseClass::PrintMessage();

        std::cout << "World!";
    }
};
```

We've updated our overridden function to call the **MyBaseClass** implementation first. Let's see what we get if we run the application now:

Figure 10.11: The functionality of both implementations

Since we start our overriding function implementation by calling the base functionality, we first output **Hello**, then return to process the logic in the derived function. This will print **Hello World!**, in its entirety, to the console. This can be very useful. You can define any common functionality in the base implementation, then go on to specialize it in a derived implementation.

Using video games as an example once again, an item system could make use of this. Say we defined a base class called **Item** that contained some generic members, including a **Use** function that takes some energy from the player. We could then go on to inherit from this to create as many derived items types as we want, implementing the **Use** function in each. Perhaps for a **Health Potion** item, we give the player some health; or for a **Torch** item, we create a light. Both of these derived classes can not only be stored in a common container of type **Item***, but could call the base implementation of **Use** before their own.

Pure Virtual Functions/Abstract Classes

Overriding a normal **virtual** function is optional; however, if we want to force our users to implement a virtual function in the derived class, we can make it pure virtual in the base class. A pure virtual function does not have an implementation in the base class, it is merely declared. The syntax for a pure virtual function is as follows:

```
virtual void MyFunction() = 0;
```

When a class contains one or more pure virtual functions, it becomes an abstract class. This is a class that cannot be directly instantiated. Here's an example:

```
class MyAbstractClass
{
    virtual void MyPureVirtualFunction() = 0;
};
```

```
class MyDerivedClass : public MyAbstractClass
{
    void MyPureVirtualFunction() override
    {
        std::cout << "Hello World!";
    }
};

int main()
{
    MyAbstractClass myAbstractClass;
}
```

In this code, we've defined a pure virtual function in a base class. We then inherit from this class in **MyDerivedClass** and provide a definition for the function. In our main function, we try to instantiate an instance of the abstract class. Let's run this and see what the compiler gives us:

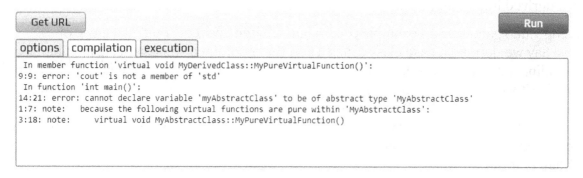

Figure 10.12: Trying to instantiate an abstract class

The compiler is not happy with us trying to instantiate this class because there's no definition of the function. If we were to instead instantiate our derived class, the compiler would be fine with that because we've provided a definition. If we were to omit that definition from our derived class, it too would become abstract and thus would not be able to be instantiated directly.

If we don't want to provide a definition in the base class, but still want to make overriding the function optional, we can give it an empty body:

```
virtual void MyPureVirtualFunction() {}
```

If we update our code to declare **MyPureVirtualFunction** (as we did earlier), our code would compile. Since we've given it an empty body, the class does not become abstract; we just have a function that doesn't do anything.

Abstract classes can be very useful to control what our users can and can't instantiate. A good example of this is with an object system in something like a video game engine. It's typical to have a base class called something like **Object**. This will define the shared features all objects will have, such as a unique GUID, and will act as a base class for all further objects—a **player** object. Since the base class is purely there to provide shared functionality and properties, but isn't useful on its own, we can make it an abstract class to ensure it can't be directly instantiated. It can only be inherited from to create derived classes.

Exercise 68: Virtual Functions

Let's put this new understanding of virtual functions to use; the **shape** example will work nicely. We've been declaring a base **Shape** class and inheriting from it to create specialized shapes such as a circle and a square. Our shape class on its own isn't very useful; it contains nothing specific and its main purpose is to provide shared functionality and members—a perfect candidate for an abstract class.

> **Note**
>
> The complete code for this exercise can be found here: https://packt.live/2D7zNd2.

We'll make this class abstract and provide a virtual function for calculating the area of a shape:

1. Let's start by defining our base **Shape** class. We want our shared members to be declared here; an integer to store the shape's area and a function to calculate it. We can make use of some access modifiers to ensure those variables that don't need to be public aren't:

```
#include <iostream>
#include <string>

class Shape
{
public:
    virtual int CalculateArea() = 0;

protected:
    int area = 0;
};
```

2. Now we'll declare our first derived class, **Square**. This derived class wants to override the **CalculateArea** function with the appropriate calculation and provide its own variable for the square's height. We'll inherit from **Shape** publicly:

```
class Square : public Shape
{
public:
    int height = 0;

    int CalculateArea() override
    {
        area = height * height;
        return area;
    }
};
```

3. Next, create another derived class, **Circle**. This will be similar to our **Square** class, but instead of providing a **height** variable, we'll provide a **radius** variable. We'll also update the calculation within the **CalculateArea** function:

```
class Circle : public Shape
{
public:
    int radius = 0;

    int CalculateArea() override
    {
        area = 3.14 * (radius * radius);
        return area;
    }
};
```

4. In our **main** function, we're now going to instantiate these derived classes, setting the member variable we declared for them, and calling the **CalculateArea** function. We'll start with **Square**:

```
int main()
{
    Square square;
    square.height = 10;
    std::cout << "Square Area: " << square.CalculateArea()
              << std::endl;
```

5. Finally, we'll do the same for our **Circle** class, finishing off our application:

```
Circle circle;
circle.radius = 10;
std::cout << "Circle Area: " << circle.CalculateArea()
          << std::endl;
}
```

6. Run the application. You will obtain the following output:

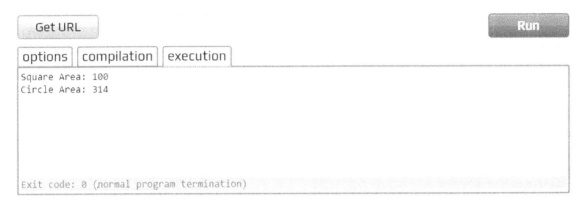

Figure 10.13: We overrode CalculateArea, specializing that function in each derived class

As we can see, our overridden **CalculateArea** functions have been successfully called for each derived class. Our base class, **Shape**, provided generic basic information, and we made the **CalculateArea** function pure virtual to ensure that it cannot be directly instantiated. If you tried to do so in this application, you would be given a compiler error. Even this trivial example shows how this powerful feature can be used to control what objects can and can't be instantiated, and to create specialized versions of classes that share a similar interface.

Polymorphism

We've now seen how we can use inheritance to create generic, base versions of objects, then specialize them in derived classes. Some of the many benefits of this include reduced code repetition, the ability to implement a common interface, and polymorphism.

Polymorphism allows us to call different implementations of the same function depending on which inheriting object we're calling the function on. We can do this because we can store derived types in a pointer variable of their base type. When we do this, we limit ourselves to only being able to access the members declared in the base, but when it's called, we'll get the implementations of the derived class.

Let's take a look at some code to see this in action:

```cpp
// Polymorphism.
#include <iostream>
#include <string>

class MyClassA
{
public:
    virtual std::string GetString() = 0;
};

class MyClassB: public MyClassA
{
public:
    std::string GetString() override
    {
        return "Hello ";
    }
};

class MyClassC: public MyClassA
{
public:
    std::string GetString() override
    {
        return " world!";
    }
};

int main()
{
    MyClassA * myClass = new MyClassB();
    std::cout << myClass->GetString();
    myClass = new MyClassC();
    std::cout << myClass->GetString();

    delete myClass;
    myClass = nullptr;
}
```

We've created two derived objects here, **MyClassB** and **MyClassC**, both inheriting from **MyClassA**. Since these objects share that common base class, **MyClassA**, we can store them in a pointer to this type (**MyClassA***) and access any members declared in that base class. When we call them, however, we get their derived implementations.

If we run the code, we can see this in action:

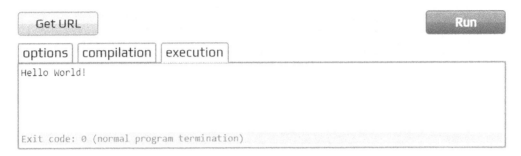

Figure 10.14: We've called two different implementations of a function from the same object type

Despite calling the function on the same variable, **myClass**, we get different results because it's storing a different derived class. This is polymorphism in action. It's important to note that polymorphism only works with non-value types—that is, references and pointers. With regard to polymorphism, they act largely the same; however, a reference cannot be legally null. This means that **dynamic_cast** will instead throw an exception on a failed cast rather than returning **nullptr**.

Casting is important and will be covered in the next part of the chapter, but before we get to that, let's continue building on the previous exercise. We'll store our derived shape classes polymorphically and see how we get different implementations depending on the derived type that was initially stored.

Exercise 69: Polymorphism

In *Exercise 68, Virtual Functions*, we used virtual overridden functions to provide multiple implementations of **GetArea()**. Let's do something similar, but this time we'll store these types polymorphically. We'll see how, even though we have two variables of the same type, because we assigned different derived classes, the implementations of our function calls will differ.

> **Note**
>
> The complete code for this exercise can be found here: https://packt.live/2OBx5Bz.

1. Copy the code of the previous exercise into your compiler.

2. Next, give the member variables in **Square** and **Circle** default values:

```
class Square : public Shape
{
public:
    int height = 10;
    int CalculateArea() override
    {
        area = height * height;
        return area;
    }
};


class Circle : public Shape
{
public:
    int radius = 10;
    int CalculateArea() override
    {
        area = 3.14 * (radius * radius);
        return area;
    }
};
```

3. Now we can implement polymorphism. We're currently instantiating an instance of each of our derived classes. The **square** variable is of type **Square**, and the **circle** variable is of type **Circle**. Let's change this so both of them are of type **Shape*—** that is, a pointer to a **Shape** object:

```
Shape* square = new Square();
Shape* circle = new Circle();
```

> **Note**
>
> Although we're using raw pointers here, you could also use smart pointers, as covered in the previous chapter. Raw pointers are used here for simplicity to keep the focus on the topic at hand.

4. Since we're now working with pointers to the base class, we can no longer access the **height** and **radius** variables. This will be covered in the next part, where we look at casting. For now, remove those calls.

5. Finally, with our square and circle variables now pointers, we need to change how we access the **CalculateArea** methods. We need to use the **->** operator instead of the . operator. We also need to delete the pointer:

```
std::cout << "Square Area: " << square->CalculateArea()
          << std::endl;
std::cout << "Circle Area: " << circle->CalculateArea()
          << std::endl;
delete square;
square = nullptr;
delete circle;
circle = nullptr;
```

> **Note**
>
> Deleting the pointer here isn't strictly necessary because our application is about to terminate anyway. It's always good practice, however, to match any calls to **new** with a call to **delete**. It'll save potential memory leaks.

6. Run the program. You will obtain the following output:

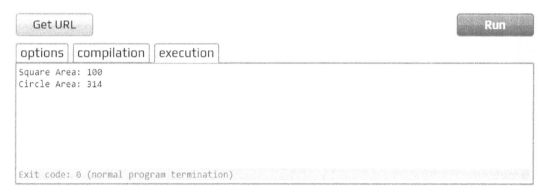

Figure 10.15: Using polymorphism, we've stored our derived types as pointers to their base

In this application, we show how we can store inherited types polymorphically as pointers to their base. When we then call functions on this object, we get the implementation provided by the derived class. If an overridden implementation isn't provided, we revert to calling the base class implementation.

Casting between Types

Now that we can store and interact with types polymorphically, we need to know how to cast between them. Casting is the process of converting an object from one type to another. This is important if we're storing derived types in a collection whose type is the base. In this case, we would need to cast from a base to a derived type. This is called a down-cast and requires a type check. We can also cast from a derived type to a base class, and this is called an up-cast. These are always allowed.

Consider the following:

```cpp
// Casting.
#include <iostream>
#include <string>

class MyClassA
{
public:
    int myInt = 0;
};

class MyClassB: public MyClassA
{
public:
    std::string myString = "";
};

int main()
{
    MyClassA * myClass = new MyClassB();
    std::cout << myClass->myInt << std::endl;
    std::cout << myClass->myString << std::endl;
    delete myClass;
    myClass = nullptr;
}
```

In this example, we have **MyClassB** inheriting from **MyClassA**. We instantiate **MyClassB**, store it in a pointer to **MyClassA**, then try to access members from both. What will we get if we run this application?

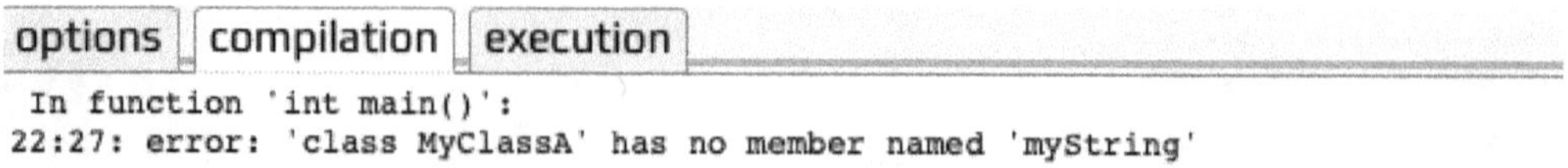

```
 options   compilation   execution

  In function 'int main()':
 22:27: error: 'class MyClassA' has no member named 'myString'
```

Figure 10.16: We're unable to access the members declared in the derived class from the base

We get a compilation error. Since we're working with a **MyClassA** object, we can only access members from that class. In order to access our derived members, we need to cast to the type. We're going to cover three types of cast in this chapter: **static_cast**, **dynamic_cast**, and C-style casts.

Static Cast

Let's start with a **static_cast**. A **static_cast** is used when you are sure you're working with an object of a certain type. As such, no checks are done. In our example, for instance, we're clearly storing an object of type **MyClassB**, so we can **static_cast** to that type safely.

The syntax for **static_cast** is as follows:

```
static_cast<type_to_cast_to*>(object_to_cast_from);
```

If we apply that to the previous code example, we can cast to our derived type, and then accessing the members isn't an issue:

```cpp
int main()
{
    MyClassA* myClass = new MyClassB();
    std::cout << myClass->myInt << std::endl;
    MyClassB* myClassB = static_cast<MyClassB*>(myClass);
    std::cout << myClassB->myString << std::endl;

    delete myClass;
    myClass = nullptr;

    delete myClassB;
    myClassB = nullptr;
}
```

This code will now compile fine, and we're able to access the **myString** member of our object.

Dynamic Cast

The second cast, **dynamic_cast**, is used when we aren't sure what type of object we're working with. If we try a dynamic cast and it fails, **nullptr** is returned. We can then check if our object is valid.

The syntax for **dynamic_cast** is as follows:

```
dynamic_cast<type_to_cast_to*>(object_to_cast);
```

For **dynamic_cast** to work when down-casting, the base class must contain at least one virtual function. If we were to try to down-cast **MyClassA** to **MyClassB** as is, we would get a compiler error, as shown in the following figure:

```
MyClassB* myClassB = dynamic_cast<MyClassB*>(myClass);
if (myClassB != nullptr)
{
std::cout << myClassB->myString << std::endl;
}
```

Error is as follows:

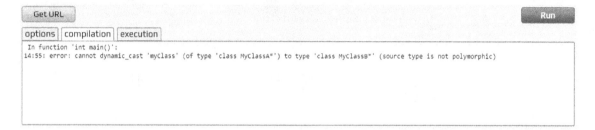

```
In function 'int main()':
14:55: error: cannot dynamic_cast 'myClass' (of type 'class MyClassA*') to type 'class MyClassB*' (source type is not polymorphic)
```

Figure 10.17: We're unable to downcast from MyClassA to MyClassB since it's not a polymorphic type

However, if **MyClassA** was to contain a **virtual** function—and thus be a polymorphic type—this would work fine. Using **dynamic_cast** is safer than **static_cast** because it will return a null pointer if the cast fails.

C-Style Cast

Finally, C-style casts, or regular casts, try a number of different casts and take the first one that works. This doesn't include **dynamic_cast**, however, so it is as unsafe as **static_cast**.

The syntax for a C-style cast is as follows:

```
(type_to_cast_to *) object_to_cast
```

For example, if we were to cast **MyClassA** to **MyClassB** using a C-style cast, we would do this:

```
MyClassB* myClassB = (MyClassB*)myClass;
```

Since we know that **myClass** is of type **MyClassB**, this cast is OK and results in a usable object.

Which cast you use will depend on your scenario. Aim to use the various C++ style casts when writing C++, choosing **static_cast** when you're sure of the type, and **dynamic_cast** when you're not. There are also other C++ casts available, such as **const_cast** and **reinterpret_cast**, but they're outside the scope of this chapter.

> **Note**
>
> If you want to do further reading on these other C++ casts, head to https://packt. live/37tJksD.

To put our newfound casting skills into practice, let's build on the previous exercise.

Exercise 70: Casting

For our last exercise of the chapter, we're going to extend our shape application once more. In the previous exercise, we moved to store our various shape types polymorphically. Instead of storing them as their individual types, we stored them as pointers to their base class and accessed their **CalculateArea** function through polymorphism. One thing we had to do, however, was to give their radius and height variables default values because we had no way to set them. Let's remedy that with casting. We'll use **dynamic_cast** for this.

> **Note**
>
> The complete code for this exercise can be found here: https://packt.live/37svU07.

1. Copy the code of *Exercise 69, Polymorphism* into the compiler window.

2. We'll start by changing the values of the **area**, **height**, and **radius** variables in class **Shape**, **Square**, and **Circle** respectively back to **0**:

```
//[...]
public:
    int area = 0;
//[...]
public:
    int height = 0;
//[...]
public:
    int radius = 0;
//[...]
```

3. Now we need to cast our **Shape*** types to their derived types. Since we named our square and circle types appropriately, we can be sure of their type. Because of this, we'll use **static_cast**. In **main()**, we'll first cast our square variable to type **Square***, after it's defined:

```
Square* square2 = static_cast<Square*>(square);
```

4. With our object now of type Square, we can access the height variable and set it to 10, like before:

```
square2->height = 10;
```

5. Now, do the same for our **Circle** class:

```
Circle* circle2 = static_cast<Circle*>(circle);
circle2->radius = 10;
```

6. Run the program:

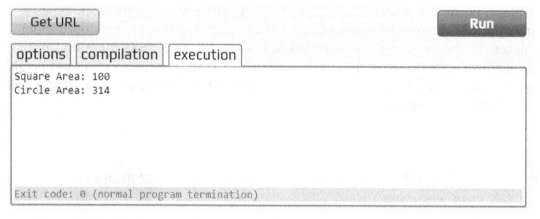

Figure 10.18: Casting to our derived type allows us to call members specific to them

In this exercise, we've seen how we can cast from a base type to a derived type to access derived members. This works the same way the other way around as well—from derived to base—although we're then only able to access members declared in the base class. Knowing how to cast between types is key when we start to work with polymorphism and inheritance.

Activity 10: An Encyclopedia Application

To finish our work on advanced object-oriented principles, we're going to do an activity in which we create a small encyclopedia application that will display various bits of information on a selection of animals. A base class will be created to define an underlying structure, and we'll extend this with individual animal records, making use of polymorphism to fetch their data. The output will look as follows:

Figure 10.19: Users can view information on various animals

Note

The complete code for this activity can be found here: https://packt.live/2ODU5Ad.

Here are the steps to help you perform the activity:

1. Start by including all the files that you'll need for the application.

2. Create a struct, **AnimalInfo**, that can store **Name**, **Origin**, **Life Expectancy**, and **Weight.**

3. Create a function to print that data out in a neat format. Name it **PrintAnimalInfo.**

4. Now, create the base class for our animals. Name it **Animal**. It should provide a member variable of type **AnimalInfo**, and a function to return it. Be sure to use appropriate access modifiers.

5. Next, create the first derived class, **Lion**. This class will inherit from **Animal**, be final, and fill out the **AnimalInfo** member in its constructor.

6. Next, create the second derived class, **Tiger**. Fill out the same data.

7. Create the final derived class, **Bear**, also filling out the **AnimalInfo** member.

8. Define the **main** function. Declare a vector of pointers to the base **Animal** type and add one of each of the animal-derived types.

9. Output the application title.

10. Create the main outer loop for the application and output a message to the user prompting them to select an index.

11. Output the possible selections to the user. Use a **for** loop for this, and each option should include an index and the name of the animal. Also, include an option for the user to be able to quit the application by entering **-1**.

12. Fetch the user input and convert it to an integer.

13. Check whether the user entered **-1** and thus wants to quit the application. Handle this if they do.

14. Next, check that the user entered an invalid index. An invalid index is one that's less than **-1** and greater than the size of the animal vector **-1** (because indices start at 0, not 1). If they did, output an error message and have them choose again.

15. If the user input a valid index, make a call to the **PrintAnimalInfo** created earlier, passing in the animal's info that you'll get from the vector.

16. Outside of the **main** loop, clean up the pointers. This means deleting their memory, setting them to **0**, and then clearing the vector.

> **Note**
>
> The solution for this activity can be found on page 559.

Summary

In this chapter, we've covered some further topics on OOP, starting with inheritance. We saw how we can use this to define behaviors in a base class, then inherit from that to create a derived class. Our derived classes specialize these more generic base classes, inheriting any public and protected members while defining their own as well. We can go on to create chains of inheritance or inherit from more than one class at a time to create complex objects.

We then looked at virtual member functions. When we declare functions in base classes, we can mark them as virtual, meaning their implementation can be overridden. Derived classes can provide their own implementations for virtual functions, should they wish to. If, however, a function is marked as pure virtual—and thus the base class is abstract—then the deriving class must provide a definition or become abstract as well.

This led to polymorphism and type casting. With objects that share a similar interface-the members declared in shared base classes—we can store them as a pointer to their base type. When we do so, we only have access to the members declared in the base class, but when we call them, we will get the derived class's implementation. If we want to then access specific members, we need to cast back to our derived type, and we covered the different methods of doing so: **static_cast**, **dynamic_cast**, and C-style casts.

We finished the chapter by creating an encyclopedia application for a zoo. By making use of the OOP topics covered in the chapter, we defined a base class for an animal and created a number of derived classes. We then allowed the user to select an animal via an index and printed various bits of information.

In the final part of this book, we're going to be looking at further advanced concepts, including templates, containers and iterators, and exception handling. Templates allow us to create highly reusable code and open a whole world of possibilities. We looked at a couple of basic containers, arrays and vectors, so we'll be extending that by looking at more standard library containers and iterators. Finally, exception handling is something that we will cover in *Chapter 13*, *Exception Handling in C++*. Handling exceptions is key to creating stable software that doesn't crash when it finds itself in a bad state.

11

Templates

Overview

This chapter covers an overview of templates and gives some examples of how they can be used and where. By the end of this chapter, you will feel confident enough to implement template types and functions where they may be applicable and have some foundational knowledge you can build from.

Introduction

In the previous chapters, **OOP** was introduced, along with examples and use cases. Classes and best practices for creating them were covered in detail. In this chapter, we are going to look at another powerful feature of OOP—templates.

Templates allow the reuse of code for different data types. An example of the use of templates is the C++ standard template library (or STL). This library is a set of template classes that provide generic containers and algorithms. The library can be used with any data type, and this is achieved using template functions and classes. In this chapter, we will cover the creation of template classes and template functions to allow the creation of reusable code.

Specifically, we will be describing the following topics: template classes, template functions, and template specialization.

At its core, a template is a form of generic programming. It allows us to reuse a set of functionality, without that functionality needing to be specific to one type. For example, a class could hold data and provide some functionality to a variable of type **int**. If we needed to perform the same functionality on a variable of the **float** type, then we would need to duplicate that code, replacing **int** with **float**. However, with templates, we can reuse that code and allow the compiler to generate the code we need for each type. We will begin by showing how a template can be declared and then go into more detail with examples and exercises.

Syntax

Creating templates involves the use of a new C++ keyword: **template**. This keyword lets the compiler know that this class or function is intended to be used as a template, and that instances of a template parameter in a template *definition* should be replaced with the actual data type provided by a template *instantiation*:

```
template <typename T>
template <class T>
```

In the preceding examples, **T** is the template parameter. Anywhere that type **T** is used within a template class or function, it will be replaced by the actual type. This will become clearer with some examples. **T** is a very common name for a template parameter, but the name can be anything you wish.

Template Classes

An example of a very simple template class is provided here:

```
template<typename T>
class Position
{
public:
    Position(T x, T y)
    {
        m_x = x;
        m_y = y;
    }

    T const getX() { return m_x; }
    T const getY() { return m_y; }

private:
    T m_x;
    T m_y;
};
```

Notice the use of the template syntax. In this case, we are declaring that anywhere that **T** appears can be replaced with a type we choose when we create an instance of this class. This class is a simple holder for 2D positional values. Depending on the precision required, these positional values might be stored as **int**, **float**, or even **long** types. Through the use of templates, this class can be used for all of these types by passing the intended type when creating the class instance. Let's test this with a small exercise.

Exercise 71: Creating Different Types for the Position Objects

Using the preceding template class, write a **main** function that creates a few different **Position** objects. Each should use a different template parameter (**T**'s replacement) and then print out the type of a member variable that is now the type of the template parameter. To get the type of a variable, we can use the **typeid** operator contained in the **<typeinfo>** header.

> **Note**
>
> The complete code for the exercise can be found at https://packt.live/2rhi6Vm.

Here are the steps to complete the exercise:

1. Declare a **Position** object that replaces **T** with **int**:

```
int main()
{
    Position<int> intPosition(1, 3);
```

2. Declare a **Position** object that replaces **T** with **float**:

```
    Position<float> floatPosition(1.5f, 3.14f);
```

3. Declare a **Position** object that replaces **T** with **long**:

```
    Position<long> longPosition(1, 3);
```

4. Include the **<typeinfo>** header at the top of our file:

```
#include <typeinfo>
```

5. Output the types of our **m_x** variables in each instance of **Position**:

```
    cout << "type: " << typeid(intPosition.getX()).name() <<   " X: "
         << intPosition.getX() << " Y: " << intPosition.getY()
         << endl;

    cout << "type: " << typeid(floatPosition.getX()).name() <<   " X: "
         << floatPosition.getX() << " Y: " << floatPosition.getY()
         << endl;

    cout << "type: " << typeid(longPosition.getX()).name() <<   " X: "
         << longPosition.getX() << " Y: " << longPosition.getY()
         << endl;
```

6. The complete program looks like this:

```
#include <iostream>
#include <string>
#include <typeinfo>

using namespace std;

template<typename T>

class Position
{
```

```cpp
public:
    Position(T x, T y)
    {
        m_x = x;
        m_y = y;
    }

    T const getX() { return m_x; }
    T const getY() { return m_y; }

private:
    T m_x;
    T m_y;
};

int main()
{
    Position<int> intPosition(1, 3);
    Position<float> floatPosition(1.5f, 3.14f);
    Position<long> longPosition(1, 3);

    cout << "type: " << typeid(intPosition.getX()).name() << " X: "
        << intPosition.getX() << " Y: " << intPosition.getY()
        << endl;

    cout << "type: " << typeid(floatPosition.getX()).name() << " X: "
        << floatPosition.getX() << " Y: " << floatPosition.getY()
        << endl;

    cout << "type: " << typeid(longPosition.getX()).name() << " X: "
        << longPosition.getX() << " Y: " << longPosition.getY()
        << endl;

    return 0;
}
```

Once you run the preceding code, you will obtain the following output:

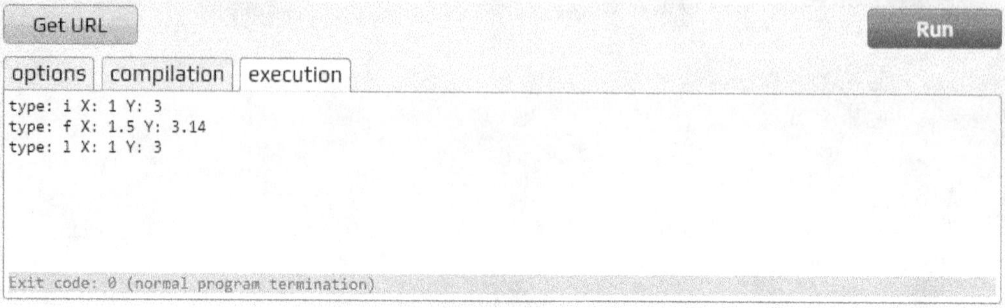

Figure 11.1: The three Position types

In our exercise, three **Position** types have been created, each with a different type for the template parameter: **int**, **float** and **long**. The **#include <typeinfo>** line gives access to the name of the passed-in type through the **name()** function (take note that these names cannot be guaranteed to be the same between compilers). Printing the value from this function by passing the **x** value from the **Position** class shows that the type of **T** has indeed been replaced with the passed-in type to the template class. The output shows that **i**, **f**, and **l** are, in the case of this compiler, the names for **int**, **float**, and **long**, respectively.

Multiple Template Parameters

In the preceding section, we saw a single template parameter being used in the examples. However, multiple template parameters can also be used. In the following example, there is an additional template parameter, **U**, that is used as a datatype for the **z** rotation in the **Position** class:

```cpp
#include <iostream>
#include <typeinfo>

using namespace std;

template<typename T, typename U>

class Position
{
public:
    Position(T x, T y, U zRot)
    {
        m_x = x;
        m_y = y;
        m_zRotation = zRot;
```

```
    }

    T const getX() { return m_x; }
    T const getY() { return m_y; }
    U const getZRotation() { return m_zRotation; }

private:
    T m_x;
    T m_y;
    U m_zRotation;
};
```

Just like **T**, anywhere that **U** is used will be replaced by another type when we create an instance of our class. The preceding class is almost the same as before, but now there is a **getZRotation** function that doesn't return the type that **T** will refer to. Instead, it returns the type that **U** will refer to. We can test this with a **main** function that again prints the types of the values within our class once an instance has been created:

```
int main()
{
    Position<int, float> intPosition(1, 3, 80.0f);
    Position<float, int> floatPosition(1.0f, 3.0f, 80);
    Position<long, float> longPosition(1.0, 3.0, 80.0f);

    cout << "type: " << typeid(intPosition.getX()).name() <<  " X: "
         << intPosition.getX() << " Y: " << intPosition.getY() << endl;

    cout << "type: " << typeid(floatPosition.getX()).name() <<  " X: "
         << floatPosition.getX() << " Y: " << floatPosition.getY() << endl;

    cout << "type: " << typeid(longPosition.getX()).name() <<  " X: "
         << longPosition.getX() << " Y: " << longPosition.getY() << endl;

    cout << "type: " << typeid(intPosition.getZRotation()).name()
         <<  " Z Rot: " << intPosition.getZRotation() << endl;

    cout << "type: " << typeid(floatPosition.getZRotation()).name()
         <<  " Z Rot: " << floatPosition.getZRotation() << endl;

    cout << "type: " << typeid(longPosition.getZRotation()).name()
         <<  " Z Rot: " << longPosition.getZRotation() << endl;

    return 0;
}
```

The preceding code yields the following output:

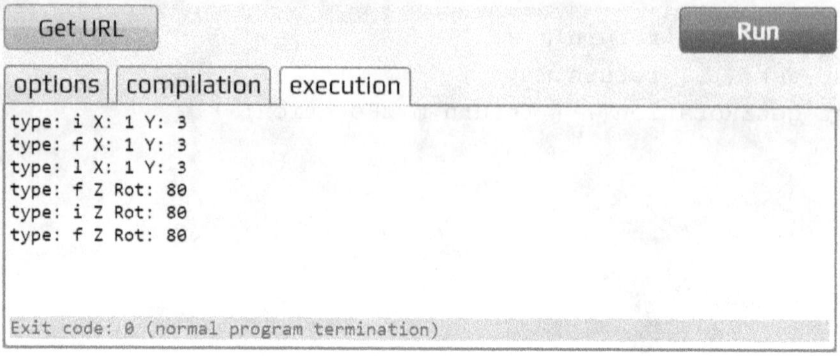
Get URL
Run
options
compilation
execution
type: i X: 1 Y: 3
type: f X: 1 Y: 3
type: l X: 1 Y: 3
type: f Z Rot: 80
type: i Z Rot: 80
type: f Z Rot: 80
Exit code: 0 (normal program termination)

Figure 11.2: Output for type U

Class templates are extremely powerful and can help with code reuse throughout your C++ applications. Whenever we know that some functionality a class performs on a type would be useful for more than just that one type, then we have a candidate for a template class. Template classes aren't the only way we can achieve this reuse, though; another way is through the use of **template functions**.

Template Functions

Having a class that can utilize many different datatypes is very useful, and yet sometimes, it is a smaller piece of code that needs to be reused in a "templated" way. This is where **template functions** come in. Template functions allow a specific function to be generic, rather than a whole class. Here is an example of a template function that returns the largest value between two numbers of the same type:

```
template<typename T>

T getLargest(T t1, T t2)
{
    if(t1 > t2)
    {
        return t1;
    }
    else
    {
        return t2;
    }
}
```

The syntax used here is the same as when declaring a template class, but it is placed above a function signature instead of a class declaration. Furthermore, just as with template classes, anywhere that **T** appears, it will be replaced by the type of the template parameter.

In the following exercise, we will be using the **getLargest** class to compare the **x** and **y** variables of the **Position** class created previously.

Exercise 72: Comparing Position Values Using a Template Function

The **getLargest** function in the preceding example can be used to compare the **x** and **y** variables of the **Position** class. Unlike we did in creating an instance of a class, we don't have to pass the type into the function when we use it. The compiler will have created a version of the function that works for each type when the program is compiled. Let's write an example that will help this make sense.

> **Note**
>
> The complete code for the exercise can be found at https://packt.live/2O7pICT.

Here are the steps to complete the exercise:

1. First, we begin with the **Position** class:

```
#include <iostream>
#include <typeinfo>

using namespace std;

template<typename T, typename U>
class Position
{
public:
    Position(T x, T y, U zRot)
    {
        m_x = x;
        m_y = y;
        m_zRotation = zRot;
    }

        T const getX() { return m_x; }
        T const getY() { return m_y; }
        U const getZRotation() { return m_zRotation; }
```

```
    private:
        T m_x;
        T m_y;
        U m_zRotation;
};
```

2. After this class, we can add the **getLargest** function:

```
template<typename T>
T getLargest(T t1, T t2)
{
    if(t1 > t2)
    {
        return t1;
    }
    else
    {
        return t2;
    }
}
```

3. And finally, we can create some **Position** objects and pass the **x** value to **getLargest** while comparing the **m_zRotation** values of the **int** and **long** **Position** instances:

```
int main()
{
    Position<int, float> intPosition(1, 3, 80.5f);
    Position<float, int> floatPosition(2.5f, 3.14f, 80);
    Position<long, float> longPosition(5, 3, 200);
    cout << "largest is: " << getLargest(intPosition.getX(),
        intPosition.getY()) << endl;

    cout << "largest is: " << getLargest(floatPosition.getX(),
        floatPosition.getY()) << endl;

    cout << "largest is: " << getLargest(longPosition.getX(),
        longPosition.getY()) << endl;

    cout << "largest ZRot is:" << getLargest(intPosition.
        getZRotation(), longPosition.getZRotation()) << endl;

    return 0;
}
```

When you run the complete code, you should obtain the following output:

Figure 11.3: Output containing a comparison of the x and y variables

We can see that we did not need to specify which type we were passing to the template function; the compiler did this work for us. Also, note that the function did not base its type on the **T** value of the instance we used, but on the actual type of the member variable we passed in. This is made clear by comparing the **z** rotation value to the **x** position value, which is of a different type - the compiler still created the correct function for us.

Template Specialization

While templates are largely designed to make classes more generic, there are occasions where one particular datatype needs to have its own implementation. Template specialization allows us to create templates that work in the generic way we have come to understand, but can behave differently for a specific datatype. This is useful in many instances, such as for algorithms that are fast for the majority of datatypes, but may be slow or inefficient in a particular case. To illustrate this, here is a simple **compare** function that uses **strcmp** in the case of C-style strings and effects a comparison using the *equality operator* for other types.

Template function:

```
template<typename T>
bool compare(T t1, T t2)
{
    return t1 == t2;
}
```

This is an example where we need a special circumstance–and, hence, a specialization–because, since **const char*** is a pointer, the equality operator would only compare the pointer addresses and not the content of the strings:

Specialized template function:

```
template <>
bool compare<const char*>(const char* c1, const char* c2)
{
    return strcmp(c1, c2) == 0;
}
```

Observe that when using a specialized template function, the concrete data type is used in place of the generic **T** but it is not passed in as a template parameter to template <>; instead, it is passed in after the function name. The following example tests these functions:

```
#include <iostream>
#include <string.h>

using namespace std;

template<typename T>
bool compare(T t1, T t2)
{
    return t1 == t2;
}

template <>
bool compare<const char*>(const char* c1, const char* c2)
{
    return strcmp(c1, c2) == 0;
}

const char* TRUE_STR = "TRUE";
const char* FALSE_STR = "FALSE";
```

```
int main()
{
    cout << (compare(1, 1) ? TRUE_STR : FALSE_STR) << endl;
    cout << (compare("hello","hello") ? TRUE_STR : FALSE_STR) << endl;
    cout << (compare(1, 2) ? TRUE_STR : FALSE_STR) << endl;
    cout << (compare("hello","goodbye") ? TRUE_STR : FALSE_STR) << endl;

    return 0;
}
```

The preceding code would yield the following output:

Figure 11.4: Output when comparing strings using strcmp and other types using the equality operator

The same can be achieved using classes instead of functions, as outlined in the following example:

```
#include <iostream>
using namespace std;

template <class T>

class MyClass
{
public:
    MyClass() { cout << "My class generic" << endl; }
};

template <>
class MyClass <int>
{
public:
    MyClass() { cout << "My class int specialization" << endl; }
```

```
};

int main()
{
    MyClass<float> floatClass;
    MyClass<int> intClass;

    return 0;
}
```

The preceding code yields the following output:

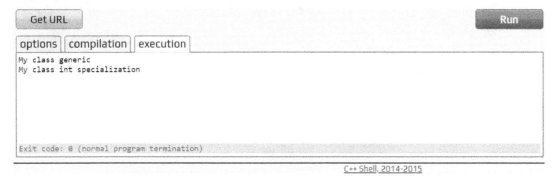

Figure 11.5: Output when using classes instead of functions

Additional Template Considerations

There are a few points that you need to consider when creating and using template classes. These are briefly described here.

Forcing Accepted Types

When creating our template classes, it is worth keeping in mind that an assumption has been made that the passed-in parameter is of a type that can be used in the context we want. This is not always the case, and measures need to be taken to ensure that things behave as intended—for example, if we have a template function that sums values together and we pass it a string or a custom type. Unfortunately, we cannot set the types we want to accept in the template declaration. There are ways to achieve this, yet a lot of the options are very usage-specific and outside the scope of this book. It is worth keeping in mind how an invalid type might be handled if you know it is possible that a type will be used that will certainly cause major issues.

Templates and Default Constructors

Another assumption made in the preceding examples is that any template parameter type has a default constructor. This is because a template class, just like any other, still has the responsibility of calling the default constructors of its member variables, and if given a type without a default constructor, it will fail to compile. Using the **Position** class as an example (as it does not have a default constructor), we can see what would happen if we were to pass that type into another template class as a template parameter:

```cpp
#include <iostream>
using namespace std;

template<typename T>
class Position
{
public:
    Position(T x, T y)
    {
        m_x = x;
        m_y = y;
    }

    T const getX() { return m_x; }
    T const getY() { return m_y; }

private:
    T m_x;
    T m_y;
};
```

The class has been simplified again to its original form. The following is an example of a template class that could have a position as its template parameter type:

```cpp
template<class T>

class PositionHolder
{
public:
    PositionHolder()
    {
    }
```

```
    T getPosition() { return m_position; }

private:
    T m_position;
};

int main()
{
    PositionHolder<Position<float>> positionHolder;

    return 0;
}
```

PositionHolder is a new template class that will be used to wrap **Position<T>** types. Running this code will produce something like the following compiler error:

```
error: no matching function for call to 'Position<float>::Position()'
```

We can deduce from this that an attempt to call the default constructor for **Position** has been made and, since **Position** does not have one, this has led to a compiler error. One option to fix this error is to make the **PositionHolder** constructor a templated function that can pass the values of the correct type to the constructor of **Position<T>** in the initialization list:

```
template<typename U>

PositionHolder(U x, U y) : m_position(x,y)
{
}
```

Creating **PositionHolder** now requires passing in the values of the variables that the **T** parameter requires in its constructor. Essentially, we now give **PositionHolder** the responsibility of passing appropriate values to the constructor of **T**:

```
int main()
{
    PositionHolder<Position<float>> positionHolder(20.0f, 30.0f);

    return 0;
}
```

This works, but it would quickly become unwieldy, and any updates to the **Position** constructor would mean an update to the **PositionHolder** constructor and that any type that **PositionHolder** can contain would need this two-parameter constructor. A better option is to define a copy constructor in **Position** and call that instead. Here is the **Position** class copy constructor:

```
Position(const T& t)
{
    m_x = t.m_x;
    m_y = t.m_y;
}
```

And now, **PositionHolder** can use this copy constructor in its own constructor, as follows:

```
PositionHolder(const T& t) : m_position(t)
{
}
```

Now, when we want to add a **Position** object to **PositionHolder**, we can construct a new position to copy from, or just add an existing **Position** object, depending on the circumstances:

```
int main()
{
    PositionHolder<Position<float>> positionHolder(Position<float>(20.0f,
30.0f));

    return 0;
}
```

Now the stored position can be created from another position, and it is up to the template parameter type to define its own copy constructor. Note that in the preceding case, the copy constructor would not need to be defined, as a shallow copy would suffice, but this is not always the case and should be kept in mind.

Creating a Generic Queue

Armed with this new template knowledge, we can now attempt to create something practical. In coming chapters, we will cover the containers from the **STL**, but before that, it is useful to have an idea of how some of them may work on a simpler level. Then, if thesituation arises that one of them is not quite right for our needs, we can write something more suited to us that still gives us the nice-to-use interface of the STL.

What Is a Queue?

We can define a queue as a container with a **first in**, **first out** (**FIFO**) data structure. Elements are inserted at the back and deleted from the front. Queues are useful for many things, such as scheduling tasks that can be acted upon and then removed. Think of queues just like when you queue in a shop. If you are first in the queue, then you will be served first.

For our example, we will be basing our queue on the STL queue and trying to implement everything that it provides already. That being said, the STL queue provides the following functions:

- **empty()**: Returns a bool to indicate whether the queue is empty.

- **size()**: Returns the queue's current size or number of elements.

- **swap()**: Swaps the contents of two queues (we will not implement this one here, but you could attempt this yourself as an extension task).

- **emplace()**: Adds an element to the end of the queue (again, we will not implement this, as it is outside the scope of this chapter).

- **front()** and **back()**: Return a pointer to the first and last elements in the queue, respectively.

- **push(element)** and **pop()**: Push an element to the end of the queue and delete the first element, respectively.

Here is the initial class definition that the remainder of the example will be built from:

```
template<class T>

class Queue
{
public:

private:
};
```

Looking at the functions we need to implement, we can see that we are going to need to store the first and last elements in the queue so that they can be returned from **front()** and **back()**. As we move further into this chapter, we will cover the use of dynamic memory to store our queue elements. When working with this dynamic memory, we will be allocating memory to hold our data and then returning a pointer to the first element in this chunk of memory. Therefore, **front()** will simply be the pointer to our queue data, and **back()** will point to one past the last constructed element of our data decremented by one (in other words, the last constructed element).

The following is a diagram of how elements will be laid out in our queue:

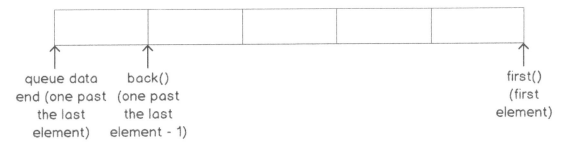

queue data
end (one past
the last
element)

back()
(one past
the last
element - 1)

first()
(first
element)

Figure 11.6: Elements being laid out in the queue

With this in mind, here is the updated class to reflect this:

```
template<class T>

class Queue
{
public:
    T* front() { return queueData; }
    const T* front() const { return queueData; }

    T* back() { return queueDataEnd - 1; }
    const T* back() const { return queueDataEnd - 1; }

private:
    T* queueData;
    T* queueDataEnd;
};
```

Notice that there are **const** and non-**const** versions of the **front()** and **back()** member functions. This allows us to use both **const** and non-**const** queues. We now need to define the **size()** function, but we don't actually need to store this as we can work it out from the pointers to the first and one past the last element (**queueData** and **queueDataEnd**). **Subtracting one pointer from another gives the number of elements between the locations of those two pointers; this value is of the ptrdiff_t type.**

The **size** function will need to return a value of a type that we know can store any number of elements in our queue. In this following snippet, **size_t** can store the maximum size of a theoretically possible object of any type (including array), and our **Queue** class with an implemented **size()** function now becomes the following:

```
template<class T>

class Queue
```

```
{
public:
    T* front() { return queueData; }
    const T* front() const { return queueData; }
    T* back() { return queueDataEnd - 1; }
    const T* back() const { return queueDataEnd - 1; }
        size_t size() const { return queueDataEnd - queueData; }

private:
    T* queueData;
    T* queueDataEnd;
};
```

We can also now trivially create the **empty()** function by checking whether **size()** returns **0**:

```
bool empty() const { return size() == 0; }
```

Implementing Constructors and Destructors in the Queue

For this queue, we are going to write two constructors: a default constructor that creates an empty queue (first and last elements are both 0), and a constructor that takes a size value and allocates enough memory to store that many elements of **T**. The initialization process will use a function that we will call **init()** that has the responsibility of allocating memory for our elements. Here is the updated class with these constructors (the **init** function will be covered later):

```
template<class T>
class Queue
{
public:

    Queue() { init(); }
    explicit Queue(size_t numElements, const T& initialValue = T())
    {
        init(numElements, initialValue);
    }
    T* front() { return queueData; }
    const T* front() const { return queueData; }
    T* back() { return queueDataEnd - 1; }
    const T* back() const { return queueDataEnd - 1; }

    size_t size() const { return queueDataEnd - queueData; }
```

```
    bool empty() const { return size() == 0; }

private:
    void init() {}
    void init(size_t numElements, const T& initialValue) {}
    T* queueData;
    T* queueDataEnd;
};
```

Note that the **Queue** constructor that takes a size has a default parameter of **initialValue** that uses the default constructor of **T**. This is used when no initial value is passed to the constructor. The **explicit** keyword is also used to ensure that the compiler cannot implicitly construct this type to convert from one type to another if passed as a parameter:

```
    explicit Queue(size_t numElements, const T& initialValue = T())
    {
        init(numElements, initialValue);
    }
```

Also note that there are two **init()** functions: one is overloaded to take two parameters, and will be used by the constructor that also takes two parameters, as shown:

```
void init() {}
void init(size_t numElements, const T& initialValue) {}
```

We now have constructors but, of course, we are going to need a destructor and its **init()** equivalent, **destroy()**. Here is the updated class with a destructor and the skeleton of our **destroy()** function:

```
template<class T>

class Queue
{
public:
    Queue() { init(); }
    explicit Queue(size_t numElements, const T& initialValue = T())
    {
        init(numElements, initialValue);
    }
    ~Queue() { destroy(); }

    T* front() { return queueData; }
    const T* front() const { return queueData; }
```

```
    T* back() { return queueDataEnd - 1; }
    const T* back() const { return queueDataEnd - 1; }
    size_t size() const { return queueDataEnd - queueData; }
    bool empty() const { return size() == 0; }

private:
    void init() {}
    void init(size_t numElements, const T& initialValue) {}
    void destroy() {}
    T* queueData;
    T* queueDataEnd;
};
```

The **destroy** function will have the responsibility of deallocating memory and destroying any elements in our queue. The **init** functions will make use of two functions contained in the **<memory>** header: **uninitialized_fill** and **uninitialized_copy**. Now, **uninitialized_fill** copies a value to an uninitialized memory area defined by a range [first, last), and **uninitialized_copy** copies a range of values [first, last) to an uninitialized memory area. Before we update our class to have one of the **init** functions, use the **uninitialized_fill** function that we need to cover what we will use to allocate our memory.

Dynamic Memory

We would like our queue to be able to grow whenever a new element is pushed onto it, just like the STL version. Our first thought may be to use the new **T[]** array initializer to allocate memory. However, this would give us the same problem outlined earlier in this chapter, which is that the new **T[]** array would call the default constructor for **T** and, therefore, **T** would be limited to types that have a default constructor. We would rather this was not the case, and consequently, we must find another option for allocating memory for our container.

Allocators

Using the **<memory>** header gives us access to the **allocator<T>** type. This type allows us to allocate a block of memory that can store objects of **T** and, additionally, not initialize the objects. Using the **allocator<T>** type also allows us to allocate more memory than we currently need so that we can remove the overhead of initializing memory, and only do so when the queue has grown too large. Creating twice as much storage as we need whenever the queue needs to grow is a good strategy. If the queue never ends up larger than that, then the overhead of allocating more memory will have been removed; note that the new **T[]** array would not allow us to make this optimization.

One caveat to **allocator<T>** is that we now need to keep track of the partition between initialized and uninitialized memory, and so our class becomes slightly more complex; but the benefits are still clear.

We can update our class to have an **allocator<T>** variable as a member so that we can make use of it, and a new pointer that will point to one past the end of the allocated memory:

```
#include <iostream>
// need the memory header
#include <memory>

using namespace std;

template<class T>

class Queue
{
public:
    Queue() { init(); }
    explicit Queue(size_t numElements, const T& initialValue = T())
    {
        init(numElements, initialValue);
    }
    ~Queue() { destroy(); }
    T* front() { return queueData; }
    const T* front() const { return queueData; }
    T* back() { return queueDataEnd - 1; }
    const T* back() const { return queueDataEnd - 1; }
    size_t size() const { return queueDataEnd - queueData; }
    bool empty() const { return size() == 0; }

private:
    void init() {}
```

```
    void init(size_t numElements, const T& initialValue) {}

    void destroy() {}

    // the allocator object
    allocator<T> alloc;

    T* queueData;
    T* queueDataEnd;
    T* memLimit; // one past the end of allocated memory
};
```

In the preceding example, we have added the memory header, an **allocator<T>** member variable, and a pointer to one past the end of the allocated memory. Using the **allocator<T>** member variable allows us to implement our **init()** functions to allocate memory and use **uninitialized_fill** to copy an initial value to it:

```
void init()
{
    queueData = queueDataEnd = memLimit = 0;
}

void init(size_t numElements, const T& initialValue)
{
    queueData = alloc.allocate(numElements);
    queueDataEnd = memLimit = queueData + numElements;
    uninitialized_fill(queueData, queueDataEnd, initialValue);
}
```

The **init** function that takes no parameters just sets all our pointers to **0**, creating an empty queue with no allocated memory. The second **init** function allocates sufficient memory to hold **numElements** of our **T** objects. From the **allocate** function, it returns a pointer to the first element of our data. To acquire the other pointers we need for one past the end of the last constructed element and the end of the memory limit, we simply increment **numElements** to the **queueData** pointer (first element) and assign it to both the **queueDataEnd** and **memLimit** pointers. These willnow both point to one past the last constructed element, which, at this point, is one past the allocated memory. Then, we use **uninitialized_fill** to copy the initial element into the memory chunk using **queueData** and **queueDataEnd** as the first and last in the range, respectively. The following example is our **destroy** function; it uses the **destroy** allocator and deallocates functions to clean up our class:

```
void destroy()
{
```

```
    if (queueData != 0)
    {
        T* it = queueDataEnd;
        while (it != queueData)
        {
            alloc.destroy(--it);
        }
        alloc.deallocate(queueData, memLimit - queueData);
    }

    queueData = queueDataEnd = memLimit = 0;
}
```

This function loops backward through our **queueData**, calls the destructor of any constructed elements, and then uses the **deallocate** function to free the allocated memory. The second parameter into **deallocate** is the size of the memory we wish to free. We kept track of the first and one past the allocated memory so that we can get the pointer difference and use that as the second parameter of the **deallocate** function.

Resizing and Appending

Now that we have an allocator, we can use it to create functions that will resize our memory chunk, when needed, and construct objects in the available memory. We will call these functions **resize()** and **append()**. As outlined previously, we are going to double the amount of allocated memory whenever the queue is resized. Here are the functions in their entirety:

```
void resize()
{
    size_t newSize = max(2 * (queueDataEnd - queueData), ptrdiff_t(1));
    T* newData = alloc.allocate(newSize);
    T* newDataEnd = uninitialized_copy(queueData, queueDataEnd, newData);
    destroy();
    queueData = newData;
    queueDataEnd = newDataEnd;
    memLimit = queueData + newSize;
}

void append(const T& newValue)
{
    alloc.construct(queueDataEnd++, newValue);
}
```

The **resize()** function first calculates how much memory will need to be allocated and, since the queue could be empty, it uses the **max** function to ensure that we are always allocating enough space for at least one element (2 multiplied by 0 is still 0). This **newSize** amount of memory is then allocated using the allocator, and **uninitialized_copy** copies the existing **queueData** into the new memory area. The **destroy** function is then called to delete the existing data before reassigning the new pointers to our member pointers. Our member pointers now correctly point to the newly allocated memory space and its start and limits. **append()** uses the **construct** function of the allocator to construct an element in the first available space in the allocated memory, after the constructed elements.

Pushing and Popping

Now we come to the interface side of our **Queue**. These are the functions that anyone using the queue will utilize, and they allow elements to be added and removed from our queue. A lot of the complexity has already been written, so there is not a whole lot to these functions. However, there is one thing to keep in mind: we are creating a FIFO container. Therefore, when **pop** is called, the first element that was pushed into the container will be the first to be removed. What this means is that we need to destroy the first element in our queue and then shift all the remaining elements across and also decrement the pointer to the last element (**queueDataEnd**). Here is the **pop()** function, which implements this functionality in a very simple way:

```
void pop()
{
    if (queueData != 0)
    {
        alloc.destroy(queueData);
        for (int i = 0; i < size(); i++)
        {
            queueData[i] = queueData[i + 1];
        }

        queueDataEnd -= 1;
    }
}
```

As this loop goes along, it assigns the element at **i** to the element at **i + 1**, so element **1** will be shifted into element **0**, and **2** into **1**, and so on. It then decrements the pointer to **queueDataEnd** as the queue is now one element smaller.

Pushing elements uses our existing **resize** and **append** functions in the following way:

```
void push(const T& element)
{
    if (queueDataEnd == memLimit)
        resize();
        append(element);
}
```

If there is sufficient space in our allocated memory, then the queue will not be resized. Either way, an element will be appended to the queue. Calling **append** after a call to **resize** (if needed) ensures that we will have enough space to do the append without checking first.

Finalizing and Testing

Finally, our **Queue** implements all the functionality we set out for it. You will recall in the chapter on constructors, where the **Rule of Three** was discussed, that if a class needs to implement a destructor, then it will almost always need to implement a copy constructor and overload the assignment operator. We will not go into detail about copy constructors and assignment operators as they have already been covered, but we will go over the creation of a new **init()** function that can be used when implementing them:

```
void init(T* front, T* back)
{
    queueData = alloc.allocate(back - front);
    memLimit = queueDataEnd = uninitialized_copy(front, back, queueData);
}
```

Given pointers to the start and end of a block of memory, this overloaded **init()** function allocates space and then copies the elements over to it. You can see how this will be useful in a copy constructor and overloaded assignment operator; it simplifies these functions significantly, as we don't have to rewrite any of our **init** code when copying:

```
Queue(const Queue& q) { init(q.front(), q.back()); }
Queue& operator=(const Queue& rhs)
{
    if (&rhs != this)
    {
```

```
            destroy();
            init(rhs.front(), rhs.back());
        }
        return *this;
    }
```

Everything is now in place and we can finally test the functionality of our queue. The following is a very simple test of a queue of **int** values:

Example 11_01.cpp

```
113 int main()
114 {
115     Queue<int> testQueue;
116     testQueue.push(1);
117     testQueue.push(2);
118     cout << "queue contains values: ";
119
120     for (auto it = testQueue.front(); it != testQueue.back() + 1; ++it)
121     {
122         cout << *it << " ";
123     }
124
125     cout << endl;
126     cout << "queue contains " << testQueue.size() << " elements" << endl;
127     testQueue.pop();
128     cout << "queue contains values: ";
129
130     for (auto it = testQueue.front(); it != testQueue.back() + 1; ++it)
131     {
132         cout << *it << " ";
133     }
134
135     cout << endl;
136     cout << "queue contains " << testQueue.size() << " elements" << endl;
137
138     testQueue.push(9);
139     testQueue.push(50);
140
141     cout << "queue contains values: ";
        // [...]
163     return 0;
164 }
```

The complete code for this example can be found at: https://packt.
live/2O8A9WR

When you run the preceding code with the complete and updated **Queue** class, you will obtain the following output:

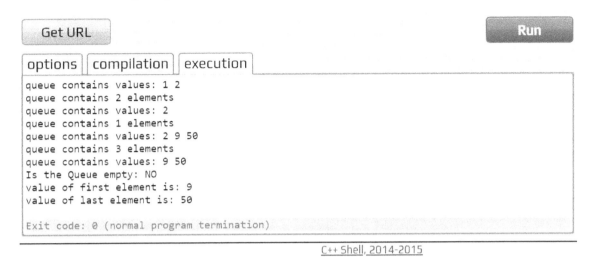

Figure 11.7: Output when testing the queue

Activity 11: Creating a Generic Stack

Queues have a **FIFO** data structure, whereas a stack has a **last in**, **first out** (**LIFO**) data structure. Think of a stack data structure just like a stack of magazines. In this stack, you remove magazines from the top (we wouldn't grab the magazine from the bottom of the stack), and the top is also the last magazine that was added to the stack. In this activity, you will create a stack data structure. All the elements of how this can be done are outlined in the *Creating a Generic Queue* section of this chapter, with the most important difference contained in the **pop()** function. The **front()** and **back()** functions will also be renamed **top()** and **bottom()**, respectively, and will point to the correct positions within the stack.

> **Note**
>
> The complete code for the activity can be found at https://packt.live/2r9XgYi.

Here are some steps that will help to complete the activity:

1. Write a generic stack using the generic queue example as a base.

2. Alter the **pop()** function to handle a LIFO data structure.

3. Test the stack in a **main** function, outputting data to test whether the stack works correctly.

Upon successful completion of the activity, you should obtain output similar to the following:

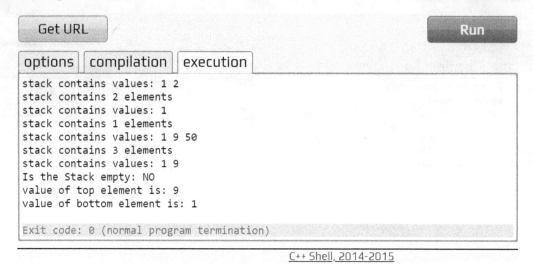

```
Get URL                                                    Run

options   compilation   execution
stack contains values: 1 2
stack contains 2 elements
stack contains values: 1
stack contains 1 elements
stack contains values: 1 9 50
stack contains 3 elements
stack contains values: 1 9
Is the Stack empty: NO
value of top element is: 9
value of bottom element is: 1

Exit code: 0 (normal program termination)
```

C++ Shell, 2014-2015

Figure 11.8: Final output for the activity

Note

The solution to this activity can be found on page 564.

Summary

Templates are a complex subject, yet through this chapter, we have discovered that this complexity can create amazingly reusable code. The **Queue** class created here can hold a queue of any elements without any changes to its internals, which is a huge benefit when writing code that needs to be reused in many areas. While not as fully functional, robust, or performant as STL queues, it still gives insight into how a rudimentary version of an STL container can be recreated without too much work, if the STL is unavailable to us or, for some reason, does not suit our needs. We looked at template functions and classes and discovered how powerful they can be when used correctly, along with areas that we might want to be mindful of.

In the next chapter, we are going to cover the STL itself and look closely at the containers it provides. The STL will become invaluable to your future programming efforts in C++. It does a lot of the hard work for us, meaning we will not have to keep implementing low-level memory operations like the ones we have been using in the chapter exercises and examples so far. We can take advantage of the powerful implementations of common algorithms and containers that the STL provides for us.

12

Containers and Iterators

Overview

This chapter will provide an overview of using the containers and iterators provided by the C++ standard library. The library provides us with lots of algorithms and ways of storing data so that we can focus on writing practical code, while being confident that a tested and robust library is powering our programs.

Introduction

In the previous chapters of this course, we gave examples and offered exercises that did not utilize the C++ standard library. This can lead to a lot of code to often do very little. We stuck with raw arrays to help with understanding the fundamentals of the language; however, in this chapter, we will cover powerful features that will allow you to write complex behavior and functionality with a surprisingly small amount of code. C++ really becomes a joy to work with once you introduce the standard library into your projects and, handily, it is provided with any C++ compiler. We can do away with using raw arrays and writing our own queues and stacks and, instead, use pre-existing implementations, all with a common interface. To begin our journey, we will start by explaining what a container is and discussing their different types, before moving onto iterators and how they can make using these containers very natural and efficient.

Containers

Containers in the context of the C++ standard library are a set of common data structures. These structures take the form of lists, stacks, arrays, and more. Containers can store data and objects and can be categorized into a few different types. These types, and the container classes associated with them, are sequential containers—string, vector, list, deque, and array.

A String Is a Container

In C++, strings are a class type, meaning that they are an object that has member variables and functions to act upon them; they are a container in the standard library just like any other. Underneath the string class interface is a C-style character array, and the string class provides the functionality to access a single byte in this sequence. The benefit of using strings over standard character arrays is that a lot of the algorithms that can be used in other containers, such as sorting and searching, can also be applied to strings. If we were to use a standard C-style character array to hold our strings, like we have in the preceding chapters, then we would not be able to take advantage of these pre-written algorithms and we would have to write our own.

Each of the containers provided by the standard library has a set of constructors that provide flexibility in how we initialize our containers. This chapter will cover these when a new container is introduced. Some of the constructors are not going to be immediately useful to us, but they are worth knowing about for the future.

String Constructors

The string class has several different constructors that can be utilized:

- **`string()`** ;: We can use this to create an empty string with no characters.

- **`string(const string& str)`** ;: We can use this to construct a string from a copy of another string.

- **`string(const string& str, size_t pos, size_t len = npos)`** ;: We can use this to construct a string from a substring of an existing string.

- **`string(const char* s)`** ;: We can use this to construct a string using a copy of the C-style char array pointed to by **s**.

- **`string(const char* s, size_t pos, size_t n)`** ;: We can use this to construct a string using a copy of a C-style **char** array pointed to by **s** with a specific number of elements to copy (**n**).

- **`string(size_t n, char c)`** ;: We can use this to construct a string of size **n** chars initialized to a copy of **c**.

- **`template <class InputIterator> string (InputIterator first, InputIterator last)`** ;: We can use this to construct a string with a range between the first and last iterators.

We will implement a few of these strings in the following exercise.

Exercise 73: Creating Strings

As shown in the *String Constructors* section, there are numerous ways to construct strings. We can try these out and print their values. First, open a new file on cpp.sh and create a basic **main** function that also includes **<iostream>** and **<string>**. We will also declare that we are using the **std** namespace, because string lives within this namespace, and we can avoid needing to type the scope operator and the namespace.

> **Note**
>
> The complete code for this exercise can be found at https://packt.live/2rXH6ln.

Here are the steps to complete the exercise:

1. Start with the **main** function:

    ```cpp
    #include <iostream>
    #include <string>

    using namespace std;

    int main()
    {
        return 0;
    }
    ```

2. Create an empty string using the **string()** constructor:

    ```cpp
    string str;
    ```

3. Create a string using a C-style character array with **string(const char* s)**:

    ```cpp
    string str1("Hello, I'm a string!");
    ```

4. Create a string from a copy of another string with **string(const string& str);**:

    ```cpp
    string str2(str1);
    ```

5. Create a string from a substring of an existing string with **string(const string& str, size_t pos, size_t len = npos)**:

    ```cpp
    string str3(str1, 0, 5);
    ```

6. Create a string from a substring of a C-style char array with **string(const char* s, size_t pos, size_t n)**:

    ```cpp
    string str4("Hello, I'm a string!", 0, 5);
    ```

7. Create a string using a character and the length required with **string(size_t n, char c)**:

    ```cpp
    string str5(10, 'x');
    ```

8. Create a string from a substring of an existing string, but use iterators to miss out the first and last characters with the **<class InputIterator> string (InputIterator first, InputIterator last)** template:

    ```cpp
    string str6(str4.begin() + 1, str4.end() - 1);
    ```

9. Write the following output commands:

```
cout << str << endl;
cout << str1 << endl;
cout << str2 << endl;
cout << str3 << endl;
cout << str4 << endl;
cout << str5 << endl;
cout << str6 << endl;
```

10. Here is the complete program:

```
#include <iostream>
#include <string>

using namespace std;

int main()
{
    string str;
    string str1("Hello, I'm a string!");
    string str2(str1);
    string str3(str1, 0, 5);
    string str4("Hello, I'm a string!", 0, 5);
    string str5(10, 'x');
    string str6(str4.begin() + 1, str4.end() - 1);
    cout << str << endl;
    cout << str1 << endl;
    cout << str2 << endl;
    cout << str3 << endl;
    cout << str4 << endl;
    cout << str5 << endl;
    cout << str6 << endl;

    return 0;
}
```

11. Run the complete program. You should obtain the following output:

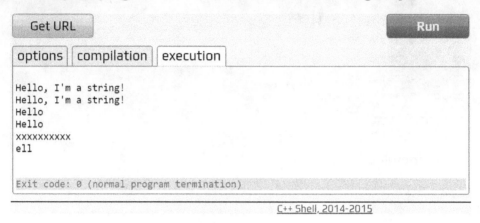

Figure 12.1: Output strings

All of these constructors give us a lot of flexibility and allow us to be in control of how we initialize strings.

Assigning to Strings

Strings can also be initialized using the assignment operator, as well as through constructors. There are a few different overloads available, as outlined here:

- **string& operator= (const string& str)** ;: Initialize from a copy of an existing string

- **string& operator= (const char* s)** ;: Initialize from a copy of a C-style character array

- **string& operator= (char c)** ;: Initialize with a **char**

The following snippet shows some examples of assigning to strings. We don't need to go into too much detail here, but it is good to know that when we want to assign a string to another string or initialize a string from an existing string, then the standard library has us covered:

```cpp
#include <iostream>
#include <string>

using namespace std;

int main()
{
    string str = "Hello, I'm a string!";
    string str1 = str;
```

```
        string str2;
        str2 = 'x';
        cout << str << endl;
        cout << str1 << endl;
        cout << str2 << endl;

        return 0;
}
```

The preceding code yields the following output:

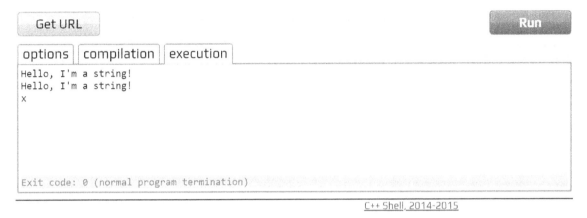

Figure 12.2: Output when using the assignment operator

It is extremely common to see strings initialized in the way that this example does with **str**. **Hello, I'm a string!** is actually a character array, so we are initializing a string from a copy of a C-style char array.

Operations on Strings

The string class provides many different operations to manipulate the underlying byte sequence. You may recognize some of them as similar to the generic queue in *Chapter 11, Templates*. Operations on strings can be very useful. We may need to append a character to our strings to help us identify them, or we may need to remove extraneous characters that aren't needed in our program, when the place we read the strings from stores them in that way. Let's look at some of the string operations we can use:

- **push_back(char c)**: Pushes a character (c) onto the end of a string.

- **pop_back()**: Deletes the last character of a string.

- **capacity()**: Provides the current capacity of the string. This does not necessarily correspond to the current size of the string because, just like the queue described in *Chapter 11, Templates*, it may have pre-allocated extra memory.

- **resize(size_t n) & resize(size_t n, char c)**: Resizes the string. If the value is less than the current string size, anything after that size in the char sequence will be removed. The overloaded function takes a char, c, and initializes any new elements as copies of c.

- **shrink_to_fit()**: Sets the capacity of the string to its current size.

- **reserve(size_t n)**: Changes the string's capacity to allow n chars.

Here is an example of all of these functions used in a simple program:

```cpp
#include <iostream>
#include <string>

using namespace std;

int main()
{
    string str("Hello, I'm a string");
    str.push_back('!');
    str.push_back('!');
    cout << str << endl;
    str.pop_back();
    cout << str << endl;

    // notice this will keep existing contents and append x for the rest
    str.resize(25, 'x');

    // reserve space for 50 chars - capacity()
    str.reserve(50);

    // notice that ! is pushed after the last char not
    //the end of allocated space
    str.push_back('!');
    cout << str << endl;
    cout << str.capacity() << endl;
    cout << str.size() << endl;
    str.shrink_to_fit();

    // note : shrink_to_fit is not guaranteed to be exactly size()
```

```
    // depending on compiler implementation
    cout << str.capacity() << endl;

    return 0;
}
```

The preceding code will yield the following output:

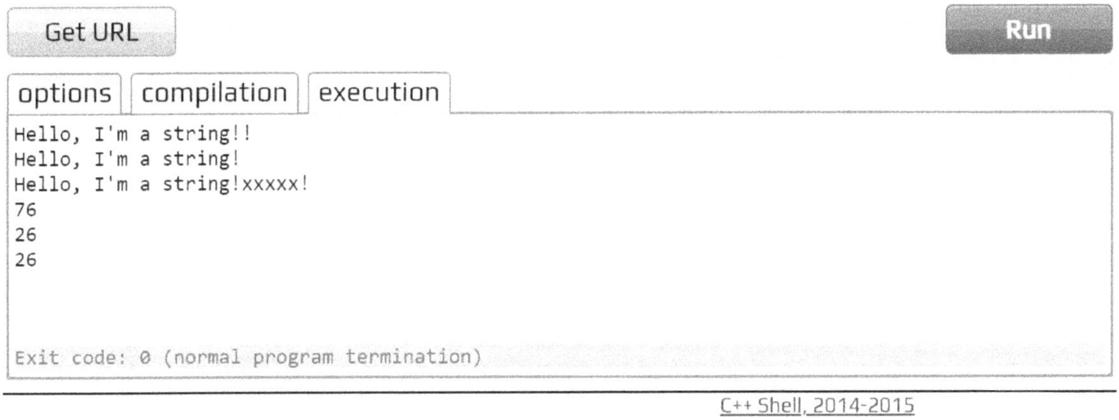

Figure 12.3: Output when performing push back operations on strings

Iterators

Just like the other containers we will cover, strings have iterators that can be utilized to allow traversal through a string in loops.

Iterators from strings and most standard library containers can be accessed through the following functions:

- **begin()**: An iterator to the beginning of the string
- **end()**: An iterator to the end of the string
- **rbegin()**: A reverse iterator to the beginning of the string
- **rend()**: A reverse iterator to the end of the string

The type of an iterator for containers in the standard library can be obtained using the name of the class plus the scope operator and iterator or the reverse iterator, depending on which type is needed. For strings, this means an iterator can be obtained using **string::iterator** or **string::reverse_iterator**. These iterators can be stored as variables for reuse or used in a **for** loop, where they exist within the scope of the for loop.

The following is a simple example of using these iterators to loop and display the contents of a string:

```cpp
#include <iostream>
#include <string>

using namespace std;

int main()
{
    string str("Hello, I'm a string");

    for(string::iterator it = str.begin(); it != str.end(); it++)
    {
        cout << *it;
    }

    cout << endl;

    for(string::reverse_iterator rit = str.rbegin(); rit != str.rend();
        rit++)
    {
        cout << *rit;
    }

    cout << endl;

    return 0;
}
```

The preceding code yields the following output:

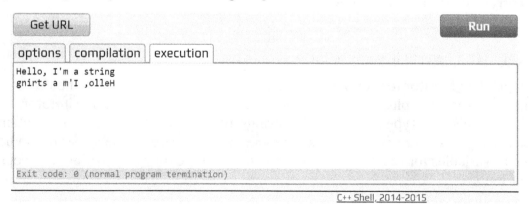

Figure 12.4: Output when using the string iterators and reverse iterators

Note that a reverse iterator allows us to use an incrementing for loop while still moving in the reverse direction through a container. Both of these iterators are known as bidirectional, meaning we can iterate in either direction for both of them, so we can loop in both directions through either of these iterator types, if required.

Further Research

The string class has many useful operations that can make them extremely powerful to work with compared to a C-style character array. There are functions to find certain characters within the string, remove or replace characters within a string, copy a string into a character array, and append a string onto another string. Additionally, the string class provides overloaded operators such as **+=** to append to a string and **+** to concatenate strings. Rather than listing all of these functions here with examples, it would be a good idea to research these functions and apply them to an example program of your own.

Exercise 74: Is It a Palindrome?

Because strings behave just like the other containers in the standard library, we can make use of common algorithms present in the **<algorithm>** header. This enables complex manipulation with very minimal code.

The following exercise shows how we can write a function to check whether or not a string is a palindrome, utilizing a selection of algorithms.

> **Note**
>
> The complete code for this exercise can be found at https://packt.live/37tTYQ3.

Here are the steps to complete the exercise:

1. Our first task is to allow the user to input the text to be checked. We will use the **std::getline** function to read from **std::cin** and store this in a string. Here is our main function with this in place:

```
#include <iostream>
#include <string>
#include <algorithm>

using namespace std;

int main()
{
```

```
    string str;
    getline(cin, str);
    return 0;
}
```

2. Now we must create the stub of our **isPalindrome** function and place it above our **main** function. This function will take a **const** reference to a string and return a **bool**:

```
bool isPalindrome(const string& str)
{
    return false;
}

int main()
{
    string str;

    getline(cin, str);

    cout << "'" << str << "'" << " is a palindrome? "
        << (isPalindrome(str) ? "YES" : "NO") << endl;
    return 0;
}
```

Test this by inputting a string to check. Of course, it will say **NO** at this point, but we will know everything is compiling fine so far.

3. There are some characters that we would like to ignore in our palindrome check, such as spaces and punctuation. The following code implements this:

```
bool isPalindrome(const string& str)
{
    // make a copy of the string
    string s(str.begin(), str.end());

    // remove any spaces or punctuation
    s.erase(remove_if(s.begin (), s.end (), [](const char& c) { return
    ispunct(c) || isspace(c);}), s.end());
```

There are a lot of palindromes that include punctuation and spaces that, if considered, would invalidate the palindrome. We will choose to ignore these completely and only check the letters. To do this, we will make a copy of our passed-in string using the range constructor, and then use the **remove_if** algorithm to give us a range containing only the elements that are not spaces or punctuation.

The **remove_if** algorithm shifts any elements that do not satisfy the predicate we give it to the end of the container, and leaves the elements that do in a range at the start of the container. It then returns an iterator we can use that points to the last element in the range we want. We can use this iterator as the first parameter into the string's **erase** function to delete all the elements past the range we care about.

Now that we have removed the elements we don't need we can now move onto lower casing our remaining elements; as for our palindrome check, we want it to be case-insensitive. To do this, we can use the **transform** algorithm. This algorithm allows us to call a function on each element in a range. We are going to be using a provided function called **tolower** on each of the elements in the range.

4. Write the following code to incorporate the **transform** algorithm in the **isPalindrome** function:

```
// lower case what's left
transform(s.begin(), s.end(), s.begin(), ::tolower);
```

5. Now that we have a range of characters that are lowercase and do not contain any punctuation or spaces, we can create a reversed version of the string. To do this, we will use the range constructor again, but this time we will pass in the reverse iterators. We can then compare these two strings and see whether they match. If they do, then we have a palindrome:

```
// create a reversed version of the string
string sr(s.rbegin(), s.rend());

// compare them
return (s == sr);
}
```

6. Now we can test our palindrome checker in a new **main** function. We will initialize our string to a classic palindrome, "Never odd or even", and then pass it into our function and display whether it is a palindrome or not:

```cpp
int main()
{
    string str = "Never odd or even";

    cout << "'" << str << "'" << " is a palindrome? "
         << (isPalindrome(str) ? "YES" : "NO") << endl;

    return 0;
}
```

7. Here is the complete code:

```cpp
#include <iostream>
#include <string>
#include <algorithm>

using namespace std;

bool isPalindrome(const string & str) {

    // make a copy of the string
    string s(str.begin(), str.end());
    // remove any spaces or punctuation
    s.erase(remove_if(s.begin(), s.end(), [](const char & c) {
    return ispunct(c) || isspace(c); }), s.end());

    // lower case what's left
    transform(s.begin(), s.end(), s.begin(), ::tolower);

    // create a reversed version of the string
    string sr(s.rbegin(), s.rend());

    // compare them
    return (s == sr);
}

int main()
{
    string str = "Never odd or even";
```

```
            cout << "'" << str << "'" << " is a palindrome? "
                 << (isPalindrome(str) ? "YES" : "NO") << endl;

            return 0;
        }
```

8. Run the complete code. You will obtain the following output:

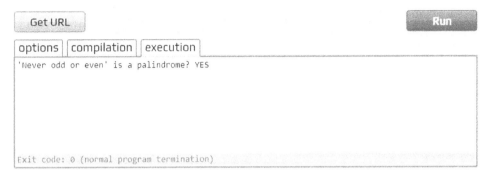

Figure 12.5: Palindrome

Strings are usually a much better choice than using character arrays. They provide a lot of useful functionality and generally are much more pleasant to work with. The standard library also upgrades another type we use a lot: arrays. Let's move onto covering the alternative to arrays—vectors.

Vectors-Handy, Resizable Arrays

Vectors implement a multi-purpose dynamic array. Remember that C++ arrays must be a fixed size; we cannot resize an array, and will have to create new arrays and copy the contents if we need to add another element. We have been doing this a lot in custom classes that we have created throughout this course. Vectors allow us to create a container that can be resized whenever we need it. The elements in a vector are stored contiguously—that is, laid out in a neighboring fashion—and therefore can be accessed through offsetting pointers to elements as well as iterators. We can make use of vectors by including the **<vector>** header.

Vector Constructors

Vectors give us a number of different constructors to use when we want to create a new vector. A selection of these constructors are outlined here:

- **vector()** ;: Constructs an empty vector.

- **vector(size_t n, const T& value = T())** ;: Constructs a vector with a number of elements (n) optionally initialized using a constructor that takes t as an argument, or **T**'s default constructor by default.

- **template <class InputIterator> vector(InputIterator first, InputIterator last)** ;: Constructs a vector from the range between the first and last iterators.

- **vector(const vector& other)** ;: Constructs a vector by copying another vector (copy constructor).

- **vector (initializer_list<value_type> il)** ;: Constructs a vector using an initializer list.

The following code snippet shows these constructors in use:

```
#include <iostream>
#include <vector>

using namespace std;

int main()
{
    // default constructed empty vector
    vector<int> intVector;
    vector<int> initializerListIntVector = {1,2,3};

    // default constructed vector of 5 floats
    vector<float> floatVector(5);

    // vector of 5 floats initialized to 1.0f
    vector<float> floatVectorAllOne(5, 1.0f);

    // vector constructed from an existing vector
    vector<float> anotherFloatVector(floatVector);

    // range constructed vector
    vector<float> rangeConstructedFloatVector(anotherFloatVector.begin(),
    anotherFloatVector.end());

    return 0;
}
```

Each of the constructors is used in this snippet for your reference. All of these constructors are useful in certain situations, so take the time to learn them to ensure you are using the correct one for your programs.

Vector Assignment

Vectors can also have a new value assigned to them using the vector overloaded assignment operator, **vector& operator=(const vector& other)**. Here's an example:

```
#include <iostream>
#include <vector>

using namespace std;

int main()
{
    // default constructed vector of 5 floats
    vector<float> floatVector(5);
    vector<float> floatVectorAssigned = floatVector;
    return 0;
}
```

When assigning a new value to a vector, it must have a valid conversion. If not, the compiler will report an error on that line. For example, **vector<int>** cannot be assigned to **vector<float>**. However, if you are using the range constructor, and a conversion exists between two types, then they can be constructed as outlined in the following snippet:

```
#include <iostream>
#include <vector>

using namespace std;

int main()
{
    // default constructed vector of 5 floats
    vector<float> floatVector(5);

    vector<int> intVector(floatVector.begin(), floatVector.end());

    return 0;
}
```

Here, we have constructed an **int** vector using a range of **float**s. Since these types can be converted, the constructor handles this correctly.

Exercise 75: Accessing Elements in a Vector

We know from the introduction to this chapter that a vector is a sequential container, so our elements are available to be iterated over sequentially and can be accessed by index. Vectors really do behave very much like raw arrays and are almost always a better option than arrays when you need a sequential container. To introduce vectors, we will create a small program that fills a vector and accesses an element by index, and then also iterates over the vector and all of the values of the elements within:

> **Note**
>
> The complete code for this exercise can be found at https://packt.live/2QQtalv.

1. Start with a new file on **cpp.sh** and add a main function. To get access to vectors, we need to include the vector header and iostream so we can print our values:

```
#include <iostream>
#include <vector>

using namespace std;
int main()
{
    return 0;
}
```

2. Now we can create our vector and prefill it with some values using the initializer list constructor, the **(initializer_list<value_type> il)** vector:

```
int main()
{
    vector<int> vec = {1,2,3,4,5,6,7,8,9,10};

    return 0;
}
```

3. When we want to iterate over the elements in a container, we can use the range **for** loop. In this case, it would look like the following:

```
for(auto v : vec)
{
    cout << v << " ";
}
```

The **auto** keyword allows us to let the compiler work out what is contained within our vector. It then loops through all the elements and sequentially returns them as the element here called **v**.

4. We can also now access an element in our vector through an index. Grab the number 4, which, in our zero-indexed vector, is at index **3**:

```
cout << vec[3];
```

5. When we run the program, we should see all of our **vec** values printed along with the number 4. Here is the code:

```cpp
#include <iostream>
#include <vector>

using namespace std;

int main()
{
    vector<int> vec = {1,2,3,4,5,6,7,8,9,10};

    for(auto v : vec)
    {
        cout << v << " ";
    }

    cout << vec[3];

    return 0;
}
```

6. Run the code. You will obtain the following output:

Figure 12.6: Accessing elements of a vector

Accessing elements of a vector is obviously very important, yet vectors allow us to perform many other operations. The next section will give you an overview of these operations.

Operations on Vectors

The majority of useful operations on vectors involve adding and removing elements within them. This is the essence of a vector and is what makes them a good choice over a standard array. Just like strings, we will begin to see some commonalities between operations on the various containers we will cover. Here are some useful functions that can be applied to vectors:

- **`push_back()`**: Pushes an element on to the back of a vector.
- **`pop_back()`**: Removes and destroys the last element in a vector.
- **`insert(const_iterator pos, const T& val)`**: Inserts the **val** element at the position specified by the **pos** iterator.
- **`erase(const_iterator pos)` & `erase(const_iterator first, const_iterator last)`**: Erases an element at the **pos** iterator or a range between the first and last iterators.
- **`clear()`**: Removes and destroys all elements of a vector.
- **`emplace()`**: Similar to **insert**, but whereas insert takes a reference to an already constructed element, emplace constructs a new element and grows the vector to accommodate it.

Similar to strings, vectors also expose functions to get their capacity, resize them, and reserve memory.

Searching Vectors

A lot of programming involves finding a specific element or range of elements based on some specific logic. We may want to find all elements of a **vector<int>** that have a value less than 10. We may want to search a vector for one specific element that meets our criteria. The algorithms contained in the standard library <algorithm> header can be applied to our vectors to allow us to search for specific elements easily and with a minimal amount of code. The most important algorithms for searching through vectors are **std::find** and **std::find_if**.

These algorithms take iterators that search a range of elements in a vector and return an iterator to the first element that matches the criteria. If no element matches the criteria, then an iterator to the end of the vector is returned. This can be compared when checking whether an element exists or not. Look at the following example, which checks whether a specific **int** is contained within a **vector<int>**:

```cpp
#include <iostream>
#include <algorithm>     // std::find
#include <vector>

using namespace std;

bool contains(const int value, const vector<int>& vec)
{
    return (find(vec.begin(), vec.end(), value) != vec.end());
}
```

In the preceding function, the find algorithm takes an iterator to the start of the range we wish to search. Since we want to search the entire vector, we pass in **begin()**, which is the start of the vector, and then end for the end of the vector. This constitutes the whole array. The final parameter is value, and that is the **int** we wish to find. The value returned from this function is then compared to **end()**. If it is equal, then we know it is not contained within the vector because **end()** points to one past the last element, not an element itself. The following snippet uses this function to check for the number 9 in a vector of integers:

```cpp
int main()
{
    vector<int> vec = {1,2,3,4,5,6,7,8,9,10};

    const int numToCheck = 9;

    cout << "Vector contains " << numToCheck << " "
         << (contains(numToCheck, vec) ? "YES" : "NO");
    cout << endl;

    return 0;
}
```

The output for this check should be:

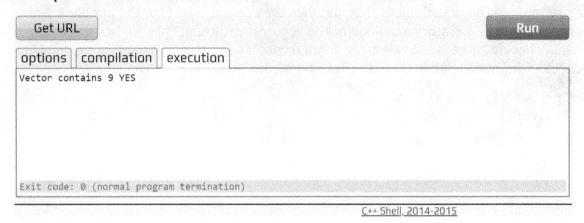

Figure 12.7: Output for the find algorithm

Additionally, we can use the **std::distance** function to return the index of the element within the vector by getting the offset from the beginning of the vector to the found element. The following snippet checks whether an element is contained in a vector and returns its index, if so. If no element was found, then it returns **-1**, which we can check against:

```
#include <iostream>
#include <algorithm>    // std::find
#include <vector>

using namespace std;

long contains(const int value, const vector<int>& vec)
{
    vector<int>::const_iterator it = find(vec.begin(), vec.end(), value);

    if(it != vec.end()) // we found the element
        return distance(vec.begin(), it);

    return -1;
}
```

In this function, the **find** algorithm is used in a similar manner as before, but this time the iterator to the found element is stored in **it**. The same check for **it** being equal to **end** is performed (not found), and if the element has been found, the distance function returns the index, which is the number of elements between the first element in the array and the element that was found.

The following snippet makes use of this function to check whether the number 9 is contained in our vector, and if so, we can get its index:

```cpp
int main()
{
    vector<int> vec = {1,2,3,4,5,6,7,8,9,10};
    const int numToCheck = 9;
    long index = contains(numToCheck, vec);
    cout << "Vector contains " << numToCheck << " "
        << (index != -1 ? "YES" : "NO");
    if(index != -1)
        cout << " and its index is " << index;

    cout << endl;

    return 0;
}
```

The preceding code would yield the following output:

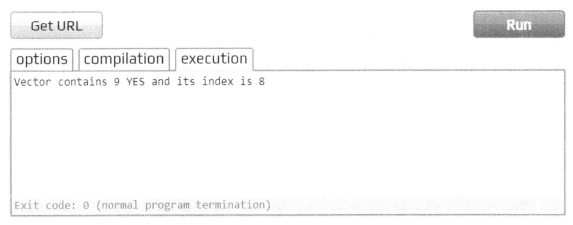

Figure 12.8: Checking for elements in a vector

We can take this one step further and create a template function that can find an element of any type from a vector of that type. The following example shows just how powerful the standard library is when it comes to writing minimal and generic code:

```
template<typename T>
long contains(const T& value, const vector<T>& vec)
{
    auto it = find(vec.begin(), vec.end(), value);

    if(it != vec.end()) // we found the element
        return distance(vec.begin(), it);
    return -1;
}
```

Here, we replaced the **int** iterator with the **auto** keyword. This means we will be given the correct type of iterator even though it is not explicitly typed. Additionally, the function is now a template function, and any types have been replaced with **T**. Now if we run the same snippet as before, but with the new **contains()** function, we should get the same result, without needing to explicitly use an **int** vector-only **contains()** function.

Exercise 76: Sorting Vectors with a Custom Comparison

Sorting vectors is another common operation. There are built-in comparisons that can be used for trivial sorts, such as sorting by ascending and descending order on a vector of integers. There may be times where we would like to sort our vector based on something more granular, such as ascending or descending order based on one particular variable in a custom type.

> **Note**
>
> The complete code for this exercise can be found at https://packt.live/2tXeDN2.

Implement this using a Track object, and sort the tracks based on track length:

1. First, we will write a simple class track that has a name, length, and popularity rating:

```
#include <iostream>
#include <algorithm>

using namespace std;
```

```
class Track
{
public:
    Track(float length, string name, int popularity) :
        m_trackLength(length), m_trackName(name),
        m_popularityRating(popularity) {}
    float getLength() const { return m_trackLength; }
    string getName() const { return m_trackName; }
    int getPopularity() const { return m_popularityRating; }

private:
    float m_trackLength;
    string m_trackName;
    int m_popularityRating;
};
```

2. From this, we can create a vector of tracks that we will sort using our custom comparison:

```
int main()
{
    vector<Track> tracks;
    tracks.push_back(Track(199.0f, "God's Plan", 100));
    tracks.push_back(Track(227.0f, "Hold On, We're Going Home", 95));
    tracks.push_back(Track(182.0f, "The Motto", 80));

    return 0;
}
```

3. A custom comparison is essentially a function that takes two parameters of the same type and returns a **bool**. How we define this function is up to us, but for our current program, we just want to sort track length in ascending order so we can compare track length values:

```
bool trackLengthCompare(const Track& t1, const Track& t2)
{
    return (t1.getLength() < t2.getLength());
}
```

4. Now, we can use this within the sort algorithm to sort our tracks in ascending order and then print them out. We can pass the custom sort function as a parameter to the sort function, along with iterators to the start and end of our vector:

```
sort(tracks.begin(), tracks.end(), trackLengthCompare);
```

5. We can test this code in our **main** function and also print out the values once they are sorted:

```cpp
int main()
{
    vector<Track> tracks;

    tracks.push_back(Track(199.0f, "God's Plan", 100));
    tracks.push_back(Track(227.0f, "Hold On, We're Going Home", 95));
    tracks.push_back(Track(182.0f, "The Motto", 80));
    sort(tracks.begin(), tracks.end(), trackLengthCompare);

    for (auto t : tracks)
    {
        cout << t.getName() << endl;
    }

    return 0;
}
```

Here is the complete code:

```cpp
#include<iostream>
#include<string>
#include<algorithm>

using namespace std;

class Track
{
public:
    Track(float length, string name, int popularity) :
            m_trackLength(length), m_trackName(name),
            m_popularityRating(popularity) {}
    float getLength() const { return m_trackLength; }
    string getName() const { return m_trackName; }
    int getPopularity() const { return m_popularityRating; }

private:
    float m_trackLength;
    string m_trackName;
    int m_popularityRating;};
```

```
bool trackLengthCompare(const Track& t1, const Track& t2)
{
    return (t1.getLength() < t2.getLength());
}

int main()
{
    vector<Track> tracks;
    tracks.push_back(Track(199.0f, "God's Plan", 100));
    tracks.push_back(Track(227.0f, "Hold On, We're Going Home", 95));
    tracks.push_back(Track(182.0f, "The Motto", 80));
    sort(tracks.begin(), tracks.end(), trackLengthCompare);

    for (auto t : tracks)
    {
        cout << t.getName() << endl;
    }

    return 0;
}
```

Once you run the code, you will obtain the following output:

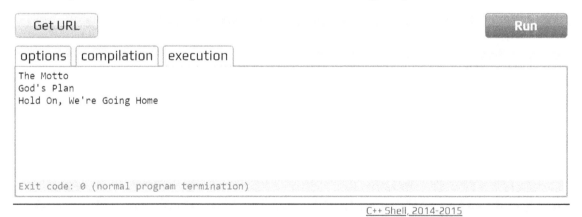

Figure 12.9: Output for sorting with a custom comparison

Now that we understand how to use the sort function, try extending this exercise with the following extra functionality:

6. Write a comparison for the popularity rating:

```
bool trackPopularityCompare(const Track& t1, const Track& t2)
{
    return (t1.getPopularity () < t2.getPopularity());
}
```

7. Sort by track length in descending order:

```
bool trackLengthCompare(const Track& t1, const Track& t2)
{
    return (t1.getLength() > t2.getLength());
}
```

8. Sort by name length:

```
bool trackNameLengthCompare(const Track& t1, const Track& t2)
{
    return (t1.getName().size() < t2.getName().size());
}
```

Map/Unordered Map: Our Associative Containers

Maps and unordered maps are associative containers. Elements within a map/ unordered map are associated with a key and are accessed through this key. No two elements within a map/unordered map can have the same key. Internally, maps are sorted by keys using an internal comparison object. Conversely, elements in an unordered map are not sorted by keys, but are stored in a fashion that allows fast retrieval of elements by their key. Maps are generally more suited for iterating over and looking up keys, whereas unordered maps are more efficient at accessing elements directly by their associated key. If you end up looping through your data and using each element in some way, then a map is most suitable; if you are mostly grabbing an element from the container by its key and not looping over the entire collection, then an unordered map is the most suitable.

Constructing Maps and Unordered Maps

Here is a selection of constructors to use when constructing maps:

- **map()**: A default constructor, an empty map

- **map(const map& x)**: Constructs a map from a copy of another map

- **template <class InputIterator>; map (InputIterator first, InputIterator last)**: Constructs a map from a range

- **map (initializer_list<value_type> il)**: Constructs a map using an initializer list

Here is an example snippet that shows how the aforementioned constructors can be used:

```cpp
#include <iostream>
#include <map>

using namespace std;

int main()
{
    map<int, int> myMap;
    map<int, int> copiedMap(myMap);
    map<int, int> rangeMap(copiedMap.begin(), copiedMap.end());
    map<int, int> initList = { {1,2}, {2,3}, {3,4} };
}
```

When declaring a map, we need to pass in two template parameters, as shown in the preceding snippet. The first is the type we would like the keys in our map to be. These are the identifiers we will associate with the second parameter type; the value. This tying together of a key and a value is the 'associative' part of associative containers.

Unordered maps, of course, have a similar set of constructors, some with the added option of specifying the minimum number of buckets to use for the internal hash table, used to retrieve elements by a key. Buckets internally partition the sequence of the container into smaller subsequences. If this value is not specified, then this is determined automatically. These are the constructors for unordered maps:

- **unordered_map(size_type n)**: Constructs an unordered map with an optional minimum bucket size

- **unordered_map(const unordered_map& x)**: Constructs an unordered map from a copy of another unordered map

- **template <class InputIterator>unordered_map (InputIterator first, InputIterator last)**: Constructs an unordered map from a range

- **unordered_map (initializer_list<value_type> il, size_type n)**: Constructs an unordered map from an initializer list with an optional minimum bucket size

Here is an example snippet in which each of the aforementioned maps is implemented:

```cpp
#include <iostream>
#include <unordered_map>

using namespace std;

int main()
{
    unordered_map<int, int> myUnorderedMap;
    unordered_map<int, int> copiedUnorderedMap(myUnorderedMap);
    unordered_map<int, int> rangeUnorderedMap(copiedUnorderedMap.begin(),
    copiedUnorderedMap.end());
    unordered_map<int, int> initList = { {1,2}, {2,3}, {3,4} };
}
```

Operations on Maps and Unordered Maps

Maps and unordered maps expose similar operations as other containers, such as strings and vectors. Something unique to these containers is that when adding an element into a **map/unordered_map** we use **std::pair**; which we will hereafter refer to as a key-value pair. We can create key-value pairs using **std::make_pair**. The following example shows how to insert elements into a map and an unordered map. Notice the use of **std::pair** when inserting the elements. This key-value pair is an association of a key and a value:

```cpp
#include <iostream>
#include <unordered_map>
#include <map>

using namespace std;

int main()
{
    unordered_map<int, int> myUnorderedMap;
    map<int, int> myMap;
    myUnorderedMap.insert(make_pair(1, 2));
    myMap.insert(make_pair(1, 2));
}
```

When traversing a map, the iterator will point to a key-value pair inside the map. Each element in a map or unordered map is a key-value pair, with the key type of the pair being our declared key template parameter type, and the value being our value template parameter type (in the preceding case, the key is an `int` and the value is also an `int`). We can access the key using first, and the value using second.

The following example shows the simple traversal and printing of a map (the same applies to unordered maps):

```cpp
#include <iostream>
#include <map>
#include <string>

using namespace std;

int main()
{
    map<string, string> myStringMap =
    {
        {"Hello", "Hola"},
        {"Goodbye", "Adiós"},
        {"Programmer", "Programación"}
    };

    for (const auto& loc : myStringMap)
    {
        cout << loc.first << " In Spanish is " << loc.second << endl;
    }
}
```

When you run the preceding code, you will obtain the following output:

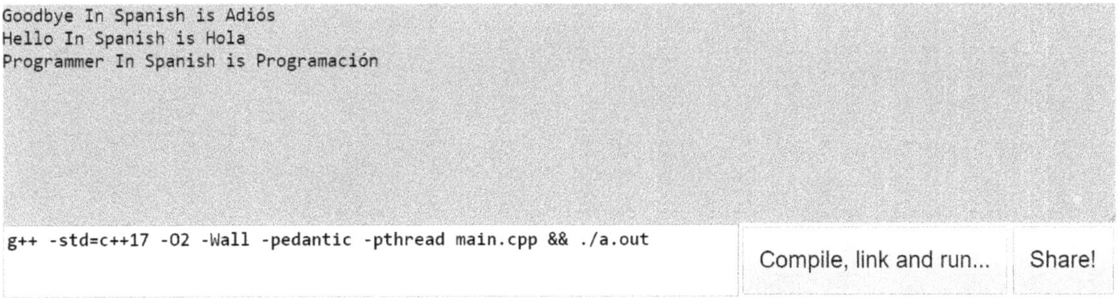

```
Goodbye In Spanish is Adiós
Hello In Spanish is Hola
Programmer In Spanish is Programación




g++ -std=c++17 -O2 -Wall -pedantic -pthread main.cpp && ./a.out
                                          Compile, link and run...    Share!
```

Figure 12.10: Traversal and printing of a map

In this example, the map is prefilled using the initializer list constructor. When using the initializer list, values are separated with commas and braces to make up a key-value pair:

```
{"Hello", "Hola"},
```

The example then uses the ranged **for** loop to go through each element and print its first and second keys and values, respectively.

Exercise 77: Map Quiz

As well as built-in types such as floats and integers, we can also use custom types as keys. One requirement of key custom types is that we need to implement a comparison by either overloading the **<** operator, or creating a custom object that can be passed in as a template parameter when declaring a map. This is required so that the map knows how to sort its keys.

> **Note**
>
> The complete code for this exercise can be found at https://packt.live/2FkP6js.

Let's write something practical using a map—in this case, a quiz with multiple choices that shows our score at the end:

1. First, we will create our custom key type called **Question**. This will have member variables for the question itself, its question number (we will use this in the comparison object), and the index of the correct answer:

```cpp
#include <iostream>
#include <map>
#include <string>
#include <vector>

using namespace std;

class Question
{
public:

    Question(int questionNumber, string question, int answerIndex):
            m_questionNumber(questionNumber), m_question(question),
            m_answerIndex(answerIndex) {}

    int getQuestionNumber() const
```

```
    {
        return m_questionNumber;
    }

    string getQuestion() const
    {
        return m_question;
    }
    int getAnswerIndex() const
    {
        return m_answerIndex;
    }

private:

    int m_questionNumber;
    string m_question;
    int m_answerIndex;
};
```

2. Next, we will create the custom comparison object that the map will use to sort the keys:

```
struct QuestionCompare
{
    bool operator() (const Question& lhs, const Question& rhs) const
    {
        return lhs.getQuestionNumber() < rhs.getQuestionNumber();
    }
};
```

We now have a few steps to create our quiz, so we must declare our map. The key for our map will be our custom **Question** type. The value part of the key-value pair in our container can also be a container. This means that we can have a key-value pair of the **<int, vector<int>>** or **<float, map<int, int>>** types. We will make use of the ability of the value part of a pair to be a container for our multiple choices by using a vector of strings as our value type. Finally, we will use the custom comparison object as the final template parameter:

```
int main()
{
    map<Question, vector<string>, QuestionCompare> quiz;
```

3. Now we can create our **Question** objects and vector of strings containing the answers, and then insert them into the quiz map:

```
Question question1(1, "Which two actors directed themselves
in movies and won Oscars 2 for Best Actor?", 2);

vector<string> question1Answers =
{
    "Al Pacino and Timothy Hutton",
    "Jack Nicholson and Kevin Spacey",
    "Laurence Olivier and Roberto Benigni",
    "Tom Hanks and Paul Newman"
};


Question question2(2, "\"After all, tomorrow is another day!\"
was the last line 12 in which Oscar-winning Best Picture?", 0);

vector<string> question2Answers =
{
    "Gone With the Wind",
    "Great Expectations",
    "Harold and Maude",
    "The Matrix"
};


quiz.insert(make_pair(question1, question1Answers));
quiz.insert(make_pair(question2, question2Answers));
```

4. Now we can create our main loop, which will ask our questions and then wait for input. We will first get an iterator for our map and then continue to ask questions, take answers, and increment our iterator until it matches **quiz.end()**:

```
cout << "Welcome to the movie quiz" << endl;
cout << "Type your answer between 1-4 and press enter:"
        << endl;
map<Question, vector<string>>::
    iterator quizIterator = quiz.begin();
vector<bool> correctAnswers;

while (quizIterator != quiz.end())
{
    cout << quizIterator->first.getQuestion() << endl;
    int answerIndex = 1;


    for(auto answer : quizIterator->second)
```

```
                {
                    cout << answerIndex << " : " << answer << endl;
                    answerIndex++;
                }

                int answer;
                cin >> answer;
```

5. We will push any correct answers onto a vector of **bool** values and then use the size of that vector to output the score at the end:

```
                int correctAnswer = quizIterator->first.getAnswerIndex();
                bool wasCorrect = answer - 1 == correctAnswer;

                cout << (wasCorrect ? "CORRECT!" : "INCORRECT!")
                        << " Correct answer is: "
                        << quizIterator->second[correctAnswer] << endl;

                if (wasCorrect)
                        correctAnswers.push_back(answer);
                quizIterator++;
            }
        cout << "Your score was " << correctAnswers.size()
                << " out of " << quiz.size() << endl;
        cout << "done";
    }
```

The output for a full quiz is as follows:

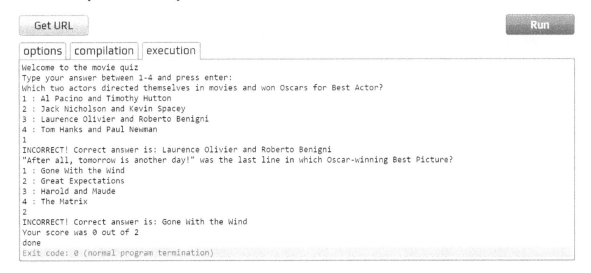

Figure 12.11: Final output

As you can see, associative containers are extremely useful for programs that rely on values which can be looked up by keys, or even just associating a specific value with another value, like the exercise does with questions and their respective possible **answer** vector.

Sets/Multisets

A set is an associative container just like a map, and, just like a map, every key is unique; it cannot have multiples of the same key. The difference with a set is that it is not a container for key-value pairs. It is essentially a container of unique keys, like a vector in which each element in the vector is unique. Once an element is added to a set, it cannot be modified; but it can be removed from the set. A multiset behaves just like a set except for allowing multiple non-unique keys.

Constructors

When constructing a set, we can also pass in the comparator used to sort the set. A comparator is a function that's used to decide how elements are to be ordered in the set. The following are a selection of constructors to use for sets and multisets (only sets are shown, for brevity):

- **set()**;: Default empty set

- **set(const key_compare& comp)**;: Empty set with the chosen comparison object

- **set(const set& x)**;: Copy constructor

- **template <class InputIterator> set (InputIterator first, InputIterator last, const key_compare& comp = key_compare())**;: Range constructor with an optional chosen comparison

- **set (initializer_list<value_type> il, const key_compare& comp = key_compare())**;: Initializer list with an optional chosen comparison

Exercise 78: A Custom Comparator for a Set

By default, a set will sort elements in ascending order, so if we were to create a set of integers, they would be sorted in ascending order. This is fine for built-in types such as **int**, but if we have our own custom type, then we must define how the elements are sorted. We can define which property of that type is used for sorting and even change the default sorting from ascending to descending. In this exercise, we will create a class called Person that contains a name and an age. We will then create a custom comparison for the set to sort the Person elements by age, in descending order:

> **Note**
>
> The complete code for this exercise can be found at https://packt.live/2D6re26.

1. First, we will write the **Person** class. It is very simple:

```cpp
class Person
{
public:
    Person(string name, int age)
    {
        m_name = name;
        m_age = age;
    }

    string getName() const { return m_name; }
    int getAge() const { return m_age; }

private:
    string m_name;
    int m_age;
};
```

2. Now, create a custom comparator. Here, we will use a functor, which is an *object* that can be used like a *function*. The functor will be used to compare each element in the set, when it is added, to decide the order. A comparator takes two elements and returns a **bool**:

```cpp
struct customComparator
{
    bool operator() (const Person& a, const Person& b) const
    {
        return (a.getAge() > b.getAge());
    }
};
```

3. Now we can create some **Person** objects, add them to the set, and then print them. Here is the full source code:

```cpp
#include <iostream>
#include <string>
#include <set>

using namespace std;

class Person
{
public:
    Person(string name, int age)
    {
        m_name = name;
        m_age = age;
    }

    string getName() const
    {
        return m_name;
    }

    int getAge() const {
    return m_age;
    }

private:
    string m_name;
    int m_age;
```

```
};

struct customComparator
    {
        bool operator()(const Person & a,
        const Person & b) const {
        return (a.getAge() > b.getAge());
    }
};

int main()
{
    set < Person, customComparator > personSet;
    Person a("bob", 35);
    Person b("bob", 25);
    personSet.insert(a);
    personSet.insert(b);

    for (auto person: personSet)
    {
        cout << person.getAge() << endl;
    }
}
```

4. Run the complete code. You should obtain the following output:

Figure 12.12: Output for the custom comparator for a set

Operations

Sets have a few additional useful operations along with equivalents for getting the size, as well as inserting and obtaining iterators that are exposed with other containers:

- **count(const T& val);**: Returns the number of elements that match **val** within the set. Remember that a set's elements are all unique, so this function can only return 1 at most. This is useful for finding whether a key exists within the set.

- **lower_bound(const T& val);**: Returns an iterator to **val**, if it exists, or to a value that definitely will not go before **val** in the set based on the comparison object.

- **upper_bound(const T& val);**: Returns an iterator to **val**, if it exists, or to a value that definitely will go after **val** in the set based on the comparison object.

- **equal_range(const T& val);**: Returns an iterator of pairs with the upper and lower bounds of a range that contains **val**. Again, since elements in a set are unique, this will return an iterator to **val** if it exists.

In the following exercise, we will use a set to obtain the number of unique elements in a multiset.

Exercise 79: Using a Set to Get the Number of Unique Elements in a Multiset

Since a set does not allow non-unique elements but a multiset does, we can use a set to get the number of unique elements in a multiset by inserting each element in the multiset. If we try to add an element that already exists in the set, then it will not be added. After trying to add all the elements, we can then count how many elements are contained in the set. This will be the number of unique elements:

> **Note**
>
> The complete code for this exercise can be found at https://packt.live/2OqKyMs.

1. In a new **main** function, we can declare our set and multiset:

```
#include <iostream>
#include <string>
#include <set>
#include <stdlib.h>

using namespace std;

int main()
```

```
{
    set<int> intSet;
    multiset<int> intMultiset;
```

2. We can then add a bunch of random numbers into our multiset by looping and inserting into the multiset:

```
for(unsigned int i = 0; i < 100; i++)
{
    intMultiset.insert(1 + rand() % 100);
}
```

> **Note**
>
> The preceding code snippet is an example of a simple random number generation.

3. We can now iterate over this multiset and try to add each element into the set:

```
for(auto i  : intMultiset)
{
    intSet.insert(i);
}
```

4. And finally, we can print the number of elements in our set using the **size** function:

```
    cout << "there are " << intSet.size()
        << " unique elements in the multiset";
}
```

5. Here is the complete code:

```
#include <iostream>
#include <string>
#include <set>
#include <stdlib.h>

using namespace std;

int main()
{
    set < int > intSet;
    multiset < int > intMultiset;
    for (unsigned int i = 0; i < 100; i++)
    {
        intMultiset.insert(1 + rand() % 100);
```

```
        }
        for (auto i: intMultiset)
        {
            intSet.insert(i);
        }
        cout << "there are " << intSet.size()
            << " unique elements in the multiset";
    }
```

6. Here is the possible output from our program:

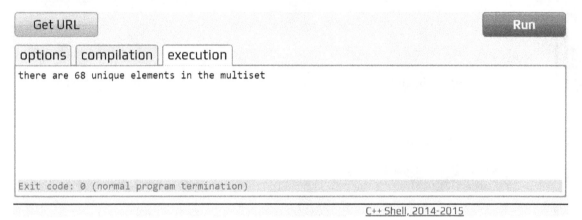

Figure 12.13: Final output of the exercise

Queues/Stacks

Queues are a type of container with a first-in-first-out behavior. Conversely, a stack is a container with a last-in-first-out behavior. When adding elements to a queue, they are added to the end of the queue, and elements will be popped or peeked from the front. When adding elements to a stack, we can think of them as being added to the top, and then elements will also be popped or peeked from the top. This is the difference between first-in-first-out and last-in-first-out. Both of these containers are very useful when elements need to be retrieved and removed in a particular order; the end-of-chapter activity will utilize a queue to handle going through elements in a defined order.

Constructors

When constructing a queue, we can also decide what the underlying container for that queue will be. The same applies to a stack. If we do not choose a container type for ourselves then, by default, **std::deque** will be used.

The template declaration of a queue and a stack uses the following syntax:

```
template <class T, class Container = deque<T> > class queue;
template <class T, class Container = deque<T> > class stack;
```

We can see that the container defaults to **deque** for both types.

Constructors for both stack and queue are minimal and, usually, we will want to use the default constructors for these types and an optional custom container object:

- **queue()** ;: Constructs an empty queue
- **stack()** ;: Constructs an empty stack

Operations

Both queue and stack support the following operations:

- **empty()** ;: Returns whether the container is empty
- **size()** ;: Returns the number of elements within the container
- **push()** ;: Inserts an element
- **pop()** ;: Removes an element

Queues specifically expose the subsequent functions:

- **front()** ;: The next element in the queue
- **back()** ;: The last element in the queue

Stacks expose the **top()** function, which is the last-in-first-out equivalent of the **front()** function of the **queue**.

You've seen an implementation of queues and stacks in the previous chapter. You are encouraged to experiment further with your own implementations here.

Activity 12: Converting RPG Combat to Use Standard Library Containers

Now that we have learned about the different containers the standard library provides, we can improve a previous activity, **RPG Combat** (included in *Chapter 11, Templates*) by using containers, instead of raw arrays, and also a queue to create a gauntlet of monsters for us to fight. This activity will help show just how much we can do with containers with a relatively small amount of code. All the functions we have previously utilized raw arrays for will be much shorter using the standard library containers and we won't need to implement copy constructors and assignment operators; the standard library containers will handle copying themselves. Once you successfully complete the activity, you should obtain the following output:

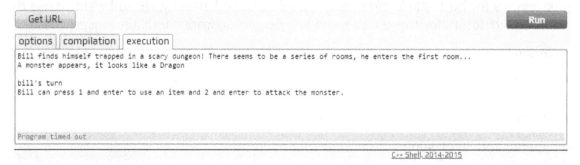

Figure 12.14: Final output of the activity

> **Note**
>
> The complete code for this activity can be found at https://packt.live/2pCMg55.

Here are the steps to complete the activity:

1. Alter the **Attack**, **Item**, and **Character** classes to use strings instead of **char** arrays.

2. Remove any now unneeded copy constructor, destructor, and assignment implementations.

3. Get the **Character** class to take vectors of **Attack** and **Item** instead of raw arrays.

4. Implement the **attack** and **defend** functions to use vectors instead of arrays and update the display function to utilize the vectors.

5. In the main function, implement a queue that holds different **Character** types for the player to fight.

6. Fight each monster in the queue until the queue is empty and display a **win** string. Also, allow the use of items and a default attack.

> **Note**
>
> The solution to this activity can be found on page 567.

Summary

There are many containers we can make use of in C++, and each has its own very specific purpose. Although these specifics are important, it is also important to realize just how similar the interface into these containers really is. This common interface helps us to write less code and also quickly understand how to use containers we may not have used before. This is very powerful and is the foundation of writing solid C++ code. In the next and final chapter of this book, we will look into handling exceptions.

13

Exception Handling in C++

Overview

This chapter introduces exception handling, the mechanism used by C++ for reporting and recovering from unexpected events in a program. By the end of this chapter, you will be able to recognize the kinds of events for which exception handling is appropriate; know when to throw exceptions and when to return an error code; write robust code using exception handling; Use RAII with exception handling to automatically reclaim resources after an unexpected event; and recover from and continue execution after unexpected events.

Introduction

Previous chapters introduced C++ flow-of-control statements and variable declarations. We have had a taste of object-oriented programming and created data structures out of dynamic variables. In this chapter, we turn our attention to how C++ can help a developer handle situations that arise when something unexpectedly goes wrong in a program.

An invalid number input by the user, an unanticipated timeout awaiting a response, and a logic error are all examples of events in a program. Some of these events, such as the input error, may occur so frequently or predictably that they must be anticipated and handled, or else the program will be unusable. Other events, such as the timeout, happen rarely, and never when the program and the system within which it runs are working perfectly. Still other events, such as the logic error, are never meant to happen at all, but sometimes they do anyway.

The user input error event is an expected event. It is handled with specific code; a "user input error" dialog box might be shown, and the program will loop back to await the input again. The code to recover from a user input error is likely to be lexically near to the code that detected the error because its action depends strongly on the particular event that occurred. Ordinary flow-of-control statements are appropriate for handling expected events. After an expected event has been handled, the code can continue on the path of normal execution as if the event had not happened.

A logic error is an *unexpected* event. It is impossible to write specific code to handle unexpected events because the events are literally unexpected–they aren't supposed to happen.

Another reason why it isn't possible to write specific code to handle unexpected events is because of the great number of possible unexpected events that might occur in every statement. Every function call could potentially have logic errors, argument errors, and runtime errors. If you had to write specific code to handle each event in each place that it might occur, the program would be 99.9 percent event handlers, and nothing would get done.

A third reason why specific code to handle unexpected events can't be written is because these events block the forward progress of the program. A program can't fix a logic error (because it is unexpected), so it can't progress past the test for the logic error. This leaves the program with a limited number of ways to handle an unexpected event.

The program could halt, it could retry a block of code representing some computation to see if the unexpected event goes away, or it could abandon the computation with the unexpected event in it and try to do something else. These handling actions are relatively generic. Each action may be appropriate for many distinct unexpected events.

C++ exception handling is designed for unexpected events–that is, for responding to events that:

- Occur infrequently and unpredictably

- Prevent forward progress of the program

You can, of course, use exception handling for *expected* events, but it's not the right tool for the job. You can also use exception handling to return from a function, but it will be slower and harder to explain to colleagues. Exception handling is not meant for these jobs, any more than a hammer is meant for turning screws. It is *possible* to pound in screws with a hammer, but it is difficult and inefficient to do so.

Responding to Unexpected Events

Unexpected events may be detected anywhere in a program, but they are typically detected in library functions that interact with the operating system and the external world. Calls to these functions are usually found nested many levels deep in the function call stack.

An unexpected event blocks the forward progress of the program's current computation. The program could choose to halt abruptly when faced with an unexpected event, but if it wants to be able to do anything other than halt (including simply saving work and printing a message), it must abandon the current computation and return to higher-level code that kicks off new computations. It is in this higher-level code that the program can decide whether execution can continue or must be stopped.

There are two ways this can happen. Traditionally, the function that detected the unexpected event can stop what it's doing, manually clean up any resources it's using, and return an error code to its caller. The caller, in turn, cleans up and returns the error code to its caller. The error code is passed up the calling chain step-by-step, like a bucket brigade, until it arrives at code capable of responding to it, as shown in the following figure:

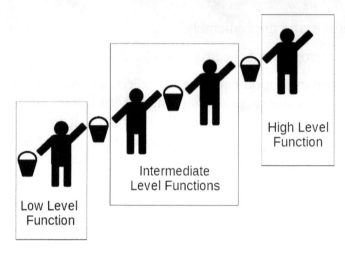

Figure 13.1: Visualizing the step-by-step return of error codes

The step-by-step return of error codes is fraught with risk. If a function does not capture the return code of all called functions, it may attempt to continue instead of passing the error code to its caller, as visualized in the following figure:

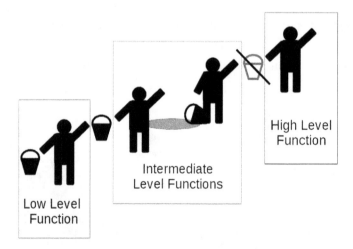

Figure: 13.2: Intermediate-level function dropping an error code

Attempting to continue execution after an unexpected event generally causes a cascade of more and more serious unexpected events until the operating system forcibly stops the program. If a function does not delete dynamic variables, close open file handles, and release other resources, these resources leak, causing the program or the operating system to eventually become unstable and crash.

The other way to return execution to high-level code is with C++ exception handling. Exception handling has three parts. A **throw** statement "throws" an exception, signaling the occurrence of an unexpected event. The C++ runtime system "unwinds" the function call stack, calling the destructors of every local variable, without returning control to the function containing the local variable. Then a **try/catch** block "catches" the exception, ending the unwinding process and allowing execution to continue.

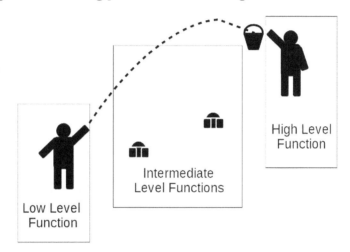

Figure 13.3: Visualizing throwing and catching of exceptions

A thrown exception cannot be ignored like a returned error code. The exception is either caught by a **try/catch** block, or the C++ runtime system terminates the program.

As the C++ runtime system unwinds the stack while processing the thrown exception, it calls the destructors of all local variables. Resources wrapped in smart pointers or C++ classes are deleted and thus do not leak. The developer does not have to write complex flow-of-control code to handle both the normal execution case and the unexpected error case, as they would have to do when error codes are returned step-by-step. These features make exception handling a better way to process unexpected events.

Throwing Exceptions

A **throw** statement throws an exception, signaling to the C++ runtime system that an unexpected event has occurred. The **throw** statement consists of the **throw** keyword followed by an expression of any type. The exception thrown has the same type as the expression. C++ provides a library of exception types that are class instances derived from **std::exception**, but a program is not limited to throwing these or any other class instances; a program can throw an **int** or a **char*** or any other desired type. Here are a few examples of **throw** statements:

- Throw an exception of type **std::exception**:

```
throw std::exception;
```

- Throw an exception of type **std::logic_error**, a class derived from **std::exception**. The exception has an optional text string that describes the specific exception:

```
throw std::logic_error("This should not be executed");
```

- Throw an exception of type **std::runtime_error**, a class derived from **std::exception**. The exception has an integer error code and an optional text string that further describes the specific exception. The integer code is an operating system-specific error:

```
throw std::runtime_error(LastError(), "in OpenFile()");
```

- Throw the Linux **errno** pseudo-variable as an exception of type **int**. The value of the integer is an operating system-specific error code:

```
throw errno;
```

- Throw an exception of type **char const***. The contents of the string describe the exception:

```
throw "i before e except after c";
```

Most of the standard exceptions that a developer will use are either **std::logic_error** and its derivations or **std::runtime_error** and its derivations, particularly **std::system_error**. The remainder of the standard exceptions are thrown by C++ standard library functions. The intent of the standard has never been clear as to why one exception is a **logic_error**, another is a **runtime_error**, and yet another is neither. This is simply not one of the better-designed parts of C++.

The use of standard exceptions is problematic in low-memory situations since most standard exceptions may allocate dynamic variables when constructed. The **what** argument to standard exceptions has no defined meaning. It's just a bit of text inserted into the string returned by the **what()** member function of **std::exception**.

Uncaught Exceptions

Exceptions are thrown by **throw** statements and caught by **catch** clauses in a **try/catch** block. We will look at catching exceptions later.

If a thrown exception is not caught by a **try/catch** block, the C++ runtime system terminates the program. Throwing an exception is better than calling **exit()** or **abort()** to terminate program execution because it documents that an unexpected event has occurred. Throwing an exception also allows the program to be improved later by catching the exception and making a decision about whether to terminate the program or continue.

Exercise 80: Throwing Uncaught Exceptions

In this exercise, we will see what happens when we throw an exception that is not caught by the **catch** clause of a **try/catch** block:

> **Note**
>
> The complete code for the exercise can be found here: https://packt.live/37tOlS4.

1. Type in the skeleton of the **main()** function. It looks like this:

```
#include <iostream>

using namespace std;

int main()
{
    return 0;
}
```

2. Inside **main()**, insert a **throw** statement. This consists of the **throw** keyword followed by an expression of any type. Exceptions are often class instances derived from the C++ standard library **std::exception** class, but any type of expression will do. You can throw an integer, such as an error number, or even a null-terminated text string describing the exception:

```
throw "An exception of some type";
```

3. The completed program looks like this:

```cpp
#include <iostream>

using namespace std;

int main()
{
    throw "An exception of some type";

    return 0;
}
```

4. Run the program. While the precise message printed varies by operating system and compiler, the output from the tutorialspoint online compiler looks like this:

```
$g++ -o main *.cpp
$main
terminate called after throwing an instance of 'char const*'
timeout: the monitored command dumped core
sh: line 1: 30049 Aborted                      timeout 10s main
```

Figure 13.4: Output of the program in exercise 80

What happened here? When an exception is thrown and not caught, the C++ runtime system calls the standard library **terminate()** function. **terminate()** does not return; it instead causes the program to exit, signaling the abnormal termination to the operating system. On Linux, this kind of abnormal termination dumps a core file for debugging.

5. Following **using namespace std;**, add an **int** function called **deeply_nested()**. The function skeleton looks like this:

```cpp
int deeply_nested()
{
    return 0;
}
```

6. Add code to throw the **int** value **123**. Then output **"in deeply_nested after throw"**. The completed function looks like this:

```cpp
int deeply_nested()
{
    throw 123;
```

```
      cout << "in deeply_nested() after throw" << endl;
      return 0;
}
```

7. Following **deeply_nested()**, add another **int** function called **intermediate()**. Its skeleton looks like this:

```
int intermediate()
{
      return 0;
}
```

8. Add a call to **deeply_nested()**. Don't forget to capture the returned value from **deeply_nested()** in an **int** variable called **rc** (which stands for return code). Output the message **"in intermediate(), after deeply_nested()"**. Then, return the return code from **deeply_nested()** that is in **rc**. The complete function looks like this:

```
int intermediate()
{
      int rc = deeply_nested();
      cout << "in intermediate(), after deeply_nested()";
      return rc;
}
```

9. In **main()**, replace the **throw** statement with a call to **intermediate()**. Don't capture the return code from **intermediate()**:

```
      intermediate();
```

10. The updated program looks like this:

```
#include <iostream>

using namespace std;

int deeply_nested()
{
      throw 123;
      cout << "in deeply_nested() after throw" << endl;
      return 0;
}

int intermediate()
{
      int rc = deeply_nested();
```

```
        cout << "in intermediate(), after deeply_nested()";
        return rc;
}


int main()
{
    intermediate();

    return 0;
}
```

11. Run the program. While the precise message printed varies by operating system and compiler, the output from the tutorialspoint online compiler looks like this:

```
$g++ -o main *.cpp
$main
terminate called after throwing an instance of 'int'
timeout: the monitored command dumped core
sh: line 1: 143250 Aborted                    timeout 10s main
```

Figure 13.5: Output of the updated program in exercise 80

What happened here? **main()** called **intermediate()**, which called **deeply_nested()**. This is intended to represent the normal behavior of programs, which typically execute functions nested many layers deep when an exception is thrown. Execution of the code in **deeply_nested()** stops when the **throw** statement is executed. The C++ runtime system starts looking for a **try/catch** block to catch the exception. There is none in **deeply_nested()**, none in **intermediate()**, and none in **main()**, so the C++ runtime system calls **terminate()**. The output is produced by the operating system and may vary from one operating system or compiler version to the next. Notice that none of the output statements that follow the **throw** are executed, indicating that the execution of the functions stopped after the **throw** statement.

> **Note**
>
> Another thing to notice about this program is the return codes. **deeply_nested()** returns a code, possibly describing an error. So does **intermediate()**. But **main()** doesn't capture the return code from **intermediate()**, so the error information is lost if no exception is thrown. Exceptions reliably stop a program if they are not caught, and they reliably transport error information from the **throw** statement to the site of the **catch** clause.

Catching Exceptions

The code to catch an exception is called a **try/catch** block. It consists of two parts; the **try** block–consisting of the **try** keyword, followed by a statement list surrounded by curly braces–is a block of statements controlled by the **try/catch** block. Following the **try** block is one or more **catch** clauses. Each **catch** clause consists of the **catch** keyword, followed by a parenthesized variable declaration, declaring the type of exception to be caught by the **catch** clause. The last **catch** clause may be **catch (...)**, which catches every exception not previously caught.

Here is a sample **try/catch** block:

```
try
{
    auto p = make_unique<char[]>(100);
}
catch (std::exception& e)
{
    cout << e.what() << endl;
}
```

The **try** block contains the single statement:

```
    auto p = make_unique<char[]>(100);
```

This statement might throw an exception of type **std::bad_alloc** if there is insufficient memory to create the dynamic variable. The statement(s) in the **try** block are executed. If no exception occurs, execution continues with the statement following the last **catch** clause.

There is one **catch** clause in the sample **try/catch** block, which handles any exception whose type is derived from **std::exception**, including **std::bad_alloc**. If an exception occurs, the type of the exception is compared to the type of the first **catch** clause. If the type of the exception can construct or initialize the variable of the **catch** clause, the way an actual function argument constructs a formal argument, that **catch** clause begins to execute. The executable statement in the sample **catch** clause prints out a description of the exception using the **std::exception::what()** member function:

```
    cout << e.what() << endl;
```

After the compound statement in the **catch** clause is executed, the exception is considered handled. Execution continues at the location following the last **catch** clause.

If the type of the thrown exception cannot construct the variable in the first **catch** clause, the next **catch** clause is compared. The order of the **catch** clauses matters. The C++ runtime system matches a thrown exception against **catch** clauses from top to bottom. The exception is caught by the first **catch** clause in which the exception can be constructed. The order of the **catch** clauses should be from the most specific to the most general, with **catch (...)**, being the most general, at the end of the list.

If no **catch** clause matches the type of the thrown exception, the search for a **try/catch** block continues in the scope (delimited by curly brackets) enclosing the **try/catch** block.

Exercise 81: try/catch Blocks

This exercise shows the basic form of a **try/catch** block. The purpose of a **try/catch** block is to process some or all thrown exceptions to decide whether the execution of the program can continue:

> **Note**
>
> The complete code for the exercise can be found here: https://packt.live/2sa34l1.

1. Enter the skeleton of the **main()** function. The code looks like this:

```
#include <iostream>

using namespace std;

int main()
{
    return 0;
}
```

2. Type in the function **deeply_nested()** from the previous exercise. The code looks like this:

```
int deeply_nested()
{
    throw 123;
    return 0;
}
```

3. Inside **main()**, create a **try/catch** block. Inside the **try** block, call **deeply_nested()**. Add a **catch** block to catch all exceptions using the catch clause **catch(...)**. Inside the **catch** block, output the **"in catch ..."** string. The code looks like this:

```
try
{
    deeply_nested();
}
catch (...)
{
    cout << "in catch ..." << endl;
}
```

4. After the **try/catch** block, output the **"in main(), after try/catch"** string. The code looks like this:

```
cout << "in main(), after try/catch" << endl;
```

5. The complete program looks like this:

```
#include <iostream>

using namespace std;

int deeply_nested()
{
    throw 123;
    return 0;
}

int main()
{
    try
    {
        deeply_nested();
    }
    catch (...)
```

```
    {
        cout << "in catch ..." << endl;
    }

    cout << "in main(), after try/catch" << endl;
    return 0;
}
```

6. Run the program. Its output looks like this:

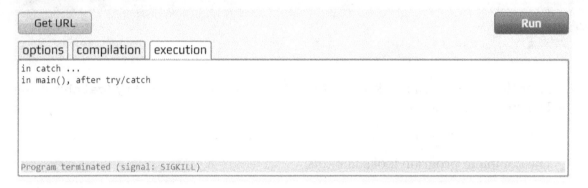

Figure 13.6: Output of the program in exercise 81

Notice that the program did not call **terminate()** and did not end with an abnormal termination message from the operating system. **main()** called **deeply_nested()**. The exception thrown in **deeply_nested()** was caught by the **catch(...)** clause, which printed the message **"in catch ..."**, so normal program execution continued in main() after the **catch** clause and printed the message **"in main(), after try/catch"**.

Don't erase the program. The next exercise is going to build on it.

Certain C++ statements and certain functions of the C++ standard library throw exceptions. All of the exceptions thrown by C++ statements and functions are instances of classes derived from **std::exception**, which can be found in the **<exception>** header. A useful feature of exceptions derived from **std::exception** is that they provide member functions you can call to get more information about the exception. To access these member functions, a **catch** clause must assign the caught exception to a variable.

The **catch** clause to catch an exception of type **std::exception** and put a reference to it in a variable called **e** (for exception, of course), is:

```
    catch (std::exception& e)
```

You might have caught the same exception by value using the **catch** statement:

```
catch (std::exception e)
```

But this would require the exception to be copied. Thrown exceptions live in memory reserved for this purpose so that a dynamic variable is not needed to hold the exception. This is important because one exception thrown by C++ is the **bad_alloc** exception, which occurs when memory can't be allocated. Copying an exception might require a dynamic variable to be created, which would crash the program if it is out of memory.

Exercise 82: Exceptions Thrown by C++

Not every exception is thrown by a **throw** statement in the developer's own code. Some exceptions are thrown by C++ statements and standard library functions. In this exercise, we will catch an exception thrown by a C++ standard library function:

> **Note**
>
> The complete code for the exercise can be found here: https://packt.live/2KNtmQy.

1. Start with the complete program from the last exercise. In case you need to re-enter it, it looks like this:

```
#include <iostream>

using namespace std;

int deeply_nested()
{
    throw 123;
    return 0;
}

int main()
{
    try
```

```
    {
        deeply_nested();
    }
    catch (...)
    {
        cout << "in catch ..." << endl;
    }
    cout << "in main(), after try/catch" << endl;
    return 0;
}
```

2. Below the **include** for header **<iostream>**, add an **include** for **<exception>** and an **include** for **<string>**. This is the code:

```
#include <exception>
#include <string>
```

3. In **deeply_nested()**, replace the **throw** statement with the following statement:

```
        string("xyzzy").at(100);
```

What this statement does is create a standard library character string, initialize it to a five-letter word, and then ask for the 100th character of the string. Obviously, this is not possible, so the **at()** member function throws an exception.

The program so far looks like this:

```
#include <iostream>
#include <exception>
#include <string>

using namespace std;

int deeply_nested()
{
    string("xyzzy").at(100);
    return 0;
}

int main()
{
    try
    {
        deeply_nested();
    }
```

```
        catch (...)
        {
            cout << "in catch ..." << endl;
        }

        cout << "in main(), after try/catch" << endl;
        return 0;
    }
```

4. Run the program. Its output is the same as that of the previous exercise:

Figure 13.7: Output for the program in exercise 82

5. Before the **catch(...)** clause in **main()**, add a new **catch** clause. Catch the **exception** type (remember, this is **std::exception**, because of the **using namespace std** statement) in the reference variable, **e**. Inside the **catch** clause, output the value returned by **e.what()**, which prints a text string describing the exception. The new **catch** clause looks like this:

```
        catch (exception& e)
        {
            cout << "caught " << e.what() << endl;
        }
```

6. The updated program looks like this:

```
    #include <iostream>
    #include <exception>
    #include <string>

    using namespace std;

    int deeply_nested()
    {
        string("xyzzy").at(100);
```

```
        return 0;
    }


    int main()
    {
        try
        {
            deeply_nested();
        }
        catch (exception& e)
        {
            cout << "caught " << e.what() << endl;
        }
        catch (...)
        {
            cout << "in catch ..." << endl;
        }

        cout << "in main(), after try/catch" << endl;
        return 0;
    }
```

7. Run the program. It produces the following output:

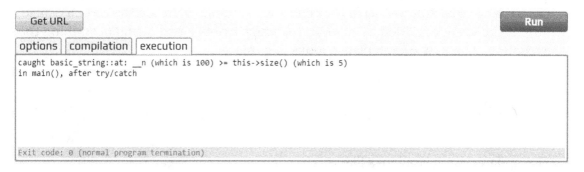

Figure 13.8: Output of the revised program in exercise 82

main() called **deeply_nested()**. Inside **deeply_nested()**, the statement **string("xyzzy").at(100)**; threw an exception of a type derived from **std::exception**. What type is the exception? It is an instance of class **out_of_range**, which is derived from class **logic_error**, which is derived from class **exception**. This exception was first matched against **std::exception&**. The reference to the derived class could initialize the reference to the base class, so this **catch** clause was executed, producing the first line of output.

After the exception was caught, execution continued with the line following the **try/catch** block, which printed the second output line, as expected. The **catch(...)** clause was not executed because C++ had already matched the thrown exception to the previous **catch** clause and executed the statements of the **catch** clause.

8. If the program had contained a **catch** clause for **logic_error** or **out_of_range** before the **catch (exception& e)** clause, that **catch** clause would have been executed instead. But if the **catch (exception& e)** clause had come first, it would have been executed. Remember, **catch** clauses are examined in order. The first **catch** clause that matches the exception is executed, not the one that is the best match.

Unwinding the Stack

Unwinding the stack is the process of destroying the local variables of each scope on the stack and looking for a **try/catch** block.

The following is exactly what the C++ runtime system does when it processes a thrown exception. Unwinding the stack begins in the innermost dynamically nested scope. This is the scope (delimited by curly braces) surrounding the **throw** statement. It is called a dynamically nested scope because the stack of function scopes on the function stack changes dynamically during program execution as one function calls another.

For each scope on the function activation stack, the C++ runtime system performs the following steps, repeating as long as there are more scopes:

- All the local variables in the current scope are destroyed. C++ keeps track of exactly what variables need to be destroyed in each scope. If a class that is being constructed throws an exception, just the base classes and member variables that have been constructed are destroyed. If only some of the variables in a block are constructed, only those variables are destroyed.

- If the current scope is a function scope, the function's activation record is popped off the stack, and the C++ runtime system processes the next enclosing scope.

- If the current scope is anything other than a **try** block, C++ continues processing with the next enclosing scope.

- Otherwise, the current scope is a **try** block. The C++ runtime system compares each **catch** clause in turn against the type of the thrown exception. If the type of the thrown exception can be constructed into the variable in the **catch** clause, the **catch** clause variable is constructed in the same way as a function formal argument, and the **catch** clause is executed. Execution then continues with the statement immediately following the last **catch** block, and this process is done.

- If the thrown exception cannot be constructed into any of the **catch** clauses, C++ processes the next enclosing scope.

- If there are no (more) scopes, the exception is uncaught. The C++ runtime system calls **terminate()**, then returns control to the operating system, indicating an abnormal termination status.

RAII (Resource Acquisition Is Initialization) and Exception Handling

Make no mistake, the stack unwinding behavior of C++ exceptions is extremely powerful. The C++ standard library defines many classes that acquire resources, own those resources, and release those resources when the class instance is destroyed. This idiom, where a class owns a resource and releases it on deletion, is called RAII (Resource Acquisition Is Initialization). Smart pointers, which we saw in chapter 8, are RAII classes that delete the dynamic variable they own. Any smart pointers or other RAII class instances that own resources in a scope release those resources before the scope is exited so the resources do not leak.

The combination of exception handling and RAII frees the developer from coding two different pathways to delete owned resources: one followed when execution is successful, and a second path followed when an unexpected event occurs. The developer only needs to use smart pointers and the other RAII classes of the C++ standard library. The C++ rules about destroying objects when leaving a scope and the behavior of RAII classes manage the release of resources automatically, with no explicit coding.

The next exercise uses code instrumented with noisy class instances to demonstrate the stack unwinding process in action.

Exercise 83: Unwinding the Stack

In this exercise, we will create a program that invokes functions to produce dynamically nested variable scopes. The program throws an exception to illustrate how the stack unwinding process occurs:

> **Note**
>
> The complete code for the exercise can be found here: https://packt.live/2pGj9xP.

1. Enter the skeleton **main()** function. The code looks like this:

```
#include <iostream>

using namespace std;

int main()
{
    return 0;
}
```

2. Add **include** directives for headers **<exception>** and **<memory>** libraries. This program throws an exception derived from **std::exception**, and it needs the smart pointers defined in **<memory>**:

```
#include <exception>
#include <memory>
```

3. Type in the definition for our old friend class **noisy**. The code looks like this:

```
class noisy
{
    char const* s_;
public:
    noisy(char const* s) { cout << "constructing " << (s_ = s) <<
endl; }
    ~noisy() { cout << "destroying " << s_ << endl; }
};
```

4. Type in the **int** function **deeply_nested()**. Its skeleton looks like this:

```
int deeply_nested()
{
    return 0;
}
```

5. In **deeply_nested()**, create a smart pointer to a dynamic **noisy** variable using **make_unique()**. The code looks like this:

```
    auto n = make_unique<noisy>("deeply_nested");
```

6. Throw a logic error. **logic_error** takes a null-terminated string constructor argument. This can be anything you like; try **"totally illogical"**:

```
    throw logic_error("totally illogical");
```

7. Enter the **int** function **intermediate()**. Its skeleton looks like this:

```
int intermediate()
{
    return 0;
}
```

8. Create a local instance of class **noisy**. Its argument can be **"intermediate"**. The destructor for class **noisy** prints a message. It is a stand-in for classes that release resources explicitly in their destructor:

```
noisy n("intermediate");
```

9. Add a call to **deeply_nested()**. Capture the returned value from **deeply_ nested()** in the **int** variable **rc**. Output the message **"after calling deeply_ nested"**. Return **rc**:

```
int rc = deeply_nested();
cout << "after calling deeply_nested()" << endl;
return rc;
```

10. In function **main()**, add a **try/catch** block. It should have a **catch** clause for class exception. The skeleton of the **try/catch** block looks like this:

```
try
{
}
catch (exception& e)
{
}
```

11. In the **try** block, construct a smart pointer to a dynamic **noisy** instance with constructor argument **"try in main"**:

```
auto n = make_unique<noisy>("try in main");
```

12. Call **intermediate()** and print out the return code:

```
int rc = intermediate();
cout << "intermediate() returned " << rc << endl;
```

13. In the **catch** clause, output **e.what()** so we will know what exception was caught:

```
cout << "in catch: exception: " << e.what() << endl;
```

14. After the **try/catch** block, output the string **"ending main()"**:

```
cout << "ending main" << endl;
```

15. The completed program looks like this:

```cpp
#include <iostream>
#include <exception>
#include <memory>

using namespace std;

class noisy
{
    char const* s_;
public:
    noisy(char const* s) { cout << "constructing " << (s_ = s) <<
endl; }
    ~noisy() { cout << "destroying " << s_ << endl; }
};

int deeply_nested()
{
    auto n = make_unique<noisy>("deeply_nested");
    throw logic_error("totally illogical");
    return 0;
}

int intermediate()
{
    noisy n("intermediate");
    int rc = deeply_nested();
    cout << "after calling deeply_nested()" << endl;
    return rc;
}

int main()
{
    try
    {
        auto n = make_unique<noisy>("try in main");
        int rc = intermediate();
        cout << "intermediate() returned " << rc << endl;
```

```
    }
    catch (exception& e)
    {
        cout << "in catch: exception: " << e.what() << endl;
    }
    cout << "ending main" << endl;

    return 0;
}
```

16. Compile and run the program. Its output looks like this:

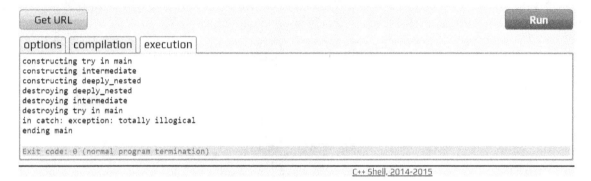

Figure 13.9: Output of the program in exercise 83

The **try** block in **main()** constructed a dynamic instance of **noisy** (first line of the output). **main()** called **intermediate()**, representing many layers of function calls. **intermediate()** constructed an instance of **noisy** (second line). **intermediate()** called **deeply_nested()**, which constructed a dynamic **noisy** instance (third line). At this point, the function call stack frames look like this:

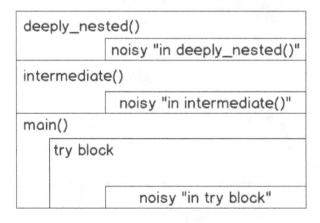

Figure 13.10: The function call stack

deeply_nested() threw an exception. We know that happened because the **noisy** instance in **deeply_nested()** was destroyed (fourth line), but the output statement in **intermediate()** wasn't executed. There was no **try/catch** block in **intermediate()**, so the **noisy** instance in **intermediate()** was destroyed (fifth line). There is a **try/catch** block in **main()**. The dynamic instance of **noisy** in the **try/catch** block is destroyed (sixth line). The type of the exception is **std::logic_error**, which is derived from **std::exception**. There is a **catch** clause for exception, so the **catch** clause was executed (seventh line). Execution continues with the output statement after the **try/catch** block (eighth line).

Notice that **deeply_nested()** and **intermediate()** return values as well as throwing an exception. Because an exception was thrown, the code that returns the value was not executed.

17. There is an unfortunate 'gotcha' in this highly desirable automatic stack unwinding process. Replace the **try/catch** block in **main()** with the contents of the **try** block, so that **main()** looks like this:

```
int main()
{
    auto n = make_unique<noisy>("try in main");

    int rc = intermediate();
    cout << "intermediate() returned " << rc << endl;
    cout << "ending main" << endl;

    return 0;
}
```

18. Compile and run the program again. If you see the same output, breathe a sigh of relief. However, you may see output similar to the following:

Figure 13.11: Output of the modified program in exercise 83

None of the **noisy** instances were destroyed. What happened? It turns out that the C++ standard permits the implementation not to unwind the stack when an exception is uncaught.

> **Note**
>
> Every program that uses exception handling should put at least a minimal **try/catch** block around the contents of **main()**, so that an unexpected exception unwinds the stack.
>
> In the summative activity of this chapter, you will explore how a program can catch exceptions and make the choice to either continue or terminate program execution after an unexpected event.

Activity 13: Handling Exceptions

Imagine you want to write a program that does some arbitrary thing over and over, until some termination condition that you don't control occurs. You might call a **bool** function called **do_something()** to perform the program's action. You continue as long as **do_something()** returns **true** and end the program when **do_something()** finally returns **false**. Your program might look like this:

```
#include <iostream>

using namespace std;

int main()
{
    bool continue_flag;
    do
    {
        continue_flag = do_something();
    }
    while (continue_flag == true);

    return 0;
}
```

OK, that was easy. Let's raise the stakes.

Say that the thing your program does is monitor the safe operation of a 200-megawatt nuclear power reactor. Your **do_something()** function is now called **reactor_safety_check()**. It reads sensors and sets controls to keep the reactor from blowing up and irradiating London, England. It's a really important program that needs to keep running no matter what. This program can only stop running if it senses that the control rods are pushed all the way in and the core temperature is below 100° C, which is when **reactor_safety_check()** returns **false**.

As the chief main loop software engineer, you have learned that the team that implemented the reactor safety check code chose to throw a **std::runtime_error** exception on runtime errors such as *trouble reading sensors*. Your electrical engineers have assured you that these errors are a transitory glitch. Even if one iteration of the program reports a **runtime_error** exception, the next time through, the error will likely not appear.

Because you have a suspicious mind, you searched the source code for **throw** statements and found, to your dismay, that there are a few. You don't know what these other exceptions imply, but the risk they pose if not caught is obviously grave. You are aware of another function, called **SCRAM()**, which pushes the control rods in all the way, vents steam, and starts the emergency feedwater pumps, which is about all you can do when the reactor is not under control.

Your mom and your sister live in London, so even if you would prefer not to have this responsibility, you dare not quit. It's up to you to prevent a core meltdown or the more serious event that nuclear reactor engineers euphemistically call "prompt critical rapid disassembly," which implies a small thermonuclear explosion.

Write a program that repeatedly calls the **bool** function **reactor_safety_check()**. Handle the **runtime_error** exception by continuing the **main** loop. Handle other exceptions by calling **SCRAM()** and exiting.

> **Note**
>
> The complete code for the exercise can be found here: https://packt.live/33chUEq.

Here are some steps for completing the activity:

1. Write a test version of **reactor_safety_check()** that occasionally throws exceptions to test your code. Here's a hint for writing **reactor_safety_check()**. If you create a static **int** variable called **count**, and increment **count** each time **reactor_safety_check()** is called, you can use **count** to decide what to do in **reactor_safety_check()**. For instance, maybe you want to throw a glitch exception every 17th time **reactor_safety_check()** is called.

2. You will want to catch all possible exceptions, not just **std::runtime_error**, because you don't want the loop to terminate while the reactor is still running.

3. You can assume that after you call **SCRAM()**, you don't have to monitor the reactor any longer because there's nothing else that can be done. This is typical of error recovery actions, which take place on a best-effort basis.

> **Note**
>
> The solution to this activity can be found on page 574.

Summary

The traditional way of informing a program about unexpected events is using an error return code from the function that detected the event. This way is fraught with risk because developers do not always remember to check return codes. Exceptions overcome this risk because an exception is either caught or it terminates the program.

The features of C++ exception handling are designed to process unexpected events during program execution.

A thrown exception unwinds the stack, calling the destructor of each variable in each scope as it is unwound. Using the RAII idiom, classes that own resources (such as dynamic variables, open file handles, mutexes, and so on) can release these resources. Because resources are released as the stack is unwound, it is safe to continue program execution after catching an exception.

A **try/catch** block can catch exceptions. The **catch** clauses can choose either to continue or halt program execution.

This is the end of the book, *The C++ Workshop*, but it is only the beginning of your learning. We described the flow-of-control statements of C++ in the first few chapters. If you want to be able to use these statements, you will need to practice writing programs and executing them on your own on one of the online C++ compilers, or on your C++ IDE of choice. This book has presented you with several concepts and related exercises. However, only through repeated practice will you be able to fully appreciate and utilize the skills you've learned.

We looked at the basic types of variables in C++, but there are variations. For instance, the **int** type comes in **short int**, **long int**, and **long long int** varieties, plus unsigned variations of all of these. There are three floating-point types, **float**, **double**, and **long double**. There are arrays and structs to try out, and classes with member functions.

Dynamic variables let you build arbitrarily large data structures in memory, as long as you avoid the deadly sins of dynamic variables. Smart pointers and RAII will help you there.

It may take you years to feel comfortable with object-oriented programming if your previous programming experience doesn't include objects. Entire books have been written on this topic alone.

C++ has a standard library containing algorithms and data structures packaged as template functions and classes. We didn't have space to teach template programming in this introductory book, but it's a subject that's well worth learning about, once you feel comfortable with the basics.

You have used C++ output statements, but you have really only scratched the surface of the C++ I/O streams interface. It is uniquely powerful and flexible, so it's worth learning more about.

C++ exception handling is a powerful tool compressed into just two statements. It's worth mastering, and there's a lot we weren't able to tell you.

In fact, virtually every C++ statement, declaration, expression, and directive has wrinkles that we weren't able to cover. The C++ standard itself runs over 1,500 pages. We urge you to look up statements as you practice, to see what additional knowledge might help you. It's something that even very experienced C++ developers do, so don't be ashamed to keep improving your knowledge.

How long until you have a journeyman's knowledge of C++? Not a week—even with our excellent book. With only self-study, it takes most people two full-time years of practice to arrive at the point where they are comfortable. The authors think you have a tremendous head start from completing this book, but keep practicing.

Appendix

About

This section is included to assist the students to perform the activities present in the book. It includes detailed steps that are to be performed by the students to complete and achieve the objectives of the book.

Chapter 1: Your First C++ Application

Activity 1: Write Your Own C++ Application

Solution:

1. Define your age bracket thresholds using **#defines**.

2. Define a name for each group using **#defines**.

   Here is the code required for steps 1 and 2:

   ```cpp
   // Activity 1.
   #include <iostream>
   #include <string>

   #define GROUP_1_THRESHOLD 12
   #define GROUP_2_THRESHOLD 28

   #define GROUP_1_NAME "Group A"
   #define GROUP_2_NAME "Group B"
   #define GROUP_3_NAME "Group C"
   ```

3. Output a text string asking the user for their name and capture the response in a variable.

4. Output text asking the user for their age and capture the response in a variable.

5. Write a function that will accept age as a parameter and return the appropriate group name.

6. Output the user's name, and the group that they have been assigned to.

   Here is the code required to perform steps 3-6:

   ```cpp
   std::string GetGroup(int age);

   int main()
   {
       std::string name = "";
       int age = 0;
       std::string group = "";

       std::cout << "Please enter your name: ";
       getline(std::cin, name);
   ```

```cpp
        std::cout << "And please enter your age: ";
        std::cin >> age;

        group = GetGroup(age);
        std::cout << "Welcome "<< name << ". You are in "
                << group << ".\n";
    }

    std::string GetGroup(int age)
    {
        if (age <= GROUP_1_THRESHOLD)
        {
            return GROUP_1_NAME;
        }

        else if (age <= GROUP_2_THRESHOLD)
        {
            return GROUP_2_NAME;
        }

         else
        {
            return GROUP_3_NAME;
        }
    }
```

7. Run the complete code. You will obtain the following output:

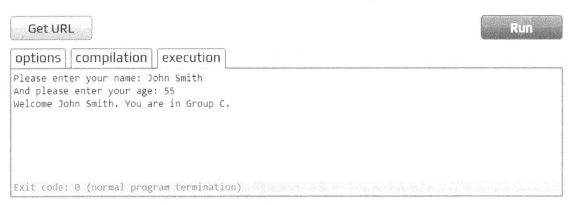

Figure 1.20: Our program asked for the user's name and age,
and assigned them to the appropriate group

Chapter 2: Control Flow

Activity 2: Creating a Number-Guessing Game Using Loops and Conditional Statements

Solution:

1. Declare all the variables we'll need. This includes **guessCount**, **minNumber**, **maxNumber**, and **randomNumber**:

```
// Activity 2: Number guessing game.
#include <iostream>
#include <string>

int main()
{
    // Declare variables.
    int guessCount = 0;
    int minNumber = 0;
    int maxNumber = 0;
    int randomNumber = 0;

    std::string input = "";
    bool bIsRunning = true;
```

2. Create a main outer loop that will run the application:

```
while (bIsRunning)
{
}
```

3. Present the user with some introductory text (**"Enter the number of guesses"**) and get from them the following: a number of guesses, a minimum number, and a maximum number:

```
while (bIsRunning)
{
    // Output instructions and get user inputs.
    std::cout << "***Number guessing game***\n";
    std::cout << "\nEnter the number of guesses: ";
    getline(std::cin, input);
    guessCount = std::stoi(input);
```

```
std::cout << "Enter the minimum number: ";
getline(std::cin, input);
minNumber = std::stoi(input);

std::cout <<"Enter the maximum number: ";
getline(std::cin, input);
maxNumber = std::stoi(input);
}
```

> **Note**
>
> We do no checking here to ensure that the maximum number is greater than the minimum number. This for the sake of brevity in the code, but when writing production code, it's always necessary to sanity check user input such as this.

4. Generate a random number within the range specified by the user:

```
while (bIsRunning)
{
    // Output instructions and get user inputs.
    //[…]
    // Generate random number within range.
    srand((unsigned)time(0));
    randomNumber = rand() % (maxNumber - minNumber + 1)
    + minNumber;
}
```

> **Note**
>
> We used this same approach to generate random numbers earlier in the chapter, so head back to *Exercise 2.3, Refactor an if/else Chain into switch/case*, for a reminder if necessary.

5. Create a loop that will iterate the number of times that the user specified as their guess count.

6. Inside the **count** loop, fetch the user's guess.

7. Inside the **count** loop, check whether the user's guess is correct, or too high/low. We can use **break** here to exit when the correct value has been guessed.

8. When the number has been found, or the user has run out of guesses, present them with the option to either continue or exit the application.

The code to perform steps 5-8 is as follows:

```
while  (bIsRunning)
{
    // Output instructions and get user inputs.
    // […]
    // Generate random number within range.
    // […]
    // Process user guesses.

    for (int i = 0; i < guessCount; ++i)
    {
        int guess = 0;
        std::cout << "\nEnter your guess: ";
        getline(std::cin, input);
        guess = std::stoi(input);

        if (guess == randomNumber)
        {
            std::cout << "Well done, you guessed the number!\n";
            break;
        }
        int guessesRemaining = guessCount - (i + 1);

        std::cout << "Your guess was too "
                  << (guess < randomNumber ? "low. " : "high. ");

        std::cout << "You have " << guessesRemaining
                  << (guessesRemaining > 1 ? " guesses" : "
                  guess") << " remaining";
```

```
        }

        std::cout << "\nEnter 0 to exit, or any number
                to play again: ";
        getline(std::cin, input);

        if (std::stoi(input) == 0)
        {
            bIsRunning = false;
        }
    }
}
```

9. Run the complete code. You will obtain the following output:

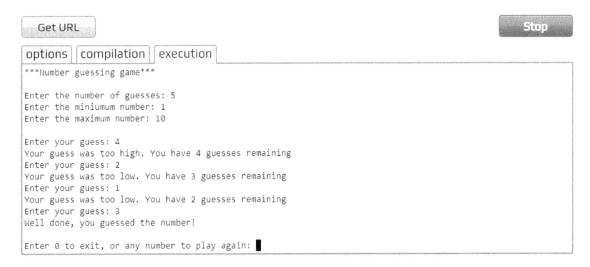

Figure 2.18: Number-guessing game output

Chapter 3: Built-in Data Types

Activity 3: Sign-Up Application

Solution:

1. Start by including the various headers that the application will need:

```
// Activity 3: SignUp Application.
#include <iostream>
#include <string>
#include <vector>
#include <stdexcept>
```

2. Next, define the class that will represent a record in the system. This is going to be a person, containing both a name and an age. Also, declare a vector of this type to store these records. A vector is used for the flexibility it gives in not having to declare an array size upfront:

```
struct Person
{
    int age = 0;
    std::string name = "";
};
std::vector<Person> records;
```

3. Now, you can start adding some functions to add and fetch records; first, add. A record consists of a name and age, so write a function that will accept those two as parameters, create a record object, and add it to our record vector. Name this function **AddRecord**:

```
void AddRecord(std::string newName, int newAge)
{
    Person newRecord;
    newRecord.name = newName;
    newRecord.age = newAge;
    records.push_back(newRecord);
    std::cout << "\nUser record added successfully.\n\n";
};
```

4. Add a function to fetch a record. This function should accept one parameter, a user ID, and return the record for that user. Name this function **FetchRecord**:

```
Person FetchRecord(int userID)
{
    return records.at(userID);
};
```

5. Enter the **main** function and start the body of the application. Start with an outer **main** loop, as you used in the previous chapter, and output some options to the user. You will give them three options: **Add Record**, **Fetch Record**, and **Quit**:

```
int main()
{
    std::cout << "User SignUp Application\n" << std::endl;
    bool bIsRunning = true;
    while (bIsRunning)
    {
        std::cout << "Please select an option:\n";
        std::cout << "1: Add Record\n";
        std::cout << "2: Fetch Record\n";
        std::cout << "3: Quit\n\n";
```

6. Present these options to the user and then capture their input:

```
        std::cout << "Enter option: ";
        std::string inputString;
        std::getline(std::cin, inputString);
```

7. There are three possible branches now, depending on user input, which we'll handle with a **switch** statement. Case 1 is adding a record, and to do so, you'll get the user's name and age, and then make a call to our **AddRecord** function:

```
        // Determine user selection.
        switch (std::stoi(inputString))
        {
            case 1:
            {
                std::string name = "";
                int age = 0;
                std::cout << "\nAdd User. Please enter
                        user name and age:\n";
                std::cout << "Name: ";
                std::getline(std::cin, name);
                std::cout << "Age: ";
                std::getline(std::cin, inputString);
```

```
            age = std::stoi(inputString);
            AddRecord(name, age);
        }
        break;
```

8. The next case is the user wanting to fetch a record. For this, you need to get a **userID** from the user, and then make a call to **FetchRecord**, outputting its result:

```
case 2:
{
    int userID = 0;
    std::cout << "\nPlease enter user ID:\n";
    std::cout << "User ID: ";
    std::getline(std::cin, inputString);
    userID = std::stoi(inputString);
    Person person;
    try
    {
        person = FetchRecord(userID);
    }
    catch (const std::out_of_range& oor)
    {
        std::cout << "\nError: Invalid UserID.\n\n";
    break;
    }
    std::cout << "User Name: " << person.name << "\n";
    std::cout << "User Age: " << person.age << "\n\n";
}
break;
```

9. The next case is when the user wants to exit the application. This one is fairly simple; you just need to exit our **main** loop:

```
case 3:
    bIsRunning = false;
    break
```

10. Finally, add a default case. This will handle invalid options entered by the user. All you'll do here is output an error message and send them back to the start of the application:

```
default:
    std::cout << "\n\nError: Invalid option
                  selection.\n\n";
break;
    }
  }
}
```

With all of this in place, the application should be ready to go.

11. Run the complete code. You will obtain the following output:

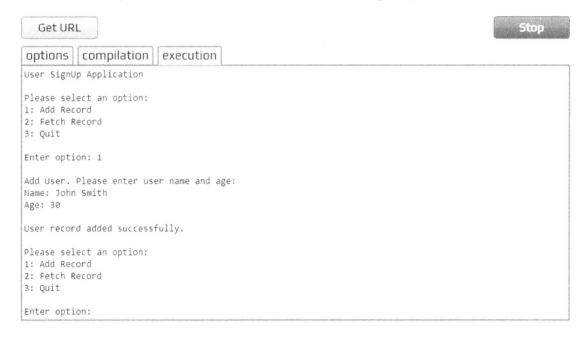

Figure 3.27: Our application allows the user to add records and then recall them via an ID

This application is by far our most complex yet and pulls together everything we've learned so far; from functions, to control flow, classes, scope, IO, and so on. We can now see how all these different elements come together to allow us to build complex systems. And this is just the beginning. We've only covered the absolute basics, and we can already see how these pieces can be put together to solve real-world problems.

Chapter 4: Operators

Activity 4: Fizz Buzz

Solution:

1. As usual, we'll start by including the headers we need for the application and starting our main loop:

```
// Activity 4: Fizz Buzz.
#include <iostream>

int main()
{
```

2. Next, we'll define our loop. We want to print 100 numbers, so we need to iterate 100 times, starting at 1:

```
for (int i = 1; i <= 100; ++i)
{
```

3. The **Fizz Buzz** application tells us that for multiples of 3, we'll print **Fizz**, and for multiples of 5, we'll print **Buzz** instead. However, a number can be a multiple of 3 and 5 at the same time; for example, 15 is a multiple of both, so we'll next define a Boolean value, **multiple**, which will help us to keep track of this, giving it an initial value of **false**:

```
bool multiple = false;
```

4. Next, we can check whether our current loop value, **i**, is a multiple of 3. If so, we'll print the word **Fizz** and set our multiple Boolean value to **true**:

```
if (i % 3 == 0)
{
    std::cout << "Fizz";
    multiple = true;
}
```

5. We can then do the same for **Buzz**, checking whether **i** is a multiple of 5 instead. Again, we'll set our **multiple** Boolean value to **true** if so:

```
if (i % 5 == 0)
{
    std::cout << "Buzz";
    multiple = true;
}
```

6. Now that we've checked whether our number is a multiple of either 3 or 5 and have a Boolean that will be **true** if so, we can use this to determine whether we print the normal number. If we've reached this point with our **multiple bool** still being **false**, then we know we need to print the normal number, **i**:

```
if (!multiple)
    {
        std::cout << i;
    }
```

7. Finally, we'll do a little bit of formatting. If we're not on our final iteration of the loop, we'll print a comma followed by a space. This will just make our application a little neater when printed:

```
if (i < 100)
        {
            std::cout << ", ";
        }
    }
}
```

8. Let's run the application now and see it in action. We should see numbers leading up to 100. Multiples of 3 will be replaced by **Fizz**, multiples of 5 by **Buzz**, and multiples of both by **FizzBuzz**.

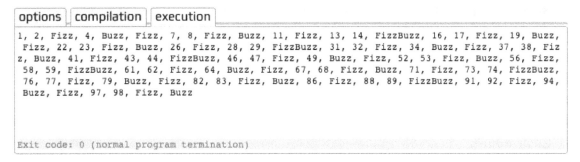

Figure 4.16: The Fizz Buzz application – a common coding test exercise

Chapter 5: Pointers and References

Activity 5: Using Pointers and References to Manipulate an Array of Strings

Solution:

1. Enter the skeleton **main()** function:

```
#include <iostream>
using namespace std;

int main()
{
    return 0;
}
```

2. Above **main()**, create an array of strings:

```
char const* array[26]
{    "alpha", "bravo", "charlie", "delta", "echo"    };
```

The array must be 26 elements long or the program might crash for certain valid arguments.

3. Enter the skeleton of the **printarray()** function. Define the arguments. Since we are printing an array of literal strings, the pointers are of type **char const****. The **count** argument is an **int&**. Define the return type, which is specified as **int** in the assignment:

```
int printarray(char const** begin, char const** end, int& count)
{
    return 1;
}
```

4. Clear **count**:

```
count = 0;
```

5. Enter code to detect errors in the arguments:

```
if (begin == nullptr || end == nullptr ||
    begin > end || end-begin > 26)
{
    return 0;
}
```

6. Enter a loop to control printing:

```
for (count = 0; begin < end; ++begin)
{
    if (*begin != nullptr)
    {
        ++count;
        cout << *begin << endl;
    }
}
```

There are several ways to do this. One way, which is self-documenting, is to use a **for** loop because the **for** loop has an initial condition, a continuation condition, and an increment. It helps you remember all the parts needed for tasks like this one. Since the **for** loop doesn't have anything else to do initially, move setting the count to zero into the initialization slot of the **for** statement.

7. Inside **main()**, write some tests:

```
int count;
if (printarray(nullptr, nullptr, count) == 0 || count != 0)
{
    cout << "error in printarray() call 1" << endl;
}
else
{
    cout << "count = " << count << endl;
}
```

All the other tests are going to look pretty much the same:

```
if (printarray(array, &array[4], count) == 0 || count != 4)
{
    cout << "error in printarray() call 2" << endl;
}

else
{
    cout << "count = " << count << endl;
}
if (printarray(&array[4], &array[3], count) == 0 || count != 0)
{
```

```
            cout << "error in printarray() call 3" << endl;
    }

    else
    {
        cout << "count = " << count << endl;
    }

    if (printarray(&array[4], &array[10], count) == 0 || count != 1)
    {
        cout << "error in printarray() call 4" << endl;
    }
    else
    {
        cout << "count = " << count << endl;
    }
    if (printarray(&array[0], &array[100], count) == 0 || count != 0)
    {
        cout << "error in printarray() call 5" << endl;
    }
    else
    {
        cout << "count = " << count << endl;
    }
```

8. Run the program. The output looks like this:

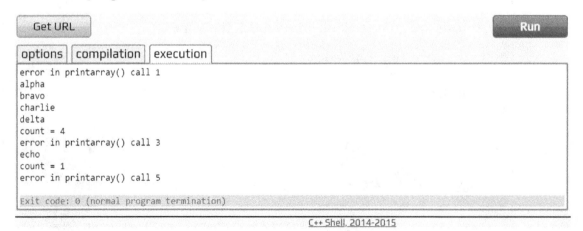

Figure 5.13: Using Pointers and References to Manipulate an Array of Strings

Chapter 6: Dynamic Variables

Activity 6: Creating Binary Search Trees of Class Instances

Solution:

1. Start with the skeleton **main()** function:

```
#include <iostream>
using namespace std;
int main()
{
    return 0;
}
```

Add a definition for **struct numeric_tree**. It requires an **int value_** member, and pointers to the left and right subtrees, which are themselves **numeric_tree** instances:

```
struct numeric_tree
{
    int value_;
    numeric_tree* left_;
    numeric_tree* right_;
};
```

2. The root of the tree is called **root**. It's a pointer to **numeric_tree**:

```
numeric_tree* root = nullptr;
```

3. The **add()** function takes as arguments an **int** value to be added, and a pointer to the address of a pointer to **tree**—that is, a pointer to pointer:

```
void add(int v, numeric_tree** pp)
{
}
```

4. For the **add()** function, understand that the added item will always be added to a subtree that is equal to **nullptr**:

```
    *pp = new numeric_tree;
    (*pp)->value_ = v;
    (*pp)->left_ = (*pp)->right_ = nullptr;
```

5. The function **delete_tree()** is most easily implemented as a recursive function:

```
void delete_tree(numeric_tree* item)
{
    if (item == nullptr)
    {
        return;
    }
    else
    {
        delete_tree(item->left_);
        delete_tree(item->right_);
        cout << "deleting " << item->value_ << endl;
        delete item;
    }
}
```

6. The **find()** function takes as arguments an **int** value to be added, and a pointer to the address of a pointer to **numeric_tree**—that is, a pointer to pointer. **find()** returns a pointer-to-pointer. **find()** can be implemented either recursively or iteratively. The recursive version is as follows:

```
numeric_tree** find(int v, numeric_tree** pp)
{
}
```

7. The **find()** function uses the recursive description of binary search trees. If the variable that **pp** points to is **nullptr**, then **find()** has located the insertion point, which is returned:

```
if (*pp == nullptr)
{
    return pp;
}
```

8. If the **v** argument is less than the **value_** member of the current item, then **find()** recurses down the left subtree. Otherwise, it recurses down the right subtree:

```
else if (v < (*pp)->value_)
{
    return find(v, &((*pp)->left_));
}
else
{
    return find(v, &((*pp)->right_));
}
```

9. The completed **find()** function looks like this:

```
numeric_tree** find(int v, numeric_tree** pp)
{
    if (*pp == nullptr)
    {
        return pp;
    }

    else if (v < (*pp)->value_)
    {
        return find(v, &((*pp)->left_));
    }

    else
    {
        return find(v, &((*pp)->right_));
    }
}
```

10. The **print()** function was previously described. It is best implemented recursively; **print()** looks like this:

```
void print(numeric_tree* item)
{
    if (item == nullptr)
    {
        return;
    }

    else
    {
        print(item->left_);
        cout << item->value_ << " ";
        print(item->right_);
    }
}
```

Using the recursive definition of the binary search tree, if the pointer is **nullptr**, there is nothing to print. Otherwise, print the left subtree (where the values are lower), then print the value of the current item and then print the right subtree (where the values are greater).

11. Inside **main()**, items can be added one item at a time, but I chose to automate the process using a **for** loop to insert each item from an array of **int** values. The **for** loop calls **add()** for each value:

```
int insert_order[] { 4, 2, 1, 3, 6, 5 };
for (int i = 0; i < 6; ++i)
{
    int v = insert_order[i];
    add(v, find(v, &root));
}
```

12. It's appropriate to print the newly constructed tree. As you might expect, it looks like this:

```
print(root);
cout << endl;
```

Notice that **print()** doesn't output **endl**, so that has to be done after. You could wrap **print()** inside another function with a name such as **print_tree()** if you wanted to hide this detail.

13. The tree is a dynamic data structure. When you're done with it, it must be deleted. The **delete_tree()** function does that:

```
delete_tree(root);
```

14. The output of the program depends on your implementation choices. However, the output of the model program is as follows:

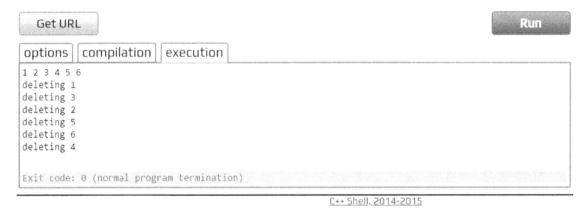

Figure 6.18: Output for creating binary search trees of class instances

Chapter 7: Ownership and Lifetime Of Dynamic Variables

Activity 7: Storing the Words of a Book Using Dynamic Variables

Solution:

1. Start with the skeleton **main()** program. It might look like this:

```
#include <iostream>
#include <memory>

using namespace std;

int main()
{
    return 0;
}
```

2. Define the **word** class:

```
class word
{
    friend class line;
    unique_ptr<char[]> ptr_;
    int letters_;
    int spaces_;
    word* next_;

public:
    word(char const* srcp, int l, int spaces);
    void to_string(char* dstp);
    int size();
};// end word
```

There is a **unique_ptr<>** to **char** array that holds the letters of the word, and a count of letters and spaces. Finally, since the words in a line are going to be a linked list, there is a next pointer.

The constructor copies in the word string and the count of letters and spaces. The destructor of **word** is built by the compiler. Yay for smart pointers. **to_string()** copies the word onto a **char** buffer. Elsewhere in the program, something sizes the **char** buffer, but for testing, you can just use **char buf[100]**. **size()** returns the number of characters in the word plus the number of spaces. To determine the size of a line, walk the linked list of words in the line and add up the sizes of all the words.

Define the **line** class:

```
class line
{
    friend class page;
    word* head_;
    line* next_;

public:
    line(char const* str);
    ~line();
    void append(word* w);
    void to_string(char* dstp);
    int size();
};// end line
```

This contains a head node for the word list and a next pointer because the book is a linked list of lines. The **line** class has the same structure as the **word** class. The constructor converts a string into a word list. The destructor deletes the word list, because line holds an owned pointer to the list. **to_string()** converts a word list into a null-terminated string in a buffer. **size()** produces the number of characters in the line.

Making the classes as similar as possible helps you to remember what you have to do. **line** has an additional function, **append()**, which adds a new word onto the end of the word list of **line**.

3. Class **page** contains the head node for the linked list of lines. The destructor is just like the destructor of **line**. Now, **append()** is just like the **append()** function of **line**. The constructor is empty, because the book is built externally. **print()** puts out a book on **cout**:

```
class page
{
    line* head_;

public:
    page();
    ~page();
    void append(line* lp);
    void print();
};// end page
```

4. Let's look next at the contents of **main()**. The range-based **for** loop fetches the strings that comprise the book one at a time. As the lines are processed, they are each output, to give something to compare the reconstructed output against.

   Why print single quotes (the '****'' characters) around the lines? This is done so that you can see that the leading and trailing spaces are correctly printed. The next line creates a **unique_ptr<>** instance to a **line** object. The string pointer is passed to the constructor, which builds the words that make up that line.

   The next line appends the **line** instance to the page. After the loop, the program puts a blank line onto the output to separate the two copies of the book. The final line invokes **page::print()**, which prints out all the lines of the book:

```
page pg;

for (auto* p : book)
{
    cout << '\'' << p << '\'' << endl;
    auto l = make_unique<line>(p);
    pg.append(l.release());
}
cout << endl;
pg.print();
```

5. The implementation of the **word** class looks like this:

```
word::word(char const* srcp, int l, int spaces)
    : ptr_(make_unique<char[]>(l+1)),
    letters_(l),
    spaces_(spaces)
{
    char* dstp;

    for(dstp = ptr_.get(); l > 0; --l)
    {
        *dstp++ = *srcp++;
    }

    *dstp = '\0';
}
```

The constructor initializer list includes making a **unique_ptr<>** to a **char** array big enough to hold the non-space characters of the word. The constructor body is a simple loop to copy characters from **srcp** into the buffer pointed to by **ptr_**. Notice that the array has room for **1 + 1** characters, which must include a null termination. In the **for** loop, **dstp** is declared outside the loop because it needs to be alive to set the trailing null termination. If **dstp** had been declared in the **for** statement, it would have gone out of scope at the closing bracket of the **for** loop.

6. **word::to_string()** copies the characters of the word, followed by any trailing spaces, into the buffer pointed to by **dstp**. A null termination is added to the end:

```
void word::to_string(char* dstp)
{
    char* srcp = ptr_.get();

    for (int letters = letters_; letters > 0; --letters)
    {
        *dstp++ = *srcp++;
    }

    for (int spaces = spaces_; spaces > 0; --spaces)
    {
        *dstp++ = ' ';
    }

    *dstp = '\0';
}
```

7. **size()** returns the number of letters plus the number of spaces that were saved when word was constructed:

```
int word::size()
{
    return letters_ + spaces_;
}
```

8. The constructor for the **line** class steps three pointers through the **str** input string. **bp** is the pointer to the beginning of the word. **ewp** (**end of word pointer**) is stepped forward from bp until the first non-word character. **esp** (**end of spaces pointer**) is stepped from **ewp** to the first non-space character. Then, a new word is created and appended to the current line. Finally, **bp** is advanced to **esp**, and the loop repeats:

```cpp
line::line(char const* str)
    : head_(nullptr),
    next_(nullptr)
{
    char const* bp;  // pointer to beginning
    char const* ewp; // pointer to end of word
    char const* esp; // pointer to end of spaces

    for (bp = str; *bp != '\0'; bp = esp)
    {
        for (ewp = bp; *ewp != '\0' && *ewp != ' '; ++ewp)
        {
            // empty
        }

        for (esp = ewp; *esp != '\0' && *esp == ' '; ++esp)
        {
            // empty
        }

        append(new word(bp, ewp-bp, esp-ewp));
    }
}
```

9. **line**'s destructor is straightforward. **head_** owns the list of **word** instances. Each **word** is removed from the list and then deleted:

```cpp
line::~line()
{
    while (head_ != nullptr)
    {
        auto wp = head_;
        head_ = head_->next_;
        delete wp;
    }
}
```

10. **append()** is similar to the **append()** functions for linked lists that we have seen before. It uses the pointer-to-a-pointer idiom to point to the pointer that needs updating:

```
void line::append(word* w)
{
    word** wpp = &head_;

    while((*wpp) != nullptr)
    {
        wpp = &((*wpp)->next_);
    }

    *wpp = w;
}
```

11. **line::to_string()** uses **word::to_string()** to put the text of each word onto the buffer pointed to by **dstp**:

```
void line::to_string(char* dstp)
{
    for (word* wp = head_; wp != nullptr; wp = wp->next_)
    {
        wp->to_string(dstp);
        dstp = dstp + wp->size();
    }

    *dstp = '\0';
}
```

12. **line::size()** walks the list of words adding up the sizes of each word. It adds 1 for the null termination:

```
int line::size()
{
    int size = 1;// for null terminator

    for (word* wp = head_; wp != nullptr; wp = wp->next_)
    {
        size = size + wp->size();
    }

    return size;
}
```

13. **page**'s constructor is empty. This has an initializer list that sets the head node of the list of lines to **nullptr**:

```
page::page():head_(nullptr)
{
    // empty
}
```

14. **page**'s destructor has exactly the same form as that of **line**'s:

```
page::~page()
{
    while (head_ != nullptr)
    {
        auto lp = head_;
        head_ = head_->next_;
        delete lp;
    }
}
```

15. **page::append()** is the same as **line::append()**:

```
void page::append(line* lp)
{
    line** lpp = &head_;

    while((*lpp) != nullptr)
    {
        lpp = &((*lpp)->next_);


    }
    *lpp = lp;
}
```

16. **print()** walks the **line** list. For each **line**, **print()** creates a dynamic buffer sized to hold all the text of the words on that **line**, and then asks **line::to_string()** to fill in the **buffer**. Finally, the contents of the **buffer** are printed on the console:

```
void page::print()
{
    for (line* lp = head_; lp != nullptr; lp = lp->next_)
    {
        auto buffer = make_unique<char[]>(lp->size());
        lp->to_string(buffer.get());
```

```
                cout << '\'' << buffer.get() << '\'' << endl;
        }

    char const* book[]
    {
        "What a piece of work is man,",
        "  How noble in reason, how infinite in faculty,",
        "In form and moving how express and admirable,",
        "  In action how like an Angel, In apprehension how like a god.",
        "The beauty of the world.    The paragon of animals.",
    };
```

17. Compile and run the program if you haven't done so already. Its output looks like this:

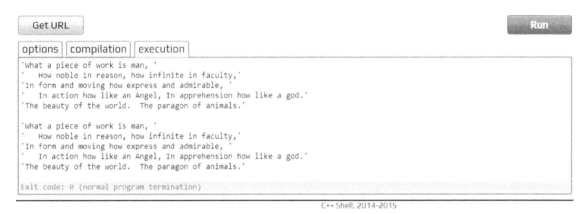

Figure 7.12: Storing the words of a book using dynamic variables

Chapter 8: Classes and Structs

Activity 8: Creating a Video Clip Class

Solution:

1. Create the **VideoClip** class outline:

```
1. Create the VideoClip class outline:
#include <iostream>
#include <string>

using namespace std;

class VideoClip
{
public:
};

int main()
{
    return 0;
}
```

2. Create member variables for the video length and video name:

```
#include <iostream>
#include <string>
using namespace std;
class VideoClip
{
public:
    float m_videoLength;
    string m_videoName;
};

int main()
{
return 0;
}
```

3. Write a default constructor that initializes the video length and name to default values:

```cpp
#include <iostream>
#include <string>
using namespace std;

class VideoClip
{
public:
    VideoClip()
    {
        m_videoLength = 0;
        m_videoName = "NOT SET";
    }

    float m_videoLength;
    string m_videoName;
};

int main()
{
    return 0;
}
```

4. Write a parameterized constructor that sets the video length and name to the passed-in parameters:

```cpp
#include <iostream>
#include <string>

using namespace std;

class VideoClip
{
public:
    VideoClip()
    {
        m_videoLength = 0;
        m_videoName = "NOT SET";
    }
    VideoClip(float videoLength, string videoName)
    {
```

```
            m_videoLength = videoLength;
            m_videoName = videoName;
        }
        float m_videoLength;
        string m_videoName;
};

int main()
{
    return 0;
}
```

5. Create a data **char** array and data size member variables and initialize them in both constructors:

```
#include <iostream>
#include <string>
#include <cstring>

using namespace std;

class VideoClip
{
public:
    VideoClip()
    {
        m_videoLength = 0;
        m_videoName = "NOT SET";
        m_dataLength = 0;
        m_data = 0;
    }

    VideoClip(float videoLength, string videoName, const char* data)
    {
        m_videoLength = videoLength;
        m_videoName = videoName;
        m_dataLength= strlen(data);
        m_data = new char[m_dataLength + 1];
        strcpy(m_data, data);
    }

    float m_videoLength;
    string m_videoName;
```

```
    int m_dataLength;
    char* m_data;
};

int main()
{
    return 0;
}
```

6. Create a copy constructor that correctly handles the copying of the data array:

```
    VideoClip(const VideoClip& vc)
    {
        m_videoLength = vc.m_videoLength;
        m_videoName = vc.m_videoName;
        m_dataLength = vc.m_dataLength;
        m_data = new char[m_dataLength + 1];
        strcpy(m_data, vc.m_data);
    }

    float m_videoLength;
    string m_videoName;
    int m_dataLength;
    char* m_data;
};

int main()
{
    return 0;
}
```

7. Create a copy assignment operator overload that correctly handles the copying of the data array:

```
    VideoClip& operator=(const VideoClip& rhs)
    {
        if(this != &rhs)
        {
            m_videoLength = rhs.m_videoLength;
            m_videoName = rhs.m_videoName;
            m_dataLength = rhs.m_dataLength;
            char* newData = new char[m_dataLength];
            strcpy(newData, rhs.m_data);
            delete[] m_data;
```

```
                m_data = newData;
            }
        return *this;
    }

    float m_videoLength;
    string m_videoName;

    int m_dataLength;
    char* m_data;
};

int main()
{
    return 0;
}
```

8. Write a destructor that deletes the allocated data array:

```
    ~VideoClip()
    {
        delete[] m_data;
    }

    float m_videoLength;
    string m_videoName;
    int m_dataLength;
    char* m_data;
};

int main()
{
    return 0;
}
```

9. Update the **main** function to create three different **videoClip** instances and output their values:

```
int main()
{
    VideoClip vc1(10.0f, "Halloween (2019)",
                "dfhdhfidghirhgkhrfkghfkg");
    VideoClip vc2(20.0f, "Halloween (1978)", "jkghdfjkhgjhgfjdfg");
```

```
    VideoClip vc3(50.0f, "The Shining", "kotriothgrngirgr");

    cout << vc1.m_videoLength << " " << vc1.m_videoName << " "
        << vc1.m_data << endl;

    cout << vc2.m_videoLength << " " << vc2.m_videoName << " "
        << vc2.m_data << endl;

    cout << vc3.m_videoLength << " " << vc3.m_videoName << " "
        << vc3.m_data << endl;

    return 0;
}
```

10. Test the copy constructor and copy assignment operators within the **main** function by initializing a video clip using an existing instance and also initializing an instance of a video clip with its constructor and then later assigning it to another existing instance:

```
int main()
{
    VideoClip vc1(10.0f, "Halloween (2019)",
                    "dfhdhfidghirhgkhrfkghfkg");
    VideoClip vc2(20.0f, "Halloween (1978)", "jkghdfjkhgjhgfjdfg");
    VideoClip vc3(50.0f, "The Shining", "kotriothgrngirgr");

    cout << vc1.m_videoLength << " " << vc1.m_videoName << " "
        << vc1.m_data << endl;

    cout << vc2.m_videoLength << " " << vc2.m_videoName << " "
        << vc2.m_data << endl;

    cout << vc3.m_videoLength << " " << vc3.m_videoName << " "
        << vc3.m_data << endl;

    VideoClip vc4 = vc1;
    vc2 = vc4;

    cout << vc1.m_videoLength << " " << vc1.m_videoName << " "
        << vc1.m_data << endl;

    cout << vc2.m_videoLength << " " << vc2.m_videoName << " "
        << vc2.m_data << endl;

    cout << vc3.m_videoLength << " " << vc3.m_videoName << " "
        << vc3.m_data << endl;
```

```
        cout << vc4.m_videoLength << " " << vc4.m_videoName << " "
            << vc4.m_data << endl;

    return 0;
}
```

When you run the complete code, you will obtain the following output:

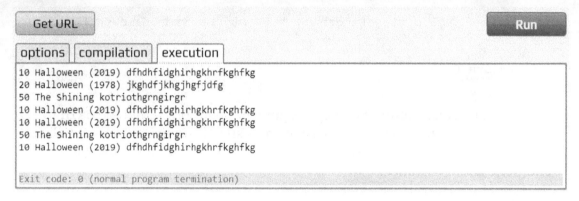

Figure 8.12: A possible output from the VideoClip class

Chapter 9: Object-Oriented Principles

Activity 9: A Basic RPG Combat System

Solution:

1. Create classes for characters, attacks, and items with a **name** variable in each class that can be set in the constructor:

```cpp
#include <iostream>
#include <cstring>
using namespace std;
class Attack
{
public:
    Attack(const char* name)
    {
        m_name = new char[strlen(name) + 1];
        strcpy(m_name, name);
    }
    ~Attack()
    {
        delete[] m_name;
    }
private:
    char* m_name;
};
class Item
{
public:
    Item(const char* name)
    {
        m_name = new char[strlen(name) + 1];
        strcpy(m_name, name);
    }
    ~Item()
    {
        delete[] m_name;
    }
private:
    char* m_name;
};
class Character
```

```
{
public:
    Character(const char* name)
    {
        m_name = new char[strlen(name) + 1];
        strcpy(m_name, name);
    }
    ~Character()
    {
        delete[] m_name;
    }
private:
    char* m_name;
};
int main()
{
    return 0;
}
```

2. Give attacks an attack statistic variable (**attackStat**) and items a heal statistic variable (**healStat**). Add appropriate getters and setters and constructor additions:

```
class Attack
{
public:
    Attack(const char* name, int attackStat)
    {
        m_name = new char[strlen(name) + 1];
        strcpy(m_name, name);
        m_attackStat = attackStat;
    }

    ~Attack()
    {
        delete[] m_name;
    }
    int getAttackStat() const { return m_attackStat; }
    char* getName() const { return m_name; }
private:
    char* m_name;
    int m_attackStat;
};
```

```cpp
class Item
{
public:
    Item(const char* name, int healStat)
    {
        m_name = new char[strlen(name) + 1];
        strcpy(m_name, name);
        m_healStat = healStat;
    }
    ~Item()
    {
        delete[] m_name;
    }
    int getHealStat() const { return m_healStat; }
    char* getName() const { return m_name; }
private:
    char* m_name;
    int m_healStat;
};
class Character
{
public:
    Character(const char* name)
    {
        m_name = new char[strlen(name) + 1];
        strcpy(m_name, name);
    }
    ~Character()
    {
        delete[] m_name;
    }
private:
    char* m_name;
};
```

3. Let characters accept an array of attacks and items in their constructor and store them to be looked up by name when they need to be used:

```cpp
class Character
{
public:
    Character(const char* name, Attack* attacks, Item* items)
    {
```

```
        m_name = new char[strlen(name) + 1];
        strcpy(m_name, name);
        m_attacksLength = sizeof(attacks)/sizeof(&attacks[0]);
        m_itemsLength = sizeof(items)/sizeof(&items[0]);
        m_attacks = new Attack*[m_attacksLength];
        m_items = new Item*[m_itemsLength];
        int i = 0;

        for(i = 0; i < m_attacksLength; i++)
        {
            Attack* attack = new Attack(attacks[i]);
            m_attacks[0] = attack;
        }

        for(i = 0; i < m_itemsLength; i++)
        {
            Item* item = new Item(items[i]);
            m_items[0] = item;
        }
    }

    ~Character()
    {
        delete[] m_name;
    }

private:
    char* m_name;
    Attack** m_attacks;
    Item** m_items;
    int m_attacksLength;
    int m_itemsLength;
};
```

4. Add a health variable to the **Character** class and create functions to attack other characters, use items, and react to attacks:

```
class Character
{
public:
    Character(const char* name, Attack* attacks, Item* items)
    {
        m_health = 100;
```

```cpp
        m_name = new char[strlen(name) + 1];
        strcpy(m_name, name);
        m_attacksLength = sizeof(attacks)/sizeof(&attacks[0]);
        m_itemsLength = sizeof(items)/sizeof(&items[0]);
        m_attacks = new Attack*[m_attacksLength];
        m_items = new Item*[m_itemsLength];
        int i = 0;
        for(i = 0; i < m_attacksLength; i++)
        {
            Attack* attack = new Attack(attacks[i]);
            m_attacks[0] = attack;
        }
        for(i = 0; i < m_itemsLength; i++)
        {
            Item* item = new Item(items[i]);
            m_items[0] = item;
        }
    }
    ~Character()
    {
        delete[] m_name;
    }

    void DoAttack(string moveName, Character& other)
    {
        other.DoDefend(GetAttackAmount(moveName));
    }
    void UseItem(string itemName)
    {
        m_health += GetItemValue(itemName);
    }

private:
    void DoDefend(int attackValue)
    {
        m_health -= attackValue;
    }
    int GetAttackAmount(string attackName)
    {
        for(int i = 0; i < m_attacksLength; i++)
        {
            if(m_attacks[i]->getName() == attackName)
```

```cpp
            {
                return m_attacks[i]->getAttackStat();
            }
        }
        return 0;
    }
    int GetItemValue(string itemName)
    {
        for(int i = 0; i < m_itemsLength; i++)
        {
            if(m_items[i]->getName() == itemName)
            {
                return m_items[i]->getHealStat();
            }
        }
        return 0;
    }

    char* m_name;
    Attack** m_attacks;
    Item** m_items;
    int m_health;
    int m_attacksLength;
    int m_itemsLength;
};
```

5. Create member variables called **strengthMultiplier** and **defenceMultiplier**. These should affect a character's attacking and defending statistics:

```cpp
class Character
{
public:
    Character(const char* name, int strengthMultiplier, int
    defenceMultiplier, Attack* attacks, Item* items)
    {
        m_health = 100;

        m_name = new char[strlen(name) + 1];
        strcpy(m_name, name);

        m_strengthMultiplier = strengthMultiplier;
        m_defenceMultiplier = defenceMultiplier;
        m_attacksLength = sizeof(attacks)/sizeof(&attacks[0]);
```

```cpp
        m_itemsLength = sizeof(items)/sizeof(&items[0]);
        m_attacks = new Attack*[m_attacksLength];
        m_items = new Item*[m_itemsLength];
        int i = 0;
        for(i = 0; i < m_attacksLength; i++)
        {
            Attack* attack = new Attack(attacks[i]);
            m_attacks[0] = attack;
        }

        for(i = 0; i < m_itemsLength; i++)
        {
            Item* item = new Item(items[i]);
            m_items[0] = item;
        }
    }
    ~Character()
    {
        delete[] m_name;
        delete[] m_attacks;
        delete[] m_items;
    }
    const char* getName() { return m_name; }

    void DoAttack(string moveName, Character& other)
    {
        cout << m_name << " attacks " << other.getName()
            << " with " << moveName << endl;
        other.DoDefend(GetAttackAmount(moveName) *
                        m_strengthMultiplier);
    }
    void UseItem(string itemName)
    {
        m_health += GetItemValue(itemName);
    }
private:
    void DoDefend(int attackValue)
    {
        int damage = attackValue / m_defenceMultiplier;
        m_health -= damage;
        cout << m_name << " takes " << damage << " damage" << endl;
    }
    int GetAttackAmount(string attackName)
```

```
{
    for(int i = 0; i < m_attacksLength; i++)
    {
        if(m_attacks[i]->getName() == attackName)
        {
            return m_attacks[i]->getAttackStat();
        }
    }
    return 0;
}
int GetItemValue(string itemName)
{
    for(int i = 0; i < m_itemsLength; i++)
    {
        if(m_items[i]->getName() == itemName)
        {
            return m_items[i]->getHealStat();
        }
    }
    return 0;
}
char* m_name;
Attack** m_attacks;
Item** m_items;
int m_health;
int m_strengthMultiplier;
int m_defenceMultiplier;
int m_attacksLength;
int m_itemsLength;
};
```

6. Create a function in the **Character** class to print a character's name and other statistics to the console:

```
void Display()
{
    cout << m_name << endl;
    cout << "Health = " << m_health << endl;
    cout << "Strength Multiplier = " << m_strengthMultiplier
        << endl;
```

```
            cout << "Defence Multiplier = " << m_defenceMultiplier
                << endl;
            cout << "Attacks:" << endl;
            for(int i = 0; i < m_attacksLength; i++)
            cout << m_attacks[i]->getName() << " : "
                << m_attacks[igetAttackStat() << endl;
            cout << "Items:" << endl;
            for(int i = 0; i < m_itemsLength; i++)
            cout << m_items[i]->getName() << " : "
                << m_items[i]->getHealStat() << endl;
    }
```

7. Test everything in the main function with a few different characters:

```
int main()
{
    Attack billAttacks[] = { {"Sword To The Face", 20} };
    Item billItems[] = { {"Old Grog", 20} };
    Attack dragonAttacks[] = {{"Flame Breath", 50}};
    Item dragonItems[] = {{"Scale Oil", 20}};
    Character bill("Bill", 10, 5, billAttacks, billItems);
    bill.Display();
    Character dragon("Dragon", 10, 5, dragonAttacks, dragonItems);
    dragon.Display();
    bill.Display();
    bill.DoAttack("Sword To The Face", dragon);
    dragon.Display();
    dragon.DoAttack("Flame Breath", bill);
    bill.Display();
    return 0;
}
```

8.   Run the complete code. You should obtain the following output:

Figure 9.11: RPG combat system

Chapter 10: Advanced Object-Oriented Principles

Activity 10: An Encyclopedia Application

Solution:

1. Start by including all the files that we'll need for the application:

```
// Activity 10: Encyclopedia Application.
#include <iostream>
#include <string>
#include <vector>
```

2. Create a struct, **AnimalInfo**, that can store name, origin, life expectancy, and weight:

```
struct AnimalInfo
{
    std::string name = "";
    std::string origin = "";
    int lifeExpectancy = 0;
    float weight = 0;
};
```

3. Create a function to print that data out in a neat format. Name it **PrintAnimalInfo**:

```
void PrintAnimalInfo(AnimalInfo info)
{
    std::cout << "Name: " << info.name << std::endl;
    std::cout << "Origin: " << info.origin << std::endl;
    std::cout << "Life Expectancy: " << info.lifeExpectancy
              << std::endl;
    std::cout << "Weight: " << info.weight << std::endl;
}
```

4. Now, create the base class for our animals. Name it **Animal**. It should provide a member variable of type **AnimalInfo**, and a function to return it. Be sure to use appropriate access modifiers:

```
class Animal
{
public:
```

```
    AnimalInfo GetAnimalInfo() const { return animalInfo; };

protected:
    AnimalInfo animalInfo;
};
```

5. Next, create the first derived class, **Lion**. This class will inherit from **Animal**, be final, and fill out the **AnimalInfo** member in its constructor:

```
class Lion final : public Animal
{
public:
    Lion()
    {
        animalInfo.name = "Lion";
        animalInfo.origin = "Africa";
        animalInfo.lifeExpectancy = 12;
        animalInfo.weight = 190;
    }
};
```

6. Next, create the second derived class, **Tiger**. Fill out the same data:

```
class Tiger final : public Animal
{
public:
    Tiger()
    {
        animalInfo.name = "Tiger";
        animalInfo.origin = "Africa";
        animalInfo.lifeExpectancy = 17;
        animalInfo.weight = 220;
    }
};
```

7. Create the final derived class, **Bear**, also filling out the **AnimalInfo** member:

```
class Bear final : public Animal
{
public:
    Bear()
    {
        animalInfo.name = "Bear";
        animalInfo.origin = "Eurasia";
        animalInfo.lifeExpectancy = 22;
```

```
                animalInfo.weight = 270;
        }
    };
```

8. Define the **main** function. Declare a vector of pointers to the base **Animal** type and add one of each of the animal derived types:

```
int main()
{
    std::vector<Animal*> animals;
    animals.push_back(new Lion());
    animals.push_back(new Tiger());
    animals.push_back(new Bear());
```

9. Output the application title:

```
    std::cout << "**Animal Encyclopedia**\n";
```

10. Create the **main** outer loop for the application and output a message to the user prompting them to select an index:

```
    bool bIsRunning = true;
    while (bIsRunning)
    {
        std::cout << "\nSelect animal for more information\n\n";
```

11. Output the possible selections to the user. Use a **for** loop for this, and each option should include an index and the name of the animal. Also include an option for the user to be able to quit the application by entering **-1**:

```
        for (size_t i = 0; i < animals.size(); ++i)
        {
            std::cout << i << ") " << animals[i]->GetAnimalInfo().name
                      << std::endl;
        }
        std::cout << "\n-1) Quit Application\n";
```

12. Fetch the user input and convert it to an integer:

```
        // Get user input
        std::string input;
        int userChoice;
        getline(std::cin, input);
        userChoice = std::stoi(input);
```

13. Check whether the user entered **-1** and thus wants to quite the application. Handle this if they do:

```
// Sanity user input
if (userChoice == -1)
{
    bIsRunning = false;
}
```

14. Next, check that the user entered an invalid index. An invalid index is one that's less than **-1** and greater than the size of the animal vector **-1** (because indices start at 0, not 1). If they did, output an error message and have them choose again:

```
else if (userChoice < -1 || userChoice >
        ((int)animals.size() - 1))
{
    std::cout << "\nInvalid Index. Please enter another.\n";
}
```

15. If the user input a valid index, make a call to the **PrintAnimalInfo** created earlier, passing in the animal's info that you'll get from the vector:

```
else
{
    // Print animal info
    std::cout << std::endl;
    PrintAnimalInfo(animals[userChoice]->GetAnimalInfo());
}
}
```

16. Outside of the main loop, clean up the pointers. This includes deleting their memory, setting them to **0**, and then clearing the vector:

```
// Cleanup.
for (size_t i = 0; i < animals.size(); ++i)
{
    delete animals[i];
    animals[i] = nullptr;
}

animals.clear();
}
```

17. Run the complete code. You will obtain the following output:

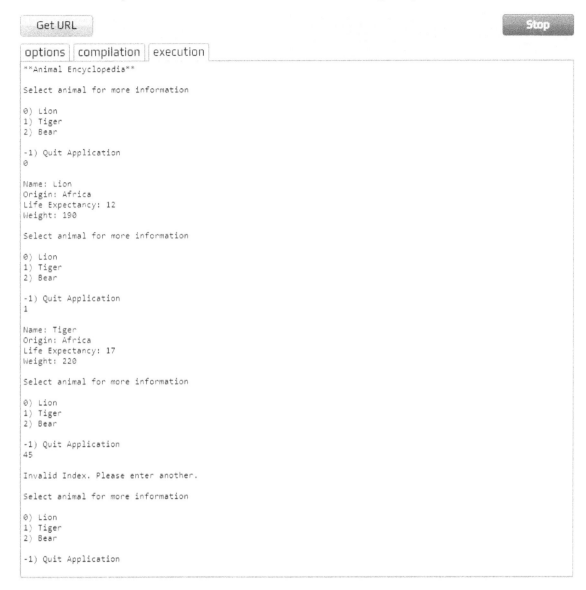

Figure 10.19: Users can view information on various animals

This application makes use of inheritance and polymorphism to simplify the storage of our animal types. By storing pointers to their base class, we can store them in a single collection, meaning we can iterate over them in a single loop and call their shared members polymorphically. Inheritance, polymorphism, and casting are important concepts, especially as we build bigger and more flexible applications. Being comfortable with them will allow us to get the most out of C++.

Chapter 11: Templates

Activity 11: Creating a Generic Stack

Solution:

1. Write a generic stack using the generic queue example as a base:

```cpp
#include <iostream>
#include <memory>

using namespace std;
template<class T>

class Stack
{
    public:
        Stack() { init(); }
        explicit Stack(size_t numElements,
                    const T& initialValue = T())
        {
            init(numElements, initialValue);
        }
        Stack(const Stack& q) { init(q.bottom(), q.top()); }
        Stack& operator=(const Stack& rhs)
        {
            if (&rhs != this)
            {
                destroy();
                init(rhs.bottom(), rhs.top());
            }
            return *this;
        }
        ~Stack() { destroy(); }
        T* top() { return stackDataEnd - 1; }
        const T* top() const { return stackDataEnd - 1; }
        T* bottom() { return stackData; }
        const T* bottom() const { return stackData; }
        size_t size() const { return stackDataEnd - stackData; }
        bool empty() const { return size() == 0; }
```

2. Alter the **pop ()** function to handle a LIFO data structure:

```
void pop()
    {
        if (top() != 0)
        {
            alloc.destroy(top());
            stackDataEnd -= 1;
        }
    }
```

> **Note**
>
> As mentioned in the activity brief, the solution involves reusing the code provided in the *Creating a Generic Queue* section. Hence, only the block that is altered is included in step 2. The complete code can be found here: https://packt. live/2r9XgYi.

3. Test the stack in a **main** function, outputting data to test whether the stack works correctly:

Activity 11.cpp

```
104 int main()
105 {
106     Stack<int> testStack;
107     testStack.push(1);
108     testStack.push(2);
109     cout << "stack contains values: ";
110
111     for (auto it = testStack.bottom(); it != testStack.top() + 1; ++it)
112     {
113         cout << *it << " ";
114     }
115
116     cout << endl;
117     cout << "stack contains " << testStack.size() << " elements" << endl;
118     testStack.pop();
119     cout << "stack contains values: ";
120
121     for (auto it = testStack.bottom(); it != testStack.top() + 1; ++it)
122     {
123         cout << *it << " ";
124     }
        //[…]
151     return 0;
152 }
```

The complete code for this step can be found at: https://packt.live/2r7Clp8

4. When you successfully run the complete code, you will obtain the following output:

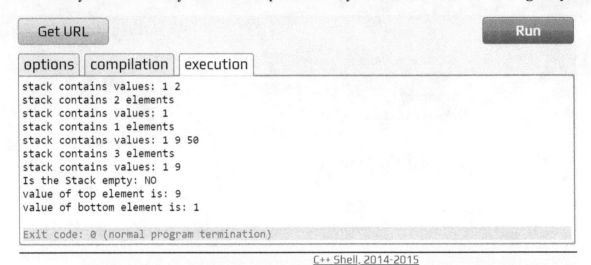

Figure 11.08: Final output of the activity

Chapter 12: Containers and Iterators

Activity 12: Converting RPG Combat to Use Standard Library Containers

Solution:

1. Alter the **Attack**, **Item**, and **Character** classes to use strings instead of char arrays (the **Attack** class is shown here):

```
class Attack
{
public:

    Attack(string name, int attackStat)
    {
        m_name = name;
        m_attackStat = attackStat;
    }
    int getAttackStat() const { return m_attackStat; }
    string getName() const { return m_name; }

private:
    string m_name;
    int m_attackStat;
};
```

2. Remove any now unneeded copy constructor, destructor, and assignment implementations (the **Item** class is shown here):

```
class Item
{
public:

    Item(string name, int healStat)
    {
        m_name = name;
        strcpy(m_name, name);
        m_healStat = healStat;
    }
    int getHealStat() const { return m_healStat; }
    string getName() const { return m_name; }
```

```cpp
private:
    string m_name;
    int m_healStat;
};
```

3. Get the **Character** class to take vectors of **Attack** and **Item** instead of raw arrays:

```cpp
class Character
{
public:
    Character(string name, int strengthMultiplier,
            int defenceMultiplier,
    vector<Attack> attacks, vector<Item> items)
    {
        m_health = 100;
        m_name = name;
        m_strengthMultiplier = strengthMultiplier;
        m_defenceMultiplier = defenceMultiplier;
        m_attacks.insert(m_attacks.begin(), attacks.begin(),
                    attacks.end());
        m_items.insert(m_items.begin(), items.begin(), items.end());
    }
```

4. Implement the **attack** and **defend** functions to use vectors instead of arrays, and update the display function to utilize the vectors:

```cpp
    void DoAttack(string moveName, Character& other)
    {
        cout << m_name << " attacks " << other.getName() << " with "
            << moveName << endl;
        other.DoDefend(GetAttackAmount(moveName) *
                    m_strengthMultiplier);
    }

    void DoAttack(Character& other)
    {
        string attackName =
        m_attacks[m_indexOfDefaultAttack].getName();
        cout << m_name << " attacks " << other.getName() << " with "
            << attackName <<endl;
        other.DoDefend(GetAttackAmount(attackName) *
                    m_strengthMultiplier);
    }

    void UseItem(string itemName)
    {
        int itemValue = GetItemValue(itemName);
```

```cpp
        cout << m_name << " uses " << itemName << " and gains "
            << itemValue << "health" << endl;
        m_health += itemValue;
    }

    bool isDead() { return m_health <= 0; }

    void Display()
    {
        cout << m_name << endl;
        cout << "Health = " << m_health << endl;
        cout << "Strength Multiplier = " << m_strengthMultiplier
            << endl;
        cout << "Defence Multiplier = " << m_defenceMultiplier
            << endl;
        cout << "Attacks:" << endl;

        for(auto attack : m_attacks)
            cout << attack.getName() << " : "
                << attack.getAttackStat() << endl;
        cout << "Items:" << endl;

        for(auto item : m_items)
            cout << item.getName() << " : " << item.getHealStat()
                << endl;
    }

private:
    void DoDefend(int attackValue)
    {
        int damage = attackValue / m_defenceMultiplier;
        m_health -= damage;
        cout << m_name << " takes " << damage << " damage" << endl;
    }

    int GetAttackAmount(string attackName)
    {
        auto it = find_if(m_attacks.begin(), m_attacks.end(),
                    [attackName](const Attack& attack){ return
                    attack.getName() == attackName; });
        return (it != m_attacks.end()) ? (*it).getAttackStat() : 0;
    }

    int GetItemValue(string itemName)
    {
```

```
                 auto it = find_if(m_items.begin(), m_items.end(),
                            [itemName](const Item& item){ return item.
                            getName() == itemName; });
             return (it != m_items.end()) ? (*it).getHealStat() : 0;
    }

    string m_name;
    vector<Attack> m_attacks;
    vector<Item> m_items;
    int m_health;
    int m_strengthMultiplier;
    int m_defenceMultiplier;
    int m_indexOfDefaultAttack;
};
```

5. In the **main** function, implement a queue that holds different **Character** types for the player to fight:

```
int main()
{
    // Bill the player
    vector<Attack> billAttacks = { {"Sword To The Face", 20} };
    vector<Item> billItems = { {"Old Grog", 50} };
    Character bill("Bill", 2, 2, billAttacks, billItems);

    // Dragon
    vector<Attack> dragonAttacks = {{"Flame Breath", 20}};
    vector<Item> dragonItems = {{"Scale Oil", 20}};
    Character dragon("Dragon", 2, 1, dragonAttacks, dragonItems);

    // Zombie
    vector<Attack> zombieAttacks = {{"Bite", 50}};
    vector<Item> zombieItems = {{"Rotten Flesh", 20}};
    Character zombie("Zombie", 1, 3, zombieAttacks, zombieItems);

    // Witch
    vector<Attack> witchAttacks = {{"Super Spell", 50}};
```

```
vector<Item> witchItems = {{"Cure Potion", 20}};
Character witch("Witch", 1, 5, witchAttacks, witchItems);
queue<Character> monsters;
monsters.push(dragon);
monsters.push(zombie);
monsters.push(witch);
```

6. Fight each monster in the queue until the queue is empty and display a **win** string. Also, allow the use of items and a default attack:

```
bool playerTurn = true;
bool gameOver = false;
cout << "Bill finds himself trapped in a scary dungeon!
        There seems to be a series of rooms, he enters
        the first room..." << endl;

while(!monsters.empty() && !gameOver)
{
    Character currentMonster = monsters.front();
    cout << "A monster appears, it looks like a "
        << currentMonster.getName() << endl;
    while(!currentMonster.isDead())
    {
        cout << endl;
        if(playerTurn)
        {
            cout << "bill's turn" << endl;
            cout << "Bill can press 1 and enter to use
                    an item and 2 and enter to attack the
                    monster." << endl;

            bool madeChoice = false;
            while(!madeChoice)
            {
                int choice;
                cin >> choice;
                switch(choice)
                {
                    case 1:
                        bill.UseItem("Old Grog");
```

```
                            madeChoice = true;
                    break;
                    case 2:
                        bill.DoAttack(currentMonster);
                        madeChoice = true;
                    break;
                    default:
                    break;
                }
            }
        }
        else
        {

            cout << currentMonster.getName() << "'s turn" << endl;
            currentMonster.DoAttack(bill);

        }
        cout << "Bills health is " << bill.getHealth() << endl;
        cout << currentMonster.getName() << "'s health is "
              << currentMonster.getHealth() << endl;

        if(currentMonster.isDead())
        {
            cout << currentMonster.getName() << " is defeated"
                  << endl;

            monsters.pop();
        }

        if(bill.isDead())
        {
            gameOver = true;
            break;
        }
        playerTurn = !playerTurn;

}
```

```
    }

    if(monsters.empty())
    {
        cout << "You win";
    }

    if(gameOver)
    {
        cout << "You lose";
    }
    return 0;
}
```

7. Run the complete code. You should receive the following output:

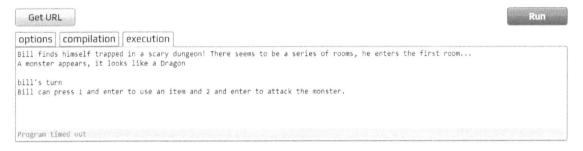

Figure 12.14: Final output of the activity

Chapter 13: Exception Handling in C++

Activity 13: Handling Exceptions

Solution:

1. Start with the sample program shown at the beginning of the activity:

```
#include <iostream>
using namespace std;
int main()
{
    bool continue_flag;

    do
    {
        continue_flag = do_something();
    }
    while (continue_flag == true);

    return 0;
}
```

2. **std::runtime_error**, the exception signaled for sensor errors, is defined in the **<stdexcept>** header, so we need to include **<stdexcept>**. Depending on the compiler, we may also need to include the **<exception>** header:

```
#include <exception>
#include <stdexcept>
```

3. In the main loop, replace the call to **do_something()** with a **try...catch** block. The skeleton **try...catch** block is shown here:

```
        try
        {
        }
        catch (exception& e)
        {
        }
```

4. In the **try** block, call **reactor_safety_check()** and save its value in the **continue_flag** variable:

```
            continue_flag = reactor_safety_check();
```

5. Add a **catch** clause that catches **runtime_error**. It must come before the **catch** clause that catches the **exception**. This **catch** clause could be empty, but it is probably best if it outputs a message describing the **exception**:

```
catch (runtime_error& e)
{
    cout << "caught runtime error " << e.what() << endl;
}
```

6. Add a **catch** clause that catches all other C++ exceptions. These exceptions are unexpected, so call **SCRAM()** to shut down the reactor, then **break**, to end the enclosing **do** loop. Instead of **break**, setting **continue_flag** to **false** would have the same effect:

```
catch (...)
{
    cout << "caught unknown exception type" << endl;
    SCRAM();
    break;
}
```

7. Add a **catch** clause that catches all other exceptions. This is a good idea because an exception may be of any type, and we don't want our reactor safety check to exit with the reactor still running. In this **catch** clause, call **SCRAM()**, then **break**:

```
catch (exception& e)
{
    cout << "caught unknown exception type" << endl;
    SCRAM();
    break;
}
```

8. After the **try...catch** block, output the message **"main() exiting"** so we know the program stopped in a controlled way:

```
cout << "main() exiting" << endl;
```

9. Above **main()**, insert a **void** function called **SCRAM()**. **SCRAM()** prints a message. Here's an example of what it might look like:

```
void SCRAM()
{
    cout << "SCRAM! I mean it. Get away from here!" << endl;
}
```

10. Add a **bool** function, **reactor_safety_check()**. It looks like this:

```
bool reactor_safety_check()
{
    static int count = 0;
    ++count;

    if (count % 17 == 0)
    {
        throw runtime_error("Sensor glitch");
    }

    else if (count % 69 == 0)
    {
        throw 123;
        //throw exception();
    }

    else if (count % 199 == 0)
    {
        return false;
    }

    return true;
}
```

Note that **reactor_safety_check()** might throw either an **std::exception** or an exception of some unexpected type, and you should test your code in both ways.

11. Compile and run the completed program. While different students' programs will produce somewhat different output, this program produces the following:

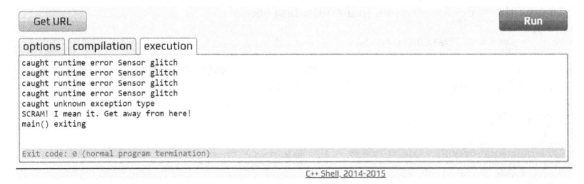

Figure 13.11: Final output of the activity

What's going on here? The **do** loop calls **reactor_safety_check()**. Most of the time, **reactor_safety_check()** returns normally, but sometimes it throws an exception, presumably because of a sensor glitch. This exception is reported, and execution is allowed to continue, which causes the loop to repeat the call to **reactor_safety_check()**. Our test version of **reactor_safety_check()** calls some other exception type sometimes. The program doesn't know what to do when another type of exception occurs, so it takes the only course of action that promises not to irradiate eight million Londoners—it scrams the reactor and breaks out of the loop.

Index

About

All major keywords used in this book are captured alphabetically in this section. Each one is accompanied by the page number of where they appear.

www.ingramcontent.com/pod-product-compliance
Lightning Source LLC
Chambersburg PA
CBHW060635060326
40690CB00020B/4409